THE AGENCY AND THE HILL

The Center *for the* Study *of* Intelligence

Central Intelligence Agency

Washington, DC 20505

Library of Congress Cataloguing-in-Publications Data

Snider, L. Britt

The Agency and the Hill:CIA's Relationship with Congress, 1946–2004/

L. Britt Snider

Includes bibliographic references, index.

ISBN 978-1-929667-17-8 (pbk.:alk paper)

1. Intelligence—United States. 2. Congress.

3. Intelligence history. 4. Intelligence oversight.

5. Intelligence organization. 6. Intelligence management.

7. Intelligence policy.

Typeset in Times.

Printed by Imaging and Publication Support, CIA.

THE AGENCY AND THE HILL:

CIA's Relationship with Congress, 1946–2004

L Britt Snider

Center for the Study of Intelligence

Central Intelligence Agency

Washington, DC

2008

CONTENTS

APPENDICES

BIBLIOGRAPHY

PREFACE

This is a study of the CIA's relationship with Congress. It encompasses the period from the creation of the Agency until 2004—the era of the DCIs. When Congress created a new position in December 2004—the director of national intelligence—to supersede the director of central intelligence (DCI) as head of the US Intelligence Community, it necessarily changed the dynamic between the CIA and the Congress. While the director of the Agency would continue to represent its interests on Capitol Hill, he or she would no longer speak as the head of US intelligence. While 2008 is too early to assess how this change will affect the Agency's relationship with Congress, it is safe to say it will never be quite the same.

This study is not organized as one might expect. It does not describe what occurred between the Agency and Congress in chronological order nor does it purport to describe every interaction that occurred over the period encompassed by the study. Rather it attempts to describe what the relationship was like over time and then look at what it produced in seven discrete areas.

I took this approach for several reasons. First, I found that telling the story in chronological sequence tended to obscure the lessons of the past, rather than illuminate them. Taking everything at once and bringing it forward made it more difficult to discern what was happening. The forest obscured the trees, if you will. Moreover, not everything that transpired in the course of the relationship can be considered historically significant. Even if it were possible to recount every interaction that took place between the Agency and Congress over the 58-year period covered by this study (and it isn't), readers would be wasting their time delving into it.

"Slicing and dicing" the subject matter in this way, however, did inevitably lead to a degree of duplication. I tried to deal with this problem by limiting the explanatory material in each chapter to that which was necessary to understanding the points being made in that chapter, even if the same explanatory material were also needed (to a lesser or greater extent) to understand the points being made in other chapters. Hopefully, the reader will bear this in mind (and remain tolerant) where the duplication occurs.

An element of subjectivity was also involved in choosing the examples used in the study. Several factors influenced my choices here. First, I wanted to confine myself to episodes that were historically significant and/or would best highlight the issues identified. I also chose episodes, where possible, that had some prior public context. Without it, not only would more explanation be required, but the chances of having it declassified would be practically nil. My intent was to produce an unclassified study, something that could be read by Agency employees outside the office. Readers may be surprised to learn that this created less of a problem than one might expect, since most of the significant interaction that has occurred between Congress and the Agency involves matters that have previously been disclosed in some manner.

The reader should not expect to find, however, detailed descriptions of the episodes chosen for the narrative. In order to keep the study to a manageable length, I deliberately tried to distill the descriptions of the events I chose into readable summaries. What I am principally concerned with here is the congressional involvement in these episodes, not with what the Agency did or did not do that prompted Congress to become involved. Indeed, books have been written about many of the episodes described here. I am not attempting to replicate what is already in the public domain with respect to the Agency's past, but rather to describe how the Agency engaged with Congress with respect to its past. Readers who want more detail concerning the Agency's activities alluded to in the study will need to consult other sources.

The study is divided into two major parts.

Part I describes how Congress and the Agency related to each other over the period covered by the study. As it happens, this period conveniently breaks down into two major segments: the years before the creation of the select committees on intelligence (1946–76) and the years after the creation of these committees (1976–2004). The arrangements that Congress put in place during the earlier period to provide oversight and tend to the needs of the Agency were distinctly different from those put in place in the mid-1970s and beyond. Over the entire period, moreover, the Agency shared intelligence with the Congress and had other interaction with its members that affected the relationship. This, too, is described in part I.

Part II describes what the relationship produced over time in seven discrete areas: legislation affecting the Agency; programs and budget; oversight of analysis; oversight of collection; oversight of covert action; oversight of security and personnel matters; and the Senate confirmation process. It highlights what the principal issues have been for Congress in each area as well as how those issues have been handled.

My principal objective in undertaking this study was not so much to describe as to explain—to write something that would help CIA employees better understand the Agency's relationship with Congress, not only to help them appreciate the past but to provide a guide to the future. At the end of each chapter appears a section titled "Author's Commentary" that contains my observations with respect to the topics covered in that chapter. The opinions expressed here are solely mine and should not be seen as necessarily reflecting the views of the Center for the Study of Intelligence or the Central Intelligence Agency.

In preparing this study, I have had access to classified Agency records. Within this body of material, the research done in the early 1990s by former Agency historian Gerald K. Haines proved especially useful. Classified monographs and interviews prepared by the Center for the Study of Intelligence were also unusually helpful. Inasmuch as this is an unclassified study, however, with a few exceptions only *unclassified* materials are cited in the footnotes. Where classified sources are involved, I typically refer to them in the text as "Agency records" or, in some cases, omit any source identification at all. While I recognize that from a reader's standpoint this may be far from ideal, it was necessary to keep the study at an unclassified level.

While these documents were extremely useful, I was also struck by the relative paucity of documentation available at the CIA concerning its relations with Congress before the mid-1970s, testament in and of itself to the informal, highly personal nature of the relationship during that period. Information was routinely communicated by DCIs to members of Congress without anyone else being present. As such, there was no one to memorialize for the Agency's records what had been said. Even where memos were prepared, they were often so cursory it was impossible to know what had actually been communicated.

In addition to the classified materials, numerous public sources were consulted. Two books have thus far been written on the subject of congressional oversight of intelligence, and both are cited frequently in this study: Smist's *Congress Oversees the United States Intelligence Community* and Barrett's *The CIA and Congress*. Indeed, both provide information that is not otherwise found in the Agency's files. Numerous other books reviewed by the author have dealt with aspects of the CIA's relations with Congress. The most notable of these are Woodward's *Veil*; Prados's *Lost Crusader* and *Presidents' Secret Wars*; and Ranelagh's *The Agency*. Several former DCIs have written memoirs that have useful insights: Helms, *A Look Over My Shoulder*; Gates, *From the Shadows*; and, most recently, Tenet, *At the Center of the Storm*.

I also did a limited number of interviews for the study, primarily with CIA officials who had recently been involved in managing the relationship with Congress and who had not been previously interviewed by the Center's historians. Sadly, these did not include the personal recollections of Stanley M. Moskowitz, who twice served as the Agency's liaison with the Congress under DCIs Woolsey and Tenet. While Stan had agreed to be interviewed for this project, he passed away unexpectedly on 29 June 2006 before the interview could be scheduled.

I did not seek access to records held by the select intelligence committees, given their past reluctance (under their respective committee rules) to provide such access to outsiders. It is my hope that one day they will see fit to write their own histories and make them available to the public.

—L. Britt Snider

PART I

WHAT THE RELATIONSHIP WAS LIKE

CHAPTER 1

THE NATURE OF THE RELATIONSHIP, 1946–76

This chapter describes the relationship between the Agency and Congress from the establishment of the Central Intelligence Group in 1946 until the creation of the select committees on intelligence in the mid-1970s. It focuses upon the institutional arrangements that Congress put in place to oversee and provide funding for the Agency during this period, the episodes that produced challenges to those arrangements, and the policies and procedures that each side instituted during this period to govern its relationship with the other.

The Central Intelligence Group (1946–47)

At the end of the Second World War, President Truman, prompted by a desire to avoid another Pearl Harbor, decided to create, for the first time in the nation's history, a permanent, peacetime intelligence capability outside of the military. He did this in January 1946, in the form of a letter addressed to the secretaries of state, war, and the navy. The new organization would be known as the Central Intelligence Group (CIG), headed by a director of central intelligence (DCI). It would serve as the "action arm" of a "National Intelligence Authority" composed of the aforesaid secretaries as well as a representative of the president. CIG would collect, analyze, and disseminate intelligence, according to Truman's directive, and would receive its staff and funding from the Departments of State, War, and the Navy. Truman established the CIG without consulting Congress or obtaining congressional approval.[1]

Prior to this, intelligence organizations within the US government had always been tied to the military, often created to deal with a particular war or crisis only to wane and disappear from the scene after the war or crisis was over. Even the wartime predecessor of the CIG—the civilian-run Office of Strategic Services (OSS)—had been placed under the jurisdiction of the Joint Chiefs of Staff and had taken its marching orders from them.[2] As such, intelligence organizations had until this point received little scrutiny from the Con-

---

[1] Leary, The Central Intelligence Agency, 18-21; Pforzheimer interview, 9 July 1996, 2.
[2] Troy, *Donovan and the CIA*, 423, 427–28, 431–34, 436–42.

gress. Their appropriations were part of a larger appropriation for the military, and any inquiries concerning their activities would be answered by their military superiors.[3] In short, there was no need for Congress to establish an oversight arrangement for intelligence activities apart from that already in place for the military.

With the creation of the CIG, however, the need appeared to change. While CIG largely managed to avoid interacting with Congress during most of its short existence,[4] it found the need to engage over its first budget. CIG funding was concealed in the budgets of the State, War, and Navy Departments, but these funds had to be identified and justified to the House and Senate Appropriations Committees. In early 1947, DCI Hoyt Vandenberg sought, on grounds of security, to have the CIG's funding request considered by a much smaller subset of the two committees. Although objections were initially heard on the House side, both appropriations committee chairmen—John Tabor (R-NY) in the House, and Styles Bridges (R-NH) in the Senate—ultimately accommodated Vandenberg by appointing small, ad hoc subcommittees to hear the CIG's budget request for FY 1948.[5] CIG subsequently denied budgetary information to other members of Congress on the basis they were not on these special subcommittees.[6]

Even with this limited review of the CIG's budget request, Congressman Tabor later bemoaned to Secretary of State George Marshall that he had had to deal with 26 people in Congress in order to secure the FY 1948 appropriation for CIG. Marshall agreed that in the future, "knowledge of that [CIG] fund and an accounting of it" should be "confined to a very few congressional leaders." Indeed, Marshall reportedly said that Tabor believed "the allotment of funds for intelligence activities should be appropriated in a lump sum and controlled by one person."[7]

Apart from this interaction over its initial budget request, there were stirrings in Congress within months of Truman's having created the CIG that the new agency should have independent statutory authority as well as its own budget. Indeed, bills to accomplish this were introduced in both the House and Senate the year CIG was created.[8]

---

[3] Ibid., 436-42.

[4] The CIG's second in command at the time, COL E.K. Wright, told his staff to avoid contact with Congress where possible. "A good rule is this," he wrote, "never initiate letters to Members of Congress." Quoted in unpublished CIA draft manuscript, Vol. I, 6, hereinafter cited as "CIA draft study" together with the appropriate volume number and page number.

[5] CIA draft study, Vol. I, 7.

[6] Ibid.

[7] Barrett, CIA and Congress, 21, 23.

[8] *New York Times*, 18 December 1946, 12.

Meanwhile, the first DCIs, Sidney Souers and Vandenberg, during their short tenures, came to the same conclusion. CIG needed its own budget, as well as its own personnel authorities.

Congress, moreover, had enacted legislation in 1944 that in effect provided that any independent agency created by executive order that was to last more than a year needed its own appropriation.[9] While CIG lawyers had begun drafting authorizing legislation for the agency in the fall of 1946, nothing had yet come of it. By the beginning of 1947, in fact, CIG was technically in violation of the law. The Bureau of the Budget (the predecessor of the Office of Management and Budget) ruled, however, that CIG could continue operating inasmuch as it intended to seek statutory authorization later in the year.[10]

Coincidentally, the White House had initiated an effort in January 1947 to draft legislation to provide for the unification of the military services under a new Department of Defense. This provided an opportunity for Vandenberg to recommend provisions be added to the bill giving CIG independent statutory authority. He also wanted CIG to have its own appropriation, authority to hire and fire its own personnel, and authority to protect its sources and methods.[11]

While Vandenberg did not get all he wanted into the bill, after several months of hearings and limited floor debate in both houses, the National Security Act of 1947 passed Congress on 25 July.[12] Section 202 of the act provided for the establishment of an independent Central Intelligence Agency that would collect, analyze, and share intelligence across the government and "perform such other functions and duties related to intelligence affecting the national security as the National Security Council may from time to time direct." President Truman signed the bill into law the following day.

The Early Oversight Arrangements: 1947–56

Most of the congressional hearings regarding the creation of the CIA were closed to the public, and what floor debate occurred with respect to section 202 centered on CIA's domestic role and on the appointment of its director rather than its operational role overseas. Even in these formative stages, Professor Barrett notes, "a strong sense emerged [in Congress] . . . that only a handful of legislative leaders should know much about . . . the CIA."[13]

---

[9] This law was known as the Independent Offices Appropriations Act for Fiscal Year 1945.

[10] Pforzheimer interview, 9 July 1996, 16–19, 48–49, 68–69.

[11] Lyle Miller, *Legislative History of the Central Intelligence Agency: National Security Act of 1947*, 33–36.

[12] Chapter 5 contains a discussion of the key issues raised with respect to the bill.

[13] Barrett, *CIA and Congress*, 20.

Once CIA was a reality, of course, Congress had to decide how to deal with it, if only to determine which committees would authorize and appropriate funds for it each year. As a practical matter, though, this occurred almost by default. It was apparent, to begin with, that the appropriations committees on each side would have responsibility for the CIA appropriations. It was also apparent that the Senate Armed Services Committee (SASC), which had handled the authorizing legislation on the Senate side, would claim jurisdiction over the agency it had created. On the House side, however, the Committee on Expenditures in the Executive Departments (a predecessor of the Committee on Governmental Affairs) had handled the authorizing legislation and might have asserted jurisdiction. It chose not to do so, however, allowing jurisdiction over the CIA to pass quietly to the Senate committee's counterpart, the House Armed Services Committee (HASC). All of this happened without formal action by either house.[14]

Principal responsibility for the CIA thus fell to some of the most, if not the most, powerful members of Congress at the time—the chairmen and ranking members of the appropriations and armed services committees on each side. Protected by a congressional seniority system that kept them in place as long as they kept getting elected, most stayed in their positions for many years, and the longer they stayed, the greater their influence became. From 1951 until 1969, for example, the SASC had only two chairmen: Richard Russell (D-GA) in 1951–53 and again in 1955–69; and Leverett Saltonstall (R-MA) in 1953–54. The Senate Appropriations Committee (SAC) had but three chairmen during this period: Kenneth McKellar (D-TN) in 1949–53; Styles H. Bridges (R-NH) in 1953–54; and Carl Hayden (D-AZ) in 1955–69. A similar situation obtained in the House of Representatives. Carl Vinson (D-GA) chaired the HASC from 1955 until 1965 and was succeeded by L. Mendel Rivers (D-SC), who served until 1971. Clarence Cannon (D-MO) chaired the House Appropriations Committee (HAC) from 1955 until 1964; his successor, George Mahon (D-TX), served until 1976. [See Appendix B for a complete listing of the committee chairmen with responsibility for the CIA.]

Limiting even further the number of members exposed to the Agency's operations during this early period was the fact that several of the legislators involved served on both the armed services and appropriations committees of their respective bodies. The most conspicuous example was Senator Russell, who served as a member of the SAC the entire time he chaired the SASC. When he finally gave up the chair of the SASC in 1969 to Senator John Stennis (D-MS), Russell became chair of the SAC, swapping places with Stennis who had been its chair.

---

[14] Ibid., 26; Pforzheimer interview, 9 July 1996, 84–85.

Senators Richard Russell (l) and Leverett Saltonstall. Between them, they chaired the powerful Armed Services Committee for 20 years, 1951–70.

(US Senate Historical Collection)

Whatever their party affiliation, virtually all the men who chaired these powerful committees had attained their positions because they were support-ers of a strong national defense. Where foreign affairs were concerned, they were inclined to support the president. All had been through the Second World War and now, like the rest of the country, faced a growing but uncertain threat from the Soviet Union. The introduction to the 1954 report of the Doolittle Commission (see page 11) provides an apt description of where most of them were coming from.

> *It is now clear that we are facing an implacable enemy whose avowed objective is world domination by whatever means and at whatever cost. There are no rules in such a game. Hitherto accept-able norms of human conduct do not apply. If the U.S. is to survive, longstanding American concepts of "fair play" must be reconsid-ered. We must develop effective espionage and counterespionage services, and must learn to subvert, sabotage and destroy our ene-mies by more clever, more sophisticated and more effective methods than those used against us. It may become necessary that the Amer-ican people be made acquainted with, understand and support this fundamentally repugnant philosophy.[15]*

The CIA, of course, was the agency Congress created to bear the brunt of this "fundamentally repugnant" mission, and as far as its overseers were concerned, it needed a certain latitude to do its work. As Senator Russell told his Senate colleagues in 1956, if there were one agency of the government whose activities "had to be taken on faith," it was the CIA.[16] Above all, it was important to members like Russell that Congress—which they knew to be a political, and at times a chaotic, institution—not make CIA's job any harder. At all costs, its operations must be protected.

To ensure security, each of the four committees involved in overseeing the Agency initially adopted similar organizational arrangements. Ad hoc, undesignated subcommittees were created in each committee to handle the CIA. The chairman and ranking member of the full committee made themselves chairman and ranking member of the subcommittee, and asked a few members from the full committee in whom they had particular trust to join them. During 1951–52, the informal subcommittee in the SASC that handled the Agency consisted of five senators. When the Republicans gained control in 1953–54, the subcommittee was reduced to just three: the chairman and ranking member of the full committee, plus one. In the beginning, these informal subcommittees were supported by only one or two staff members, who were typically senior staff from the full committees. When control of the House or Senate shifted between the parties, these staff members remained involved, at times even staying in the same position.[17]

Precisely because the leaders of the CIA subcommittees were also the leaders of the full committees, they had many demands on their time. Not surprisingly, formal meetings of the subcommittees during this early period were rare. The CIA subcommittee of the SASC, for example, met only once during 1951.[18] When the subcommittees did meet, it was always in secret, often convened on short notice by word of mouth, and the venue was varied in order not to attract attention. Typically, no transcripts were made. Often the only record of such meetings was a memorandum that one of the Agency participants prepared.[19] Since none of the subcommittees had places to store classified information, any documents made available to the members—and any notes taken by members—were returned to the CIA for safekeeping.

Apart from these practical limitations, formal meetings were not seen by either side as the place for sensitive matters to be dealt with. As one partici-

---

[15] Quoted in CIA draft study, Vol. II, 1.
[16] Barrett, *CIA and Congress*, 225.
[17] Ibid., 26–27.
[18] CIA draft study, Vol. 1, 38.
[19] Warner interview, 27 September 1996, 42.

Meeting of the Senate Armed Services Committee, probably from the mid-1960s. From the left are Senators Stennis, Russel, Smith, Thurmond, and Saltonstall.

Stennis, Russell, Smith, and Saltonstall were members of SASC's CIA subcommittee. Stennis, Russell, and Saltonstall were also members of the Appropriations Committee, with the latter two also being members of the SAC's CIA subcommittee.

(US Senate Historical Collection)

pant, Senator Saltonstall, later recalled, the meetings were "dominated by the committee chairmen. . . . Members would ask few questions which dealt with internal agency matters or with specific operations. The most sensitive discussions were reserved for one-to-one sessions between [the DCI] and individual committee chairmen."[20] The tête-à-têtes Saltonstall is referring to would sometimes take place at the members' offices or after work, at their residences, or over breakfast or lunch at the Agency, whenever they could be worked into the members' busy schedules. While the committee chairmen accepted their responsibility to put through the Agency's appropriation each year—a responsibility seen to by their respective staffs—they had neither the time nor the interest in plumbing the details of its budget.

"There were very loose reins on us at the time," CIA legislative counsel Walter L. Pforzheimer later recalled, "because the Congress believed in us and

---

[20] Ranelagh, *The Agency*, 282.

what we were doing. It wasn't that we were attempting to hide anything. Our main problem was, we couldn't get them to sit still and listen."[21]

Despite the difficulty the Agency often had in getting the attention of its overseers during this early period, it never took them for granted. They might be too busy to see the DCI, but the DCI had better not be too busy to see them. Above all, the Agency knew the chairmen of its subcommittees did not want to be surprised. They may not need to know the details of what the Agency was doing, but they wanted to know enough, if an operation came to light, that they could say they had known about it. For the most part, they relied upon DCIs to tell them what they needed to know.

They also jealously guarded their role over the Agency, objecting to any effort from the outside to impose broader, more intrusive oversight and seeing to it that other congressional committees did not cause problems. In 1948, for example, the Agency, supported by its overseers in the Senate, resisted an invitation by Senator Harry F. Byrd Sr. (D-VA), to meet with the Joint Committee on Reduction of Nonessential Federal Expenditures that was looking at across-the-board reductions in the size of government agencies. According to the notes of the Agency's legislative counsel at the time, "Nothing can be served by such a meeting since Byrd's committee has no jurisdiction over CIA's affairs."[22]

In 1950, the Agency, again with the support of its Senate overseers, was able to avoid an inquiry by the Senate Expenditures Committee into efficiency in the executive branch departments in general.[23] The Agency had more difficulty dealing with the repeated assaults of Wisconsin Senator Joseph R. McCarthy during the early 1950s, in part because of the fervor McCarthy generated in the Senate as a whole and in part because certain of the Agency's overseers in the Senate—notably Senator Bridges, chairman of the SAC during part of this period—supported McCarthy's efforts to root out communists and homosexuals in the government. While others among its congressional overseers provided quiet support, the Agency was essentially left on its own to fend off McCarthy's charges and resist his efforts to investigate the Agency. For the most part, it was able to do so. [24]

Most members of Congress during this early period were oblivious to the oversight arrangements that had been put in place for the Agency. The Agency did not appear on their "radar screens" at all. Of those who were aware, most

---

[21] Pforzheimer interview, 11 January 1988, 16.

[22] CIA draft study, Vol. I., 29.

[23] Ibid., 39.

[24] For a more detailed description of the Agency's dealings with Senator McCarthy, see chapter 10, and Barrett, CIA and Congress, 64–81, 177–96.

seemed content to let the powerful members who controlled the oversight sub-committees run the show where CIA was concerned. Occasionally, though, members who were not on one of the Agency subcommittees got into the act, typically after an Agency failure had become public. In fact, as early as April 1948—less than a year after CIA was created—after allegations appeared in the press that CIA had failed to warn of rioting in Bogota that had threatened US diplomats (see chapter 7), a resolution was introduced in the House calling for creation of a joint intelligence committee of nine senators and nine congressmen to replace the existing structure. The congressman who introduced the resolution, Edward J. Devitt (R-MN), even claimed that DCI Roscoe Hillenkoetter had approved the idea; the resolution went nowhere.[25]

In time, however, as the number of the Agency's actual or perceived failures began to mount—for example, the failure to predict the Soviet atomic bomb test in 1949 and the failure to predict the invasion of South Korea by the North in 1950—and members became increasingly aware of just how large the Agency had grown in a short period of time (see chapter 6), doubts about the efficacy of the existing oversight arrangements began to appear with greater frequency.

The Mansfield Resolutions: 1953–55

The first sign of serious discontent appeared in the Senate in 1953, when a first-term Senator from Montana, Mike Mansfield, offered a resolution to replace the current system with an 18-member joint committee on intelligence, akin to the Joint Atomic Energy Committee (JAEC), which at the time was the focal point in Congress for matters relating to nuclear weapons. This was a disciplined committee with a professional staff, whose competence and ability to keep secrets made it a preferred model for Mansfield. His resolution, however, attracted little attention and even less support among his colleagues. DCI Allen Dulles took no public position on the proposal and, based upon the assurance he had received from SASC Chairman Saltonstall, confidently predicted to insiders at the Agency that the bill would never make it out of committee.[26]

While Saltonstall proved true to his word, Dulles became concerned that unless the existing oversight committees did something more to assert their institutional role over the CIA, Mansfield's resolution might attract greater support over time. Accordingly, in January 1954, he suggested to Saltonstall and HASC Chairman Dewey Short (R-MO) that they formally designate CIA

---

[25] Barrett, *CIA and Congress*, 38–39.
[26] Ibid., 172–73; CIA draft study, Vol. I., 47.

subcommittees that would meet regularly to review the Agency's activities. Neither initially expressed interest in Dulles's suggestion.[27]

But in March 1954, when Mansfield introduced his joint committee resolution for a second time—this time calling for a 10-member committee—he accompanied his proposal with a critique of the Agency and its congressional overseers, indeed, the most withering critique that had been heard in either house to that point. "Until we create some sort of 'watchdog' committee," Mansfield concluded, "we will have nothing but continued anxiety about the Central Intelligence Agency and its widespread activities."[28] Apparently stung by this criticism, Saltonstall agreed with Dulles's earlier suggestion that he formally designate a subcommittee on CIA affairs. He also immediately scheduled a hearing with the DCI. Citing these innovations to the Senate Rules Committee a few weeks later, Saltonstall succeeded in derailing the Mansfield resolution for a second time.[29]

CIA officials continued to worry, however, that unless Congress perceived that the Agency was subject to credible oversight from the outside, Mansfield's proposal might eventually carry the day. To provide such credibility, CIA agreed, in June 1954, to submit to an investigation of its "structure and administration" by a special task force of the Government Organization Commission chaired by former President Herbert Hoover. Congress had established the Hoover Commission, as it was known, to review government organization as a whole, and by submitting itself to review by one of its task forces (headed by retired general, Mark W. Clark), the Agency hoped to deflect further reform efforts within Congress.[30] This strategy ultimately backfired, however, when the Clark task force—whose report would go to the Congress—decided that it needed to look into CIA's operational activities. To preempt this effort, President Eisenhower, at Dulles's urging, instituted a separate investigation, headed by LTG James H. Doolittle, to delve into this area. Completing its work well ahead of the Clark task force, the Doolittle Commission publicly stated that while there were areas for improvement, overall, the Agency was doing "a creditable job." The Clark task force, which reported a few months later, expressed concern over the "lack of intelligence data from behind the Iron Curtain"—a comment that caused considerable consternation within the Agency itself—but in the end the task force also gave the Agency a modestly favorable review in its public report.[31]

---

[27] CIA draft study, Vol. I, 48.
[28] Barrett, *CIA and Congress*, 174.
[29] CIA draft study, Vol. I, 48.
[30] Ibid., 49.
[31] Barrett, *CIA and Congress*, 211–13.

When it came to the oversight arrangements for the CIA, the Clark task force, came up with a new suggestion: that a small, bipartisan committee composed of respected lawmakers and "public-spirited citizens" be set up to oversee the Agency. The larger Hoover Commission, of which the Clark task force was a part, preferred Mansfield's approach, recommending as part of its June 1955 report, that Congress establish a joint intelligence committee.[32]

For a while in late 1954, DCI Dulles actually entertained endorsing the concept of a joint committee, but the hostility of President Eisenhower to the idea (he intensely disliked the JAEC) reportedly put an end to any further thoughts of this nature. In a public speech delivered in January 1955, Dulles said the Agency preferred the existing oversight arrangements to a joint committee.[33]

On 15 January 1955, Mansfield offered his joint committee resolution for a third time. This time it provided for a committee composed of 12 members, all of whom would be currently serving on one of the CIA subcommittees and would be supported by an independent professional staff. In introducing the resolution, Mansfield denounced what he saw as CIA's immunity from "regular, methodical review" by the Congress. In describing his intent to the *New York Times*, Mansfield said he had "no desire to pry into necessary secrets of the CIA" but only wanted to reform the current "hodgepodge system" of infrequent and cursory oversight.[34]

CIA officials spent the balance of the year trying to bolster oversight (and the perception of oversight) by the SASC and HASC. At the urging of Dulles, the HASC chairman, Carl Vinson, designated a special subcommittee to handle CIA affairs, while Senator Russell, who had regained the chairmanship of the SASC as a result of the mid-term elections, continued the practice begun a year earlier by then-Chairman Saltonstall. Indeed, in February 1955, Russell for the first time publicly revealed the existence and membership of the subcommittee, declaring that it had kept a "close check" on CIA for some time.[35] Not all in Congress were persuaded by these machinations, however. For example, the chairman of the House Judiciary Committee, Emmanuel Celler (D-NY) announced his support for the joint committee proposal in November 1955, and longtime CIA supporter Senator Harry Byrd conceded that even he was wavering.[36]

In the face of the Hoover Commission's endorsement of the joint committee proposal and what appeared to be growing sentiment for it within Congress,

---

[32] Barrett, *CIA and Congress*, 213.

[33] Ibid., 209–10.

[34] CIA draft study, Vol. I, 51.

[35] Barrett, *CIA and Congress*, 210–11; CIA draft study, Vol. I. 51–52.

[36] CIA draft study, Vol. I, 52.

Dulles met with Eisenhower in August 1955 to confirm the president's continued opposition to the idea. Dulles expressed his concern that a joint oversight committee with a permanent staff, allowed to probe deeply into Agency operations, would inevitably create a problem. Not only were there security risks involved, Dulles argued, but such probing would "tend to create doubt abroad as to the security of the United States' handling of material handed over by foreign sources, and would result in the inevitable stoppage of [the] flow of certain sensitive information." Dulles apparently had little difficulty convincing Eisenhower, who had long opposed the idea.[37]

Debate in the Senate: 1956

When the Senate reconvened in January 1956, the third version of the Mansfield resolution was still pending.[38] By this point, fully a third of the Senate had signed on as co-sponsors, including many members of non-CIA subcommittees on the SASC as well as the ranking member of the SAC. Fearing the resolution could garner even more support, Dulles encouraged Senator Russell to hold another meeting of the CIA subcommittee as "a good psychological move" in terms of arguing against the need for a joint committee. He also provided talking points for supportive members to use in speaking against such a committee.[39]

On 16 January 1956, Russell wrote to the chairman of the Senate Rules Committee, where the resolution had been referred.

> *It is difficult for me to foresee that increased staff scrutiny of CIA operations would result in either substantial savings or a significant increase in available intelligence information. . . . If there is one agency of the government in which we must take some matters on faith, without a constant examination of its methods and sources, it is the CIA.[40]*

For his part, President Eisenhower sought to head off the Mansfield resolution by creating an eight-member White House board to do oversight of the CIA and other intelligence agencies: the President's Board of Consultants on Foreign Intelligence Activities. Rather than assuage the concerns of Mansfield and others in the Senate, however, some saw the creation of the White House

---

[37] CIA draft study, Vol. I, 53.
[38] For a detailed description of this episode, see Barrett, *CIA and Congress*, 223–33.
[39] CIA draft study, Vol. I, 55.
[40] Smist, *Congress Oversees*, 6.

board as a signal from the administration that Congress was not up to the job itself.[41]

Indeed, when the Senate Rules Committee considered the Mansfield resolution later the same month, it shocked the administration as well as the Agency's overseers on the Hill by reporting the resolution to the floor by a 7–2 vote. Among other things, the majority report stated,

> *The CIA has unquestionably placed itself above other government agencies. There has been no regular methodical review of this agency, other than a briefing which is supplied to a selected few members of selected such* [sic] *committees.*[42]

This unexpected action by the Rules Committee led Eisenhower and Dulles to redouble their efforts to ensure the Mansfield resolution never became law. In the Senate, Eisenhower sent word to the Republican Policy Committee that he was "very much opposed" to the resolution because intelligence operations were "the most delicate things in the Government . . . too sensitive for Congress to take up."[43] Again, however, the suggestion that Congress lacked the competence to handle sensitive matters annoyed several Republican senators. The president received a more favorable reaction in the House, where House Speaker Sam Rayburn (D-TX) as well as Majority Leader John McCormack (D-MA) supported his position. HASC Chairman Carl Vinson also circulated a letter to all House members explaining his opposition to the joint committee. One by one, the congressmen who had earlier expressed support for the proposal began signaling their opposition to it in their public statements.[44]

Notwithstanding the diminishing prospect that the House would ultimately go along with the Mansfield resolution, the Senate as a whole took it up on 9–10 April 1956—the first and only time prior to 1976 that the existing oversight arrangements for the CIA were actually debated on the floor of the House or Senate. As one would expect, the debate featured the proponent of the resolution (Mansfield) engaging the principal defenders of the status quo—in this case, the chairman and ranking member of the SASC, Senators Russell and Saltonstall, respectively.

During the first day of debate, Mansfield came right to the point and asked Saltonstall how many times the CIA had requested meetings with its oversight subcommittees and how many times Saltonstall had requested briefings from the CIA. Saltonstall replied that it happened at least twice a year in the SASC

---

[41] Barrett, *CIA and Congress*, 226–27; CIA draft study, Vol. I., 56.

[42] CIA draft study, Vol. I, 56.

[43] Ibid., 57.

[44] Ibid., 59.

and once a year in the SAC. When Mansfield then asked how often the DCI (Dulles at the time) had refused to answer the subcommittees' questions, Saltonstall replied,

> *The difficulty in connection with asking questions and obtaining information is that we might obtain information which I personally would rather not have, unless it was essential for me as Member of Congress to have it. . . . It is not a question of reluctance on the part of CIA officials to speak to us. Instead, it is a question of our reluctance, if you will, to seek information and knowledge on subjects which I personally, as a Member of Congress and as a citizen, would rather not have.[45]*

Speaking to the Senate as a whole, Mansfield replied, "Mr. President, I think the Senator's answer tells the whole story."[46]

The next day, however, when debate on the resolution resumed, Senator Russell took the floor and said he had yet to hear one substantial argument for changing the existing oversight arrangements. While he candidly conceded that CIA personnel had wasted money and had "not been able to penetrate behind the Iron Curtain," he noted that CIA had developed information "of vital value," which, on two or three occasions, had been "well worth the total cost of administration of all our security agencies."[47]

Responding to the implication of Mansfield's proposal that his committee was not doing its job, Russell had this to say:

> *We have had before us the head of the Central Intelligence Agency and his staff. We have never had them fail to respond to a single question we have asked them. . . . We have asked him very searching questions about some activities which it almost chills the marrow of a man to hear about. . . . I doubt very much whether the heads of the many independent agencies* [in the federal government] *have spent more time with the committees to which they are supposed to report, over the course of an average year, than Mr. Dulles, as Director, has spent before my committee.*

> [Nevertheless] *I shall endeavor, to the best of my ability, to keep in touch with what the CIA is doing. I do not mean to say by that that I intend to undertake to find out whether or not we have an agent in some foreign country—perhaps a satellite—who is tapping the tele-*

---

[45] Barrett, *CIA and Congress*, 230.
[46] Ibid.
[47] Ibid., 230.

*phone of some foreign embassy, or anything of that nature. How-
ever, I shall undertake to exercise as close supervision of this
Agency as is ordinarily exercised by the parent committees of the
Congress in dealing with agencies which are responsible to them.[48]*

Responding later to a suggestion by Senator Wayne Morse that all senators,
indeed all citizens, be made aware of the CIA's activities, Senator Russell
strenuously objected:

We have not told the country [and will not do so in the future] *. . .
because if there is anything in the United States which should be
held sacred behind the curtain of classified matter, it is the information of this Agency. . . . It would be better to abolish it out of hand
than it would be to adopt a theory that such information should be
available to every member of Congress and to the members of the
staff of any committee.*

SAC Chairman Carl Hayden added,

*How would it be possible to keep the American people fully
informed and at the same time keep our Communist enemies in Moscow in the dark?[49]*

In the ensuing vote, the barons of the Senate prevailed, 59–27. As Mansfield later explained, "What you had was a brash freshman going up against
the high brass."[50] Mansfield confided to CIA liaison John Warner that the
next time he tried this, he would "line up with the pros—the professional poli-
ticians."[51]

Subsequent Developments: 1956–59

While the public "dust-up" over the Mansfield resolution did not result in a
change to the existing oversight arrangements, the debate did prompt SAC
Chairman Hayden to formally designate his committee's CIA subcommittee.
While his counterpart in the House, HAC Chairman Cannon, continued to use
an undesignated subcommittee he expanded its professional staff and sought
increasingly more detailed information about the Agency's program and budget. At CIA's urging, the subcommittees would also sometimes publish

---

[48] Ibid., 231.
[49] Ibid., 231–32.
[50] Ibid., 233.
[51] CIA draft study, Vol. I, 60.

notices of their meetings, if only to demonstrate to the outside world such meetings were occurring.[52]

But in the Senate, even these modest efforts to improve the outside perception of their stewardship of the Agency, were belied by what was taking place. Russell appointed himself, Saltonstall, Byrd, Bridges, and Lyndon Johnson (D-TX) to the SASC subcommittee. Appointed by Hayden to the SAC subcommittee were, again, Russell, Bridges and Byrd. Not surprisingly, the subcommittees of the SASC and SAC began conducting their business at the same meetings.[53] Moreover, their meetings were rare. Despite the Agency's efforts to get its Senate committees to meet more frequently, the SAC subcommittee met once in 1956 and not at all in 1957. In 1958, the sole budget hearing for the Agency in the Senate was a joint meeting of the SASC and SAC subcommittees and was "off the record" (in other words, no transcript was made). While CIA notes of the meeting reflect that the discussion "covered the world situation in considerable detail and the Senators appeared to be impressed with the information given them," they asked no questions about the Agency's operations, tactics, or finances.[54]

Walter L. Pforzheimer, CIA legislative counsel at the time, described the situation during this period this way:

> We allowed Congress to set the pace. We briefed in whatever detail they wanted. But one of the problems was, you couldn't get Congress to get interested.[55]

While the Agency struggled for the attention of its oversight committees where its budget was concerned, the DCI's appearances on the Hill, principally to provide substantive analysis and to explain the Agency's role in predicting well-publicized events around the world (or, more often, failing to do so), actually grew more frequent. In 1956, DCI Dulles testified before both armed services committees on the suspected "bomber gap" with the Soviet Union. Later the same year, he testified before the Senate Foreign Relations Committee (SFRC) on developments in Eastern Europe. In 1957, the HAC held three closed-door hearings on the CIA's performance. Later in the year, after the Soviets unexpectedly put a satellite into space for the first time, Dulles was brought before the SASC to explain what the Agency knew about the Soviet missile capability. In 1958, he appeared 27 times before 16 different committees. While this testimony principally involved the Sputnik launch

---

[52] Warner interview, 27 September 1996, 18.
[53] Karalekas, *History*, 66–67.
[54] CIA draft study, Vol. I, 63.
[55] CIA draft study, Vol. II, 7.

and Soviet military capabilities, several committees also probed the failure of the CIA to predict the coup that had taken place in Iraq that year. The army had overthrown and murdered the pro-Western monarch, King Faisal, sending shock waves through other pro-Western Arab governments, which feared the same could happen to them, and the CIA had apparently known nothing about it. This perceived failure prompted Mansfield, who was now the majority whip in the Senate, to offer for the fourth time his joint intelligence committee resolution as a fix to the problem, but once the hullabaloo over the coup in Iraq quieted down, he did not pursue it. (For a more detailed discussion of Congress's inquiries into these intelligence failures, see chapter 7.)

Indeed, in midsummer 1958, the Agency's increased visibility on the Hill and the criticism that frequently attended these appearances caused CIA officials to consider how they might improve the Agency's standing on Capitol Hill. "Unless some method is established at a very early date to provide the general membership of the Congress at least with a general statement of [the Agency's] competence," CIA Inspector General Lyman Kirkpatrick warned Dulles, "We shall inevitably find ourselves with a Congressional watchdog committee."[56] In the ensuing months, CIA stepped up its briefings of congressional committees and developed a comprehensive "tasks and functions" briefing for use on Capitol Hill. It also suggested to its subcommittee chairmen that they brief their full committees on the Agency's operations and accomplishments.[57]

Increased CIA interaction with the Hill, and the threat that sensitive information might be compromised as a result, concerned President Eisenhower, however, who told Dulles in December 1958 that he was testifying entirely too often before Congress, especially "non-oversight" committees. Dulles agreed that in the future he would testify before such committees only if he first obtained the permission of the chairmen of the House or Senate CIA subcommittees and would provide only oral briefings to these committees, in other words, intelligence documents would not be left on the Hill.[58]

Meanwhile, Dulles sought to improve the interaction with the CIA subcommittees. Taken aback by criticism relayed by a member of the HAC staff in December 1958 that Chairman Cannon was tired of the Agency's "hiding behind a cloak of secrecy," Dulles offered to brief the HAC whenever it wanted in as much detail as it wanted. He subsequently made the same offer to the HASC, SAC, and SASC, but it did not result in appreciable change.[59] All

---

[56] CIA draft study, Vol. I, 65.

[57] Ibid., 67.

[58] Ibid., 71.

[59] Ibid., 68–69.

told, Dulles and his senior assistants appeared 31 times before Congress in 1959, four more occasions than in the preceding year.

Dulles's efforts to cultivate the subcommittees continued into the following year, but more often than not his efforts to have the subcommittees hold hearings were met with indifference. They were "fully occupied" with other matters, the staff of the HASC subcommittee told him. Indeed, one exasperated House staff member wondered to the Agency's legislative liaison why the Agency needed more meetings anyway, since they always got all the money they asked for.[60]

The Issue of GAO Audits: 1959–62

The General Accounting Office (GAO) was an arm of the Congress used to conduct audits and performance reviews of executive branch agencies, but its authority to audit the expenditures of the CIA (or conduct performance reviews) was not made clear in the charter of either agency. RADM Hillenkoetter had taken the position in 1948 that the Agency's statutory authority to spend appropriated funds for operational purposes without the requirement of a "voucher"—a document showing how the funds had been spent— in effect exempted such funds from audit by the GAO. The law, he pointed out, said the certificate of the director would be the "final accounting" required for such funds. Hillenkoetter had allowed the GAO, however, to audit "vouchered expenditures" for nonoperational purposes, in other words where the Agency maintained receipts showing how the funds were spent, for example, TDY funds to attend conferences.[61]

In early 1959, however, the comptroller general (head of the GAO) informed the HASC that GAO planned to terminate even these limited kinds of audits because CIA refused to provide meaningful access to its information. This, in turn, led the committee to urge that CIA and GAO try to work out their differences. After several months of negotiation, Dulles agreed to ground rules that would allow the GAO to conduct a limited audit of the Agency on a trial basis. Sixteen months later, however, GAO wrote the committee again saying it was terminating its effort because it lacked meaningful access. After several months more of pressing the parties to find a solution, the HASC finally agreed that GAO could withdraw. In July 1962, all of its audit activities at the Agency were abandoned.[62]

---

[60] Ibid., 89.
[61] Ibid., 93.
[62] Ibid., 95.

Shootdown of the U-2: 1960

While DCI Dulles had told selected members about the U-2 program in 1955 (see chapter 8), most members of Congress knew nothing of the program until Francis Gary Powers was shot down in one of these spy planes over the Soviet Union on 1 May 1960. This prompted a flurry of briefings by the CIA in the weeks that followed and, to a limited degree, raised the issue of the adequacy of the existing oversight arrangements. *Aviation Week*, for example, editorialized that "the need for a congressional or some other 'watchdog' operation over CIA was never more apparent."[63]

But most of the assessments of CIA's performance that came out of Congress at the time, including those of the CIA subcommittees, were overwhelmingly supportive (see chapter 8). Subsequent efforts to institute new oversight arrangements received limited traction as a result. In September, the HASC created the Special Subcommittee to Investigate National Intelligence Activities, but it fell dormant after one inconclusive hearing with the CIA.[64] In the Senate, Eugene McCarthy (D-WI) described the U-2 episode as only the latest in a series of CIA blunders and again offered the joint intelligence committee as a solution to what he viewed as a failure of congressional oversight. A few weeks later, in a meeting of congressional leaders with President Eisenhower to discuss the forthcoming closed-door hearings on the U-2 before the two foreign relations committees, Mansfield took the opportunity to raise the joint intelligence committee idea personally with the president, only to receive a firm but polite turndown.[65] Apparently undeterred by the president's reaction, Mansfield offered another bill after the hearings, renewing his call for a joint committee, but, apparently recognizing it had little chance of being enacted, chose not to pursue it.[66]

The Bay of Pigs: 1961

Like the shootdown of the U-2, the disaster at the Bay of Pigs in April 1961 (see chapter 9) prompted renewed calls for a joint intelligence committee. Senator McCarthy reintroduced his proposal in the Senate, while four congressmen offered similar resolutions in the House.[67] Moreover, the House Rules Committee created a special subcommittee to explore whether a full-scale investigation of the CIA was called for in the wake of the Cuban fiasco.

---

[63] Barrett, *CIA and Congress*, 422.
[64] CIA draft study, Vol. I, 82.
[65] Barrett, *CIA and Congress*, 412.
[66] CIA draft study, Vol. I, 83.
[67] Ibid., 87.

In this case, however, the Agency had, for the first time, given advance notice to at least two of its oversight committees, and President Kennedy had separately advised Senator William Fulbright (D-AR), chairman of the SFRC. Dulles appeared before the HAC subcommittee in January, several months in advance of the operation and, according to an internal CIA memo, "gave a fairly detailed picture of CIA action with respect to Cuba . . . mentioning the two-pronged program of propaganda . . . [and] the paramilitary effort, and indicating the number of Cubans being trained and the supply efforts and the bases."[68] In March, he appeared before the HASC subcommittee and described the invasion plans in even greater detail. According to an internal CIA memo, the subcommittee "seemed satisfied with what they had heard."[69] According to CIA Legislative Counsel John Warner, Dulles also briefed the leaders of the SASC subcommittee on the operation. Of those members of Congress who learned of the Bay of Pigs in advance, only one, Senator Fulbright, is recorded as raising objections.[70]

So, while the Bay of Pigs had been the Agency's most stunning public failure to that point, Congress could not claim to have been uninformed about it. On 1–2 May 1961, the SFRC did hold two days of relatively contentious closed hearings following the operation, and the HAC and HASC subcommittees followed up with closed hearings of their own. But the congressional participants in these hearings were relatively restrained in their public criticisms of the Agency. Indeed, while certain members professed to understand the president's need to replace Dulles after the debacle, they also made a point of signaling their personal regard for him.[71]

Senator Mansfield, who was now the majority leader and a supporter of the new president, also sought to calm the Senate's reaction to the Bay of Pigs. Telling the press that, "this is no time for a congressional investigation," he refused to support McCarthy's resolution to create a joint intelligence committee, an idea that until this point, Mansfield had largely been identified with.[72]

President Kennedy also took several actions in the aftermath of the Bay of Pigs that dampened what might otherwise have been an occasion for an energetic congressional response. First, he appointed a blue-ribbon commission chaired by retired Army General Maxwell Taylor to investigate the operation; the commission would have access to CIA operational records (something Congress did not have). Second, within three weeks of the Bay of Pigs, he

---

[68] Ibid., 84.
[69] Ibid.; Barrett, *CIA and Congress*, 440–45.
[70] Barrett, *CIA and Congress*, 445, 448.
[71] Ibid., 452–53.
[72] Ibid., 455.

reestablished the internal oversight board for intelligence within the White House. Redesignated the President's Foreign Intelligence Advisory Board (PFIAB), it replaced the defunct Board of Consultants on Foreign Intelligence Activities that Eisenhower had established five years earlier.

The Remainder of the 1960s: A Period of Quiescence

Interest in reforming the existing oversight arrangements did not die after the Bay of Pigs. Senator McCarthy continued to reintroduce his joint intelligence committee proposal each year, which various senators and congressmen continued to tout as the "panacea" for the shortcomings perceived in the existing arrangements. But those espousing reform remained relatively few, and fewer still were willing to devote the time and energy to an issue that was evidently so stacked against them. The leaders of the CIA subcommittees seemed as determined as ever to maintain their control over Agency oversight and, in this regard, had the publicly stated support of Presidents Kennedy and Johnson.[73] Without some event that would crystallize concern more generally within the Congress, reform still appeared remote.

But such a "crystallizing" event did not occur for the rest of the decade. There were events that raised questions in Congress about the Agency's role or performance—the Ramparts episode in 1967 or the Cuban missile crisis of 1962, for example[74]—but none provoked the sort of powerful and widespread reaction needed to overturn the existing oversight arrangements. While there were "skirmishes" with the Foreign Relations Committee in the Senate during the period, as well as occasional defections to the joint committee concept on the part of influential members (see below), the powerful barons who controlled the CIA subcommittees continued to hold sway in both houses.

The Agency, for its part, continued to urge its committees to exercise their oversight responsibilities more actively—and more visibly—and expanded its substantive intelligence support to other committees.

McCone's Early Interaction with the Congress

While new DCI John McCone followed the line that Dulles had taken in public—that the issue of a joint committee was up to Congress to decide—he actively defended the existing oversight arrangements in his early public com-

---

[73] CIA draft study, Vol. I, 91.

[74] See chapter 8 for a discussion of the *Ramparts* disclosures and chapter 10 for a discussion of the Cuban missile crisis.

ments. He told the *New York Times* in January 1962 that the CIA "has been at all times responsive to the calls of these [CIA] subcommittees and in addition has brought to their attention matters the Agency felt should be properly considered by them."[75] In private, however, he, like Dulles, encouraged the subcommittees to meet more frequently with Agency representatives, receive substantive intelligence briefings, and learn more of CIA's operations. While the subcommittees seemed initially amenable to McCone's suggestions, scheduling several hearings in early 1962, as the session wore on, interest in having regular meetings waned in the press of other business.

Senator Fulbright complained publicly in March 1962 that, contrasted with the oversight subcommittees, his committee, the SFRC, was not getting enough attention from the CIA, contending that the committee needed greater access to intelligence to do its job. This led McCone to propose to Senator Russell that he allow one or two members of the SFRC to attend meetings of the SASC subcommittee, but Russell demurred.[76] Still, the Agency ended the year with a record 32 congressional briefings for the year, including 12 for their oversight subcommittees.[77]

The "Dust-up" with Congressman Lindsay: 1963-64

In April 1963, following McCone's refusal to provide information to Rep. John Lindsay (R-NY) concerning the CIA's operations in Europe, Lindsay publicly expressed his "profound displeasure" with the Agency, and in August he introduced legislation to establish a joint intelligence committee to investigate the CIA's operational performance, analytical capability, and administrative practices.[78]

Within CIA itself, Lindsay's initiative led to a reappraisal of the Agency's opposition to a joint committee. In a memo to McCone, Agency General Counsel Lawrence Houston argued that despite its shortcomings, the existing system had matured. "Our own subcommittees have been better formalized, their jurisdiction has been more clearly recognized, and we have made considerable efforts to have more frequent and complete hearings." Houston went on to argue that a joint committee would likely not protect CIA's interests as well as the existing system did and that to endorse the joint committee at this point would be "bitterly resented as criticism of the way [our current overseers] handle their responsibilities."[79]

---

[75] Ibid.
[76] Ibid., 93–94.
[77] Ibid., 101.
[78] Ibid., 94.
[79] Ibid., 92.

For his part, McCone decried "this continued prattle about a watchdog committee." His greatest fear, he told associates, was that such a committee would hire a staff of disgruntled ex-CIA employees who would wreak havoc upon their old employer.[80]

In February 1964, Lindsay continued his assault by writing an article for *Esquire* magazine—accompanied by a similar article by Senator McCarthy—that criticized the Agency and argued for a joint committee to oversee it. McCone was livid, privately denouncing the essays as "a series of absolute misstatements" and calling the authors "sons of bitches." He even threatened to resign in protest of the royalties he presumed Lindsay and McCarthy had gotten for writing their criticism. Once tempers had cooled, however, McCone approved a conciliatory approach to Lindsay, allowing Agency officials to meet with him and apologize for the Agency's previous failure to provide him with information. At the same time, CIA successfully worked behind the scenes to ensure that Lindsay's proposal, then pending before the House Rules Committee, never saw the light of day.[81]

CIA Interaction with the Congress: 1963–66

For the remainder of his tenure as DCI, McCone continued to encourage the CIA subcommittees, particularly those in the Senate, to involve themselves to a greater extent in the Agency's affairs. He was also prepared to brief other committees on substantive issues so long as it could be done without antagonizing the leaders of the CIA subcommittees.

When VADM William Raborn became DCI in 1965, CIA General Counsel Lawrence Houston advised him that while no statute required it, CIA "must continue to inform the [oversight] Subcommittees currently and fully . . . [and] should not withhold information from them unless directed to do so by the President." In the past, Houston went on to note, the Agency had given its subcommittees any information about its activities they had requested, including activities and projects "of a most sensitive nature."[82]

The number of appearances Agency officers made on the Hill fluctuated from year to year, more often the result of world events (see chapters 4 and 5) than its own efforts to promote interaction. Moreover, while there were occasional stirrings of discontent in Congress with respect to the Agency's performance during this period, none prompted calls for change in the existing

---

[80] David Robarge, *John McCone as Director of Central Intelligence*, 75 (classified biography).
[81] CIA draft study, Vol. I, 95.
[82] CIA draft study, Vol. II, 10.

oversight arrangements. In 1963, CIA records reflect a total of 30 substantive briefings to congressional committees. The following year, the number shrunk to 13, but the Agency did meet on nine occasions during the year with its four oversight subcommittees. By this point, staff on the subcommittees had grown to four or five professionals on each subcommittee, still small but twice as large as the staffs had been a decade earlier.[83]

In 1965, the total of substantive briefings provided by the Agency rose to a record 53, which included 34 meetings with its subcommittees during the year, leading John Warner, its legislative counsel, to write incoming DCI Richard Helms in mid-June 1966 that the Agency's standing with the Hill was "better than ever."[84]

The SFRC Asserts Its Right to Oversee the CIA: 1966

Notwithstanding Warner's glowing assessment, not all members were happy with the existing state of affairs. Frustrated by the inability of the SFRC to obtain more information from the CIA about the situation in South Vietnam, Senator Eugene McCarthy introduced a resolution in January 1966 calling for a review by the SFRC of CIA's impact on foreign policy. When the full committee considered the proposal in May, it reported out, at the behest of its chairman, Senator Fulbright, an amended resolution that called for the addition of three members of the SFRC to the CIA subcommittee of the SASC.[85]

Senator Russell, who still chaired the SASC and its CIA subcommittee, reacted negatively, promising a floor fight when the SFRC resolution reached the floor. Majority Leader Mansfield, wishing to avoid this result, asked Russell and SAC Chairman Hayden to meet with Fulbright to come up with a compromise. Mansfield himself suggested a separate three-person subcommittee be established on the SFRC to do oversight of intelligence operations. CIA was so alarmed by this suggestion that it sought and obtained White House intervention to oppose the idea. Russell also expressed his displeasure. As a result, neither the SFRC resolution nor any compromise plan made it to the Senate floor that year.[86]

To appease the dissidents on the SFRC, however, Russell afterwards invited Mansfield, Fulbright, and Senator Bourke Hickenlooper (R-IA), the SFRC's ranking minority member, to begin attending meetings of his CIA subcommit-

---

[83] Ibid., Vol. I, 104–6; Warner interview, 27 September 1996, 31.

[84] CIA draft study, Vol. I, 108.

[85] CIA draft study, Vol. II, 24–25.

[86] Ibid., 25–26.

tee. Initially, the three were receptive to Russell's invitation, but all soon stopped attending, because, as Fulbright complained, "they [the CIA] never reveal anything of significance [at these meetings]."[87]

1971: A Pivotal Year

By the end of 1971, senior officials at the Agency clearly saw the old system of oversight coming to an end. Largely as a result of the Vietnam War and the growing mistrust of the executive branch, Congress, like the public generally, was becoming more disillusioned and suspicious. Younger, antiwar members were being elected to seats in Congress and did not have the same reverence for the institution or for its traditions of seniority. CIA, because of the secrecy in which it necessarily had to operate, was peculiarly vulnerable to this sense of mistrust. Some in Congress suspected the Nixon White House was using the CIA to carry out its policies in Southeast Asia to avoid congressional scrutiny.

To make matters worse, the Agency's aging congressional overseers, who had protected it for a quarter of a century, were passing from the scene. Senator Russell died in January 1971. Carl Hayden and Mendel Rivers were also gone by this point. Those who remained in charge were relatively old—SAC chairman Allen Ellender (D-LA) was 81; HAC chairman George Mahon (D-TX), 72; SASC chairman John Stennis, 71; and HASC chairman Edward Hebert (D-LA), 71—and, for the most part, resisted changing their old patterns of behavior. When a public furor broke out in February 1971, for example, over Senator Stuart Symington's (D-MO) acknowledgment that CIA had, for years, been conducting a "secret war" in Laos (see chapter 9), SASC Chairman Stennis chose to handle it quietly, behind the scenes. The SASC subcommittee, in fact, held no meetings at all in 1971. And after the Senate introduced a rash of legislative proposals following Symington's disclosure (mandating everything from disclosing the Agency's budget to barring CIA from conducting paramilitary activities abroad), Stennis made certain none saw the light of day. At the same time he warned DCI Helms informally that unless the Agency disentangled itself from Laos, it faced the possibility that Congress would intervene to curtail its activities around the globe and that he might not be able to stop it.[88] Apparently taking Stennis's admonition to heart, Helms sought permission from the Nixon administration to terminate the program.

---

[87] Ibid., 26–27.
[88] Hathaway and Smith, *Richard Helms*, 179–80.

In the House, the CIA's overseers proved more amenable to accommodating the growing demand for change. After the Democratic Party caucus, at the urging of younger members, adopted a new policy in 1971 that limited members to a single subcommittee chairmanship, HASC Chairman Hebert created a new special subcommittee on intelligence to which he appointed Lucien Nedzi (D-MI), a younger, energetic congressman as chairman. Nedzi was given the job, Hebert explained to the CIA legislative counsel, because he enjoyed the confidence of the "younger and more restive members."[89]

In any event, by the end of 1971, as CIA Legislative Counsel John Maury perceptively noted in his yearend report,

> *The congressional power structure, which has for a quarter of a century served to shield the Agency from intrusion or attack by the rank-and-file membership, is in a state of flux. . . . One need not go far down the seniority lists of the committees over which* [the aging leaders] *preside to find members of substantially different temperament and outlook. They include men who have over the years become increasingly suspicious or jealous of the secretive manner in which the Agency oversight committees have exercised their responsibilities. And their ranks are being periodically reinforced by newly elected younger members. Many of these feel that because of the increasingly important role of the Agency in providing inputs to crucial policy decisions its information and its activities should be more broadly accessible to the Legislative branch, and some of them appear to have been infected by the anti-establishment and anti-Agency campaigns of the "New Left." Faced with the resulting pressures, our aging and harassed protectors and benefactors on the Hill can no longer be expected to hold the old lines.*[90]

Congressional Inquiries into Watergate: 1973–74

On the night of 16 June 1972, five men were arrested at the Watergate Hotel in Washington DC, caught burglarizing the offices of the Democratic National Committee. All, it turned out, had connections with the CIA. One, James McCord, was a retired Agency security officer, and the other four were Cuban exiles who either had been, or still were, on the Agency's payroll. Information found on the burglars also connected them to another former Agency

---

[89] CIA draft study, Vol. II, 43.
[90] Hathaway and Smith, *Richard Helms, 181.*

employee, E. Howard Hunt, who worked at the Nixon White House as the head of a small unit that investigated security leaks.

As the criminal investigation of the burglary proceeded, it came to light that CIA had provided certain kinds of assistance to Hunt. The Agency at Hunt's request had provided a psychological profile of Daniel Ellsberg, the Pentagon official who had earlier leaked the Pentagon Papers to the press. Later, Hunt and G. Gordon Liddy used Agency-provided disguises, fake ID cards, and miniature cameras to scout out the office of Ellsberg's psychiatrist in California. Film taken of the office was then sent to CIA to be developed. While CIA was unwitting of Hunt's purposes, it terminated its assistance to him at that point, uncomfortable with what he might be doing.[91]

Raising further suspicion regarding the Agency's involvement, the ongoing investigations later revealed that the White House had attempted to use the CIA as part of its effort to cover up its involvement in the affair. The White House had asked CIA to intervene with the FBI to stop its investigation of the Mexican connections of two of the Watergate burglars. White House Counsel John Dean subsequently proposed that CIA use money from its contingency fund to make bail for the burglars. While DCI Helms had steadfastly refused to allow the Agency to be used for these purposes, the fact that the White House had reportedly made such overtures to the Agency during the summer of 1972 deepened suspicion in the Congress.

First to investigate was the Nedzi subcommittee of the HASC, which in May 1973 began a series of hearings specifically focused on CIA's involvement in Watergate that lasted intermittently for more than a year. While the subcommittee eventually vindicated Helms as well as the Agency—Nedzi told Helms that both had been "badly abused" by the Nixon administration[92]—the Nedzi investigation was the most thorough, meticulous investigation of possible wrongdoing within the CIA that a congressional committee had conducted to that point.

The broader, more widely appreciated congressional investigation of Watergate, carried out by a special committee of the Senate chaired by Senator Sam Ervin (D-NC), also looked into CIA's role in the affair. But in the end, like the Nedzi subcommittee, it found no evidence of CIA's involvement beyond the unwitting assistance provided to Hunt. The vice chairman of the Watergate Committee, Senator Howard Baker (R-TN), however, remained skeptical and filed separate views to the committee's final report describing his continued misgivings on the issue.[93] Baker's statement deeply concerned DCI William

---

[91] Prados, *Lost Crusader*, 250.
[92] Hathaway and Smith, *Richard Helms*, 198.

Colby, who not only believed CIA was innocent of the charges but thought the Agency had gone out of its way to provide Baker and his staff with access to Agency personnel and pertinent documentary evidence.[94] Indeed, for the first time in its history, the Agency had allowed investigators from the Congress to review documents from its files and interview its employees. Heretofore, the Agency had provided information to congressional committees through briefings or by providing documents for review on the Hill. In any event, while the Watergate Committee did not recommend change to the oversight arrangements per se, its final report did recommend that Congress should "more closely supervise the operations of the intelligence and law enforcement 'community' . . . and, in particular, its relations with the White House."[95]

Watergate had one other consequence for CIA that ultimately had a significant bearing on the arrangements for congressional oversight, and that was the assembling of the "Family Jewels." When James Schlesinger succeeded Helms as DCI in March 1973, the criminal investigation into Watergate had been ongoing for months, and the congressional investigations were swinging into high gear. On 15 April, the Justice Department announced that it had established evidence of a White House link to the burglary of the office of Daniel Ellsberg's psychiatrist two years earlier. This led CIA to look again at the photographs they had developed for Hunt: their significance was now clear. When Schlesinger was told of this, he was outraged and wanted to know what else he had not been told about. The order went out within the Agency that the DCI wanted to know anything and everything about the Agency's past, especially any domestic activities, that might have "flap potential."[96] The CIA inspector general, in response to this order, assembled a compilation of 693 pages that became known as the "family jewels." It contained reports of mail-opening programs, surveillance of Americans, infiltration of domestic political groups, drug experiments on unwitting subjects, break-ins of homes and offices, connections with organized crime (in conjunction with plans to assassinate Cuban leader Fidel Castro), and other dubious activities (see chapter 8).

By the time the report had been assembled, however, Schlesinger had left the DCI's job to become Secretary of Defense. This meant that his putative successor, William Colby, soon to face confirmation hearings before the SASC, would have to deal with it. Colby decided that at a minimum he had to bring the "family jewels" to the attention of the SASC and HASC before he was confirmed. He did so in private meetings with Stennis and Symington of

---

[93] Ibid., 201.
[94] CIA draft study, Vol. II, 45.
[95] Hathaway and Smith, *Richard Helms*, 202.
[96] Prados, *Lost Crusader*, 259–260.

the SASC and Hebert and Nedzi of the HASC. Of the four, only Nedzi asked to see the compilation; the others relied on Colby's assurances that these were activities that had taken place in the past, had been ended, and would not be allowed in the future; they agreed they should not be part of Colby's confirmation process since he had himself played no role in them. Nedzi did, in fact, read the compilation but took no further action with respect to it within his subcommittee.[97]

Part of the quandary Nedzi faced in deciding what to do about the "family jewels" was the absence of an historical track record on what the appropriate congressional role should be in such circumstances. "It is a bit unsettling," he told an interviewer in 1973, "that 26 years after the passage of the National Security Act of 1947, the scope of real congressional oversight, as opposed to nominal congressional oversight, remains unformed and uncertain."[98]

Congressional Inquiries into the CIA Activities in Chile: 1973–74

While the investigations of Watergate were ongoing, Congress began an unrelated series of inquiries into CIA's activities that signaled even more clearly that the old system of oversight was about to change.

In September 1973, Chilean President Salvador Allende was overthrown and died in a military coup. A short time later, articles appeared in the press containing allegations by Congressman Michael Harrington (D-MA), a liberal, anti-administration member, that the CIA had been involved.

In October 1973, a House foreign affairs subcommittee, at Harrington's urging, summoned Colby to testify on the Agency's activities in Chile. While Colby appeared before the subcommittee, he refused to testify substantively in open session, saying that such testimony should more properly occur before the Nedzi subcommittee of the SASC.[99]

Testimony before Nedzi's subcommittee did not occur, however, until April 1974. When Colby did appear in closed session, he described the efforts that the Agency had made in 1970 at the direction of the Nixon administration to keep Allende from being elected president of Chile, essentially propaganda campaigns designed to discredit Allende among his supporters. Colby also assured the subcommittee that the Agency had not been involved in the 1973 coup that had resulted in Allende's death.[100]

---

[97] Ibid., 263–64.
[98] Karalekas, *History*, 100.
[99] Harold Ford, *William E. Colby as Director of Central Intelligence, 1973–76*, 70 (an internal, classified biography).

Colby chose to reveal—only to Nedzi at the time, however—that there was more to the story. The popular vote for Allende in 1970 had been less than a majority, which required, under the Chilean constitution, a vote by the Chilean legislature three weeks after the popular election. During this interim period, CIA at the express direction of President Nixon had undertaken several actions, including exploring the possibility of a coup with members of the Chilean military, to prevent Allende from coming to power. In the end, the coup never materialized, and Allende won the confirming vote in the Chilean legislature. (This disclosure to Nedzi becomes relevant later.)

In any event, after the closed hearing before the Nedzi subcommittee, Rep. Harrington asked to review the transcript of Colby's testimony pursuant to the rule of the House of Representatives that allowed all members access to hearing transcripts and records.[101] Unlike the House's CIA overseers before him, Nedzi believed he had no choice but to agree to the request. To no one's surprise, Harrington leaked the substance of Colby's testimony, claiming it proved the Agency had tried to "destabilize" the Allende candidacy in 1970.

The news stories that followed provoked a storm of criticism. For the first time, it appeared the Agency had admitted to covertly interfering in the electoral process of another democratic country. This prompted a number of bills to be introduced in each house during the summer of 1974 whose purpose was to restrict in some manner the CIA's operational activities abroad. One of these proposals, an amendment to the Foreign Assistance Act known as the Hughes-Ryan Amendment, eventually became the focus of the reformers. Requiring that the president personally approve all covert actions in the future, the amendment went on to provide that such operations could only be undertaken after a "finding" by the president that the operation at issue was necessary to the defense of the United States and that such a "finding" had been communicated to six committees of the Congress: the two armed services committees, the two foreign affairs committees, and the two appropriations committees.

Obviously, the amendment, if it became law, would involve the foreign affairs committees in oversight of the CIA in a way they had never been before, but this time the clout of the barons who had protected CIA for a quarter century had been significantly weakened. The chief counsel of the SASC advised the CIA's legislative liaison, for example, that while the committee's chairman, Senator Stennis, hoped to strip the amendment from the bill in committee, he worried that "we couldn't hold off the younger Senators much longer."[102] In fact, Stennis failed to get the amendment struck in committee

---

[100] Ibid., 70.
[101] CIA draft study, Vol. II, 47.

and sought to head it off by inviting the Senate majority and minority leaders, who were also members of the Senate Foreign Relations Committee, to participate in meetings of the CIA subcommittee. On the House side, HASC Chairman Mahon similarly offered to give the House Foreign Affairs Committee a role in overseeing intelligence activities affecting foreign policy. Neither of these efforts, however, proved enough to hold back the rushing tide. [103]

Meanwhile, if the Hughes-Ryan Amendment were not enough for the barons to contend with, a Senate government operations subcommittee held two days of hearings in early December 1974 on various bills to strengthen congressional oversight of the CIA and the Intelligence Community. Senator Baker, the lead witness at the hearings, sharply criticized the existing structure and argued again for a joint intelligence committee. Others pointed out that the CIA subcommittees never issued reports on the CIA and that Congress, in general, had little access to intelligence information. [104] While subsequent events overtook the subcommittee's legislative agenda, the hearings were nonetheless a clear indication of mounting discontent within the Senate.

By mid-December, the Hughes-Ryan Amendment had sailed through both houses of Congress. While CIA, with the support of administration officials, had doggedly sought changes to the amendment, its efforts to modify the proposal failed. In the face of overwhelming congressional support, President Ford ultimately signed it into law on 30 December 1974. [105]

Allegations of Domestic Spying and Other Abuses: 1974–75

Eight days before the Hughes-Ryan Amendment became law, the *New York Times* published a front-page story, headlined "Huge CIA Operation Reported in the U.S. Against Anti-War Forces, Other Dissidents in Nixon Years." The story dealt with many of the subjects disclosed in the "Family Jewels" (domestic wiretaps, break-ins, and mail openings; infiltration of domestic political groups; and the existence of CIA files on as many as 10,000 American citizens involved in the antiwar movement) and, indeed, for the first time, revealed the existence of the compilation to the public. [106]

President Ford, himself surprised by the report—the Agency had neglected to tell the White House of the "Family Jewels" or alert it to the publication of the *New York Times* story—reacted by announcing on 4 January 1975 the

---

[102] Ford, *William E. Colby*, 72.
[103] CIA draft study, Vol. II, 48.
[104] Ibid., 49.
[105] Ford, *William E. Colby*, 72.
[106] Prados, *Lost Crusader*, 294.

establishment of a blue-ribbon commission to be chaired by Vice President Nelson Rockefeller to investigate the allegations of CIA wrongdoing contained in the article.[107]

In Congress, in an effort to establish control of the situation, the CIA subcommittees of the SASC and SAC held a joint hearing on 15 January and called Colby to testify in response to the allegations. At the committees' request, Colby agreed that the transcript of the hearing should immediately be made public.[108] But for many in Congress, this was too little, too late. One consequence of the subcommittees' failure to maintain records of their activities over the years was that they were now unable to defend themselves when their stewardship was seriously challenged. It was apparent in any case that the old way of doing oversight no longer sufficed. The *New York Times* story was proof positive that the existing oversight arrangements did not work. The oversight subcommittees had known nothing of these activities.

Accordingly, neither House was willing to entrust the investigation of the alleged CIA abuses to its existing committee structure. On 27 January 1975, the Senate voted 82–4 to established a select committee of six Democrats and six Republicans, chaired by Frank Church (D-ID) to carry out an investigation. Not one of the leaders of the existing CIA subcommittees was appointed to the committee.[109] The House of Representatives followed suit on 19 February 1975. By a vote of 286 to 120, it created a 10-member investigating committee of seven Democrats and three Republicans.[110] Nedzi, notwithstanding his role as SASC CIA subcommittee chairman, was made chairman based upon his statement that a broader, more thoroughgoing investigation was needed and because he was seen as the most knowledgeable member of the House on intelligence matters.[111]

Although the CIA subcommittees in both houses would continue to handle the Agency's funding requirements while the investigations were ongoing, their oversight role was effectively at an end.

However, other congressional committees—held at bay for decades by the Agency's powerful protectors—were suddenly emboldened to join the fray. In addition to his numerous appearances before the two investigating committees, DCI Colby was called before seven other Senate committees during 1975, and before four additional House committees, testifying on such diverse subjects as CIA domestic spying, alleged CIA ties with drug lords in Thailand,

---

[107] Ibid., 298.
[108] Ibid., 308; William E. Colby, *Honorable Men*, 402–3.
[109] Smist, *Congress Oversees*, 31.
[110] Ibid., 134.
[111] CIA draft study, Vol. II, 113.

drug experimentation on unwitting subjects, alleged CIA activities in Chile, and the use of missionaries as intelligence sources. Indeed, when asked years later what the low point had been for him during this long, exhausting year, Colby replied without hesitation: "Bella Abzug!"

From her perch on the House Government Operations Committee, Abzug had, in her inimitable take-no-prisoners style, raked Colby over the coals for having kept a file on her. Admitting that he had "gotten sore," Colby recalled telling her that "if she were going to visit [terrorists] abroad, enemies of the United States, there was no way I was going to keep her name out of our records."[112]

Senator Frank Church
(US Senate Historical Collection)

The Church Committee: 1975–76

The Church Committee's investigation lasted 15 months. It held 126 formal hearings during this period, 21 days of public hearings, conducted over 800 interviews, and released 14 volumes of hearings and reports.[113] It focused its efforts on the alleged improprieties that had been identified in the press (collection on US persons, CIA involvement in Chile, and assassination plots). But it also expanded these inquiries into related areas (NSA surveillance of US citizens and FBI surveillance of Dr. Martin Luther King).[114]

This was the first probe of any consequence that Congress had ever conducted into Agency operations. Colby had given the Senate Watergate Committee access to documents and personnel relating to the Agency's assistance to E. Howard Hunt, but this did not entail an in-depth probe into the Agency's operational activities. Heretofore, if Congress had questions, it summoned the DCI to the Hill to explain. Now, it was asking for documents and access to Agency personnel.

---

[112] Ford, *William E. Colby*, 177–80.
[113] Smist, *Congress Oversees*, 28.
[114] For a discussion of its investigative activities relating to the Agency, see chapters 7–9.

For the most part, the Agency tried to cooperate. While some at the Agency thought the Church Committee should be told as little as possible, Colby believed that "you won't get away with stonewalling them." He thought the Agency "had a good story to tell" and that if the committee could be persuaded to stay focused on the domestic issues, the Agency might well avoid damage to its overseas operations. [115]

While the committee did not, as Colby had hoped, confine its investigation to domestic issues—for example, it looked into covert action in Chile and alleged assassination plots against foreign leaders—it did not conduct in-depth investigations of the Agency's principal mission areas: clandestine collection abroad and analysis. (See chapters 7 and 8.)

This is not to say the Church Committee posed no problems for the Agency. On the way back from his first hearing before the committee, Colby complained that he felt he was "sitting there with the handcuffs already put on me. . . . They treated me like a criminal."[116] There was also great consternation over Church's characterization of the Agency as a "rogue elephant rampaging out of control" at the committee's first public hearing[117] as well as other of his actions that the Agency regarded as attempts to sensationalize the investigation to advance his own political ambitions. Church announced his candidacy for president half way through the investigation. There were also continuing battles over the committee's access to Agency documents as well as considerable dismay over the committee's initial reports on assassination plots and covert action (see chapter 9 for a fuller description). But by the time the committee had finished its work, relations between the committee and its staff and the Agency's own staff had considerably improved.

Moreover, its final report, issued in April 1976, proved to be far more balanced from the Agency's standpoint than much of its investigative work. Colby, in fact, later characterized it as a "comprehensive and serious review of the history and present status of American intelligence."[118] While the committee concluded that CIA had, on occasion, operated outside the law and had violated the rights of US citizens, it specifically rejected its chairman's characterization that the Agency was ever "out of control" or a "rogue elephant." Rather, the committee found that "the CIA and other intelligence agencies had made important contributions to the nation's security and had generally performed their missions with dedication and distinction." On the whole, it

---

[115] CIA draft study, Vol. II, 69.
[116] Cary interview, 24 November 1987.
[117] CIA draft study, Vol. II. 68.
[118] Colby, *Honorable Men*, 442.

assessed the CIA to have been responsive to internal and external review and to direction by the executive branch.[119]

On the subject of the existing oversight arrangements within Congress, the committee found that the awareness of the Agency's overseers had been extremely limited, allowing many of the abuses identified by the committee to occur. To remedy this situation, the committee called for establishment of a permanent select committee on intelligence in the Senate to oversee CIA and the rest of the Intelligence Community. Senator Church went so far as to say this was the committee's most important recommendation inasmuch as it would go a long way to preventing abuses in the future.[120]

While some at the Agency resented the criticism in the committee's final report and worried that it would "provide our adversaries with a bottomless reservoir of material for anti-American propaganda and political exploitation," the Agency offered no official response to the report, fearing that whatever it might say could have a bearing on the formation of the new oversight committee that was expected to follow.[121]

The Nedzi/Pike Committees: 1975–76

The investigating committee the House established in February 1975 under the chairmanship of Congressman Nedzi never held a hearing. From the beginning, the other six Democrats appointed to the committee — in particular Congressman Harrington — viewed Nedzi with suspicion, given his earlier role as chairman of the HASC CIA subcommittee. As Harrington said at the time, there was a general perception that Nedzi was a "co-opted congressman."[122]

Compounding his problem, Nedzi moved slowly to organize the committee. He did not appoint a staff director until May, and his choice did not satisfy his fellow Democrats. Sealing his fate, the *New York Times* disclosed on 5 June 1975 that the Agency had briefed Nedzi on the "Family Jewels" a year earlier and that he had done nothing about it. A storm of criticism ensued, prompting Nedzi's fellow Democrats on the investigating committee to create a CIA subcommittee chaired by Representative James Stanton (D-OH) rather than Nedzi. The subcommittee never met, but Nedzi was motivated to offer his resignation as chairman. While the House subsequently voted 290–64 to reject this resignation, as a symbolic show of its support for Nedzi, he was nonethe-

---

[119] CIA draft study, Vol. II, 100.
[120] Ibid., 101.
[121] Ibid., 107.
[122] Smist, *Congress Oversees*, 150–53.

less allowed to step aside after the vote. On 17 July 1975, the House reconstituted the investigating committee under a new chairman, Otis Pike (D-NY).

Pike set to work immediately, holding the committee's first public hearing two weeks after he was appointed. Moreover, he announced he was firmly committed to finishing the investigation by 31 January 1976, at the time only six months away. Pike also indicated he would take a different focus than his Senate counterpart. Rather than focusing on abuses, he would look at the costs of intelligence and whether taxpayers were getting their money's worth. To assess this question, the Pike committee would evaluate the performance of the CIA and other intelligence agencies in terms of predicting events that had taken place around the world over the preceding 10 years. (See chapters 6–9 for further details of its investigation.) This inevitably raised the issue of the committee's access to intelligence production as well as access to the raw intelligence underlying such production and led to repeated confrontations not only with the Agency but also with the White House—confrontations exacerbated by the adversarial and acerbic attitudes that Pike and his senior staff brought to the negotiations.

Its composition also hampered the committee. Eight of the nine Democrats were seen as liberal and generally hostile to the Intelligence Community; three of the four Republicans were conservatives supportive of intelligence and were opposed to the investigation from the start. Pike thus had the support of the Democrats in taking a hard line with the executive branch and had little incentive or interest in building a consensus with his Republican members.[123]

In all, the Pike Committee conducted 28 days of public hearings. Beginning with the costs of intelligence, it then turned its attention to perceived intelligence failures by the Intelligence Community, the role of the National Security Council in covert action operations, domestic intelligence programs, and CIA internal administration. It also examined intelligence issues related to monitoring arms control agreements.

As its deadline neared, the committee staff produced a 338-page draft final report that it gave to the Agency on 19 January 1976, with one day on which to comment. The Agency's liaison protested in the strongest terms, not only to the deadline but also to the report itself, which he called "an unrelenting indictment couched in biased, pejorative and factually erroneous terms" that would give the American public a clearly distorted view.[124]

The committee nonetheless proceeded to approve release of the report on 23 January 1976 without substantial changes or an executive branch security

---

[123] Ibid., 158–62.
[124] CIA draft study, Vol. II, 146.

review, even though it had earlier agreed not to release information to the public without such review. This led the ranking minority member of the committee to take the issue to the House floor, where on 29 January 1976, the House voted 246–124, with 127 Democrats joining 119 Republicans, to suppress the publication of the report.[125]

Notwithstanding the House action, a version of the report was leaked to journalist Daniel Schorr, who gave it to the *Village Voice* newspaper, which published it on 16 February 1976 under the headline, "The Report on the CIA that President Ford Doesn't Want You to Read." Concerned by the leak, the House voted three days later to have the House Ethics Committee investigate. Ultimately, 11 days of hearings were held, and all members of the Pike Committee, as well as 32 of its staff, were compelled to testify. The source of the leak to Schorr, however, was never identified.

While the report of the Pike Committee never received the imprimatur of the House and most members largely ignored it, it did, like the Church committee report, call for the establishment of a permanent standing committee on intelligence within the House with oversight and budgetary jurisdiction over the CIA and the rest of the Intelligence Community.[126] Due to the sour taste left by the Pike Committee, however there was no immediate movement in the House to embrace this or other of its recommendations.

AUTHOR'S COMMENTARY

The Early Congressional Arrangements: 1947–76

It is not surprising that oversight of the CIA initially went to the armed services and appropriations committees on each side. In the Senate, the Armed Services Committee had developed and handled the law creating the CIA, and it naturally claimed jurisdiction over the entities it created. While principal responsibility for handling the CIA legislation in the House had rested with the Committee on Executive Expenditures, it did not have the same substantive expertise in national security matters that the House Armed Services Committee did. The appropriations committees had to be involved because they would have to put the Agency's funding through the congressional process each year. Moreover, at the point these decisions were made, while it was clear CIA would be independent of the Department of Defense, it was rela-

---

[125] Smist, *Congress Oversees*, 162–63.
[126] Ibid., 149.

tively small and its mission not fully formed. Indeed, the most controversial part of its mission, covert action—which quickly became the largest component of its funding—did not begin to take shape until a year or so after the Agency was created. Thus, Congress gave no serious consideration at the time to treating CIA as a special case for oversight requiring a separate standing committee, a select committee, or a joint committee.

Moreover, once the jurisdictional arrangements were put in place, they were difficult to change. The powerful members who led these committees were not about to give up their jurisdictional claims over the Agency. They felt this way not simply as a matter of protecting their turf, but also as a matter of protecting the Agency from disruptive forays by other congressional committees. They had set up the CIA to work secretly against the spread of communism around the world, and they were not about to let (a chaotic) Congress interfere with that mission.

The fact that CIA's overseers were powerful members of Congress at a time when deference was paid to their positions assured their ability to control things, and as a result, CIA was spared, for the most part, searching oversight of its operations during the early part of its existence. It is also beyond dispute that the involvement of these members was crucial to putting the Agency on its feet. The exponential growth that the Agency experienced between 1948 and 1953, for example, could only have been achieved by the chairmen of the armed services and appropriations committees who together had purview over the huge defense budget (from which the increases had to come). Lesser committees could not have done it, nor would ordinary rank-and-file members have had the wherewithal to push through such increases, especially for a new, largely unproven agency.

The Agency also benefited from the fact that its subcommittees were remarkably free of partisanship during this period. The chairmen and ranking minority members of its subcommittees, by and large, worked closely together, usually reaching agreement easily on the Agency's resource needs and refusing the temptation to make political "hay" of its operational or analytical failures even after they had become public. Indeed, the historical record is virtually silent with respect to any leaks from the Agency's subcommittees during this early period.

But the very fact that the Agency's protectors in Congress were among its most respected and powerful members had its costs: they were also among its busiest members. They had no time for the minutiae of budget presentations. They wanted to know the bottom line: What did the Agency need? They wanted to know what the Agency was doing—but only in general terms. They did not want to be surprised, but they had no interest in the nuts and bolts of the Agency's work either. They had no interest in micromanaging. While Agency managers welcomed this attitude, former Legislative Counsel John Warner spoke of a downside: "They never did learn enough about us to know how we really functioned. So they could not be active defenders."[127] The difficulty the Agency had in engaging with its oversight committees also made it more vulnerable to inquiries by other committees. "It's a lot easier for a DCI [to fend off other committees]," noted former Legislative Counsel George Cary, "if we have an oversight committee who isn't too busy for us . . . and is recognized to have exclusive jurisdiction over our activities."[128]

For a while, this kind of laissez-faire system sufficed. But, gradually, as their colleagues came to appreciate how large the Agency had grown, how widespread and problematic its activities seemed to be, and how little attention it seemed to be getting from its designated overseers, doubts began to grow in Congress about the efficacy of the existing arrangements. Indeed, as the record shows, from the mid-1950s until the mid-1970s, virtually every perceived intelligence failure by the Agency brought on renewed calls for better oversight by the Congress. The Agency spent an inordinate amount of its time and energy, in fact, worrying about such complaints and attempting to deal with them, both by urging its oversight subcommittees to do a better job and by working behind the scenes to scuttle every proposal for change.

Nothing the Agency tried, however, ultimately changed the dynamic that existed from the start with its oversight subcommittees. Despite its controversial mission, the Agency was still "too small a potato"—compared with the Department of Defense—for its congressional protectors to allot much of their time to. Former Legislative Counsel George Cary later reflected that the CIA subcommittee chairmen

> *had more than they could handle in overseeing the Department of Defense. That can keep Members totally occupied. The intelligence business can also keep Members totally occupied. . . .When you put those two responsibilities on one set of people, something is going to give. Something is going to come up short. The intelligence business came up short. . . . Members just didn't have enough time to do what they should have done.[129]*

Ultimately, the relative inattentiveness of its overseers did not serve the Agency's long-term interests well. It led to mistrust and resentment in much of Congress, and when the Agency's operations came under challenge on

---

[127] Warner interview, 27 September 1996, 40.
[128] Cary interview, 30 September 1983, 16.
[129] Ibid., 12.

many fronts in the early 1970s, its oversight subcommittees were in no position to defend it. Indeed, the allegations of Agency misconduct that were so prevalent during this period that critics began to question the effectiveness of the existing oversight system itself. The CIA subcommittees had never probed what the Agency was doing; they simply didn't know. Had they taken a more active role, problems might have been prevented.

However appealing cursory congressional oversight might seem, in the end it undermines congressional, as well as public, support for the Agency. Better to have overseers who understand and are able to defend the Agency's interests than to have overseers who are largely ignorant of them.

This experience also demonstrates that if oversight responsibility is placed in the hands of committees that have other significant oversight responsibilities, oversight of the Agency will likely never be more than cursory, whatever the Agency may do. Those in Congress who do oversight of the Agency ought to be members who have the time to devote to it, and they should have an appropriate number of able staff to assist them.

The Joint Committee "Panacea"

Looking back over the Agency's early history, it is remarkable how often the idea of a joint committee on intelligence was offered up in Congress as the panacea to the existing oversight arrangements. Beginning with the first Mansfield resolution in 1953 until the creation of the select committees in the mid-1970s, it was the notion of a "joint committee" that reformers always turned to, and the Agency, together with the administrations it served during this period, consistently rejected. Why was this so? Seemingly, from the standpoint of reformers, combining oversight of the CIA into a single committee would reduce, rather than increase, the amount of oversight the Agency was getting. Similarly, one would expect the Agency to find dealing with one committee preferable to dealing with four, not only to reduce the potential for damaging leaks but also to alleviate the burden of keeping multiple committees informed.

In fact, Agency records reflect that it did seriously consider whether a joint committee might better serve its interests when Mansfield first raised the idea in 1953. It was also considered at other points along the way, notably when John McCone became DCI and was confronted with the same issue. Each internal reexamination, however, always resulted in the same position: vehement opposition to a joint committee.

The model that both the reformers and the CIA had to work with in these early days provides part of the explanation. Congress had created the Joint

Atomic Energy Committee (JAEC) in 1946 to be its watchdog over the US atomic energy program, which, like the CIA, was considered a sensitive area for congressional oversight. Unlike other joint committees, the JAEC was given legislative authority to report bills to the floors of both houses and, among other things, was charged with oversight of, and authorizing appropriations for, the Atomic Energy Commission. The committee was composed of senior members on both sides for whom the JAEC was their principal preoccupation. It had a large professional staff to support it and carried out most of its work in secret. The JAEC was abolished in 1977 but during the early part of its existence enjoyed widespread respect in the Congress.

From the standpoint of the reformers, the JAEC model offered a preferable alternative to the CIA subcommittees because it was thought that, at the very least, Congress would have the benefit of an independent review of the Agency's operations by a dedicated professional staff. The Agency was concerned about a joint committee for precisely the same reason. Under the existing system, this staff capability did not exist. Staff was briefed, but it did not probe.

It is also clear from the Agency's records that its leaders were concerned about offending the powerful chairmen of its oversight subcommittees. In fact, the longer the Agency enjoyed their protection and support, the harder it was to endorse a different oversight arrangement. While the Agency might have taken a different position vis-à-vis a joint committee in 1953, there was no going back when McCone considered the issue in 1962. From time to time, members of the CIA subcommittees themselves endorsed the idea of a joint committee, but the chairmen of these subcommittees never did, and the Agency, understandably, did not wish to lose their support.

The Personalities, Attitudes, and Circumstances of the Early DCIs

The Agency's fortunes on Capitol Hill to some degree have always been a function of how the committees with responsibility for the Agency perceived the DCI: the greater the level of trust, the greater the level of comfort in terms of how the Agency is operating. But especially during the early years, when so much of the interaction between the Agency and the Congress was informal and personal, how the DCI was perceived on the Hill was a key factor in setting the terms of the relationship.

President Truman appointed four men to serve as DCI during his presidency. All were general or flag officers. RADM Sidney Souers, the first, accepted the appointment reluctantly. He had been planning to retire after the war and return to his native Missouri. The organization he was being asked to lead, the Central Intelligence Group (CIG), not only was yet to be formed, but outside influences would greatly circumscribe its activities. It would be dependent upon other agencies for its funding and operate under the authority of a committee. Not surprisingly, Souers took the first opportunity to leave, less than six months into the job. While recognizing that the CIG needed independent funding and authority that only Congress could provide, Souers did not stay long enough to broach the matter with Congress.

That task fell to his successor, LTG Hoyt Vandenberg. At the time of his appointment, Vandenberg was chairing the advisory board for the CIG, created as part of Truman's executive directive. Assertive, with wartime experience in intelligence, Vandenberg also had the advantage of being politically well-connected. He was the nephew of Senator Arthur Vandenberg (R-MI), who was elevated to the chair of the SFRC the same year his nephew became DCI. Vandenberg sought and obtained permission from the White House to seek legislation for the CIG, giving it an independent status. Fortunately for Vandenberg, there was a legislative vehicle in the works that would clearly become law—what became the National Security Act of 1947—that could be used for this purpose. Had the creation of the CIA required free-standing legislation, the bill would have attracted more attention, and its enactment would have been far less certain.

Notwithstanding his instrumental role in obtaining legislation to establish the Agency as an independent entity, however, General Vandenberg saw his future elsewhere. Two months before the National Security Act of 1947 was enacted, he resigned as DCI in order to position himself to become the first chief of staff of the Air Force, which the law also created.

To replace him, Truman appointed RADM Roscoe Hillenkoetter in May 1947. When the National Security Act passed two months later, Truman reappointed him as the first "statutory" DCI. While his confirmation was perfunctory, it probably owed much to the fact that he was already in the job. While he had had tactical intelligence experience during the war and had served as naval attaché in Paris after the war, he was relatively low-ranking (compared to Vandenberg) and was unaccustomed to dealing with the Congress or the upper reaches of official Washington. His dour, low-key style did not make it any easier for him, particularly when he had to testify at several contentious hearings in defense of the Agency's analytical performance in predicting the riots in Bogota in 1948, the Soviet atomic bomb test in 1949, and North Korea's invasion of the South in 1950 (see chapter 7). He was prone to take offense at hostile questioning, however persuasive the case he had to make. In defending the Agency's performance with regard to predicting the North Korean invasion, he also managed to bring the Truman administration into the line of fire, implying that it had failed to act on the Agency's information. This appears to have contributed to Truman's decision to replace him in October 1950 with LTG Walter Bedell "Beetle" Smith.

Smith was the best known and most accomplished of Truman's appointees as DCI. He had served as Eisenhower's chief of staff during the war and had been ambassador to the Soviet Union for three years prior to accepting the DCI position. His appointment received broad, enthusiastic acclaim within Congress. His bearing toward members was "deferential, responsive, and soldierly," according to one account, and his popularity was based more on respect than personal warmth.[130] Smith was also far more adept than his predecessor at navigating the bureaucratic shoals of the executive branch and took charge of the CIA with a blunt, no-nonsense style. His appointment also came at a critical juncture—when the war in Korea was intensifying. It fell to Smith not only to brief Congress on the war but also to keep the CIA subcommittees informed of the Agency's operational activities in support of the war effort. Having someone of Smith's stature and demeanor in charge of the Agency at this point lent credibility to both its analysis and its operational achievements. Indeed, Smith's tenure awakened many in Congress to the existence of the CIA.

When Smith's former boss, General Eisenhower, was elected president in 1952, there was naturally speculation that Smith might be asked to stay on. But Eisenhower had other plans for him, as under secretary of state. To succeed Smith, Eisenhower chose Allen Dulles, who was serving as DDCI at the time. Dulles was not only the first civilian but also the first intelligence professional to be appointed DCI. But what made his appointment truly unique was that Eisenhower appointed his brother, John Foster, as secretary of state. Rather than detracting from his credibility as DCI (by being too close to his political bosses), this happenstance only added to Dulles's charisma.

Dulles was already well known on Capitol Hill when his appointment was announced. Gregarious, bright, and engaging, he had an easy time making friends and enlisting confidants among his congressional overseers. At times, in fact, his penchant for talking with the Hill led to admonitions from the White House. There were also times when his contacts led to confrontation, notably his clashes with Senator Stuart Symington over Soviet strategic capabilities in the last half of the 1950s (see chapter 3). But overall, Dulles was a master at dealing with Congress, especially the leaders of his subcommittees. Preferring informal tête-à-têtes to formal meetings, Dulles easily ingratiated himself with these men and quickly earned their confidence.

Had they not had such confidence in Dulles, they may not have been quite so passive in their own oversight. Nor might they have shown such tenacity in

---

[130] Montague, *Bedell Smith*, 256.

fending off the reformers who were urging a more intrusive role for the Congress. Even during Dulles's most trying hour—the aftermath of the Bay of Pigs fiasco—the Agency's overseers were not among those calling for his resignation. While they understood President Kennedy's decision to fire him, they refused to lead the charge against him (see chapter 9).

Dulles's successor as DCI, John McCone, lacked his personal charm as well as his intelligence background but brought other strengths to the job. Coming on the heels of an intelligence operation that had created worldwide embarrassment for the country, the appointment of an outsider to head the Agency—a "no nonsense" Republican businessman and "hard-line" anticommunist—was intended to provide assurance that the Agency's operations were being placed in competent hands. When his nomination received more negative votes than any DCI to that juncture (12), McCone set out to prove his worth to those senators who had voted against him.

In fact, by virtue of his prior service as under secretary of the air force and as chairman of the Atomic Energy Commission, McCone already understood the dynamics of the legislative-executive relationship and had proven adept in dealing with members. While lacking the personal flair of Dulles, he did not shy away from contacts with Capitol Hill; rather he sought hard to develop them, believing that the more the Agency's overseers understood about the Agency, the better position they would be in to fend off more intrusive oversight arrangements. One congressmen described his presentations to the CIA subcommittees as "straight and unadulterated, the way we liked it."[131]

After the Kennedy assassination, President Johnson kept McCone on, but the two men had distinctly different personalities as well as policy views, differing in particular on the appropriate course of action in Vietnam. When Johnson was elected president in his own right in the fall of 1964, McCone announced his intent to resign within a few months.

To replace McCone, Johnson appointed a retired Navy admiral, William Raborn, who had headed the Navy's Polaris program. Enthusiastic, ebullient by nature, Raborn had dealt frequently and successfully with the armed services committees as a program manager and was anxious to reinstitute the same kind of relationship from his new post. His lack of experience in both intelligence and foreign affairs, however, led to occasional "faux pas" before the Congress and proved difficult for him to overcome.[132] He did not put in the time necessary to master these subjects and left it to others to run the Agency's day-to-day

---

[131] Robarge, *John McCone*, 75.
[132] White interview, 7 January 1998, 40.

operations. In time, word leaked to the press that he was ruining morale. A little over a year after being appointed, Raborn offered his resignation.

Raborn's deputy, Richard M. Helms, replaced him in June 1966 largely because he offered what Raborn did not: a career spent in intelligence and foreign affairs. Helms by this point was well known to the CIA subcommittees and, while he did not possess the effusive personality of either Dulles or Raborn, was highly regarded for his professionalism. Helms took a reserved, businesslike approach to dealing with his congressional overseers. Not one for gratuitously offering up the details of intelligence operations, however titillating they might be, he was prepared to tell the leaders of the CIA subcommittees what he believed they needed to know. Above all, he did not want them to be surprised by something that appeared in the press. Where rank-and-file members were concerned, Helms made less of an effort to ingratiate himself, but even here, he later said, he always tried to level with members, giving them the facts without embellishment. Over time, this approach earned Helms broad respect within the Congress.

During the last three years of Helms's tenure as DCI, however, a tide of mistrust and disillusionment with the government, fueled first by the war in Vietnam and later by the Watergate scandal, swept the country. Relations between the executive branch and the Congress were frostier than they had been for a long time. CIA itself was particularly susceptible to congressional mistrust, not only because it was associated with the policies of the administration but also because, in important ways, it operated in secret outside legislative control.

The old system of laissez-faire oversight was breaking down. Most of the members on both sides who had protected the Agency during its early years had died or left their positions. Even those who remained in charge grew increasingly sensitive to criticism that their committees had failed to provide adequate oversight where the Agency was concerned. When HASC Chairman Edward Hebert appointed a political liberal, a junior congressman from Michigan named Lucien Nedzi, to chair the CIA subcommittee in 1971, he signaled a clear break with the past. Nedzi, in fact, did what none of his predecessors had done—he set out to educate himself with respect to the Agency and its operations. Without other committee responsibilities to distract him, he made repeated visits to CIA Headquarters, received numerous briefings, and held frequent, substantive hearings. The Agency leadership, once it assessed him as serious and responsible, welcomed his interest and attention. For years, in fact, the Agency had sought to provide its congressional overseers with a more in-depth understanding of its work, believing that improved understanding would redound to its benefit, but rarely had they had the time.

Also marking a turning point in terms of congressional interaction with the Agency was the Watergate scandal. Not only did Nedzi's subcommittee investigate CIA's role in it, but the Senate Watergate Committee did as well. Both committees were given unprecedented access to CIA records and personnel. Fortunately for the Agency, Helms rebuffed the Nixon administration's efforts to involve it in the cover-up in the summer and fall of 1972. But Helms's refusal to cooperate obviously did not ingratiate him with the administration, and when Nixon was reelected in November 1972, Helms was told he would be replaced.

The appointment of James Schlesinger as Helms's successor in January 1973 did not attract much controversy. The Watergate burglary had seemingly been put to rest by this point, and Schlesinger was regarded as a tough-minded outsider, whose track record at the Office of Management and Budget led observers to expect him to bring greater fiscal discipline to the Agency. Soon after Schlesinger took office in January, however, the Watergate scandal began to unravel. On 9 May 1973 when Schlesinger learned for the first time that CIA had developed photographs taken during the burglary of Daniel Ellsberg's psychiatrist's office, he hit the roof, demanding to know anything else the Agency had done that might be considered improper. This, in turn, led to the 693-page collection of alleged misdeeds that came to be known as the "Family Jewels."

Nixon's choice to succeed Schlesinger was William E. Colby, who had been serving as executive director of the Agency and then deputy director for operations since 1972, first under Helms, then under Schlesinger. A lawyer by training, Colby had served in the OSS during the war and had had a long career in Agency operations. He was known to many in Congress, principally for his involvement in the Vietnam War during the 1960s; his role in the Phoenix program, a South Vietnamese program intended to identify Viet Cong and Viet Cong sympathizers in the villages of the country had brought him unwelcome notoriety. Colby had staunchly defended the Agency's involvement in the program before Congress in 1970—against charges that it had been an "assassination" program—it remained the principal issue he had to deal with at his confirmation hearing.

It was the "Family Jewels," however, that ultimately became Colby's undoing and led to the demise of the existing oversight arrangements on Capitol Hill. Although Colby had been nominated on 10 May 1973, the SASC had to put off his confirmation hearings until July while its chairman, John Stennis, recuperated from a street shooting. In the meantime, the CIA inspector general completed pulling together the "family jewels." Although Colby immediately took action to end what he regarded as the more objectionable practices, he also felt obliged to tell the chairmen of the SASC and HASC, as well as

Nedzi, of the "Family Jewels" before his confirmation hearings. All agreed that the matter should not be surfaced.

A year and a half later, however, in December 1974, the *New York Times* published a front-page story describing a "laundry list" of alleged CIA abuses, based largely on information leaked from the "Family Jewels." This, in turn, led the Senate and House to create separate committees—the Church and Pike Committees—to investigate the Agency.

Colby wanted to cooperate with the investigations—he firmly believed that Congress had a right to know about the Agency's operations—but he was also concerned with protecting them. In this regard, he was no different than most of his predecessors as DCI. But instead of oversight carried out in members' offices or over cocktails at the end of the day, Colby was facing oversight of a different kind: oversight carried out in the glare of the public spotlight, by members who had little knowledge of, or appreciation for, the work of the Agency. Rather than dealing with a supportive group of congressional veterans, Colby found members—some young firebrands—who were hostile and confrontational. Colby came back to the Agency after his first closed hearing in the Senate saying he had been "treated like a criminal."

Colby's personality undoubtedly contributed to his woes. He was not a gregarious, backslapping sort but low-key and aloof. At times he could seem cold and distant, and members had difficulty reading him. While respected as an intelligence professional, he was never seen as entirely forthcoming by the chairmen of either of the investigating committees he had to deal with.

Colby's failure to establish a better relationship with Church and Pike also owed as much to their personalities and circumstances as to his. While Senator Church had had considerable exposure to the CIA by virtue of his long service on the SFRC, he announced shortly after accepting the chairmanship of the investigating committee that he intended to run for president in the 1976 election. This inevitably led to an investigation that was more sensational, more controversial, and more political than it otherwise would have been. Indeed, that the Church Committee was able to pull together at the end and issue a credible, bipartisan final report owed more to the fact its chairman was away on the campaign trail than actively involved in its work. On the House side, Congressman Pike was appointed to lead the investigation only after it had come to light that Nedzi, who had originally been appointed to head the investigating committee, had seen the "Family Jewels" and done nothing about them. In other words, Pike was appointed precisely because he was not "tainted" by past involvement with the CIA. From the outset, he made it clear that it was "us against them"—CIA was the enemy. Pike made life miserable for the Agency for six months, ultimately reneging on his own commitment not to publish a report that had not been subject to security review by the executive branch.

Ironically, the Ford administration viewed Colby as being too forthcoming with the Church and Pike Committees and not forthcoming enough with the administration. In November 1975, the decision was made to fire him. Not surprisingly, the man chosen to replace him—George H.W. Bush—was a former member of Congress, the first ever to be nominated for the DCI's position.

Bush proved to be the calming influence President Ford had hoped for but resigned after the 1976 presidential election, too soon to play a significant role in shaping the new oversight arrangements that grew out of the Church and Pike investigations. The SSCI was still being organized in the fall of 1976; the HPSCI was not created until the following year.

While it is likely that the old system of congressional oversight would have given way during the 1970s without the Church and Pike investigations—perhaps evolving along the lines of the HASC/Nedzi model—the creation of select committees in the mid-1970s dedicated to the oversight of the CIA and other intelligence agencies was a direct result of these tumultuous investigations. The disclosure that prompted them was the *New York Times* story published in December 1974, which could not have been written if the "family jewels" had never been compiled. And the "family jewels" were compiled only because a DCI who was relatively new to the job and unused to dealing with scandal had, in a fit of anger, ordered them to be.

CHAPTER 2

THE RELATIONSHIP: 1976–2004

The Senate Select Committee on Intelligence: 1976

Within a month of the issuance of the Church Committee's final report, the Senate took up Senate Resolution 400 creating the Select Committee on Intelligence (SSCI), as the Church Committee had recommended. On 19 May 1976, the resolution passed 72–22. It gave the new committee exclusive oversight of the CIA, as well as concurrent jurisdiction with respect to the intelligence activities of other elements of the Intelligence Community. In nonbinding, hortatory language, the resolution said that agencies within the Intelligence Community were expected to keep the new committee "fully and currently informed" of their activities, including any "significant anticipated activities."

The resolution also provided that the new select committee would authorize appropriations annually for all "intelligence activities" of the government. Notably, in a concession to the leaders of the SASC, this term was defined to exclude "tactical foreign military intelligence activities serving no national policymaking function."[1] While this was clarified in 1978 to allow the new committee to make recommendations regarding the annual authorization for tactical intelligence, the SASC would retain legislative control over these funds.[2]

The new Senate committee would be a "select" committee rather than a "standing" committee. Its members would be "selected" by the Senate majority and minority leaders rather than determined in the party caucuses that preceded each new Congress. The committee's chairman and vice chairman would be selected by their respective caucus but could not, at the same time, serve as chairman or ranking minority member of a major standing committee. This was intended to ensure that other committee responsibilities would not distract the leaders of the new committee.

The new committee would have 15 members, no more than eight of whom could come from the majority party; in other words, there would always be a

---

[1] S Res, 400, § 14 (a).
[2] Smist, *Congress Oversees*, 106.

one-vote majority regardless of the proportion of the majority to the minority in the full Senate. Of those chosen for membership, eight also had to sit on standing committees with related jurisdictions: two each from Appropriations, Armed Services, Foreign Relations, and Judiciary. Members would be appointed for eight-year terms, after which they would leave the committee. This was intended to ensure members did not serve long enough to become co-opted by the intelligence agencies they were suppose to oversee. It was also expected that by rotating senators onto the committee, over time more would be exposed to intelligence work, and the perception that oversight rested with an elite few would be dispelled.

As mentioned above, the resolution also provided that instead of a ranking minority member the committee would have a vice chairman, chosen from the minority, who would preside in the absence of the chairman rather than having that responsibility pass to the next in line on the majority side. In addition, the new committee adopted rules giving minority members the same access that majority members had to information held by the committee.

The committee was authorized to hire its own staff, provided that every person hired had to receive a security clearance in accordance with DCI-approved standards and "in consultation with the DCI." This latter phrase was interpreted as providing the DCI an opportunity to comment on the hiring of particular employees without giving the DCI the right to make hiring decisions for the committee. There would not be a majority and minority staff per se, as was typical with most Senate committees; rather there would a "unified" staff to serve both sides of the aisle. The chairman and vice chairman would hire most of the staff (with each controlling certain senior positions). Members would, however, have the right to hire one member of the staff, known as a "designee," to serve his or her own interest, in addition to carrying out their duties for the committee as a whole. All members of the committee would be permitted an opportunity to review the backgrounds of proposed hires for the staff and to raise objections if they saw a potential problem.

Daniel Inouye (D-HI) was appointed as the first chairman of the SSCI, and Barry Goldwater (R-AZ) was its first vice chairman. Five of its original members—Democrats Walter Huddleston (KY), Gary Hart (CO), Robert Morgan (NC), and Republicans Goldwater and Howard Baker (TN)—had served on the Church Committee, as had 14 of its staff, including staff director William Miller.[3] Within two years, the size of the staff had grown to 50, larger than the staffs of most standing committees at the time.[4]

---

[3] Smist, *Congress Oversees*, 84–85.
[4] CIA draft study, Vol. II, 159.

Among other things, S Res. 400 also required the new committee to study the desirability of creating a joint committee on intelligence. Acting swiftly to quash this idea, the SSCI found in its first annual report to the Senate in May 1977 that "for the foreseeable future a joint committee does not seem desirable or possible."[5] This was to remain its position until the present day.

The House Permanent Select Committee on Intelligence: 1977

Despite the Senate's action, the House of Representatives did not move immediately to create a counterpart committee. There was no desire on either side of the aisle to repeat the disagreeable experience of the Pike Committee.[6] In time, however, it became apparent to newly elected House Speaker Thomas P. "Tip" O'Neill (D-MA) that a counterpart to the Senate committee was needed. There needed to be a place where the intelligence now being provided the Senate would also be provided the House. The weekly intelligence briefings that O'Neill himself was receiving were, in his view, not a satisfactory solution. Moreover, there needed to be a place where legislation passed by the Senate could be referred. (The SSCI had developed its first intelligence authorization bill in the spring of 1977 without a corresponding process in the House.)

Thus, on 17 July 1977, at O'Neill's urging, the House passed House Resolution 658 creating the Permanent Select Committee on Intelligence (HPSCI) by a vote of 227 to 171. The resolution was modeled after the Senate's but contained important differences.

The committee would be a select committee, chosen by the House Speaker and minority leader and with 13 members (rather than 15 in the Senate). But the composition would reflect the proportion in the House as a whole, rather than having a one-vote difference as in the Senate. Democrats asserted this meant they were entitled to nine seats on the new committee; the Republicans, only four. Republicans challenged these assertions, which caused many who saw the resolution as "blatantly political" to vote against it.[7] Joining them were a number of liberal Democrats who saw the resolution as a "return to the old days" when an elite few carried out the oversight responsibility in secret.

O'Neill argued that the proposed committee was needed, however, and assured House members that it would operate in a bipartisan manner. "I expect this committee to deliberate and act in a nonpartisan manner," O'Neill said on

---

[5] Smist, *Congress Oversees*, 108.

[6] Ibid., 214.

[7] Ibid., 215.

the floor. "This is a nonpartisan committee; there will be nothing partisan about its deliberations."[8] On the basis of his assurances, the resolution passed by a comfortable margin.

The resolution, like the Senate's, provided that members would serve for fixed terms, in this case, six years instead of eight. It also provided for the appointment of "cross-over" members from the Armed Services, Appropriations, Foreign Relations, and Judiciary Committees.

Reflecting the historically more partisan nature of the House, however, the resolution did not adopt the Senate's concept of creating a "vice chairman" as opposed to a ranking minority member. When the HPSCI chairman is absent, the next in line on the majority side takes control. The rules of the committee also did not provide equal access to the information the committee held. Moreover, there would be separate majority and minority staffs, hired by the chairman and ranking minority member, respectively, rather than a "unified" staff.

The jurisdiction of the HPSCI also differed from that of its Senate counterpart. It would have jurisdiction over tactical intelligence activities, both from the standpoint of oversight and budget authorization. While the House Armed Services Committee retained the right to seek sequential referral of the annual intelligence authorization bill to address tactical intelligence issues, it would not have responsibility for authorizing these funds.

The hortatory language of the Senate resolution directing intelligence agencies to keep the committee "fully and currently informed" also did not make it into the House resolution (perhaps because it was hortatory).

Like the Senate resolution, the resolution establishing the HPSCI also required it to examine the feasibility of a joint committee on intelligence, but, in view of the Senate committee's earlier rejection of the idea, no action was taken.[9]

Following the vote in the House, O'Neill appointed his longtime friend and colleague, Edward P. Boland (D-MA) as the first HPSCI chairman. Bob Wilson (R-CA) was appointed its first ranking minority member. Within two years, the committee had hired a staff of 20, none of whom had served on the Pike or Nedzi Committees.[10]

* * *

With the creation of the select committees, the CIA subcommittees on the armed services and appropriations committees on each side officially dis-

---

[8] Ibid., 216.
[9] Ibid., 237.
[10] Ibid., 232.

banded. The armed services committees continued to have concurrent oversight jurisdiction over the Defense Department (DoD) elements of the Intelligence Community, and the defense appropriations subcommittees on each side assumed responsibility for the Agency's annual appropriation, typically clearing one or two professional staff to handle the account. For several years after the select committees were created, in fact, the staff of the defense appropriations subcommittee of the HAC played an unusually active role where oversight was concerned. In time, however, as it became apparent that the select committees had a far larger, more sophisticated capability to do oversight, the defense appropriations subcommittees began deferring almost entirely to them.

All four committees, however—the armed services and appropriations committees in both houses—continued to play important roles in terms of the Agency's funding. Because funds for the Agency were contained in the DoD budget account, there had to be agreement each year between the intelligence committees and the armed services committees on the amount to be authorized for the CIA within the defense authorization. Similarly, there needed to be an appropriation for the Agency within the annual defense appropriation bill. In theory, the appropriations committees could not appropriate more than what the authorizing committees authorized, but they might appropriate less. So, they were not to be taken for granted. Perhaps of even greater importance, supplemental appropriations bills—which the Agency frequently relied upon over its history to fund its overseas operations—did not receive an authorization. While the intelligence committees were typically given an opportunity to weigh in on them, they did not officially act on them. So maintaining the support of the defense appropriations subcommittees would remain crucial for the Agency.

The organizational arrangements for intelligence oversight that each house adopted in the mid-1970s did not significantly change until 2004, nor were they seriously challenged from within. When political control of the House or Senate changed during this period, obviously the leadership of the HPSCI and SSCI would also change. Some committee chairmen established subcommittees; others did not. The number of members on each committee also fluctuated over time, as did the size and composition of their respective staffs. But the basic organizational structure of two select committees with members serving fixed terms did not change for 26 years.

What did change over this period were the policies and procedures that governed the relationship. As seen in chapter 1, until the select committees were created, relations between the Agency and the Congress were, for the most part, ad hoc and informal. (The only law on the books that addressed the relationship was the Hughes-Ryan Amendment enacted in 1974.) Congress would make requests for information, and the Agency would deal with them. Each interaction was handled as the circumstances required. Obviously, the Agency's overriding concern was keeping its principal overseers satisfied, but it also wanted to build support for itself within the Congress where it was possible to do so (see chapter 3). Balanced against these considerations was the Agency's concern for the security of its operations and the direction it received from the White House.

With the creation of the select committees, however, new legal obligations were imposed on the relationship, and over time these obligations changed and multiplied. Some came at the initiative of the executive branch; most came at the initiative of the Congress. Some were instituted in response to events that demonstrated shortcomings in the existing process; some were an effort to prevent such problems from arising. However the changes came about, the Agency's relationship with Congress increasingly came to be carried out within a formal framework, based upon law and regulation, rather than a framework built upon personal relationships. This evolution is described in the pages that follow.

1977–80: The Committees Prove Themselves

The first four years of the select committees' existence corresponded roughly with the presidency of Jimmy Carter, who took office pledging cooperation with them. Carter's vice president, Walter Mondale, had served on the Church Committee and had been instrumental in the creation of the follow-on committee. He wanted it to succeed.

The leaders of the new committees reciprocated with assurances that they intended to operate in a cooperative way. HPSCI Chairman Boland proclaimed, "This will not be an inquisition like the Church and Pike committees."[11] Daniel Inouye, his counterpart on the SSCI, pledged that the country's security would not be compromised by the work of the committee and that the committee would work to "restore responsibility and accountability to U.S. intelligence activities." In a letter to DCI Turner, Inouye said the committee viewed the Intelligence Community as "legitimate and needed" and pledged to work with Turner to strengthen it.[12]

As tangible evidence of their intent, both committees hired key staff with intelligence backgrounds. The HPSCI, for example, hired as its first staff director, Thomas Latimer, who had served in the Intelligence Community and had been a special assistant on intelligence matters to the secretary of defense.

---

[11] CIA draft study, Vol. II, 226.
[12] Ibid., 160.

To handle budget matters, the HPSCI hired James Bush, who had handled the intelligence budget at DoD. At the SSCI, Daniel Childs, who had headed the Program and Budget Division of the Intelligence Community Staff, was hired as budget director.[13]

Despite the evident goodwill in both branches, however, profound misgivings lay beneath the surface. Could committees of Congress, inherently political institutions, do hands-on oversight of intelligence activities without revealing them? At this point, no other country in the world had seen fit to entrust their legislatures with such an intrusive role. Prior to the Church and Pike Committees, intelligence information had been briefed to the Hill, but not left on the Hill, for the simple reason there was nowhere to store it. Heretofore, the number of congressmen and senators with access to Agency information at any given time had totaled 10 or 12. Now there would be 28 on the intelligence committees alone. Moreover, they would be supported by sizable staffs that had nothing else to do but look at the intelligence business. Heretofore, the limited number of congressional staff supporting the CIA subcommittees had had major responsibilities for the full committees they worked for, leaving them little time to delve into the Agency's activities.

Agency records, in fact, reflect a widespread unease among its senior officers brought about by the demands of the new committees. At a DCI morning meeting in December 1977, for example, one officer noted the large number of requests the committees were making and complained that many were ill-conceived. He went on to express the fear that the new committees may be slipping into an adversarial role vis-à-vis the Agency.[14]

While the new committees did make increasingly greater demands on the Agency, they did not aggressively challenge restrictions on their access to Agency information, at least in the beginning. Particularly when their demands touched on sensitive information that had heretofore never been shared with the Congress, the new committees were ordinarily willing to limit the number of people who had access to such information and/or to have the Agency retain such information rather than provide hard copies for the committees.[15]

Indeed, both committee chairmen understood that congressional oversight of intelligence could only work if the committees demonstrated both the capacity and the intent to protect the classified information that was shared with them. Accordingly, the leadership of both houses took great care to appoint "responsible" members.[16] Both committees also established secure

---

[13] Childs returned to the CIA in 1982 to serve as its comptroller.

[14] CIA draft study, Vol. II., 162.

[15] Ibid., 228–29.

[16] Smist, *Congress Oversees*, 93–95, 100, 224–28.

Senator Daniel Inouye (l), first chairman of the Senate Select Committee on Intelligence, and Representative Edward Boland, first chairman of the House Permanent Select Committee on Intelligence. Each was instrumental to the successful inauguration of his respective committee.

(Photos courtesy of the US Senate Historical Collection and the Office of the Clerk of the US House of Representatives.)

offices, committee rooms, and storage areas in which to carry on their operations. They also adopted procedures and policies, comparable to if not more stringent than those in the executive branch, for handling and storing classified documents.[17]

As important, both chairmen recognized that operating their respective committees out of the public spotlight and in a bipartisan way made it less likely that members might be tempted to leak information for partisan advantage. By doing their work behind closed doors and maintaining a low-profile in public, both sought to demonstrate to the Intelligence Community, as well as their parent bodies, that they intended to operate in a responsible manner to protect the secrets entrusted to them.

In time, the confidence of the executive branch in the ability and intent of the oversight committees to protect the classified information that was shared with them grew. Moreover, it became clearer what kinds of information the committees needed to do their jobs, and what sorts they ordinarily could get by without. Where issues of access did arise, they were resolved in some fashion, either by limiting the number of people with access or the manner in which access was provided.

---

[17] CIA draft study, Vol. II, 160, 226.

On the whole, the committees carried out their duties during this period in a workmanlike manner. In 1978, they developed and put through Congress the first in a succession of intelligence authorization bills and were instrumental in the passage of other legislation the administration desired (see chapter 5). They also carried out oversight inquiries into the Agency's performance of its collection and analytical missions that displayed increasing sophistication (see chapters 7 and 8).

Senator Inouye also reopened the issue of GAO audits, pressing both the Agency and GAO to negotiate ground rules allowing audits to be reinstituted. These efforts continued sporadically during 1977 and 1978, making occasional headway but never coming to fruition.[18]

When the Carter administration issued a new executive order (E.O. 12036) on intelligence activities in 1978, it officially recognized the existence of the two oversight committees and directed that they be kept "fully and currently informed" by the departments and agencies that made up the Intelligence Community.[19] This was, in fact, the first time that such a legal obligation had been imposed on US intelligence agencies, reflecting the increasing level of confidence the administration had in the two committees.

The Intelligence Oversight Act of 1980

The last year of the Carter administration provided an even clearer demonstration of how far the congressional oversight process had come. The committees proposed to establish, as a matter of law, the obligations of the Intelligence Community toward each committee, an initiative that was in itself unusual and might well have been resisted by the executive branch, had the committees been unable to prove themselves. As it was, President Carter ultimately accepted the committees' proposal and signed it into law.

The Intelligence Oversight Act of 1980, as the law was known, established general reporting requirements for the Intelligence Community vis-à-vis the two oversight committees. The basic obligation imposed by the new law was the same one Carter had imposed on intelligence agencies earlier by executive order: to keep the two committees "fully and currently informed" of their activities. The new law made clear, however, that these activities included "significant intelligence failures" as well as "significant anticipated activities." Thus, while the committees' approval was not required to initiate such activities, the law contemplated they would be advised in advance of "signifi-

---

[18] Ibid., 304.
[19] See § 3-401, Executive Order 12036.

cant activities" being undertaken by the Intelligence Community. Where covert actions were concerned, the law provided that where prior notice was not given, the president would inform the committees "in a timely fashion" and provide a statement explaining why prior notice had not be given. Most important as far as the Agency and the Carter administration were concerned, the law limited the reporting of covert actions to the two intelligence committees, reducing the number of committees that had been receiving such reports under Hughes-Ryan from eight to two.

Also important to the Carter administration, the new law provided that when the president determined it "essential . . . to meet extraordinary circumstances affecting vital interests of the United States" notice of intelligence activities (including "significant anticipated activities") could be given to the leaders of the House and Senate, as well as the leaders of the two intelligence committees—the so-called gang of eight—rather than to the full membership of the two committees.

Finally, the new law provided that the intelligence agencies were obliged to provide any documents in their possession that either committee might request and, further, that information could not be withheld on the grounds that giving it to the committee would constitute an unauthorized disclosure of intelligence sources and methods. At the same time, the law recognized that disclosures to the committees may take into account the need to protect "sensitive intelligence sources and methods or other exceptionally sensitive matters" from unauthorized disclosure. The committees interpreted this language as providing latitude in terms of *how* access to sensitive information would be provided, not *whether* it would be provided.

The Intelligence Oversight Act of 1980 was a civil statute in that it contained no criminal penalties for failing to comply with its provisions. However, it established legal obligations vis-à-vis the two oversight committees that could, and did, form the basis upon which intelligence agencies as well as their employees would be held accountable in the future.

The Mining of the Nicaraguan Harbors and the Casey Accords: 1984

When Ronald Reagan became president in 1981, his administration increasingly turned to covert action as a means of carrying out its foreign policy agenda. His choice for DCI, William J. Casey, was determined to make the Agency a player again on the world stage, and covert action was his chosen means for doing so. But Casey's aggressive use of covert action often brought him into conflict with the congressional oversight committees (see chapter 9) and, on one occasion, resulted in a formal change to the existing oversight arrangements.

In April 1984, it came to light in a press article that pursuant to a previously approved presidential finding and express authorization from the White House, the Agency had been involved in mining the principal harbors in Nicaragua in an effort to curtail commerce and pressure the Sandinista regime.

While Casey contended afterwards that both intelligence committees had been informed of these activities, the leadership of the Senate committee at the time, Senators Goldwater and Daniel Moynihan (D-NY), respectively, insisted they had not. If Casey had mentioned it, they contended, he had not called sufficient attention to it. In the end, Casey provided a grudging apology and agreed that henceforth he would more clearly spell out what the Agency was doing pursuant to an approved covert action finding. This commitment, which Reagan agreed to, was reduced to writing and became known as the "Casey Accords." It provided, among other things, that covert action findings would be accompanied by "scope papers" that would elaborate on the precise activities contemplated by the finding and include a risk/gain assessment of each such activity. In addition, when new activities were contemplated pursuant to an approved finding that might be politically sensitive or otherwise had gone to the president for an approval, the committees would be informed.[20]

Term Limits as an Issue for the SSCI: 1984

Since the resolution creating the SSCI in 1976 provided that its members had to leave the committee after eight years, when that deadline arrived in 1984, Senator Goldwater became concerned that nine or 10 of its members, including himself, would be forced to leave at the same time, having "far-reaching, negative consequences for Senate oversight of the Intelligence Community."[21] Goldwater communicated these concerns to a special Senate committee that had been established to study the Senate committee system, arguing that membership on the oversight committee required far more sophistication and knowledge than "we dreamed when we wrote Senate Resolution 400." But Goldwater could not get a consensus on this issue from his own committee and, in the absence of its backing, chose not to pursue the matter further.[22]

---

[20] CIA draft study, Vol. III, 65; Woodward, *Veil*, 358–59; Smist, *Congress Oversees*, 122–23.

[21] CIA draft study, Vol. III, 72.

[22] Ibid., 72–73.

GAO Again: 1984

The issue of GAO's relationship with the Agency also resurfaced in 1984. By this point, both committees had come to regard GAO not as an organization to supplement their oversight but as a potential competitor to their oversight. When GAO requested three National Intelligence Estimates (NIEs) from the Agency that related to work it was doing for another committee, the Agency took the position, which the oversight committees supported, that as an element of Congress, GAO had to work through the intelligence committees to obtain information from or about the Agency. The Agency would provide the NIEs to the committees, but it would be up to them whether they were shared with GAO.[23]

Continued Wrangling over Covert Action Notification: 1985–86

Despite the "Casey Accords," Casey and the committees continued to butt heads over the notification process for covert action. The committees complained that it was taking too long for them to receive findings and notifications, that they were not getting the actual texts of findings, and that the Agency was overusing the option of giving notice to the "gang of eight" rather than the full committees. They also had a special concern that CIA was transferring US military equipment to support its activities without advising them.[24]

Casey, for his part, chafed under what he saw as the unreasonable demands of the committees, which he believed unacceptably hampered the president and the DCI in their handling of foreign affairs. To deal with the problem from his standpoint, in the spring of 1985 Casey proposed to both committees new procedures to govern the notification process: he would notify the committees of all findings and memorandums of notification approved by the president by means of written "advisories" that would go to the leaders of the intelligence committees and the appropriations committees, provided that he reserved the right to brief these leaders orally when the operation was particularly sensitive. Moreover, when the president specifically directed, he could limit notice to the congressional leadership (the majority and minority leaders of the Senate and the Speaker and minority leader of the House) rather than the committees and could withhold notice from them altogether until such time as the president directed him to provide it.[25]

---

[23] Ibid., 18.
[24] Ibid., 108.
[25] Ibid.

Both committees rejected Casey's proposals. The SSCI, however, endeavored to reach a compromise, and on 17 June 1986, after months of negotiation, an agreement between Casey and the committee was formalized. The committee accepted Casey's "advisories" format and recognized the "gang of eight" option provided by existing law. At the same time, Casey would "make every reasonable effort to inform the committee of presidential findings and significant covert action activities and developments as soon as practicable." The committee would also be told of "significant transfers" of military equipment.[26] The deal worked out with the SSCI was not acceptable to the HPSCI. While the two sides continued to negotiate, the disclosure of the Iran-contra scandal in November 1986 effectively put an end to the negotiations with the HPSCI and cast doubt upon what had been agreed to with the SSCI.

Tightening Control over Intelligence Funding: 1986

While the HPSCI was unable to negotiate a compromise on covert action notifications, it did get changes enacted to the oversight statute in 1986 that considerably strengthened the control of the oversight committees over intelligence funding.[27] Although procedures had long been in place to govern the "reprogramming" of appropriated funds for different purposes, they were a matter of practice rather than law, and the HPSCI suspected the Agency was not adhering to them.

In 1986, at the initiative of HPSCI Chairman Lee Hamilton (D-IN), provisions were added to the annual authorization bill to deal with this situation. Appropriated funds could only be expended, the law would now provide, (1) if Congress had specifically authorized them; (2) if, in the case of the DCI's Contingency Reserve Fund, the DCI had given the committees prior notice of his intent to make use of such funds; or (3) if, in the case of funds being used for a purpose other than that for which they had been appropriated, the DCI (or secretary of defense) notified both committees in advance that the new purpose had been unforeseen at the time of the original appropriation and was now considered a higher priority. In addition, no funds could be spent for any intelligence activity for which Congress had denied funding, nor could funds be spent for a covert action that had not been the subject of a presidential finding.[28]

In addition, provisions were added to the law to deal with the concerns of both committees that CIA was transferring US military equipment without advising them. From here on, the law would require such notification when

---

[26] Ibid., 109.
[27] Smist, *Congress Oversees*, 257.
[28] §504, *National Security Act of 1947*, as amended.

intelligence agencies contemplated transferring defense articles or services with an aggregate value of $1 million or more to a third party outside the US government, unless the transfer was conducted openly under the Arms Export Control Act or other applicable federal statutes.[29]

Investigating the Iran-contra Affair: 1986–87

On 3 November 1986, a Lebanese magazine, *Al Shiraa*, reported that the United States had been supplying arms to Iran in hopes of winning release of the American hostages being held in the Middle East and that US National Security Advisor Robert McFarlane had visited Tehran earlier in the year to meet with Iranian officials in furtherance of the sales. On 12 November, the congressional leadership, including the leaders of the two intelligence committees, was briefed at the White House on the Iran initiative. On 21 November, DCI Casey and Deputy National Security Advisor John Poindexter testified before both intelligence committees, defending the arms sales as necessary to freeing the hostages and the beginning of a new relationship with Iran. Casey acknowledged that the Agency had provided support to what had been an NSC initiative but denied that the Agency had known about the nature of the shipments. He also suggested that, while the committees may not have been notified of the Agency's role "in a timely fashion," to have done so might have infringed upon the constitutional powers of the president.[30]

Four days later, Attorney General Edwin Meese announced at a press conference that he had found evidence in the office of LTC Oliver North, who had run the Iranian initiative for the NSC, that $12 million generated by the arms sales to Iran had been "diverted" to purchase supplies for the contras—a conglomeration of groups in Central America that were trying to overthrow the leftist Sandinista government in Nicaragua—at a time when Congress had by law expressly prohibited such assistance.

By the end of the year, no fewer than seven investigations had been launched of what had become known as the Iran-contra affair. On 26 November, Casey directed the CIA inspector general to investigate CIA's involvement. On 1 December, President Reagan established a special review board, chaired by former Senator John Tower, to investigate the NSC's involvement. Both intelligence committees announced they would conduct investigations, as did the House Appropriations and Foreign Affairs Committees. On 19

---

[29] §505, *National Security Act of 1947*, as amended.
[30] CIA draft study, Vol. III, 132.

December, Meese appointed an "independent counsel" to investigate the criminal aspects of what had happened.[31]

Within Congress, though, it soon became clear that Iran-contra did not fit comfortably within the existing committee structure in either house. Although CIA had had a role in it, the operation had been run out of the White House, which lay outside the jurisdictional purview of the intelligence committees. While the foreign affairs committees had jurisdiction over foreign policy, they were not equipped to deal with the intelligence aspects. Moreover, it was clear that a significant staff effort would be required, exceeding the extant capabilities of the existing committees. Thus, on 6 January 1987, the Senate created a special investigating committee; the House of Representatives followed suit a day later. Four members of the SSCI, including its chairman and vice chairman, were appointed to the Senate investigating committee; on the House side, five HPSCI members were appointed, including its chairman and ranking minority member.[32] All designated senior staff from the intelligence committees were to support them. Of the congressional inquiries that had been initiated, only the SSCI, under its new chairman, David Boren (D-OK), issued a report of its investigation to that point. (See chapter 9 for a detailed description of the Agency's role in the Iran-contra affair.)

Within several months of their creation, the Senate and House investigating committees realized that they would be seeking to review the same documents and interview the same witnesses. When it came time for hearings, each would presumably want to address the same issues. Thus, in March 1987, the two investigating committees decided to pool resources to conduct a joint investigation. While each side initially reserved the right to issue its own final report, a joint report was produced in November, signed by 18 Democratic and Republican members of the House and Senate, together with a minority report signed by eight Republican members. The investigation had gone on for almost a year and involved 300,000 documents reviewed, more than 500 witnesses interviewed, and 40 days of joint public hearings held.[33]

The investigation ultimately showed that knowledge of the Iran-contra operation within the CIA had been relatively limited. While some Agency officers had known of the arms sales to Iran, no documentary evidence was found to indicate anyone at the Agency had specifically known of the "diversion" of the proceeds of these sales to the contras. By the time Iran-contra was disclosed, several Agency officers had come to suspect this had happened, but they had not been specifically told. North later testified that Casey had been

---

[31] Ibid., 150.
[32] Smist, *Congress Oversees*, 259.
[33] Ibid.

aware of the diversion, but by this point Casey had died and no evidence corroborating North's testimony could be found. Notwithstanding, several Agency officers, who had been witting of North's role in organizing support for the contras from private sources, were later disciplined by DCI Webster for having deliberately withheld such information from the intelligence committees, and two senior officers were dismissed for engaging in improper activities on behalf of the contras.[34]

For the intelligence oversight committees, however, the most unsettling revelation to emerge from the investigation came during the testimony of North when he revealed that he and Casey had planned to use the profits from the arms sales to Iran to finance a self-sustaining, "off-the-shelf" organization, run by private citizens and/or private entities, to carry out covert actions around the world without involving Congress at all.[35] Casey, now deceased, was unable to confirm or deny North's testimony.

Changes to Congressional Oversight Prompted by Iran-contra: 1987–91

While the Agency's involvement in and knowledge of Iran-contra had been relatively limited, the final report of the congressional investigating committees recommended a number of changes to the system of intelligence oversight that fell to the two intelligence committees to deal with. Most involved the approval and reporting of covert actions:

- Congress should be notified, without exception, no later than 48 hours after a covert action "finding" had been approved.

- All findings should be in writing and personally approved by the president.

- Retroactive findings should be prohibited.

- Findings should specify their funding source(s).

- All findings would lapse after a year unless the president renewed them.[36]

The Iran-contra committees specifically rejected the notion that a joint committee would improve congressional oversight of intelligence but did recommend that the oversight committees bolster their capabilities by creating audit staffs to monitor the financial aspects of Agency operations. They also

---

[34] CIA draft study, Vol. III, 158.

[35] *Report of the Congressional Committees Investigating the Iran-Contra Affair*, 411–13; Smist, *Congress Oversees*, 264–65.

[36] *Report of the Congressional Committees Investigating the Iran-Contra Affair*, 423–27.

recommended that the inspector general for the CIA be made "independent" (see the discussion in the next section) and that both the IG and CIA general counsel be appointed by the president and subject to Senate confirmation.[37]

Both committees turned first to the issue they considered paramount: notification of covert actions. In their view, the Intelligence Oversight Act of 1980 envisioned prior notice being given the committees, but where that was not possible, notice would be given "in a timely fashion." Although the statute did not define this phrase, both committees were of the view that the failure of the Reagan administration to inform them within 10 months of the findings authorizing CIA support of the arms sales to Iran did not meet this standard.

The Justice Department, however, issued a legal opinion in late 1986 soon after Iran-contra was disclosed, saying that the "timely notice" provision had to be interpreted in light of the president's constitutional authority as commander-in-chief and, read as such, gave the president "virtually unfettered discretion" when to provide notice of covert actions to the two committees. While there may not have been unanimity on the committees with respect to what "timely" notice meant, there was unanimity that it did not mean this.

Apart from what "timely notice" meant, however, the Reagan administration, as well as the Bush administration that followed it, objected to changing the law to require notice, without exception, within 48 hours of a finding being signed. They contended that this requirement was too inflexible and could hamstring a future president. While they were willing to compromise on the subsidiary issues (such as requiring findings to be in writing and the prohibition of retroactive findings) they would not accept a strict 48-hour time limit.

The impasse lasted for almost four years.[38] The intelligence committees, especially the SSCI, repeatedly offered legislation to resolve the notification issue, as well as the subsidiary issues, but for one reason or another this legislation stalled on its way through the congressional process and, on one occasion, was vetoed after making it through Congress. (See chapter 5 for a detailed discussion.)

In 1991, a compromise was reached on "timely notification," and as a result, legislation to remedy the problems identified by the Iran-contra investigations was at long last enacted. The "timely notice" language remained in the law. But the conference report explaining this language required a president's commitment to notify the Congress "within a few days" of signing a finding. To withhold notice for a longer period, a president would have to assert consti-

---

[37] Ibid.
[38] Lundberg, *Congressional Oversight and Presidential Prerogative*; Conner, "Reforming Oversight of Covert Actions After the Iran-Contra Affair."

tutional authorities as commander-in-chief. The committees, for their part, disagreed in principle that the Constitution empowered a president to withhold notice from the Congress for longer than "a few days," but they recognized this was an issue for the courts to settle.

The legislation went on to define "covert action" for the first time in statute and, for the first time in the Agency's history, specifically authorized CIA to undertake such activities. Relating to some of the issues raised by Iran-contra, the new law provided that covert action findings must be in writing and personally approved by the president; that no retroactive findings would be permitted; and that findings would identify any government agency or third parties (private entities or foreign governments) being used. Finally, findings could not authorize activities that violated the Constitution or laws of the United States.[39]

GAO Audits Resurface: 1987–88

Although the Iran-contra committees had not recommended the GAO be given authority to audit CIA activities, the issue resurfaced in Congress in the wake of the scandal. In the Senate, the chairman of the Governmental Affairs Committee (which had jurisdiction over GAO) introduced legislation that would have specifically authorized the GAO to evaluate the Agency's programs and activities. In the House, a more limited bill was introduced authorizing the GAO to audit the Afghanistan covert action program. In both cases, the bills were referred to the intelligence committees where they languished.

The chairman of the SSCI at the time, David Boren (D-OK), was concerned, however, that some further action was needed if the committee was to stave off similar initiatives in the future. To create such a counterweight, he announced the formation of a small "audit staff" within the committee to conduct independent audits of ongoing covert action programs. Eager to ensure that congressional investigations remained in the hands of the oversight committees, the Agency welcomed Boren's initiative.[40]

The Creation of a Statutory Inspector General for the CIA: 1989

Another significant change to the oversight arrangements that grew out of the Iran-contra affair was the creation of a statutory inspector general (IG) at the CIA. The Iran-contra committee had recommended such action in 1987,

---

[39] §503 of the National Security Act of 1947, as amended.
[40] CIA draft study, Vol. III, 167.

and two years later, Congress enacted legislation creating the office. (See chapter 5 for a detailed description.)

While the Agency had had an IG since 1952, the IG established by the 1989 law would be different. Notably, it would now have a direct reporting relationship with the Congress. Heretofore, IG reports were seen as internal documents and not furnished the committees. Now they would be shared on request. Agency IGs would also be required to make semiannual reports of their activities, something that had not been done in the past. This would give the committees an awareness and an opportunity to inquire further, which they had not had before. Moreover, if the IG undertook an investigation of the DCI or other senior Agency officer, the committees would have to be notified. If the DCI were to terminate or quash one of the IG's investigations (an action the statute specifically allowed), the committees would also have to be told.[41] In short, the IG statute gave the committees a window into the Agency's operations that they had not had before.

By creating an independent IG within the CIA, the statute also gave the committees a place they could go within the Agency to ask for oversight inquiries that exceeded the committees' own capabilities. While, in theory, the IG could demur to such requests and/or the DCI could block them, doing so would obviously create a political problem with the committee concerned.

Statutory Recognition of the Agency's Support of Congress: 1992

The Agency, over its entire existence, had regarded the provision of substantive intelligence support to Congress as part of its mission. (See chapter 3 for a detailed description.) But until 1992, there was nothing in the law itself that made intelligence support to the Congress part of the Agency's mission.

The Intelligence Organization Act of 1992 was not meant to effect changes to the oversight arrangements per se; indeed, those arrangements had only been modified the year before. But in setting forth the responsibilities of the DCI in law, Congress took the opportunity to spell out, for the first time, the DCI's responsibility for "providing national intelligence . . . where appropriate, to the Senate and House of Representatives and the committees thereof." The law went on to say that such intelligence should be "timely, objective, independent of political considerations, and based upon all sources available to the intelligence community."[42]

---

[41] §20 of the CIA Act of 1949, as amended.
[42] §103A of the *National Security Act of 1947*, as amended.

Formalization of Notification Procedures: The Guatemala Inquiries, 1995

In 1995, the American wife of a Guatemalan guerrilla leader who had disappeared three years earlier told the two intelligence committees that the Agency had somehow been involved in his disappearance. In looking into these allegations, the SSCI discovered that a clandestine source of the Agency's within the Guatemalan military was rumored not only to have been involved in the disappearance of the guerilla leader but was also suspected of having been involved five years earlier in the death of an American citizen living in Guatemala. Both committees investigated these allegations as did the CIA inspector general and the Intelligence Oversight Board, a subcommittee of the President's Foreign Intelligence Advisory Board (see chapter 8 for more detail). The Agency's IG, in fact, undertook an even broader inquiry at the request of the intelligence committees, examining what the Agency had known about human rights abuses by any of its clandestine sources in Guatemala since 1984.

While neither investigation found evidence that the Agency's source had been involved in the death of the American in 1990 or in the disappearance of the guerrilla leader, they did find that CIA had learned of the first allegation in 1991 and, despite having several opportunities between 1991 and 1995, had failed to notify either of the intelligence committees of the potential problem. Both committees regarded this as a failure of the statutory requirement to keep them "fully and currently informed." The Intelligence Oversight Board at the White House later agreed, albeit finding the failure inadvertent rather than intentional.[43] Nonetheless, 12 Agency employees were disciplined for this failure, two of them forced to retire.

Most significant for the long term, however, were the systemic changes the Agency adopted as a result of the Guatemalan episode. In February 1996, Deutch issued new guidance for dealing with allegations of human rights abuse, or crimes of violence, by assets or foreign liaison services. In general, the guidelines provided that where such allegations could be proved or largely substantiated, further relationships would be barred unless senior CIA officials approved them as necessary to the national interest.

The Agency also established, on its own initiative, a systematic notification process to protect against another failure to notify Congress of significant information concerning its operations. Heretofore the determination of whether to notify the oversight committees of operational activities that were seen as unusual or problematic had been informal and ad hoc. Either Agency leaders themselves would see the need to advise them, or components would

---

[43] Intelligence Oversight Board, *Report on the Guatemalan Review.*

perceive a need and raise it through channels. Under the new system, instituted by DCI directive in 1996 and incorporated into Agency training programs, this process became regularized and formalized. Components would be required to systematically review operational activities on an ongoing basis for issues or problems that should be briefed to the oversight committees and provide the DCI written memoranda on the results. The DCI ultimately would decide which notifications to provide the committees as well as the content of such notifications. While the Agency continued to protect operational details to the extent possible, far more notifications began being sent to the two oversight committees than ever before.

While the practice would sometimes result in follow-up requests for briefings, or even lead one of the committees to open an investigation, the new notification system considerably reduced the chances that issues might "fall through the cracks" and lead to recrimination. Indeed, the Agency had a written record of precisely what the committees had been told. Former OCA Director John Moseman put it this way:

> *They couldn't come back to us any more when something went wrong and claim they'd never been told about it. If they had a problem with something, then it was up to them to let us know about it. If they didn't . . . well . . . it makes it hard for them to criticize us for failing to do something about it.*[44]

Procedures for "Whistleblowers" Who Wished to Contact Congress: 1998

Agency employees who wished to report perceived wrongdoing, or perceived unfairness in terms of their treatment at the hands of the Agency, had always had, in theory at least, the option of complaining to one or both of the oversight committees in Congress. But unless a complaining employee worked through Agency management to contact the congressional committees, he or she could be seen as violating the Agency's regulations governing contacts with Congress, procedures instituted not only to allow Agency management to know what was being said to Congress but also to ensure that any classified information being passed to Congress was transmitted in a secure manner. Requiring Agency employees to work through their management to contact Congress, however, naturally raised the possibility that some type of retaliatory action might be taken against the employee.

---

[44] Moseman interview, 28 December 2006.

Prior to the creation of the select committees in the mid-1970s, such complaints were rare. But from 1980 on, they became more frequent. Dealing with the conundrum presented by this practice came down to a case-by-case determination. If an employee came to one of the oversight committees directly and did not want his or her supervisors to know about it, the committees would usually respect that confidence. However, if the complaint led to the committee launching an inquiry or investigation, it might become necessary to reveal the employee's identity. The employee was typically consulted at this point before any such inquiry or investigation went forward. Moreover, once the complaining employee had been identified to the Agency, there was a tacit but firm understanding on both sides that any retaliatory action taken by the Agency against the employee (to include punishment for violating its procedures for contacting Congress) would bring the wrath of the committee upon the Agency. Indeed, at times, the committees made this clear in no uncertain terms. Agency managers, in such cases, typically complied with the committees' wishes.

In 1998, however, the intelligence committees, believing Agency regulations could be discouraging employees from coming to them, created a complex new procedure by statute that would provide Agency employees who wanted to contact them the option of first going to the Agency's IG with their complaint; the IG would have 14 days to determine whether the complaint was "credible" and, if so, forward it to the committees through the DCI. If the IG failed to forward the complaint, the employee could then contact the committees directly, provided that he or she advised Agency management of the intent to do so and was advised how to contact the committees to protect any classified information that might be part of the complaint. If the employee later perceived he or she had been the subject of retaliation for the complaint, that would become the basis for a second complaint to be processed through the same system.[45]

The law, notably, did not make this complex procedure mandatory. Rather, it left in place the option that had existed previously: contacting the committees directly but risk being charged with violating Agency regulations governing such contacts.

---

[45] *The Whistleblower Protection Act of 1998*, Title VII of the *Intelligence Authorization Act for Fiscal Year 1999*.

The Joint Inquiry into the 9/11 Attacks: 2001–2003

The 9/11 terrorist attacks led many in Congress (and across the country) to conclude there had been an intelligence failure of serious proportions. Neither intelligence committee saw fit in the painful aftermath of the attacks, however, to immediately examine what the Intelligence Community had done, or failed to do, prior to the attacks. The Speaker of the House asked HPSCI Chairman Porter Goss (R-FL) to undertake a quiet probe of these issues, but for the most part, both committees focused on what could or should be done to prevent more attacks in the future.

In the fall of 2001, the HPSCI held a series of open hearings on the US posture in terms of responding to the terrorist threat. It examined the role of the NSC in domestic counterterrorism policy, the federal components of homeland security, and the interaction of the Intelligence Community with state and local authorities. The SSCI, for its part, held several hearings on organizational reform of the Intelligence Community in light of the attacks. Both committees also participated in the larger efforts of their parent bodies to identify legislative changes—the Patriot Act of 2001 and the creation of the Department of Homeland Security, among others—that would improve the ability of the United States to predict and thwart terrorist acts.

At the beginning of 2002, however, the leadership of both committees decided it was time for them to formally assess what had happened within the Intelligence Community. To accomplish this, the committees, for the first time in their history, agreed to conduct a joint inquiry, using a separate staff of 25 professionals hired to do the investigation. While the staff of the joint inquiry would receive guidance from and support the needs of the majority and minority on both oversight committees, its work would be separate from the other work of the oversight committees. The investigation would encompass all of the agencies within the Intelligence Community and would attempt to identify what they had known about the 9/11 attacks, including the perpetrators, and what they had done with such information.

Over the course of the inquiry, the committees held nine joint hearings in open session and 13 in closed session. Its staff reviewed more than 500,000 pages of documents and interviewed more than 300 witnesses. The 422-page report of its investigation was published in December 2002.[46] While disagreement was evident in certain of the nine additional views filed to the report, no member of either committee formally voted against it. (A discussion of the

---

[46] Senate Select Committee on Intelligence and House Permanent Select Committee on Intelligence, *Joint Inquiry into Intelligence Community Activities Before and After the Terrorist Attacks of September 11, 2001*.

findings of the joint inquiry with respect to the Agency's performance is found in chapters 7–9.)

Criticism from the 9/11 Commission and an End to Term Limits: 2004

In its final report, issued in July 2004, the National Commission on Terrorist Attacks Upon the United States (the 9/11 Commission) issued a scathing indictment of the existing oversight arrangements. Finding that congressional oversight of intelligence had become "dysfunctional," the commission said that unless changes were made, "the American people will not get the security they want and need."[47] The commission went on to recommend either a joint committee on intelligence modeled on the Joint Atomic Energy Committee be created or a single committee in each house that had the power both to authorize and appropriate. It also recommended that whatever arrangements may be adopted, the oversight committees should be smaller and that term limits for their members be eliminated.[48]

In the wake of such criticism, the leaders of both Houses called for internal reviews of their respective committee structures. In the end, however, there was no sentiment in either house for the commission's principal recommendations: a joint committee on intelligence or a committee with the combined power to authorize and appropriate. Both bodies did, however, ultimately drop the term limits for members who served on the Intelligence Committees.[49] From here on, service on the two committees would be indefinite, subject to the same vagaries as service on other congressional committees.

In addition, the Senate resolution provided that at the start of each Congress the Senate majority and minority leaders, not the respective party caucuses, would chose the chairman and vice chairman of the SSCI. While this change had not been part of the 9/11 Commission's recommendations, it was explained in terms of reducing the partisanship associated with these appointments. The Senate also reduced the number of members on the SSCI to 15 (its original number) and established within the SSCI a subcommittee on oversight.

---

[47] *9/11 Commission Report*, Authorized Edition, Norton paperback, 419–20. Although the commission did not fully explain why it had found that congressional oversight of intelligence had become "dysfunctional," it is likely that members found that intense partisan divisiveness had come to infect the work of both committees. See "Author's Commentary" at the end of this chapter.

[48] Ibid., 420–21.

[49] S. Res. 445, 108th Cong., 2nd Sess., 2004; H. Res. (get cite)

AUTHOR'S COMMENTARY

What Changed When the Select Committees Were Created

As the text of this chapter indicates—and the point is reinforced repeatedly in the balance of this study—virtually everything changed once the select committees were created, from legislative initiatives affecting the Agency, to program and budget reviews, to oversight of its activities. But the fundamental thing that changed was the nature of the relationship between the Agency and the Congress.

Instead of having overseers—both members and staff—who generally saw their responsibility for the Agency as an additional duty, the Agency now had congressional overseers for whom responsibility for the Agency (and the Intelligence Community) was their exclusive focus. Not surprisingly, far more time and energy were devoted to assessing the Agency's needs and evaluating its activities, and there were more of them (both members and staff) to do it. A capability was put in place that had not existed before, and this enabled the committees to undertake many things—legislation, budget reviews, oversight inquiries—that heretofore had exceeded their ability to accomplish. This, in turn, forced the Agency itself to devote far more time and energy to managing its side of the relationship.

While the chairmen and ranking minority members (on the SSCI, its vice chairman) of the select committees continued to be the focal points for DCIs to work with, their obligations (keeping the committees "fully and currently informed," for example) now applied to the committees as a whole. Moreover, the committees insisted on access to Agency records and personnel to carry out their responsibilities as well as to document Agency activities. The era of cozy tête-à-têtes with the chairmen of their subcommittees was gone forever.

This situation had both advantages and disadvantages for the Agency. On the positive side, assuming it could prove itself, it would have stronger, more credible advocates in Congress than it had had under the old system. Assuming the committees took their responsibilities seriously and worked constructively with the Agency to solve its problems (both with legislative authority and with funding), the Agency might be able to accomplish things it could not have accomplished before. On the negative side, it was clearly going to have to expose more of its information to a larger audience on the Hill. This would not only increase the risk of its disclosure but also provide far more opportunities for Congress to second-guess what the Agency was doing. For years, other departments and agencies had complained of congressional "microman-agement," but it was a problem that, until now, CIA had managed to avoid.

But now, as the oversight process grew more intrusive and complex over the last quarter of the 20th century, CIA went from an agency with cursory oversight by the Congress to perhaps the most scrutinized agency in the executive branch. Whether this increased attention on balance contributed to or detracted from the Agency's ability to perform its mission is for others to analyze.

The Joint Committee Solution

Even after each house established the select committees on intelligence in the mid-1970s, the joint committee idea never completely went away but rather found different advocates. Now those who espoused the idea were members who favored less oversight rather than more. But those who held such views never commanded enough support in either house to constitute a significant challenge to the select committee arrangement, and the Agency itself never pushed for such change.

Why this proved to be the case may need explaining. While separate oversight committees in the House and Senate, both with relatively large staffs, pose certain practical problems for the Agency—problems that having to deal with one committee rather than two would seemingly ameliorate—the joint committee arrangement would have different, perhaps more serious problems.

On the plus side (from the Agency's standpoint), fewer people would presumably have access to its information, reducing the potential for leaks. There would also, presumably, be fewer demands made upon the Agency and fewer egos (at both the member and staff level) for the Agency to satisfy.

But having only one committee to deal with would necessarily mean putting the Agency's eggs in one basket. So long as the joint committee were supportive—both in terms of its operational activities and its resource needs—the relationship would work to the Agency's advantage. But, inevitably, if things stayed this way for long, calls would again be heard for oversight reform. The committee had been co-opted, many would say. On the other hand, if the relationship should sour, there would be nowhere for the Agency to turn. What the joint committee said and did would be the final word.

Having two committees involved in the Agency's affairs not only brings a natural check and balance to the day-to-day work of each committee—neither wants the other to see it as uninformed or arbitrary—it also provides an avenue of appeal for the Agency when it believes its interests are being slighted by one of the two committees. Assuming it can make its case to the "friendlier" committee, chances are that it can reach some kind of an accommodation that protects the Agency's equities in the issue at hand.

Having committees in both houses also gives members of both bodies who are not on the oversight committees assurances that the two committees have sorted issues out before matters come to floor, including funding for the Agency. Legislative proposals from a joint committee do not provide that level of confidence. Members do not know the extent to which their side has played in the legislation or even if it reflects the views of their members. That is why most joint committees are not given legislative authority but are set up to "study" an area of mutual concern. If they wish to propose legislation, they have to work through the standing committees of jurisdiction. If a joint committee on intelligence were to be created, it would necessarily need legislative authority, but its bills would not carry the same weight with the rank and file of Congress as those produced in the "normal" system.

Finally, by virtue of the Senate's constitutional responsibilities, there are some functions that the SSCI has that could not migrate to a joint committee. For example, only Senate committees can "advise and consent" on presidential nominations. A joint committee could not hold confirmation hearings for the DNI or other officials within the Intelligence Community. Similarly, only the Senate can ratify treaties. The longstanding role of the SSCI in providing advice to the rest of the Senate on the ability of the Intelligence Community to verify international treaties could not migrate very well to a joint committee.

Thus, from the creation of the select committees until 2004, the idea of creating a joint committee to replace the two select committees never gained much traction in either house of Congress or at the Agency itself. Ironically, when the 9/11 Commission offered the idea again in 2004, it did so as a means of strengthening the oversight being provided by the select committees, oversight that it now found had become "dysfunctional," that is, partisan and ineffectual. (See chapters 7 and 8.) Despite the commission's unusually harsh criticism, however, neither House showed interest in its recommendation. It was still not apparent to either body that a joint committee offered a better solution.

Term Limits for Members of the Select Committees

Until 2004, members of the select committees served fixed terms. Initially, the principal rationale for this policy was to prevent members of the oversight committees from being "co-opted" by the agencies they were supposed to oversee. A secondary purpose was to expose more members of Congress to the work of intelligence and dispel the notion that oversight would continue to be limited to a select few.

Over time, however, it became increasingly apparent that term limits were having a deleterious effect on the expertise of the committees and their respective staffs. Members who were able to achieve a working mastery of the subject were forced to leave the committees just when they had begun to be effective. Others, recognizing that their time on the committee was limited and that they were not destined to play a leadership role during this period, never tried to master the subject. Moreover, the turnover of members meant a turnover of staff, especially when committee leaders, who had done most of the hiring, left their positions. While both committees over their history made an effort to retain valued staff, even when their political mentors left, it was often difficult to effect such a transition.

While removing term limits had been a frequent topic of discussion on both committees, it was not until 2004, when the 9/11 Commission recommended they be abolished, that their parent bodies took such action. Removal of term limits will not, in and of itself, make members instant experts on intelligence, but it should over time make them more knowledgeable of the Agency's activities and more appreciative of its needs. It should also lead to greater continuity on their professional staffs.

At the same time, with fewer members serving on the two committees, there will be reduced awareness within their parent bodies of how the committees are conducting themselves. Over time, this could lead again to mistrust and resentment, especially if the rest of Congress should find itself shut out of the Agency's work altogether. While oversight of the Agency's operations necessarily should rest principally with the select committees, the Agency should continue to meet the legitimate needs of other committees for intelligence analysis. Otherwise, there will be problems.

The Impact of Personalities, Attitudes, and Circumstances

As this chapter indicates, the period from the creation of the select committees until 2004 was a period that saw the proliferation of laws and regulations governing the oversight relationship. Nevertheless, personalities, attitudes and circumstances often continued to determine how the relationship played out in practice.

The creation of the select committees in the mid-1970s, for example, took very different routes in the Senate and House, largely because of the experience each body had had with its respective investigating committee. The resolution creating the SSCI was brought to the floor soon after the Church Committee had issued its final report and passed by a substantial, bipartisan vote. A core group of both members and staff moved from the Church Committee to the SSCI, giving it immediate expertise and continuity in dealing with the issues the committee had identified. The House, on the other hand, did not consider the resolution creating the HPSCI until July 1977, a year and a half after the Pike Committee had disbanded, and did so only then because House Speaker O'Neill decided that a House counterpart to the SSCI was needed. House leaders wanted to stay as far away from the Pike Committee model as possible, and no members or staff from the Pike Committee moved to the new committee. But this meant the new committee had to build itself from scratch.

Both the Senate and the House leadership, in fact, were concerned that the acrimony and partisanship that had characterized the work of the investigating committees not be carried over to their new oversight committees. They also recognized that oversight of the Intelligence Community was never going to work if the committees did not protect the information that was shared with them. It was especially important that the new committees get off to the right start, with leaders who would set an appropriate, bipartisan tone. Accordingly, the first chairmen appointed to each committee were seasoned members with reputations for bipartisanship and prudence: Inouye at the SSCI and Boland at the HPSCI. Both indicated early on their intent to carry out their work in a businesslike fashion, avoid partisanship and sensationalism, and protect the secrets that were entrusted to them.

The change in administration that occurred at roughly the same time helped get things off on the right foot. Senior members of the Carter administration, notably Vice President Walter Mondale, had been instrumental in the creation of the SSCI and were proponents of greater congressional oversight. Furthermore, neither the new president nor his choice as DCI, Stansfield Turner, had experienced first hand the acrimony and frustrations of the Church and Pike investigations. Thus they were able to come to their positions (committing to the new oversight arrangements in Congress) unburdened personally by the experience of the recent past.

The SSCI, for the reasons noted above, was quicker off the mark. It had a substantial agenda left over from the Church Committee inquiry and also had responsibilities as a Senate committee—particularly advising the Senate on the ability of the Intelligence Community to verify arms control treaties—that at times necessitated a degree of involvement its House counterpart did not have. But both committees in their early years managed to carry out their responsibilities in workmanlike fashion, putting through an intelligence authorization bill each year as well as other legislation (for example, the Foreign Intelligence Surveillance Act of 1978) pertaining to their area of jurisdiction. Oversight inquiries took place behind closed doors, with few if any leaks of classified information. DCI Turner took seriously his obligation to consult and cooperate with them.

The HPSCI particularly benefited from the continuity in its leadership. Boland served as its chairman for eight years, his entire tenure on the committee. Most of the staff that he assembled at the beginning stayed with him, allowing the committee to overcome its initial deficit in staff expertise. There was also a high degree of staff continuity on the SSCI, although the leadership of the committee changed hands several times during Boland's tenure on the HPSCI. Senator Inouye left after two years, succeeded by Birch Bayh (D-IN), and when the Senate changed hands in 1980, Senator Goldwater took charge for the next four years. Perhaps at no time during the history of the oversight committees did personality and circumstance make such a difference.

Senator Barry Goldwater. Although he opposed the establishment of the Senate Select Committee on Intelligence, he served as the committee's chairman between 1980 and 1984.

(US Senate Historical Collection)

Goldwater, by this point, was 71 years old, a cantankerous veteran of 24 years in the Senate. He had run for president against Lyndon Johnson in 1964 and had been soundly defeated. He had also served on the Church Committee, where he had been an outspoken defender of the Intelligence Community, often taking issue with the committee's chairman. He had actually opposed the creation of the SSCI during the Senate's floor debate but accepted appointment to it once it was established. Even after he became chairman, however, he would offer the view (much to his staff's chagrin) that the committee was not needed.

With his appointment as SSCI chairman assured by the 1980 election, Goldwater urged President-elect Reagan to appoint Goldwater's own candidate, ADM Bobby Ray Inman, to the DCI's position. But Reagan had promised that to his campaign manager, New York lawyer and former Securities and Exchange Commission chairman, William O. Casey. Goldwater did not like it, but he accepted it. Inman was named Casey's deputy.

Casey had been in the OSS during World War II but had had limited exposure to intelligence activity since then. During the tumultuous decade of the 1970s, he had been practicing law. He and Goldwater were both hard-line anticommunists intent on rebuilding the military and intelligence communities, which they believed had suffered during the Carter years. But from the start, relations between them were strained. A few months after the Senate confirmed Casey, information came to light that he had withheld relevant information during the confirmation process. Goldwater investigated. Then came the appointment of Casey's crony, Max Hugel, as the DDO. Goldwater was outraged, and Hugel was later forced to resign.

Casey knew he was obliged to deal with the oversight committees, not only because the law required it, but because there were things he wanted from the Congress, such as funding and legislation. But he never liked this part of his duties, seeing the committees as obstacles to the president's ability to carry out his responsibilities as commander-in-chief and principal arbiter of US foreign policy. While he paid lip service to the oversight process, he came across as less than candid in his dealings with the committees. As one member later put it, "Casey treated us like mushrooms. He kept us in the dark and fed us manure."[50] Others complained they had to pull information from Casey. "He wouldn't tell you if your coat was on fire," one later commented, "if you didn't ask him."[51] Even when Casey did respond to members' questions, his answer often came in the form of an infuriating mumble, deepening their impression that he was trying to keep them in the dark. Below the surface, many perceived contempt, both for themselves and their respective institutions.

Goldwater, nevertheless, sought to work with Casey, in particular when it came to their shared concern that communist regimes were getting footholds in several Central American countries. When the HPSCI became disillusioned with the covert action program supporting the contras in Nicaragua during the early 1980s it had been Goldwater who took up the administration's cause and sought to moderate the cuts made to the program.

In April 1984, however, it came to light that the Agency had, as part of its covert operation in the country, mined the harbors of certain Nicaraguan ports in order to create economic problems for the Sandinista regime. Goldwater regarded this as an act of war and was outraged that Casey had not notified the committee before undertaking it. In fact, as the record showed, Casey had mentioned it in testimony before the committee but no one picked up on what he had said. In all probability, no one had understood it. In any event, as far as Goldwater was concerned, notice to the committee had been insufficient. Casey was forced to make an official apology and agreed to notify the com-

---

[50] CIA draft study, Vol. III, 54–55.
[51] Smist, *Congress Oversees*, 214.

mittee of any significant new activity undertaken pursuant to a previously reported covert action finding.

When Goldwater left the SSCI chair in 1985, to be replaced by another Republican, David Durenberger (MN), Casey's relationship with the committee changed, but did not improve. In particular, Durenberger's penchant for talking with the press—sometimes criticizing Casey personally, sometimes dealing with highly classified topics—led to frequent clashes between the two. By this point, Casey's own reputation for obstinacy and obfuscation was firmly entrenched on the committee.

Although impossible to prove at this juncture, it seems likely that Casey's contempt for the oversight process, as well as his inability to work with the leaders of the oversight committees, were factors that led him to allow the NSC staff at the Reagan White House to undertake the sorts of activities that eventually came to be known as "Iran-contra." When the Congress, at the initiative of the oversight committees, foreclosed further assistance to the contras in 1984, Casey supported the clandestine White House effort to circumvent the restriction by raising funds from third-party donors. Similarly, the White House decision not to tell the committees of the arms sales to Iran in 1985–86 was likely made because Casey believed they would oppose the effort. Indeed, if Oliver North's 1987 testimony to the Iran-contra committees is true, Casey had known that the proceeds generated by the arms sales had been diverted to the contras. Moreover, according to North, Casey had begun looking at the arms sales as a way of funding covert action programs without going to the committees at all.

Iran-contra stands as the most serious breach of faith with the congressional oversight process that any DCI has been a party to. Ultimately, the scandal led to the far-reaching changes in the oversight system (see chapters 5 and 9). It happened principally because Casey saw the committees as impediments to the president's foreign policy objectives rather than as collaborators in that process. Regrettably, he died in February 1987 before he could fully explain his actions.

Relations between the Agency and its congressional overseers returned to an even keel in the wake of Iran-contra, largely because of the personalities and circumstances of the individuals who assumed the key roles on each side. William Webster, a former federal judge who had headed the FBI for 10 years, became DCI in May 1987. His background was in law enforcement, and he had a reputation for impeccable integrity. For most members, his pledge during his confirmation hearings to work with the oversight committees rang true. Assuming the chair of the SSCI at that juncture was David Boren (D-OK), a conservative who had previously been governor of the state. Not only did he come to the Senate with a sense of deference toward executive authority, he prided himself on being a consensus-builder. In the tradition of the late Senator Arthur Vandenberg, Boren believed that partisanship in matters of national security should stop at the water's edge. At the HPSCI, Louis Stokes (D-OH) took the reins and, like Boren, was deferential to executive authority, having earlier served as mayor of Cleveland. Also like Boren, his leadership style was nonconfrontational.

Boren served as SSCI chairman for six years, allowing him to compile a record of legislative achievement unmatched by any of his predecessors (see chapter 5). Not only did he push through legislation remedying the shortcomings in the oversight process revealed by Iran-contra but also legislation essentially revalidating the roles and missions of US intelligence agencies in the aftermath of the Cold War. While Boren did support modest budget cuts at the end of his tenure, they were nowhere as severe as many in Congress were urging at the time. Boren's achievements owed much to his talent (and his penchant) for consensus-building and helped him hold the chair for six years.

On the HPSCI, no chairman after Boland served more than two years in the position until the tenure of Porter Goss, which began in 1997. While this meant less continuity in leadership on the House side, all of those appointed in the intervening years—Lee Hamilton (D-IN), 1985–86; Stokes, 1987–88; Anthony Beilenson (D-CA), 1989–90; Dave McCurdy (D-OK), 1991–92; Dan Glickman (D-KN), 1993–94; and Larry Combest (R-TX), 1995–96— were political moderates and less partisan than most of their House colleagues.

Also, with the exception of McCurdy, none had a confrontational style. McCurdy was seen as rising star in Democratic political circles. Bright, young, and politically ambitious, he had served on the HPSCI from 1983 to 1985 and was reappointed in 1989, serving as chair of the oversight and evaluation subcommittee. When he became chairman in January 1991, he promised to reinvigorate and intensify the committee's oversight. In fact, McCurdy followed through on his commitment, instituting a far more aggressive brand of oversight than his predecessors. He decreed that all witnesses coming before the committee would be sworn and that tardiness would not be tolerated. Above all, he expected candor. He made it clear he did not want to spend time pulling answers from witnesses or interpreting what they had said. But, to many outside observers, his apparent political ambitions tended to detract from his effectiveness.

In September 1991, McCurdy announced that he was considering a run for the presidency in 1992. A few weeks later, he injected himself into the Gates confirmation process by telling the *Washington Post* that Gates should withdraw his nomination. (SSCI Chairman Boren had already announced his support for Gates.) Then, on 18 October, McCurdy announced he would not run for president after all, committing instead to supporting the candidacy of former Arkansas governor, Bill Clinton. In fact, during his second year as HPSCI chairman, McCurdy spent a great deal of time campaigning for Clinton, apparently in hopes of winning the defense job in a new administration. But once elected, Clinton settled on McCurdy's House colleague, Les Aspin, instead. While McCurdy was rumored to be a candidate for the DCI position, he chose to publicly take himself out of the running before the job was even offered. In January 1993, Kansas congressman, Dan Glickman replaced him as HPSCI chairman, and McCurdy left the committee. Clinton announced his intent to nominate R. James Woolsey for the DCI position.

On the Senate side, Dennis DeConcini (D-AZ) replaced Boren as chairman of the SSCI. DeConcini was a lawyer by training and a former attorney general for the state of Arizona. At the time of his appointment, he had served on the committee for six years, leaving him but two years as chairman. He took the reins of the SSCI not only at the start of a new administration but also at a time when his party caucus was calling for cuts in intelligence spending in the wake of the Cold War (see chapter 6).

Woolsey, himself a lawyer in private practice with considerable experience in government, resisted such cuts, refusing to compromise what had been requested in the administration's budget. This got him off on the wrong foot with DeConcini, and their relationship continued to deteriorate for the entire two-year period that each held their respective positions, becoming public and increasingly strident in the aftermath of the Aldrich Ames espionage case (see chapter 10). Woolsey prided himself on knowing the Hill and how to work with members. He had been there before. But this sense of self-assurance came across as arrogance to many on the Hill. DeConcini found him uncompromising, stubborn and, at times, condescending. He particularly resented Woolsey taking his complaints to other senators. Woolsey, for his part, found DeConcini antagonistic and meddlesome, and too easily provoked by his (hostile) staff. While his relationship with Glickman was more cordial, Woolsey's confrontational style created obstacles for him at the HPSCI as well. In the end, he resigned after less than two years as DCI, his inability to work well with the oversight committees distinctly tarnishing his tenure.

When the Republicans won both houses in the 1994 off-year elections, new chairmen took the reins at each of the intelligence committees: Arlen Specter (PA) at the SSCI and Larry Combest (TX) at the HPSCI. Specter was also a lawyer and former state attorney general, who, like DeConcini, had served for six years on the SSCI. His would necessarily be a two-year term. Combest was a low-key conservative—a farmer and businessman—who had served on the staff of Senator John Tower (R-TX) during the 1970s.

With Woolsey's resignation, President Clinton initially offered the DCI's job to John Deutch, then serving as deputy secretary of defense, but Deutch preferred to stay where he was. When Clinton's second choice, LTG Michael Carns, fell by the wayside, however (see chapter 11), Deutch agreed to accept the job, after obtaining a commitment from Clinton that he would be a member of the cabinet.

Deutch had been a chemistry professor and former provost at the Massachusetts Institute of Technology and had served on numerous governmental panels before going to the Pentagon. In his two years as deputy defense secretary, he had established himself as a tough, knowledgeable manager, and the leaders of both intelligence committees welcomed his nomination in the wake of Woolsey's turbulent tenure.

Upon taking office, Deutch was forced to deal with the issue of whether the Agency had deliberately withheld pertinent information from the committees regarding one of its assets in Guatemala (see chapter 8). The incident had occurred before Deutch became DCI, and no evidence was found indicating the withholding had been deliberate. Nevertheless, Deutch sought to placate the committees by disciplining several of the CIA employees involved and instituting new procedures to govern the recruitment of assets with records of human rights abuse.

While these actions may have helped Deutch assuage the oversight committees they were not well received by many at the Agency. Complaints from employees regarding his detached management style also began to reach the committees. When Nora Slatkin, who was Deutch's choice for the number-three position at the Agency but who had little previous intelligence experience, began to falter in carrying out the day-to-day business of the Agency, word of her difficulties also leaked to the press. Deutch's derogatory comments to a reporter about the intellectual quality of the Agency's workforce were also made public.[52] Deutch, it appeared, did not seem happy with the Agency he had agreed to lead.

While this attitude undermined his credibility with some on the Hill, the leaders of the two oversight committees, Specter and Combest, continued to accept him at face value. In fact, Specter—a former prosecutor who relished intellectual combat in the public arena—opened a far greater percentage of the committee's deliberations to the public during his two-year tenure as chairman than any of the Agency's overseers in Congress had ever done. While most were not "headline-grabbers," Deutch was required to testify in public session more than any DCI before him. Deutch lasted only a year and a half in the job,

---

[52] Tenet, *At the Center of the Storm*, 4.

worn down not so much by his relations with Congress as by the situation he found himself in at the Agency, where he faced not only the increasing discontent in the workforce but had to contend with such highly contentious but unfounded charges that the Agency had been involved in selling crack cocaine in Los Angeles (see chapter 8).

Once again, in early 1997, the departure of a DCI roughly coincided with new leaders taking the reins at the two intelligence committees: Richard Shelby (R-AL) at the SSCI and Porter Goss at the HPSCI. Shelby, a lawyer by training, had served on the committee for two years prior to being appointed chairman. Goss, a former businessman, had served as an Agency case officer during the early part of his professional career, making him the only former CIA employee ever to become one of its principal overseers.

To replace Deutch, Clinton nominated the man who had served as his national security adviser during his first term, Anthony Lake, and from the outset, Shelby signaled his intent to cause problems for the nominee. Then-DDCI Tenet recounts in his memoir a conversation he had with Shelby shortly after Lake's nomination had been announced. "George, if you have any dirt on Tony Lake," Shelby told Tenet, "I'd sure like to have it." The request, according to Tenet, left him speechless.[53]

The confirmation hearings that followed were the most baldly political the committee had ever conducted (see chapter 11). When Lake withdrew after losing his patience, it fell to Tenet as Clinton's second nominee to cope with the change in political climate at the SSCI. While Shelby did not attempt to stall Tenet's nomination as he had Lake's, it soon became clear that he intended to position himself as the Agency's foremost critic. Many if not most of the episodes the committee looked into during Shelby's tenure (the alleged involvement in drug sales in Los Angeles, the discovery that former DCI Deutch had kept classified information on his home computer, the accidental bombing of the Chinese embassy in Belgrade) had little to do with the issues that mattered as far as the long-term future of the Agency was concerned but did give Shelby's committee opportunities for high-profile "show trials." Even issues like the failure of the Intelligence Community to predict the Indian nuclear test in 1998 (see chapter 7), which might have presented an opportunity for the committee to exercise useful, in-depth oversight, were treated as occasions for press conferences rather than prompting a serious, independent investigation by the committee. As one Agency officer close to the process later observed, "It was a game of 'pin the tail on the [Democratic] donkey' in those days."[54]

---

[53] Ibid., 6.
[54] Ott, "Partisanship and the Decline of Intelligence Oversight."

Partisanship of this kind was far from unknown on Capitol Hill, but it had not been commonplace on the SSCI, and in 2000, Shelby took a further step by publicly calling for Tenet to resign. The only other time this had happened in the Agency's history had been when Goldwater suggested that Casey should be replaced over the Hugel appointment (see chapter 10). (There had been other occasions when the chairman of an oversight committee had publicly criticized a DCI.)

Some attributed Shelby's animus toward Tenet in part to an incident that had occurred at the dedication ceremony on 26 April 1999, when the Headquarters compound was formally named the George Bush Center for Intelligence. Former OCA Director John Moseman recalled that about an hour before the ceremony was to begin he received a telephone call from Shelby's staff angrily demanding that Shelby be accorded a speaking role and place on the dais.

> *By that point it was too late to accommodate them. We already had the program set. Only President Bush, the DCI, and Congressman Portman* [the original sponsor of the legislation] *had seats on the stage. But yes—they were quite upset about it. Was it the reason he called for George* [Tenet] *to resign? No, I don't think so—but it probably contributed to it.*[55]

For Tenet, having his relationship with Shelby deteriorate to this point was both troubling and puzzling:

> *As a former Hill staffer, I understood the need to tend to Congress. It is important work. I believe in thorough and thoughtful oversight; it distinguishes this country from all other countries in the world. But I occasionally found myself wishing committees had focused more of their time on the long-term needs of U.S. intelligence rather than responding to the news of the day.*[56]

For whatever reason, Shelby proved unreceptive to Tenet's overtures. Moseman later recalled,

> *There wasn't much we could do about it . We just had to keep at it. There were things we had to deal with* [Shelby] *on and we continued to do it on a professional basis.*[57]

A year and a half after the dedication ceremony, the Republicans won back the White House in the 2000 election, and the issue of whether the incoming

---

[55] Moseman interview, 28 December 2006.
[56] Tenet, *At the Center of the Storm*, 35.
[57] Moseman interview, 28 December 2006.

Bush administration should keep Tenet on came to the fore.[58] Shelby publicly urged Bush to put "his own person there" rather than hold Tenet over as DCI, but other prominent Republicans—notably, former DCI Gates and HPSCI Chairman Goss—urged Bush to keep Tenet on. Indeed, Goss had often defended Tenet in the face of Shelby's public criticisms.[59]

When Bush chose to ignore Shelby's counsel, the senator's calls for Tenet's resignation abated. In May 2001, after control of the Senate shifted back to the Democrats because a Republican senator changed his party affiliation, the SSCI gained a new chairman, Bob Graham (D-FL), who was neither as partisan as Shelby nor as confrontational.

But Shelby remained as vice chairman and after the terrorist attacks of 9/11, which he described as a "massive failure of intelligence," renewed his calls for Tenet's resignation. Acknowledging there had also been successes on Tenet's watch and that he liked Tenet at a personal level, he told the *New York Times* on 10 September 2002, that "you could do better . . . get somebody stronger." Even after rotating off the SSCI in December 2002, Shelby continued to call for Tenet's resignation. Asserting his oft-stated position that there had been more intelligence failures on Tenet's "watch" than that of any DCI in history, he told CNN (*American Morning*, 17 July 2003) that it was time for him "to walk the plank."

Relations with HPSCI Chairman Goss were markedly different during this period, as they were with the two appropriations committees that looked after the Agency's resource needs. Indeed, Tenet increasingly turned to the appropriators for support, according to Moseman, in the face on the difficulty he was having with the SSCI.[60]

By the time Republicans regained control of the Senate in January 2003, Shelby's tenure on the SSCI had expired, and Pat Roberts (R-KS), who had served on the committee for four years, became its chair. By this point, it was clear that Tenet remained the Bush administration's choice for the job, and with war in Iraq in the offing, Roberts seemed to want a new relationship with the DCI, and Tenet reciprocated.

By the fall of 2003, however, it was clear to both Roberts and Goss—after no weapons of mass destruction (WMD) had been found in Iraq—that there had been an intelligence failure of serious proportions (see chapters 7 and 8 for more detail). The intelligence assessments prepared before the war that

---

[58] Sciolino, "As Bush Ponders Choice of Intelligence Chief, Some Suggest That No Change Is Needed."
[59] Risen, "CIA Chief Is Asked to Stay On and Agrees."
[60] Moseman interview, 28 December 2006.

had provided the Bush administration's principal justification for going to war had proved wrong. The more the committees looked into it, the more vocal (and critical) their respective chairmen became.

At the same time, Roberts and Goss were confronted with an unprecedented political situation. The 2004 presidential campaign was already in full swing, and it was apparent that the administration's use of intelligence to justify the war in Iraq would be an issue, perhaps even a decisive one, in the election. Thus, for the first time in their history, the committees were seized with an issue that had the potential for determining a presidential election. This was not lost upon Democrats on either committee. On the SSCI, Democrats pressed for committee investigations of both the Intelligence Community and the administration's use of intelligence to justify the war. On the HPSCI, Democrats simply pressed for a committee investigation of the intelligence failure.

After months of partisan bickering—during which time the Senate majority leader actually forbade the SSCI from continuing with its investigation—its leaders announced in February 2004 that the committee would carry out its investigation in phases, beginning with the performance of the Intelligence Community. The performance of the administration would be deferred until the initial phase was completed.[61]

The HPSCI undertook no investigation at all, despite the obvious significance of the intelligence failure that had occurred and the constant prodding of its Democratic members. Indeed, in the fall of 2003, Goss's stewardship of the committee, in the eyes of most observers, suddenly became far more partisan. Since taking over in 1997, he had run the committee in a relatively bipartisan, nonconfrontational way. Most of his public statements were supportive of the Agency, and the committee's work was carried out in concert with the minority. Now he seemed to be ignoring them.

Goss had already announced by this point that he would be retiring from Congress at the end of 2004. There was also speculation after the Iraqi intelligence failure that Tenet would not remain in the DCI's position much longer. In any event, in early 2004, Goss began making uncharacteristically partisan public statements, both attacking the national security record of the putative Democratic presidential nominee and focusing blame for the mistakes on Iraq on the Intelligence Community rather than the administration. Some, including SSCI Vice Chairman Jay Rockefeller (D-WV), apparently believed Goss was angling for the DCI's job should Tenet leave. Indeed, once Tenet

---

[61] For a detailed description of this period, see Snider, "Congressional Oversight of Intelligence After 9/11," published as chapter 14, *Transforming U.S. Intelligence.*

announced in the summer of 2004 his intent to resign, Rockefeller went so far as to warn the Bush White House not to nominate Goss as his replacement.[62]

Realizing that the votes for Goss were there notwithstanding Rockefeller's opposition, Bush nominated him anyway. While Rockefeller and others on the committee attempted to make an issue of Goss's earlier political statements during his confirmation hearing (see chapter 11), focusing on the issue of whether as DCI he would be politically independent of the White House, the issue never found resonance within the body as a whole. The Senate confirmed Goss, 77–17.

Notwithstanding, 2004 had been a low-water mark in the history of the two committees. To a degree, politics had always affected the way Congress carried out its intelligence oversight, but for the first 50 years of the Agency's existence, the oversight was relatively bipartisan. That began to change in the SSCI in 1997 and in the HPSCI in 2003, ultimately coming to a head in 2004 and leading the 9/11 Commission to conclude that Congress's oversight of intelligence had become "dysfunctional." In hindsight, this appears to have happened for a variety of reasons. In some cases, members appointed to the oversight committees, and to their chairs, were excessively partisan in their orientation. Some seemed to regard oversight of the intelligence function as no different than any other kind of oversight Congress exercised. The leaders of the two intelligence committees also found themselves in uniquely difficult circumstances during this period, coming under pressure from the White House and their respective leaders and caucuses to protect their party's political interests.

Whatever the reasons, the oversight process suffered as a result. Neither intelligence committee was able to get as much done. Other committees stepped into the void. The Agency itself increasingly turned to the appropriators, where it found a more sympathetic ear and a more reliable partner. The purpose of oversight also became skewed. Rather than a constructive collaboration to tackle genuine, long-term problems, oversight became a means of shifting political blame, as the circumstances required, either to the incumbent administration or away from it.

When any intelligence agency perceives this is happening, communications will suffer. No longer confident how the committees will use the information they are provided, agencies become more wary of what they share with them. The committees will still get what they ask for and are entitled to, pursuant to existing law, but the enthusiasm of senior agency officials for coming to the committees with their problems will inevitably wane.

---

[62] Rockefeller press release, 25 June 2004.

Fortunately for the Agency, politicization of the oversight process has not been the norm. Even when it has happened, members have usually acted quickly to "right the ship." Most members of the House and Senate, in fact, want their intelligence committees to operate on a bipartisan basis. They do understand the problem in doing otherwise. Perhaps the best indication of this attitude was evident in the Goss confirmation process. Had Goss not chosen to abandon his previously bipartisan approach to oversight during the last year of his tenure, his nomination would have sailed through the SSCI. As it was, the Senate confirmed him by a large margin, largely cause of that earlier record of bipartisanship.

As it happened, Goss was the only congressional overseer of the Agency ever to become its director. With his assumption of the DCI's position in September 2004, the Agency's relationship with Congress had in a sense come full circle. As it happened, Goss would also be the last DCI. He would still head the Agency but Congress would no longer look to him as the head of US intelligence. That in itself would foreshadow a change in the Agency's relationship with the Hill.

CHAPTER 3

INTELLIGENCE-SHARING AND OTHER INTERACTION

A great deal of interaction takes place between the Agency and Congress apart from the execution of Congress's institutional responsibilities for the Agency: oversight, funding, legislation, and confirmation. Indeed, this interaction may well have as great an impact on the overall relationship as the execution of Congress's institutional responsibilities for the Agency.

For example, the Agency frequently provides substantive intelligence support to congressional committees that relates to their respective jurisdictions. Chapter 7 describes several episodes in which providing such support prompted oversight inquiries by the Congress. Such episodes, however, are not the norm. For the most part, the substantive intelligence support provided to the Congress does not raise oversight issues; it is simply provided to "educate." This chapter describes the evolution of this kind of support, leaving the episodes that resulted in oversight challenges to the later chapter.

This chapter also describes how the Agency has dealt with individual members over its history: not only providing them with substantive intelligence and information about the Agency but also debriefing them on foreign intelligence they might have acquired, responding to the requests and concerns of their constituents, and hiring people on the recommendation of members. Like the provision of intelligence support to committees, how the Agency responds to a request from an individual member, especially a "rank-and-file" member whose duties do not include responsibility for the Agency, can create a lasting impression. The Agency may gain a lifelong supporter as a result of a seemingly trivial act. On the other hand, slip-ups or missteps may take on significance (for that member) far beyond their actual importance.

Over the Agency's history, the volume of this daily interaction, both at the committee and member level, has steadily increased, providing opportunities as well as pitfalls for the Agency. The first part of the chapter describes the interaction that occurred before the select committees were created in the mid-1970s, the "early period;" the second part, with the interaction that occurred after that.

The Early Period: 1947–75

Provision of Intelligence Analysis to Congressional Committees

The Agency's statutory charter charged it, among other things, with the "appropriate dissemination" of intelligence "within the government." While Congress was not specifically mentioned in the law, DCIs from the beginning accepted, as a matter of principle, the obligation to provide intelligence analysis to Congress in support of its institutional functions. There does not appear to have been a formal policy decision to this effect, either within the executive branch or within the Agency itself, and the Agency's legislative liaison during this early period, Walter L. Pforzheimer, said years later he did not think the issue had ever arisen as such.[1] There was simply recognition on the part of the Agency that Congress had a legitimate need for intelligence analysis to carry out its constitutional responsibilities. How and when such sharing would occur, however, was largely determined within the executive branch and, until the intelligence committees were created in the mid-1970s, was subject to severe constraints.

Almost immediately after its creation, the Agency began providing semi-annual written reports on the Soviet atomic program to the Joint Atomic Energy Committee (JAEC), which, at that point, was the only committee on Capitol Hill to maintain a storage area for classified information. Occasionally, the committee would ask the DCI to present these reports in person. "For many years," Pforzheimer recalled, the JAEC "was our only regular customer. . . . We received occasional requests from other congressional committees, but they are hardly worth mentioning."[2]

Nevertheless, Agency policy also stifled a more active interchange. In the spring of 1948, for example, Agency regulations required NSC approval for the release of secret or top secret material to Congress and banned the release of any information revealing intelligence sources and methods. DCI Hillenkoetter went a step further and forbade any "spontaneous dissemination" of information to the Congress—in other words, any disclosure must have prior Agency clearance.[3]

There were also practical constraints. Apart from the JAEC, no House or Senate committee had facilities approved for the storage of classified information. Accordingly, no written reports or documentary evidence could be left there overnight. At the end of the day, Agency security officers would gather up any reports, documents, transcripts, notes, tapes or carbons that might have

---

[1] Pforzheimer interview, 15 October 1996.
[2] Ibid.
[3] CIA draft study, Vol. I, 27–28.

been brought to the Hill or created by the congressional committees involved and bring them back to the Agency for safekeeping.[4]

Unclassified materials were occasionally provided. In September 1951, for example, Pforzheimer saw an opportunity to "foster and engender considerable goodwill with an extremely powerful group [of senators]" and had the Agency provide the SFRC with a collection of unclassified maps it had requested.[5]

In addition to the obvious security concerns about leaving classified documents in an unprotected environment, political concerns were a factor as well. Giving members written analysis that they might "wave around" and make use of in political debates was a concern for both the White House and the Agency's overseers in Congress. In 1959, for example, the Eisenhower White House scotched DCI Dulles's idea that a senior analyst take the Agency's "Weekly Bulletins" around to selected, influential members on the grounds that it was likely to stir up too much trouble for the administration.[6] Similarly, Senator Russell, the Agency's chief overseer in the Senate during much of the early period, forbade successive DCIs from providing anything in writing to members not on the oversight subcommittees for fear of how they would use it. When circumstances demanded that something in writing be provided to the oversight subcommittees, the Agency would prepare an unsigned "blind memo" on "non-letterhead" paper that did not identify it as the source.

Not surprisingly, what intelligence analysis Congress received from the Agency during this early period was usually briefed to it by the DCI or senior Agency officials. For the most part, such analysis fell into one of three categories: developments around the world, the threat to the United States posed by the Soviet Union, and progress reports with respect to military operations in which the United States was involved. Oversight committees as well as "nonoversight" committees received briefings on these topics, as did individual members. However, the most sensitive information bearing on these topics, including information relating to the Agency's own activities, was usually reserved for its oversight committees and even then often only for their leaders.

In 1950, after the start of the Korean War, DCI Smith began providing regular briefings on international developments to the Hill, including briefings on the progress of the war.[7] When President Eisenhower heard Smith's "round-up of the world situation" as he prepared to take office in January 1953, he was so impressed that he urged him to give the same briefing to the two foreign affairs committees.[8]

---

[4] Ibid., 21–22.
[5] Ibid., 36.
[6] Barrett, *CIA and Congress*, 322.
[7] Ibid., 82; CIA draft study, Vol. I, 36.

Five weeks later, however, after Soviet Premier Joseph Stalin suffered a debilitating stroke, the chairman of the SFRC, Alexander Wiley, asked Smith's successor, Allen Dulles, to testify about the implications for the United States if Stalin died. With such a specific focus, Dulles was worried about what he might be asked to reveal and told Eisenhower it would be "a fatal mistake" for the Agency to testify. Instead, former DCI Smith, who had now moved to a new position in the State Department, was sent to testify.[9]

During the last half of the 1950s, Congress repeatedly sought to understand the nature of the Soviet military threat as it attempted to determine what the size and nature of the country's own military forces should be. Most of the requests for such information, in fact, came from congressional committees without oversight responsibility for the Agency per se. In 1956, for example, Dulles testified several times before the SASC subcommittee on military preparedness, chaired by Stuart Symington (D-MO), which was trying to assess the relative strength of the Soviet and US strategic bomber and missile forces. Dulles's testimony on these subjects was also sought by the JAEC. Knowing these committees believed his administration was not doing enough to address the perceived gaps with the Soviets in these areas, Eisenhower initially objected to Dulles appearing before the subcommittee but ultimately acquiesced, acknowledging it had a legitimate need for the Agency's analysis.[10] Dulles's appearances before the Symington subcommittee, however, frequently brought him into conflict with its chairman (see chapter 7 for more detail).

During this period, Dulles continued to provide briefings on world events in response to congressional requests. General, tour d'horizon surveys posed less of a problem than requests for briefings on specific topics or incidents. For example, twice in 1959 Dulles agreed to brief the HFAC on recent developments around the globe but turned down its request to brief on the political situation in Eastern Europe, believing it might expose Agency operations.[11] He did agree to brief the SFRC in July 1958 with respect to the coup in Iraq, in large part to respond to criticism being leveled at the Agency for failing to predict it.[12]

In late 1959, with the approval of the Eisenhower White House, Dulles also testified at an open hearing of the Joint Economic Committee on the state of the Soviet economy, the first time a DCI had ever given public testimony before a congressional committee. While Dulles did not continue these per-

---

[8] Barrett, *CIA and Congress*, 141.

[9] Ibid.

[10] Ibid., 237.

[11] CIA draft study, Vol. I, 69–70.

[12] Barrett, *CIA and Congress*, 298.

sonal appearances, CIA continued to make unclassified analysis available to the committee for inclusion in its series of "green books," macroeconomic studies of the Soviet Union published annually. The Agency's annual contribution, in fact, was highly anticipated not only by the JEC but by scholars and historians for whom Agency reporting provided the only reliable data on the subject.[13] This support went largely unnoticed by the rest of Congress until early 1964, when DDI Ray Cline took the additional step of providing this unclassified analysis directly to journalists. Largely because the release of the analysis was widely (but erroneously) reported to have come during a "CIA press conference," DCI McCone received a harsh dressing down from SASC Chairman Russell, who told him that CIA needed to "stay in the background." "If you ever do this again," Russell warned, "I am simply not going to support the Agency in its works or its budget or anything else." Leaders of the other CIA subcommittees conveyed similar concerns to McCone.[14]

Despite this experience, McCone continued the practice of providing worldwide updates to the foreign relations committee on both sides, albeit discovering that even these informational sessions had their pitfalls. In a March 1962 briefing before the HFAC, members repeatedly chided him for ducking their questions. After the briefing, one member commented that McCone, like his predecessor, had said nothing but that at least "Mr. Dulles said it more entertainingly."[15] When McCone appeared before the defense subcommittee of the HAC in August 1964 to explain what the CIA knew about the attack on US warships in the Gulf of Tonkin, members told him they had learned more from the *New York Times* and *Washington Post* than they had from him.[16] In fairness to McCone, CIA had little involvement in, or first-hand knowledge of, these attacks at the time. In November 1963, McCone was invited to appear before a special HASC subcommittee to testify about civil defense shelters in the Soviet Union. The DCI was willing to do so, but HASC Chairman Carl Vinson protested, telling McCone that he should only provide CIA information to the CIA subcommittee of the HASC. McCone backed out, leaving the civil defense subcommittee to get what it wanted from the Defense Intelligence Agency and leaving a bad taste in the mouth of its chairman, Congressman F. Edward Hebert (D-LA).[17]

In 1965, Agency officials took the initiative when they got wind of an impending request for McCone to testify before an HFAC subcommittee on

---

[13] Kennedy, *Sunshine and Shadow*, 6–10.
[14] Robarge, *John McCone*, 76–77.
[15] CIA draft study, Vol. I, 101.
[16] Ibid., 106.
[17] Ibid., 105.

the increasingly unstable situation in the Dominican Republic. Fearing a contentious discussion involving sources and methods, the Agency prevailed upon its HAC and HASC subcommittee chairmen to intercept and block the request before it could be sent.[18]

Soon after becoming DCI in April 1965, Admiral Raborn appeared before the SFRC where its chairman, Senator Fulbright, asked him if he would provide regular briefings to the committee—perhaps as often as once a week—on the world situation. Inexperienced in congressional politics and eager to ingratiate himself, Raborn replied without hesitation that he would. After the hearing, however, his staff suggested to him that Senator Russell might have a problem with this commitment to the SFRC. When Raborn raised the matter with Russell, the senator told him he ought to try and hold the briefings to once or twice a year and under no circumstances should he discuss the Agency or its operations.[19]

Raborn's successor, Richard Helms, was far more attuned to Russell's dim view of briefings to other committees but, soon after taking office, asked Russell what he thought about the idea of gaining more support for the Agency in the Senate by seeking out a broader spectrum of its members. Helms recalled Russell's response:

> *He looked me right in the eye, and his eye got a bit glinty. He said, "If you feel any necessity to go around and talk to other Senators about the Agency's business, I certainly can't stop you. But, I'll tell you this, I will withdraw my hand and my support from your affairs."* [20]

While Helms admitted to being chastened by this exchange with Russell, he also faced a growing demand within Congress for the Agency's intelligence analysis. Increasingly mistrustful of the way the executive branch was prosecuting the war in Vietnam, Congress began to assert itself in the late 1960s, not only in the handling of the war but in other foreign policy and defense initiatives of the Johnson and Nixon administrations, such as the deployment of an ABM system in the United States and ratification of SALT I (see below). Not surprisingly, it wanted CIA's assessment of the issues it was concerned about.

By the same token, providing such briefings to the Hill often created political problems for the Johnson and Nixon administrations, leading them to discourage, if not flatly prohibit, Helms from giving them. Briefings on the progress of the war in Vietnam—where the Agency's assessments were usually

---

[18] Ibid., 109.
[19] Ibid., 110.
[20] Hathaway and Smith, *Richard Helms*, 163.

more pessimistic than those of the military—were of particular concern. Helms later recalled walking out of the White House with Johnson one afternoon in 1967, when the president took him by the arm and said in a fatherly tone, "Now, if you feel any urge to go up and testify in Congress on the whole question of civilian casualties in Vietnam, I just hope you'll pass by and have a drink with me the afternoon before." Helms added, "This was his way of conveying a message to me that he wanted to have something to say about [it]."[21]

Such admonitions obviously put Helms in an awkward position, not wanting to offend the committee requesting a briefing, but at least what the president wanted him to do was consistent with the position of Senator Russell. On several occasions during the latter half of the 1960s, in fact, Helms had Russell intervene with the SFRC to block requests for Helms's testimony on the progress of the Vietnam War on the grounds that it was an inappropriate forum for the discussion of intelligence sources and methods.[22]

Helms also sought to put limits on what the Agency briefed to the Hill by issuing an order at the beginning of his tenure that CIA analysis would be provided orally to the Hill whenever possible. If a written response were required, it should be done as a blind memo with no indication that CIA was the originator. Congressional briefings should be concise and to the point, he directed; unnecessary detail should be kept out of them.[23]

Whatever Helms might issue in the way of internal Agency policy, however, was subject to being overtaken by events on the Hill. In 1967, for example, after two senators on the SFRC requested briefings on Soviet strategic weapons, Helms checked with Senator Russell to see if he objected. After Russell himself checked with the Senate majority and minority leaders, Helms was allowed to provide the briefings so long as they did not touch on sources and methods. At the same time, Russell told the DCI that henceforth, any request for CIA briefings by individual members had to be cleared with him personally. He also told Helms not to provide written information to individual members. No briefings of staff from committees other than oversight committees would be permitted.[24]

Several months later, apparently believing he was being consistent with Russell's earlier guidance, Helms provided another one-on-one briefing on the same subject to another member of the SFRC without first clearing it with Russell. When Russell later found out, CIA records reflect he expressed "profound displeasure" to Helms.[25]

---

[21] Ibid., 5.

[22] Ibid., 172.

[23] Roberta Knapp, *The Central Intelligence Agency: The First Thirty Years*, 256 (classified history.)

[24] CIA draft study, Vol. II, 10.

Requests for briefings from the SFRC continued to complicate Helms's life throughout his tenure as DCI. In 1968, in response to a written request received from John Sherman Cooper (R-KY), a member of the SFRC, for information on Soviet and Chinese missile forces, Helms had prepared a written reply that he had sent to Russell for concurrence. Helms described what happened next:

> *The next thing I knew, I had a frantic telephone call saying Senator Russell want to see me right away. So I jumped in the car and went down to the Senate. He came off the floor and he said, "Don't you ever send a letter like that to Senator Cooper or anyone else. . . . They'll simply take that letter, come to the floor of the Senate, wave it, and say, 'I've got a letter from the [DCI] and it says so-and-so,' and it will adversely affect the debate we're having. . . . You shouldn't even consider writing letters like that." . . . He was really very shirty about it.*[26]

So long as he remained in the Senate, Russell continued to be the choke point in terms of what was furnished other Senate committees. In the spring of 1969, when Helms was asked to appear in public session before a subcommittee of the Joint Economic Committee, chaired by William Proxmire (D-WI), he consulted with Russell, who told him that he should talk to Proxmire instead and under no circumstances should he appear in public. Upon hearing from Helms what Russell had told him, Proxmire simply threw up his hands and walked away.[27]

In May 1969, Helms consulted with Russell with respect to a slightly different problem: a request from the SFRC not simply for a briefing but for copies of written analyses, including NIEs (National Intelligence Estimates), bearing upon the pending ABM issue, specifically, whether the new Soviet SS-9 ballistic missile was being equipped with multiple, independently targeted warheads, which would have indicated it was moving toward a first-strike capability. After consulting with the White House, Russell agreed that the committee could be briefed but adamantly objected to the provision of any written analysis. President Nixon, himself, later reiterated this and told Helms that he did not want CIA sending letters to the Hill on substantive matters and that oral briefings were to be as "nonspecific" as possible.[28] Helms subsequently met with Fulbright to explain the situation, telling him that NIEs could not be released without the permission of the president and that, in any

---

[25] Ibid., 12–13.
[26] Helms interview, 4 November 1983.
[27] Hathaway and Smith, *Richard Helms*, 164.
[28] Ibid., 165.

event, providing written materials to the Hill would inevitably increase the risk of leaks and embroil the Agency in partisan politics.[29]

As it turned out, however, the limits imposed on Helms made little difference. While the NIEs at issue were not given to the committee, members were briefed on their key judgments, which happened to be at odds with Secretary of Defense Melvin Laird's position that the Soviets, in fact, were trying to equip their SS-9 with multiple warheads capable of taking out US ballistic missiles and, in doing so, were seeking a first-strike capability. The Intelligence Community's disagreement with the Pentagon on this issue soon became public when portions of the NIE were leaked to the *New York Times* and embroiled the Agency—Helms, in particular—in the Senate debate on whether to fund the ABM system the Nixon administration wanted.

At a closed hearing before the SFRC on 23 June 1969, Helms testified alongside Laird. Both attempted to downplay their institutional differences, but Helms was uncomfortable with being put in the position of debating a policy issue—whether the United States should build an ABM system—with a policy official. As he later explained,

> The DCI ought to wear one hat. He should be the president's intelligence officer and give him the best objective judgment possible. He should not wear a policy hat. . . . They say that the DCI should advise the president. But I think one person should be able to say, "Here stands one man dedicated to . . . keeping the game honest."[30]

Several weeks later, when the issue of funding the ABM system moved to the floor, the Senate, for the first time in its history, held a secret, closed session to discuss the pertinent intelligence. Because only senators were permitted in the Senate chamber, the Agency prepared a paper to be read by Henry M. Jackson (D-WA) at the start of the debate that set forth the views of the Intelligence Community. By a narrow margin, the Senate voted to fund the system, notwithstanding the Intelligence Community's assessment.

Despite the numerous interventions and admonitions from Senator Russell, Agency records still reflect that the Agency provided 60 substantive briefings to Congress during 1969, including briefings to the SFRC, the JAEC, and the House Committee on Science and Astronautics.[31]

The following year a controversy developed regarding the possible Soviet expansion of submarine facilities at Cienfuegos, Cuba. Nixon's national security adviser, Henry Kissinger, told CIA to "put a lid" on any information being

---

[29] CIA draft study, Vol. II, 15.
[30] Quoted in Lunberg, *The SS-9 Controversy,* 17.
[31] CIA draft study, Vol. II, 22.

disseminated outside the executive branch about it. This created a quandary for Helms when he received a request from Mendel Rivers (D-SC), who chaired the HASC as well as the CIA subcommittee, to see any overhead photography of the Cuban facility. Helms responded by having his legislative counsel show the photographs to Rivers but urged him not to tell Kissinger, since he did not want intelligence shown to the Hill. Rivers assured the CIA representative that he would "protect the Agency," but once the meeting was over he immediately put in a call to Kissinger and told him that he would brook interference from no one in terms of access to information of concern to his committee.[32]

In early 1971, the Nixon White House set up the Legislative Interdepartmental Group to coordinate relations with Congress in the foreign affairs and national security area. CIA was represented by its legislative counsel. Among other things, the group was told to resist any effort to enact laws requiring the disclosure of national security information to the Congress. The impetus for this injunction was a request by SFRC Chairman Fulbright for all NIEs and SNIEs relating to Southeast Asia since 1945. While CIA had offered to brief Fulbright on points that may have been relevant to the study the SFRC was conducting on US involvement in Indochina, it was in no position to provide the formal estimates that had been requested. This led Kentucky Republican John Sherman Cooper, a member of the SFRC, to introduce a bill requiring that Congress be provided intelligence analysis that was necessary to its responsibilities in the foreign policy area. With the administration, along with the Agency, vigorously opposed to the bill on the grounds that it would lead to the disclosure of sensitive sources and methods, the SFRC did not seek to move it out of committee.[33]

In May 1972, President Nixon signed the first Strategic Arms Limitation Treaty (SALT I) with the Soviet Union, which capped the number of strategic nuclear weapons on each side and provided a framework to govern the future deployment of such weapons. The treaty had been in negotiation since 1969, and DCI Helms had kept the foreign relations committees as well as the CIA subcommittees apprised of developments. After the treaty had been signed and formally been sent to the Senate for ratification, Helms assured the committees that the Intelligence Community would be able to monitor Soviet compliance with the treaty, but he did not provide (nor was he requested to provide) information that would have allowed the committees to make their own independent assessments of the issue.

---

[32] Ibid., 16–17.
[33] Ibid., 39–40.

Once the treaty was ratified, the Nixon administration clamped down on any intelligence assessments going to the Hill regarding Soviet compliance with the treaty. It was later explained to the Pike Committee (see below) that the administration wished to preserve the ability to raise troublesome issues with the Soviets directly rather than have them surface (and, presumably, mushroom) in the Congress via the provision of intelligence assessments. It was not until 1975, in fact, that President Ford permitted the Agency to provide its first closed-session briefing on Soviet compliance with SALT I to a congressional committee.[34]

Notwithstanding the difficult position he was often placed in as a result of the repeated requests of the SFRC for intelligence assessments, when Helms left the job in early 1973, Chairman Fulbright told him, "In the last ten or twelve years, I think the reports of the CIA [with respect to the war in Vietnam] have proved in light of subsequent experience to have been more accurate than any other estimates that came to my attention." Senator Symington concurred: "Since the beginning [of the war] the Agency has been more accurate than anyone else in town. . . . It has operated with integrity and told it straight."[35]

Helms later observed, "If intelligence is to have any standing in the Congress, it has to have the support, as intelligence, of both sides of the aisle. And I didn't know any way to do this except to make the reports as objective, and my testimony as objective, as I was able to do." In other words, Helms said, "I leveled with the Congress. I believed they had a right to have a straight story."[36]

William Colby, who followed Helms in the DCI's job, also thought that Congress was entitled to a "straight story" and that providing substantive analysis was one way of improving the Agency's standing on the Hill, at a time when it was coming under increasing fire for a variety of actual and alleged misdeeds (see chapter 8). Accordingly, in 1975, he directed that the *National Intelligence Daily* (NID)—the Intelligence Community's daily intelligence summary with the broadest circulation in the executive branch—be delivered each day to a room on Capitol Hill, where members of the CIA subcommittees could stop by and read it. When few of them actually did so, Colby directed that a modified version be produced—a specially tailored version called the Congressional Checklist—to encourage greater readership. This, too, proved a failure, and in April 1976, with at least the Senate prepared to create a new select committee to oversee the Agency, the short-lived Congressional Checklist was dropped in favor of having the NID delivered to the appropriations and armed services committees each day, as well as the new select committee

---

[34] Ranelagh, *The Agency*, 617–18.
[35] CIA draft study, Vol. II, 14.
[36] Ibid.

in the Senate once established. The NID was left with the committees during the day and returned each evening to an Agency representative.[37]

In its final report, the Church Committee noted with approval Colby's unsuccessful effort to provide tailored intelligence support to the Congress.

With the resurgence of an active Congressional role in the foreign and national security policymaking process comes the need for members to receive high-quality, reliable, and timely information on which to base Congressional decisions and actions. Access to the best available intelligence product should be insisted upon by the legislative branch. Precisely what kinds of intelligence Congress requires . . . remains to be worked out . . . but the need and the right to it [are] *clear.*[38]

Responding to Personal Requests from the Agency's Overseers

Not surprisingly, from the beginning, the Agency paid particular attention to, and attempted to accommodate, the personal requests of the members who served on one of its oversight committees.

In 1947, within months of its creation, the Agency hired a clerical worker solely to please John Chandler "Chan" Gurney (R-SD), the chairman of the SASC at the time and one of the Agency's strongest supporters.[39]

In 1950, HAC ranking member John Tabor (R-NY) sought CIA's opinion with respect to whether a speech by Secretary of State Dean Acheson in January 1949 implying that South Korea was not of strategic importance to the United States had led to the invasion of South Korea. Legislative liaison Pforzheimer reportedly told Tabor that CIA had no intelligence with respect to North Korea's reaction to the speech.[40]

Even without a specific request, DCI Dulles made a point during his tenure of meeting personally and regularly with the leaders of the CIA subcommittees to apprise them of substantive intelligence he thought they needed to know about. Even as DDCI, Dulles had had regular meetings with SASC Chairman Russell. During Saltonstall's tenure as chairman of the SASC (1953–55), Dulles would frequently invite him for breakfast, or dinner, or drinks, either at his office at the CIA or at his own residence, a practice that continued after the chairmanship had passed back to Senator Russell. Other Agency overseers preferred to have Dulles come by their offices. HAC chair-

---

[37] Knapp, *The First Thirty Years*, 340, 357; Colby, *Honorable Men*, 357–58.
[38] Church Committee, *Final Report*, Book I, 277.
[39] CIA draft study, Vol. I, 28.
[40] Barrett, *CIA and Congress*, 86.

Allen Dulles (l) with Senator Richard Russell. The gregarious Dulles made a point of meeting personally and regularly with congressional leaders responsible for CIA oversight.

(© Bettman/Corbis)

man Clarence Cannon (D-MO), for example, frequently asked to see Dulles alone.[41] Dulles would also meet privately with Paul Kilday (D-TX), the chair of the HASC CIA subcommittee.[42] Typically, there were no papers prepared for these meetings, nor did Dulles tell the CIA legislative liaison what transpired during the course of them.

Although Dulles was masterful in terms of engaging his overseers, trying to keep them happy did not always work out in quite the way he had planned. In March 1953, for example, the Agency was supposed to send a car for Congressman Tabor, a renowned "budget-cutter" who had just become chairman of the HAC, to bring him to a meeting with Dulles. Unfortunately, while Tabor managed to identify one CIA car parked outside the Capitol, he could not find the one intended for him. This led him to write Dulles the next day:

> *Yesterday you were going to send a car up for us, and we could not find it. We approached a car that looked like it might be it. . . . On* [checking], *we found that this car was a CIA car.* [However,] *the driver said he was waiting for a lady. It looks like you have too*

---

[41] Ibid., 331.
[42] Ibid., 334.

many cars and too many chauffeurs, and that could be a very simple way of reducing requirements.[43]

In March 1954, word got back to the Agency that SAC Chairman Styles Bridges (R-NH) had been annoyed by a briefing he had asked for. According to one account quoting what Bridges had said at a Washington dinner party,

the briefing was given by young men who did not seem to be fully familiar with their subject and was given in a manner described as "blasé and disinterested." Senator Bridges said that as a result of this briefing, he felt the whole CIA setup needed looking into. . . . [Name deleted] *also quoted Bridges as saying, "I have told Allen Dulles just how I felt about the briefing given me by the CIA."*[44]

Still, Dulles would attempt to accommodate his overseers whenever he could. In late 1958, he arranged to have the Agency brief Senator Bridges and Representative Kilday as they were about to go to Western Europe on a trip together.[45]

In 1959, when Soviet Premier Khrushchev boasted during a visit to the United States that his government was able to intercept US communications, several of the Agency's overseers wanted to know whether it was true, prompting Dulles to respond personally to each of them.[46]

A large part of keeping the Agency's overseers "happy" involved not simply responding to their requests or complaints, but ensuring they were not surprised by something that might later come to light. DCI Helms later told an interviewer:

There's one thing I learned about Congress. [If] you got down there first and told members of your committee of something that had gone sour or gone wrong before they could read it in the newspapers or hear it from somebody else, they could be very understanding and stand with you and help you and so forth, if they felt they had been taken [into your confidence] and told about this in advance so that they could protect themselves against criticism from the outside. But when they were caught by surprise by one of these things by reading about it in the newspaper or being told by somebody, they really could get very flinty indeed.[47]

---

[43] Ibid., 146.
[44] Ibid., 145.
[45] CIA draft study, Vol. I, 62.
[46] Barrett, *CIA and Congress*, 342–43.
[47] Hathaway and Smith, *Richard Helms*, 64.

Dealing with Other Members of Congress at a Personal Level

While the Agency has not, over its history, devoted the same time and attention to its relations with other members of Congress, it has still taken these relationships seriously, especially those with the leadership of the House and Senate and with influential members of each body. Even requests from "ordinary" members were normally accommodated when they could be.

In a 1950 letter to DCI Smith, Senator William Benton (D-CT) said he was someone that Smith could "always . . . and surely count on." He followed up by saying, "I hope you'll tell your boys to feed stuff to my office which can be helpful to you, when I have a chance to speak on the floor."[48] (CIA records do not show what was provided in response to this request.)

In March 1952, Congressman Lansdale Sasscer (D-MD) asked CIA to write a statement of support for the Agency into a speech he was giving before a civic club. CIA accommodated by providing a draft speech that closed with the following solemn commitment: "Because of my faith in the work of the Central Intelligence Agency, I shall continue to give it complete support in every way possible."[49]

In1953, DCI Smith instituted the practice of inviting small groups of legislators, many of whom were not on the CIA subcommittees, to lunch in his private dining room at the Agency.[50] Dulles continued this practice when he became DCI and actually had his staff develop likely questions and suggested answers for these "informal" occasions. Dulles also arranged regular "courtesy calls" on the House and Senate leadership during his tenure.[51]

After Senator Margaret Chase Smith (R-ME) characterized the Agency in a 1958 speech as an uncooperative bureaucracy with the potential for causing "national scandal," Dulles made a point of seeing her personally to brief her on the Agency's relationship with its congressional oversight subcommittees. The senator told him she was not even aware such subcommittees existed and had gained respect from Dulles's briefing for his willingness to cooperate with them.[52]

Between 1947 and 1958, CIA received "hundreds" of requests from members to hire their constituents. In 1958 alone, CIA legislative liaison had 208 telephone inquiries about potential applicants and responded in writing to 168 of them.[53] Most of those referred by members of Congress were not hired,

---

[48] CIA draft study, Vol. I, 37

[49] Ibid.

[50] Barrett, *CIA and Congress*, 92.

[51] CIA draft study, Vol. I, 37.

[52] Ibid., 62.

[53] Barrett, *CIA and Congress*, 321.

occasionally leading to complaints as well as repercussions down the road. In 1958, for example, CIA's refusal to hire the son of a family friend angered the congressman who chaired the judiciary subcommittee that controlled immigration matters. Although CIA explained its reasons for rejecting the applicant, the congressman was not mollified. Two years later, when two cryptologists from NSA defected to the Soviet Union, he made a public statement implying that CIA had played a role in their hiring. When DCI Dulles telephoned him to complain about his accusations, the congressman hung up on him.[54]

Dulles and his successors in office nevertheless sought to build relationships with members where they could. In January 1959, Dulles had a special briefing on the Agency's activities put together for him to use with the leaders of Congress and other influential members.[55] In 1965, DCI McCone authorized his legislative counsel to brief a Nevada senator on the A-12, the new supersonic, high-altitude reconnaissance aircraft being tested at Nellis Air Force Base, because he feared that the sonic booms during the testing would bring on complaints from the senator's constituents.[56] In 1967, the Office of Legislative Counsel (OLC) instituted a program for briefing new members of Congress on the Agency and its activities through a series of breakfast meetings. A year later this program expanded to include selected influential members and their staffs. In addition to these informational briefings, the Agency also briefed individual members on topics of current interest to them. In its 1969 yearend report, OLC noted that 1,400 contacts with the Hill had been handled during the year, none of which, OLC proudly noted, had resulted in "a major flap."[57]

"Flaps," in fact, were always a concern for the Agency, regardless of the member it was dealing with. As Senator Russell had once noted to a senior CIA official: "There isn't a single member of the Senate that's so lowly that he can't make life unbearable for you fellows if he decides he wants to do it."[58] Keeping relations on an even keel, however, often required remarkable forbearance on the part of Agency representatives. "I have seen my colleagues wince," recalled former CIA legislative liaison John Maury, "when asked questions [by members of Congress] about how many missiles an hour can be launched from [Soviet] silos or whether our estimate of the number of their . . . submarines is based upon anything other than a wild guess." One member, Maury recalled, kept referring intermittently in his questioning to "Libya," "Lebanon," and

---

[54] Ibid., 321, 421.
[55] CIA draft study, Vol. I, 67.
[56] Warner interview, 2 November 1997, 83.
[57] CIA draft study, Vol. II, 22–23.
[58] Quoted in Maury, "CIA and the Congress;" also printed in the *Congressional Record*, Vol. 130, No. 117, 18 September 1984.

"Liberia," leaving CIA analysts to guess which country he was actually refer-ring to. Another, who had been dozing through the early part of a briefing, sud-denly awoke and demanded to know "what the hell [the Agency] was doing in covert parliamentary operations." When it was explained that the chart in front of him referred to covert "paramilitary" activities, he expressed his relief to the briefers, telling them they "don't know enough about it [parliamentary activity] . . . to be fooling around with [it]."[59]

The Agency also recognized that if it were to be successful in dealing with members, it often had to tailor its approach to them. Briefings were pitched not only to the member's level of awareness but also to his or her mental acu-ities. An assistant to DCI Helms, for example, recalled preparing a briefing paper for Helms to use with a senior southern senator whom Helms regarded as friendly but not very bright. Helms sent the first draft back saying it was entirely too complicated, so his assistant offered up a second version "dumbed down . . . to the point I had the feeling I was insulting someone's intelligence." But Helms sent this one back as well, instructing his assistant to start with the statement, "This is a cat, the cat is black." The assistant tried again, "reducing this briefing to an elementary level that I was sure would never be accepted, [but] lo and behold, that was exactly what Mr. Helms wanted."[60]

Not all of the Agency's dealings with members met with success, however. Often their requests could not be accommodated and, on more than one occa-sion, had unpleasant consequences for the Agency. Usually this happened when a member or staff requested information or favors that exceeded what the Agency (or its overseers in Congress) thought they were entitled to.

In April 1948, for example, CIA turned down a request from Representative Clare Hoffman (R-MI) for an NSC intelligence directive, not only because it was an NSC-controlled document, but because Huffman was not a member of one of its oversight committees.[61]

In April 1953, staff members from Senator Joseph McCarthy's subcommit-tee, who were traveling around Europe investigating the Radio Free Europe program, requested briefings from CIA officials in the countries they were visiting. Anxious to avoid any contact with McCarthy, DCI Dulles instructed Agency personnel to "stay as far away from them as can possibly be done." Angered by the cold shoulder they received, however, McCarthy's staff announced their intent to "crack the iron curtain" that CIA was hiding behind. When they returned to Washington, they began to request CIA records on a

---

[59] Ibid.
[60] Hathaway and Smith, *Richard Helms*, 77.
[61] CIA draft study, Vol. I, 28.

wide range of issues from periodicals to which the Agency subscribed to its relationships with corporations in Hong Kong. None were provided them.[62]

In 1955, a New York congressman, who was an outspoken supporter of democratic forces in Italy, asked Dulles to provide election support for candidates in the 1956 Italian elections. Two years later, the same congressman asked him to provide support for certain political and social organizations in Italy involved in democratic reform. Dulles demurred to both requests but agreed to pass them to the Department of State.[63]

Although no direct contact was made with the Agency, Dulles took note of a public complaint made by an Iowa congressman in 1959 that an air transport company in his district had lost an Air Force contract to Air America, a proprietary of the Agency. While deciding against briefing the congressman with respect to the Agency's relationship with the company, Dulles did raise the matter with HASC Chairman Kilday, who quietly had a third member explain it to the Iowa congressman.[64]

In fact, it was not unusual for the Agency to ask one of its overseers in Congress to intervene with other members when they came to the Agency with "off-the-wall" requests or for information that was particularly sensitive. Former CIA Executive Director Lawrence K. "Red" White later recalled,

> *If some Congressman called up and demanded something, which they did once in a while, we'd just go tell Senator Russell or the old man from Missouri* [HAC Chairman Clarence Cannon] . . . *"Say, Congressman Jones called me, and he wants this or that or the other,* [and] *we don't want to get in trouble with Mr. Jones, but what do we do about this?"* [They would say,] *"Don't worry, I'll take care of it."* [We] *would never hear any more about it.*[65]

Refusals to provide information requested by members, however, on occasion, had their consequences. In 1963, for example, Representative John Lindsay (R-NY) wrote to DCI McCone asking for certain information about the Agency's operations in Europe. Since Lindsay was not a member of either of the CIA subcommittees, McCone refused to provide answers to his questions. This infuriated Lindsay, who proceeded to express his profound displeasure with the Agency and became a leading advocate of replacing the existing oversight structure with a joint committee (see chapter 1). When the Agency

---

[62] Ibid., 42.
[63] Notes of conversations between the DCI and Congressman Victor Anfuso, 14 December 1955 and July 1957, CIA History Staff.
[64] Barrett, *CIA and Congress*, 338.
[65] White interview, 7 January 1998, 37.

Senator William Fulbright, chairman of the Senate Foreign Relations Committee. Although sometimes at odds with the Agency and its oversight committees, Fulbright called Agency analysis on Vietnam "more accurate than any other estimates that came to my attention."

(US Senate Historical Collection)

finally apologized to him a year later, he stopped criticizing the Agency publicly but continued to push for a joint committee.

DCI Raborn's refusal to respond to SFRC Chairman Fulbright's questions in the spring of 1966 about allegations the Agency was using the Fulbright scholarship program as a cover for intelligence activities (on the ground that his committee was not entitled to receive information about intelligence sources and methods) infuriated Fulbright and reportedly contributed to President Johnson's decision to replace Raborn after a little more than a year on the job.[66]

Raborn's successor, Richard Helms, also managed to get himself at odds with Fulbright soon after becoming DCI. On 18 July 1966, the *St. Louis Globe-Democrat* ran an editorial applauding the Senate's decision to bury Senator Eugene McCarthy's proposal to add three members of the SFRC to the CIA subcommittee of the SASC (see chapter 1). The author of the editorial took the occasion to label Fulbright as "crafty," a description that angered the senator and many of his colleagues. As part of a new Agency program to foster better relations with the press, Helms wrote the newspaper, praising the editorial, without taking note of, or issue with, its characterization of Ful-

---

[66] Knapp, *The First Thirty Years*, 248.

bright. Members of the Senate were surprised that Helms would write such a letter at all, much less imply agreement with the editorial's comment concerning Fulbright; several took to the floor to make speeches about it. Fulbright spoke of the need to "teach the new Director some proper conduct." Senator John Stennis (D-MS) called upon Helms to apologize. Majority Leader Mansfield pronounced himself "more than a little surprised that the 'silent service' has seen fit to write to the newspaper. . . . I think this is a matter which must be brought to the attention of Mr. Helms, so that this will not become a habit with him."[67] Helms reacted by making telephone calls to Fulbright, Stennis, and Mansfield as well as other senators who had spoken, expressing regret for any embarrassment he might have caused Fulbright. He also offered his mea culpa at his next hearing before the SFRC.[68]

Briefing and Debriefing Members with Access to Substantive Intelligence

Members of Congress frequently met with foreign officials in the United States and traveled abroad. Occasionally, these encounters involved people or places that intelligence agencies themselves had difficulty getting access to. This was especially true during the Cold War, when the Soviet Union and most of Eastern Europe were off-limits to American travelers. When members of Congress visited these "denied areas" or spoke with officials from these countries, what they learned was potentially of intelligence value.

Dulles was the first DCI to recognize this. He also saw such debriefings as an opportunity for the Agency to give members a sense they were personally contributing to the nation's security as well as a better appreciation of the Agency's work. The Agency systematically began doing this in the mid-1950s. Dulles would often meet with legislators before they left on a trip. Sometimes he would send CIA officers to accompany them. Upon their return, they would be interviewed by Agency analysts, sometimes joined by Dulles himself.

In 1955, after Senator Russell returned from an 18-day trip to the Soviet Union, Dulles, the heads of Air Force and Army intelligence, and the assistant DCI for scientific intelligence went to his office to debrief him.[69] So many members went to the Soviet Union that year, in fact, that Dulles had them debriefed in their hometowns rather than waiting for them to return to Washington.[70]

---

[67] Hathaway and Smith, *Richard Helms*, 161–62.
[68] Ibid., 162.
[69] Barrett, *CIA and Congress*, 205–6.
[70] Ibid., 206.

Even congressional delegations visiting places that were accessible to the Agency were debriefed if they happened to be led by, or involved, members of the CIA subcommittees. In 1955, for example, before Senator Saltonstall left on a trip taking him to various West European capitals, the Agency briefed him on what he could expect and advised him that CIA station chiefs would be contacting him along the way to brief him on their activities. When HAC Chairman George Mahon (D-TX) made a similar trip a year later, the Agency accorded him similar treatment.[71]

Senator Allen Ellender (D-LA) made trips to the USSR in 1955 and 1956, spending a few hours with Premier Khrushchev on the second one. In January 1957, Dulles led a debriefing of the senator that included not only CIA analysts but representatives of the State and Defense Departments as well. A few days later, Agency analysts debriefed Representative Jamie Whitten (D-MS) on his 38-day trip to the USSR and Eastern Europe. Both legislators thought the Agency was underplaying the weaknesses of Soviet society.[72]

CIA records reflect that in 1957 the Agency debriefed a total of 53 lawmakers returning from foreign travel, five being handled by Dulles personally. A similar number were debriefed in 1958.[73] Although according to CIA records, these debriefings did not produce much of intelligence interest (apart from those involving trips to the Soviet Union and Eastern Europe), they did allow the Agency to gauge the attitudes and positions of the members involved vis-à-vis the CIA. Occasionally a member would provide leads to people or organizations that could be of assistance to the Agency.

Not all of the Agency's endeavors in this area, however, generated the kind of goodwill Dulles was aiming for. In 1957, for example, after the Agency had agreed to send an escort to accompany a congresswoman on a trip to the Middle East, she spent much of her debriefing with Dulles commenting on the officer's personal and personality problems.[74] Another congressman, returning from a trip to Yugoslavia, angrily complained to Dulles about the lack of attention the US embassy paid him, as well as its "cavalier approach" to what was taking place inside the country.[75]

During the summer of 1960, after learning that Senator Frank Church had met for three hours with a Soviet diplomat, Dulles called Church to ask for a

---

[71] Ibid., 207.

[72] Ibid., 207–8.

[73] Ibid., 321.

[74] Stenographic Notes of Conversation between Dulles and Congresswoman Francis Bolton, 6 November 1957, CIA History Staff.

[75] Stenographic Notes of Conversation between Dulles and Congressman John A. Blatnik, 22 October 1957, CIA History Staff.

report of the meeting. He also offered to alert the FBI to the diplomat's activities, an offer that Church accepted.[76]

After the Creation of the Select Committees: 1976-2004

Intelligence-Sharing

In July 1976, after the SSCI was created and secure work spaces constructed, it was agreed that the committee could see publications, in addition to the NID, that were intended for general circulation within the executive branch. Among them were the *Economic Intelligence Weekly*, the *Weapons Intelligence Summary*, and the *Scientific Intelligence Digest*. At the same time, the committee acquiesced in the Agency's position that intelligence analysis tailored for officials within the executive branch—the *President's Daily Brief* (PDB), for example—would not be routinely provided, nor would intelligence cables (unevaluated intelligence reports) from the field.[77]

While the publicity given the Agency by the Church and Pike Committees was hardly favorable, it does appear to have awakened many congressional committees to the Agency's analytical capabilities. The "non-intelligence" committees, realizing what the intelligence committees would now be getting, doubled the number of their requests for the Agency's published analysis. The increased demand was such that the Agency in September 1976, with White House concurrence, had to issue guidelines limiting the provision of substantive analysis to "non-intelligence committees" to oral briefings.[78]

When the HPSCI was created in July 1977, it began receiving the same published analysis being provided its Senate counterpart. In the beginning, such analysis was delivered and retrieved at the end of the day. In time, however—and Agency records do not mark the precise point at which this occurred—substantive intelligence publications began to be left with the two intelligence committees. Both committees had built facilities to meet the DCI's security standards for the protection of SCI (sensitive compartmented information) material. Indeed, in some respects, the security procedures in place at the oversight committees exceeded those the DCI established for the executive branch as a whole. So, while questions continued to arise during the earlier years of the committees' operations in terms of the substantive intelligence to be made available to them, the absence of approved physical storage facilities was no longer a reason for denying access.

---

[76] Barrett, *CIA and Congress*, 421.
[77] CIA draft study, Vol. II, 179.
[78] Knapp, *The First Thirty Years*, 357.

Indeed, within five to 10 years of the committees' creation, most finished intelligence products intended for general consumption within the executive branch were being made available to them. These products included the NIEs and SNIEs that had been so scrupulously protected prior to the mid-1970s. There does not appear to have been a specific decision by the Agency or the executive branch that allowed for this; rather, the practice appeared to evolve for several reasons.

First, there was the changing legal framework. In 1978, the Carter administration issued a new executive order on intelligence that, among other things, directed the DCI to "facilitate the use of national foreign intelligence products by the Congress in a secure manner."[79] This was, in fact, the first time that a president had ever directed a DCI to do this. In 1980, with the enactment of the Intelligence Oversight Act (see chapter 5), the head of the CIA was obligated to keep the two oversight committees "fully and currently informed" of its activities and to provide the committees with access to "any information…in its control" that was needed for the committees to carry out their responsibilities.[80] While neither of these policy changes specifically dictated that all finished intelligence be shared with the committees, taken together, they did seem to mean that the committees could see what they wanted to see and, over time, what the committees wanted to see was almost everything.

By the early 1980s, the committees had also demonstrated that they had the capability and intent to protect the information that was shared with them. There were few leaks of finished intelligence. The committees did not allow these documents out of their control. Thus, members were unable to "wave them around on the floor," as Senator Russell had envisioned years before. Had any of this happened, the situation might have been different, but by the mid-1980s at least, the analytical products that the committees routinely wished to see were being provided in hard copy; other products were being made available on request. At the end of 1988, the Office of Congressional Affairs (OCA) reported that approximately 4,000 finished intelligence products had been provided during the year to the two intelligence committees.[81]

What this meant, then–Deputy National Security Advisor Robert M. Gates perceptively observed in 1988, was that the committees now had essentially the same access to finished intelligence as consumers within the executive branch. In an article written for *Foreign Affairs*, Gates notes,

---

[79] §1-601(c) of Executive Order 12036, 24 January 1978.
[80] See §501 and §502 of the *National Security Act of 1947*, as amended.
[81] CIA draft study, Vol. III, 148.

> *The result is that CIA finds itself in a remarkable position, involuntarily poised nearly equidistant between the executive and legislative branches. The administration knows that the CIA is in no position to withhold much information from the Congress and is extremely sensitive to Congressional demands; the Congress has enormous influence and information, yet remains suspicious and mistrustful. Such a central legislative role with respect to an intelligence service is unique in American history and in the world. And policymakers know it.*[82]

Notwithstanding the wealth of written analysis available to them, few members on either oversight committee had time to read it. Most continued to receive what intelligence analysis they were given in the form of briefings. In 1988, OCA tallied more than 1,000 such briefings to members or staff of the two committees.[83] Indeed, from the dates of their creation until the present, the two oversight committees have been given substantive intelligence briefings upon request, ranging from formal presentations made to the full committee, to one-on-one briefings with individual members, to briefings of one or more staff. When international crises occurred or developments around the world otherwise spurred congressional interest, the demands upon Agency analysts would become intense. During 1988-89, for example, the SSCI established an ad hoc "task force" for the sole purpose of following developments in the Soviet Union and Eastern Europe, as the fate of Mikhail Gorbachev and other communist leaders appeared to hang in the balance.[84] Meeting frequently with the same analysts during this two-year period, members of the task force were exposed to the stream of the Community's ongoing analysis in a way they had never been before. Briefings such as these afforded members of the two intelligence committees an opportunity not only to keep abreast of world events but also to question and look behind the analytical judgments they were hearing. This was an ability other congressional committees did not have. While other committees continued to receive intelligence briefings after the select committees were created, the intelligence sources and methods underlying the analysis were not disclosed to them.

Increasingly, though, as "non-oversight" committees began to appreciate what the intelligence committees were being given, they began turning to the committees to act as their surrogates. On four separate occasions during the early years of the SSCI's existence, for instance, the SFRC requested that the

---

[82] Gates, "The CIA and American Foreign Policy," 224–25.
[83] CIA draft study, Vol. III. 148.
[84] Lundberg, *CIA and the Fall of the Soviet Empire: The Politics of "Getting It Right,"* 29.

SSCI obtain and analyze the substantive intelligence bearing upon treaties or legislation pending before the SFRC.

- In the case of SALT II, the SSCI was asked to look at whether US intelligence could adequately monitor the treaty.

- In the case of the Panama Canal Treaty, the issue was what the Intelligence Community saw as the likely consequences of Senate ratification.

- In the case of the Iraqi poison gas attacks on the refugee camps at Shaba, the SFRC wanted to know what the Intelligence Community had been able to confirm had taken place there before it considered legislative sanctions against Iraq.

- In the case of implementing the Taiwan Relations Act, the SFRC was interested in the likely reaction of the Chinese government.

For each issue, the SSCI delivered a classified report to the SFRC, together with an unclassified summary.[85]

The provision of finished intelligence products to other committees also expanded during the 1980s. In 1987, an Office of Senate Security was established to serve as a repository for storing classified information going to other "non-oversight" committees. On the House side, several non-oversight committees established their own repositories. As a result, far more written analysis relevant to the institutional responsibilities of these committees was sent to the Hill.

The Agency also continued to provide one-on-one briefings to members who were about to leave on foreign travel or meet with foreign officials. Indeed, because of the increased awareness among members that such briefings were available to them—even if they were not on one of the oversight committees—more were requested.

In short, while the CIA had always shared intelligence analysis with the Congress, the scope and scale of such sharing reached new heights after the select intelligence committees came on the scene in the mid-1970s. Not only did intelligence-sharing with the intelligence committees burgeon, but so did intelligence-sharing with other committees and individual members, largely because of what the intelligence committees themselves were now able to get.

In 1992, what had become accepted practice was finally recognized in law with the passage of the Intelligence Organization Act that, among other things, required the DCI to provide substantive intelligence "where appropriate, to the Senate and House of Representatives, and the committees thereof."[86] Thus did

---

[85] Smist, *Congress Oversees*, 106.

the provision of intelligence support to the Congress officially become a part of the Agency's statutory mission. During the mid-1990s, the Agency began to provide finished intelligence products electronically rather than in hard copy, but the range of analysis made available did not change.

One notable innovation during the 1990s was the institution of public "worldwide threat briefings" at the beginning of each session of Congress. The Agency had long provided such tour d'horizon briefings upon request—to oversight committees and non-oversight committees alike—but in 1995, the chairman of the SSCI, Arlen Specter (R-PA), insisted that at least a part of the annual threat briefing be given in open session. This became, from that point on, an annual ritual for the DCI. While the DCI also gave the annual threat briefing to other congressional committees, only the intelligence committees held a portion of the briefing in public. OCA Director John Moseman later recalled that these briefings

> *forced us to do an enormous amount of work. Simply deciding what we could and could not say in public was a very complicated issue. But going through this exercise every year did force us to think through what we were doing. It also played into other things—the budget process, for example—it basically provided the justification for that.*[87]

When the Republican Party took control of both houses of Congress in January 1995, the Agency also took the initiative to offer weekly "hot spot" briefings to the leaders of the House and Senate on current international events. Most of those offered such briefings were too busy to schedule them, but the incoming House Speaker Newt Gingrich (R-GA) took the Agency up on its offer and regularly made time on his calendar for them. Gingrich's successor as Speaker, Dennis Hastert (R-IL), similarly made time on his schedule. Moseman later noted:

> *They obviously found the "hot spot" briefings useful, otherwise they wouldn't have put them on the schedule. [The Agency] got a lot of benefit out of them, too. They gave us a chance to cultivate a relationship we wouldn't otherwise have had. Of course, [these briefings] raised other problems—the White House was forever wanting to know what we were telling them.*[88]

---

[86] See §103 of the *National Security Act of 1947*, as amended.
[87] Moseman interview, 28 December 2006.
[88] Ibid.

Other Interaction

With the establishment of the intelligence committees, another form of inter-action with the Congress took shape: member and staff visits to Agency facilities around the world. While such visits had happened before—members of the CIA subcommittees would sometimes travel to foreign countries where they would meet with Agency personnel and receive briefings by the country team—the number of such visits proliferated after the select committees were created (more than 100 in 1988 alone), as did the amount of Agency information shared during such visits.[89] A CIA escort officer accompanied most such delegations; he or she not only facilitated the logistical arrangements but helped members obtain the information they were seeking. As a result of these visits, members and their staff often established personal relationships with the officers who escorted them or who hosted them during official visits, relationships that sometimes followed the officer once he or she returned to Headquarters for a new assignment. The committees also gained a better appreciation of the day-to-day problems in the field, of how the Agency's activities fit within the overall country-team approach, and where the Agency's assessments of the internal political situation differed from those of other agencies.

Cultivating personal relationships with the members and staffs of its oversight committees, as well as other influential members of Congress, had always been a goal of the Agency's leadership, but during the early period the "targeted" members were relatively few in number. With the creation of the intelligence committees, the number of members and staff to be cultivated multiplied severalfold. Further complicating the problem for the Agency were the term limits for service on each committee, which meant that new members and staff were continually coming aboard. It could take years to win a member over, only to have him or her leave the committee.

To encourage and promote these personal relationships, DCIs employed a variety of techniques. Casey, for example, despite his well-known aversion to dealing with Congress, and perhaps because of it, tried several approaches. In 1986, he invited new members of Congress out to the Agency for orientation briefings.[90] The same year, he began having members of the oversight committees and their staffs out to the Agency for breakfast or lunch to meet informally with senior Agency staff.[91] In December 1983, after the passage of the FOIA exemption for the Agency's operational files, he invited staff from both committees to the Agency for a party.[92] Other DCIs have adopted similar strategies,

---

[89] CIA draft study, Vol. III, 148.
[90] Ibid., 78.
[91] Ibid., 143.
[92] Woodward, *Veil*, 383–84.

at times adding wrinkles of their own. Webster and Gates, for example, held weekend "off-sites" early on in a congressional session to educate members of the oversight committees. Others chose to recognize the leaders of the oversight committees (and sometimes even long-serving staff) when they left their positions by presenting them with medals or certificates of commendation.

AUTHOR'S COMMENTARY

Significance of the Incidental Interaction with Congress

The incidental interaction that occurs with Congress apart from the exercise of its institutional responsibilities for the Agency not only affects how members perceive the Agency but can lead to repercussions for the institutional relationship as well.

For members who do not sit on one of the committees with institutional responsibility, this incidental interaction is apt to be their only personal exposure to the Agency. For them, a telephone call not returned, a letter unanswered, a constituent not hired can have significance for the relationship far beyond the matter at issue. They may not be in a position to affect the Agency's budget or otherwise call it to task, but by virtue of being members of Congress, they have a public platform from which to comment and criticize. They also have a vote in their respective chambers.

For members who do sit on one of the committees with institutional responsibility, the stakes for the Agency are higher. Small miscues can be taken as signs of larger problems. Failures to respond appropriately to a member's needs or requests can be perceived, for example, as a snub, a lack of attentiveness, a lack of candor, or evidence of incompetence. And, where these members are concerned, their positions on the oversight committees provide the wherewithal to do something about it. Hearings might be called, investigations launched, funding cut, or follow-up reports required. In short, as Senator Russell once noted, they have the ability "to make life miserable" for the miscreants (as they perceive them). Moreover, when a member of one of the oversight committees believes he or she has been slighted in some way, the leaders of the committee involved are not usually inclined to stand in their way. Most of the time, tempers cool when explanations or apologies are offered, but the Agency can never completely count on it.

By far, most of the incidental interaction that occurs with members of Congress at a personal level occurs during substantive intelligence briefings, and, these briefings have on balance, over the Agency's history, generated far more support than problems for the Agency. As former DCI Helms observed at the end of his career, members may not always agree with what the Agency has to say, but they see it as "keeping the game honest." Negative impressions, however, can also be generated. Briefers who are perceived as promoting political agendas, who can provide little information or insight beyond what is in the press, or who do not seem to have a mastery of the evidence can lead members not only to question their competence but also to wonder if this is what the Agency itself is about.

The lesson from all this is that the Agency must take even incidental interaction with the Congress seriously. Any interaction with a member, no matter how small, can potentially have consequences.

Why Congress Needs Intelligence Support

Congress has numerous functions, derived from its constitutional responsibilities, that benefit from having access to intelligence analysis. Providing for the national defense requirements of the country, for example, benefits from intelligence analysis of the foreign threat. Providing for border control and homeland security, similarly, requires knowledge of the domestic threat posed by foreign entities. Foreign assistance programs funded by Congress may well hinge on the conduct and intentions of foreign recipients. Declarations of war and/or resolutions authorizing the president to use military force abroad require consideration of the likely consequences of such action. For the Senate to provide advice and consent to treaties typically requires knowledge of the intent and capabilities of foreign signatories.

Beyond such institutional functions, members of Congress are expected to be knowledgeable of, and able to comment intelligently about, foreign policy issues, especially if they affect their home state or district. They are frequently asked about them by the press, their constituents, and their political opponents. Yet, if they are not members of the intelligence, armed services, or foreign relations committees, few opportunities exist in Congress for them to acquire basic information on foreign policy issues. While few will have the time to make themselves experts, having access to intelligence analysis can provide an expeditious means of familiarizing themselves with an issue.

Obviously, Congress has no intelligence capability of its own. It has a great many sources of information available to it, but where foreign intelligence is concerned, it must rely upon what it receives from the executive branch. Most of what it receives comes from the CIA, an agency it established and funds, but also an agency whose director (for the period covered by this study) reported to the president and was principally responsible for serving the president's needs.

During the early part of the Agency's history, the president exercised considerable control over the intelligence analysis DCIs were allowed to provide the Congress, especially if they were concerned about the sensitivity of the information or the political fallout likely to occur if it were made available to members. While presidents understood the Agency's need to keep its subcommittees happy, they were less understanding when it came to other committees. In fact, relatively little was shared with them, and the lack of secure storage facilities on Capitol Hill meant that what was shared was passed verbally, either in briefings or in one-on-one meetings.

Like other aspects of the relationship between Congress and the Agency, intelligence-sharing with the Congress changed dramatically after the creation of the select committees. It did not happen immediately nor was everything made available at the same time. By the early 1980s, however, most of the finished intelligence analysis the Intelligence Community produced was being made available to Congress. This came about not as a result of any "grand deal" struck with the executive branch but rather as a result of the evolution in the oversight process itself. By this point, not only did the committees possess the physical facilities to protect classified information, they had, for the most part, demonstrated their intent to do so. As overseers, they believed they were entitled to see what the Intelligence Community was producing. They never asked for it in terms of seeing all the finished intelligence that was being produced, nor was the president ever asked to consider it in these terms. The committees simply began asking to see publications they became aware of, and in time access to almost everything was being provided.

In retrospect, given the concerns of past presidents, it seems curious that this "sea change" in intelligence-sharing with Congress during the 1980s could have occurred without the issue being posed in some fashion to the White House. In fact, no other government in the world routinely shares intelligence with its legislature. Intelligence is meant to support the executive function, not the legislative one. In the United States, it has come to support both. To be sure, intelligence analysis is written principally for the executive branch. Congress may be able to share in such analysis, but it has no role in developing it.

The Impact of Intelligence-Sharing with the Congress

The consequences of sharing intelligence with the Congress have been, and will continue to be, far-reaching.[93]

Without question, the position of Congress vis-à-vis the executive branch has been strengthened by virtue of its access to intelligence analysis. When this analysis is at odds with administration policy, it will provide members with ammunition to challenge this policy. By the same token, having the intelligence analysis may enable members to better understand why a particular policy was adopted, thus muting the criticism the administration might otherwise have received. Congress may also be less prone to "go off half-cocked," legislating unwisely in the heat of a crisis and thereby creating problems for an administration to deal with down the road.

For the intelligence committees, access to finished intelligence allows them to see what the entire system is producing. It is the "meat" that comes out the end of the grinder, after all of the information collected around the world has been put together, processed, evaluated and put in context. If the committees are paying attention, it allows them to see what the Intelligence Community knows, and does not know, about a particular topic. It reveals where the gaps in our knowledge are and often what is needed to fill them. In this regard, having access to finished intelligence can lead to better oversight and ultimately to a stronger intelligence capability.

At the same time, the emergence of Congress as a consumer of intelligence analysis has added immeasurably to the Intelligence Community's day-to-day burdens. Whatever their commitments to executive branch policymakers, hardly a day goes by, when Congress is in session, that intelligence analysts are not also briefing on Capitol Hill. Moreover, the congressional recipients of these briefings often pose a different challenge for the analysts doing them. Members and/or their staffs are typically not as informed with respect to the subject being briefed as executive branch policymakers are, nor do they have the same perspective in terms of what the intelligence reporting means (or does not mean). Moreover, what a member may be looking for from the briefing is not simply information, but ammunition with which to challenge administration policy.

Indeed, the exponential growth in intelligence-sharing with the Congress has significantly complicated the lives of policymakers in the executive branch. Intelligence analysis, by its very nature, will sometimes undermine or seem at odds with the policy a particular administration adopts. Perhaps the administration, for perfectly valid reasons, has chosen a course of action that seems unsupported by the intelligence analysis, yet their rationale may not be apparent to members of Congress who hear the analysis. Before, policymakers rarely had to worry what was being briefed to the Hill. Now, intelligence

---

[93] For a detailed description of this topic, see Snider, *Sharing Secrets with Lawmakers.*

briefings occur with such frequency that policymakers must struggle to keep up with what Congress is being told. If they fail to do so, the next time they are testifying before Congress they risk being caught short by a member who inquires about an intelligence analysis the policymaker has not seen and wants to know how the administration's policy can be sustained in light of it. Forcing policymakers to explain why the administration's policy makes sense despite the intelligence analysis might be seen as a salutary effect of intelligence-sharing, but it also has the potential for creating hostility and resentment for the analyst whose work created the problem for the policymaker. To avoid this outcome, most intelligence analysts will advise policymakers when their analysis is apt to cause a problem on the Hill.

CHAPTER 4

ORGANIZATIONAL ARRANGEMENTS AT THE CIA

Principal responsibility for dealing with the Congress has always rested with the DCI. He has been the one to enunciate Agency policy and positions to the Hill, explain and defend Agency activities, provide its analytical assessments, and render such other support as the Congress may request.

To help him carry out these responsibilities, each director has had a staff that supported him. Over time, however, the level and nature of this staff support has varied.

One-Man Operations

In the fall of 1947, shortly after the enactment of the Agency's charter as part of the National Security Act of 1947, DCI Hillenkoetter stopped the Agency's legislative liaison, Walter Pforzheimer, in the hallway and told him he did not think he would be able to keep him on any longer because there would not be enough business between the CIA and the Congress to justify a full-time attorney.[1] Pforzheimer stayed on, nonetheless, making sure the Agency's funding got put through the congressional process each year and handling the various matters that arose with the Hill.

Walter Pforzheimer handled the Agency's (and CIG's) liaison with Congress for nine years, 1946–55.

---

[1] Pforzheimer interview, 15 October 1996.

For the first 20 years of the Agency's existence, from the days of CIG to the tenure of DCI Helms, one person—first designated as legislative liaison and later legislative counsel—was able to satisfy the demands of this role. Except for a short period in the mid-1950s when the legislative counsel reported to the Agency's inspector general, the legislative counsel was assigned to the Office of General Counsel (OGC) but operated under the direct supervision of the DCI. Pforzheimer filled this position from 1946 until 1955; Norman Paul (who reported to the IG) did so from 1956 until 1957; and John Warner did so from 1957 until 1966, during which time he also doubled as deputy general counsel.

The legislative counsel was assisted by secretaries and, as needed, by others in the General Counsel's office, but it largely fell to him to ensure that the Agency's dealings with the Hill remained on an even keel. He monitored legislative developments, arranged for briefings and hearings, ensured that congressional requests were satisfied, and, above all, shepherded the Agency's funding request through Congress each year. Occasionally, the three men who held this position found themselves the target of complaints from the Hill and, on one occasion, even the target of a congressional subpoena (see chapter 10). But overall, judging from what has been written about them, all enjoyed good relations on Capitol Hill. DCIs looked to them not simply to make sure Congress was getting what it needed but to monitor congressional sentiment towards the Agency on an ongoing basis.

In November 1966, in recognition of the increasing importance that relations with Congress had assumed, as well as the time it now took to tend to these relationships, DCI Helms moved the legislative liaison function out of OGC and made it a separate component of his own staff, known as the Office of Legislative Counsel (OLC). Warner moved out of OGC altogether at this point to become the head of the new office, which consisted of six people.[2] He remained for two years before returning to OGC and giving way to John Maury in 1968. Maury, a seasoned DO officer, served in the position until 1974, when he was replaced by his deputy, George Cary.

Although the OLC continued to handle the regular business of the Agency on the Hill, it was too small to deal with the volume of congressional requests that deluged the Agency once the Church and Pike Committees began their inquiries. Special arrangements had to be instituted. The agency assembled an ad hoc "review staff" headed by an "assistant to the DCI" to respond to the requests of the Rockefeller Commission. Thus, DCI Colby attempted to establish a process that would satisfy the new investigating committees while at the same time protect the Agency's legitimate security interests.[3]

---

[2] Hathaway and Smith, *Richard Helms*, 162; CIA draft study, Vol. II, 21.
[3] CIA draft study, Vol. II, 58.

In practice, achieving this balance proved difficult. Colby assigned experienced Agency officers to the new staff, but none had had prior dealings with Congress. Moreover, few were prepared for the hostility they encountered. One of them, assigned to deal with the especially contentious Pike Committee, later said its staff was "rude, uncivil, and acted like prosecuting attorneys. . . . They thought we all were criminals."[4] Another commented:

> *The months I spent with the Pike committee made my tour in Vietnam seem like a picnic. I would vastly prefer to fight the Viet Cong than deal with a polemical investigation by a congressional committee, which is what the Pike committee was.*[5]

Increasing their frustration, the review staff also found itself at odds with Agency components that could not understand why the investigating committees needed, or why the Agency should offer up, documents concerning their operations. As one of the review staff later noted, "We were accused [by components] of being a Benedict Arnold for even asking questions [that the Church and Pike Committees wanted to know about]."[6] The committees, for their part, complained constantly that the staff was dragging its feet. As Pike observed at one of his committee's hearings, "What we have . . . is a great deal of the language of cooperation and a great deal of . . . non-cooperation."[7]

Over time, the role of the review staff expanded from simply being a clearinghouse for documents going to the Church and Pike Committees to monitoring and evaluating their work for the DCI.[8] Indeed, because of the one-day time limit the Pike Committee mandated for the Agency to review the draft of committee's final report, it fell largely to the review staff to accomplish.

An Expanded Office of Legislative Counsel: 1976–81

When the Church and Pike investigations were over, the Agency initially continued to have a special review office to coordinate the provision of Agency documents to the Hill.[9] But the Agency continued to conduct its regular business with the Congress through OLC, and within a year OLC subsumed the role of coordinating document production as well.

---

[4] Ibid., 152.
[5] Ibid., 120.
[6] Ibid., 70.
[7] Ibid., 121.
[8] Ibid., 105–7.
[9] Ibid., 161.

With the creation of the SSCI in the summer of 1976, it became clear that OLC was too small to satisfy the Agency's future needs. To remedy the situation, the head of OLC at the time, George Cary, proposed to create an office of 32 people, divided into three staffs: legislation, liaison, and coordination and review. Although it took a while for Cary's proposal to wind its way through the Agency bureaucracy (there was a change in DCIs in early 1977), DCI Turner approved it in December 1977. Several months later, Turner named his own person, a former DO officer, Fred Hitz, to head the office.[10] At the time Hitz took over from Cary, there were 28 people assigned to OLC.[11]

Casey and Congress: 1981–86

When DCI Casey took control of the Agency in 1981, he combined what had been OLC with the existing Office of Public Affairs to form the Office of External Affairs. To head the new office, he appointed J. William "Billy" Doswell, a former newspaper publisher and lobbyist of the Virginia legislature. He, however, had neither intelligence experience nor experience in Congress. Not surprisingly, both Congress and the Agency viewed him as an outsider with little influence.[12]

Under Doswell, the congressional affairs function became the province of the Legislative Liaison Division, which itself was divided into a House and Senate branch and a legislation branch.[13] Responsibility for pushing the Agency's annual budget through Congress, however, shifted to the Agency's comptroller. The Legislative Liaison Division was left to coordinate hearings and briefings on the Hill as well as track congressional activities.

This arrangement lasted for about a year and a half. Casey became disenchanted with Doswell because he thought Doswell was not doing enough to support his position on Nicaragua. Doswell, on the other hand, thought Casey needlessly provoked confrontation with Congress.[14] He left at the end of 1982.

With Doswell gone, Casey abolished the Office of External Affairs and again made the Office of Legislative Liaison an independent element of his staff. To head the office, he chose Clair E. George, who at the time was second in command within the Directorate of Operations (DO). George, in turn, brought in DO officers to staff the office. CIA records reflect that within three months there had been an across-the-board personnel turnover.[15]

---

[10] Ibid., 162.
[11] Cary interview, 30 September 1983, 3.
[12] CIA draft study, Vol. III, 7.
[13] Ibid., 8.
[14] Woodward, *Veil*, 264.

This did not play well with the two intelligence committees. Unlike Doswell, George was the consummate insider, but Agency records reflect the staffs of the two committees generally found him unresponsive and uncooperative. Instead, they perceived they were being "gamed" by the DO; there were no longer officers in the Office of Legislative Liaison they could trust.[16]

In the spring of 1984, after the Nicaraguan harbor mining episode had come to light (see p. 60), the staff director of the SSCI actually stopped speaking with George and told Casey "he had to go."[17] In July 1984, George moved on to become the deputy director for operations, and the Agency's executive director at the time, Charles Briggs, replaced him as the head of OLL. Casey also took action to ensure that OLL was kept better informed of covert action activities so that it could, in turn, better represent the Agency's activities to the Hill.[18]

When Briggs took over, he immediately sought to improve the level of trust between OLL and the two committees. Part of the problem, he found, was the lack of stability and continuity in his own office. Committee staffers referred to OLL as "Bolivia," Briggs later recalled, "because of all the coups, changes and reorganizations" that were constantly taking place. Agency officers were not staying long enough to develop relationships. Red tape within the CIA bureaucracy was also resulting in inordinate delays in terms of satisfying the committees' requests for information. Briggs endeavored to fix both problems.[19]

Briggs remained in the job until he retired in February 1986. Replacing him was David D. Gries, a DO officer who had previously served as the National Intelligence Officer (NIO) for East Asia. Gries continued Briggs's efforts to improve relations with the Hill. Among other things, he got Casey's approval for changing the name of his office to the Office of Congressional Affairs (OCA), which both believed was a stronger, more accurate reflection of the office's mission.[20] This, in fact, has remained its name until the present day.

Despite their efforts to improve relations with the Hill, some on the oversight committees continued to regard Briggs and Gries as "doing Casey's bidding." As long as they worked for this DCI, they would be seen as part of his perceived efforts to keep the committees in the dark.[21]

---

[15] CIA draft study, Vol. III, 9.

[16] Ibid; see also Woodward, *Veil*, 319–38 for a description of George's involvement with the SSCI over the Nicaraguan harbor mining episode.

[17] CIA draft study, Vol. III, 64.

[18] Ibid., 65.

[19] Ibid., 77.

[20] Ibid., 79.

[21] Ibid., 80.

Responding to Iran-Contra: 1986–90

While the investigations of the Iran-contra affair focused on the activities of the White House staff, CIA was nonetheless a key subsidiary target. Moreover, because so many investigative bodies were looking into Iran-contra, the Agency faced an enormous challenge in terms of controlling access to its documents and personnel. Initially, DCI Casey split responsibility among his staff: OGC would monitor and support the independent counsel's criminal investigation; OCA would handle the congressional investigations; and the Agency's IG, who performed the first internal review of the Agency's involvement, would support the Tower Commission probe.[22]

Within a short time, however, these arrangements changed in response to events on the outside. The Tower Commission's probe ended relatively quickly. The White House then set up an interagency declassification and production review group to control document production within the executive branch as a whole. The Agency's role in this review group was carried out by a special "documents unit" that OCA had originally established to coordinate the production of Agency documents going to the Hill. DCI Webster also established an internal coordinating committee, chaired by the Agency's executive director, to oversee at a policy level what was being provided to the various investigations.[23]

The investigation of Iran-contra by the joint congressional committees lasted through the summer of 1987, at which time their demands for information began to diminish.

Strengthening Ties to the Hill after the Guatemala Episode: 1995

In January 1995, in response to the hostile reactions the Agency had received from both committees for its failure to notify them of a 1991 intelligence report suggesting that an Agency source in Guatemala had been present at the murder of an American citizen there (see chapter 8), the DO sent out an internal message asking its employees to list everyone in Congress with whom they had "personal ties" or a "working relationship." Saying that "the agency's standing with Congress is linked inextricably to the Hill's view of the directorate of operations . . . it is imperative to engage members in a variety of initiatives" to improve the Agency's standing. The goal, the message said, was "to insure [sic] that we communicate an accurate portrayal of signif-

---

[22] Ibid., 150–51.
[23] Ibid., 151.

icant ongoing activities—both positive and negative—as well as articulate our vision for the future."

This memo was leaked to the *New York Times* by an Agency employee who believed the directorate's initiative violated a federal law prohibiting federal agencies from lobbying Congress. An Agency spokesman disputed this allegation and described the initiative simply as an educational effort intended to supplement the work of OCA.

While not commenting on its legality, incoming SSCI Chairman Arlen Specter (R-PA) found the whole idea distasteful. "The CIA's directorate of operations would be better advised," he told the *Times*, "to improve its reputation and standing by real performance, instead of attempting to rely on factors like personal, school, or family ties."[24]

The Office of Congressional Affairs: 1988–2004

The Office of Congressional Affairs remained the focal point within the Agency for handling the day-to-day relations with Congress from 1988 until 2004. While its internal organization and staff size fluctuated during this period, its role did not significantly change. OCA continued to be the office that scheduled and coordinated briefings and hearings in Congress, ensured the needs of its committees and members were met, monitored and influenced legislation affecting the Agency's interests, and helped to deal with "flaps" when they occurred. While there were significant congressional investigations of the Agency during this period (see chapters 7–10), none required the creation of special ad hoc arrangements, such as the Church and Pike Committees or those that were put in place to respond to the Iran-contra scandal.

Moreover, after the rocky experiences of the Casey years, subsequent DCIs, for the most part, put seasoned officers at the helm of OCA—people versed in the Agency's operations, who had also worked with the Congress. John Helgerson, a veteran of the Directorate of Intelligence, headed OCA from 1988 to 1989. Following him were Norbert Garrett, a DO officer, who served from 1989 to 1991; Stan Moskowitz, another veteran of the DI, who served from 1991 to 1994; Joanne Isham, from the Community Management Staff, who served from 1994 to 1996; John H. Moseman, a former minority staff director of the SSCI, who served from 1996 to 2001; and Moskowitz who served for a second time from 2001 to 2004.

Of this succession of OCA directors, only Moseman came to the job from the outside. By virtue of his previous jobs, however, he had considerable

---

[24] Quoted in Weiner, "CIA Mission: Strengthen Ties on Capitol Hill."

background in the Agency's operations as well as an in-depth knowledge of the Congress. He also made a point of staffing OCA with seasoned Agency veterans to enhance the office's credibility, both internally and externally.[25]

AUTHOR'S COMMENTARY

The Agency's Arrangements for Dealing with the Congress

Over its history, the Agency has used a variety of staff arrangements to support its dealings with the Congress. For the most part, the volume of congressional demands at a given time, the attitude of particular DCIs toward the Hill, and finally the way DCIs want to use their congressional affairs staff (as mere conduits of information or as active promoters of the Agency's interests) have determined the nature of these arrangements. In other words, the size, shape, and responsibilities of the congressional affairs staffs have depended upon the circumstances.

Nonetheless, a few points can be drawn from this experience.

First, the fact that for the first 20 years of the Agency's existence, essentially one person (with limited help) was able to handle relations with Congress is perhaps the most telling evidence of the cursory oversight of this period. Even presuming the individuals who performed these duties were capable of keeping many balls in the air at once, there are but so many hours in a day. One of them even doubled as deputy general counsel for most of his tenure.

Second, the only time in the Agency's history that a DCI brought in someone from the outside—without experience either in the Agency or the Congress—to handle congressional affairs (Casey in 1981), it did not work. Neither institution trusted him.

The optimal solution, according to former Agency Legislative Counsel John Warner, was to have someone in the OCA position who knew both sides:

> *To the Congress, the legislative man . . . is the Agency and should be able to talk about the Agency to the Congress and vice versa. . . . So that means a guy experienced in the Agency. . . . He can learn the legislature and maybe serve a tour . . . on the* [congressional affairs] *staff, but don't just jerk up a guy right out of operations and put him in there who has been overseas most of the time. . . . He has no con-*

---

[25] Moseman interview, 31 March 2006.

*cept of what's going on. He needs experience in the Agency and. . .
some legislative experience behind him.*[26]

Finally, whatever the staff arrangement, those managing the relationship
with Congress will always find themselves "in the middle"—trying to satisfy
congressional demands while trying to protect the Agency's interests. When
the system has worked well, it has been due to these people "in the middle,"
who understand and find ways to reconcile the interests of both sides. Con-
versely, when the system has broken down, it has been because the people "in
the middle" are seen as overly protective of one side's interests, usually the
Agency's, to the detriment of the other's. For the Agency's original legislative
counsel, Walter L. Pforzheimer, being successful at his job was "only just a
question of maintaining good, honest relationships."[27]

---

[26] Warner interview, 9 October 1987, 35.

[27] Pforzheimer interview, 11 January 1988, 8.

PART II

WHAT THE RELATIONSHIP PRODUCED

CHAPTER 5

LEGISLATION

This chapter primarily deals with the statutes Congress enacted between 1946 and 2004 that affected the CIA's mission, authorities, and organization. It does not include statutes that merely authorized or appropriated funds for the Agency, imposed funding or operational restrictions, or established oversight requirements vis-à-vis the Congress. The actions of Congress with respect to the Agency's funding, as well as the imposition of operational restrictions, are covered in subsequent chapters, whereas chapters 1 and 2 dealt with the laws concerning oversight.

From the creation of the Agency in 1947 until the establishment of the permanent select committees on intelligence in the mid-1970s, there was relatively little legislation in this area. Only three statutes, in fact, fell into the aforementioned categories, and all were developed largely by the Agency and supported by the administration in power. With the advent of the select committees, however, Congress began to develop and enact more legislation affecting the Agency's mission, authorities, and organization. Not only did the annual authorization bills for intelligence developed by the select committees offer new opportunities to bring legislation affecting the CIA to the floor, but the committees themselves increasingly took the initiative to propose such legislation. This chapter will highlight the most significant enactments during the 58-year period covered by the study.

The reader should also appreciate that a considerable part of the Agency's legislative efforts over this period has been to keep laws from being enacted that it did not want. While the Agency has had mixed success in dealing with legislation of this kind, it is beyond the purview of this study to deal with these episodes. Instead, the body of this chapter, apart from the author's commentary at the end, deals only with laws that came to fruition.

The Agency's Original Charter: Section 202 of the National Security Act of 1947

As described in chapter 1, the first DCI, Sidney Souers, at the end of his short tenure as head of the CIG, recommended that CIG seek independent statutory authority from the Congress. His successor, Hoyt Vandenberg, agreed and in the fall of 1946 set his legal staff to drafting a bill modeled on the Truman directive establishing the CIG. In addition to setting out functions for the Agency, the bill would include special enabling provisions (for example, the right to hire and fire personnel and the authority to protect sensitive information and the sources and methods used to collect it) to allow the agency to carry out its mission.[1] In late 1946, Vandenberg submitted the draft legislation to the White House for inclusion in the "merger" bill that was being drafted to unify the armed services.

While the White House was amenable to including language in the bill to establish a "central intelligence agency," Vandenberg was advised that the enabling provisions he had proposed would have to wait. "All but the slightest reference" to CIA had to be removed from the merger bill," the White House advised, "because the topic of intelligence and who should control it was too controversial."[2] The White House wanted nothing in the bill "which might in any way hamper the successful passage of the Act." Before the bill was sent over, CIG contacted members of Congress whose committees would likely handle the legislation and also advised them this was sound strategy.[3]

The draft legislation sent to the Congress by the Truman administration on 26 February 1947 contained a short section providing for the establishment of a central intelligence agency (hereafter, the CIA provision) that would operate under the supervision of the National Security Council, also created by the proposed law. It would be headed by a director of central intelligence, selected from the military or civilian sectors, and would inherit the "functions, personnel, property, and records" of the CIG.[4]

The bill was referred to the Armed Services Committee in the Senate and to the Committee on Expenditures in the House, which had jurisdiction over reorganizations within the executive branch. CIG immediately began working behind the scenes with friendly members of both committees to ensure passage of the legislation.[5]

For the most part, the proposal received a positive reaction from the Congress. Uncertainty and concern about Soviet expansionism in Eastern Europe and the Middle East were growing, and an organization like the CIA was seen as necessary to containing it. But passage of the CIA provision was far from

---

[1] CIA draft study, Vol. I, 9.

[2] Ibid., 10.

[3] Ibid., 11. Also see Pforzheimer interview, 9 July 1996, 94, referring to his conversation with Senator Gurney, then chairman of the SASC.

[4] CIA draft study, Vol. I, 11.

[5] Ibid., 11–12.

certain, as various elements worked behind the scenes to scuttle it. Even former OSS Director William Donovan, who had promoted the idea of a civilian intelligence agency to President Roosevelt but was left out of the postwar planning for such an organization, told Congress that responsibility for intelligence was best assigned to the Pentagon.[6] The State Department and heads of military intelligence organizations, fearing Congress might end or curtail their own capabilities if the new agency was created, also worked behind the scenes to oppose the CIA provision.[7]

In the end, however, their objections did not carry the day. Donovan's proposal was offered in the Senate but rejected, and under pressure from the White House, the Secretaries of State, War, and the Navy sent a letter to the Congress assuring it that they did not see the creation of CIA as impinging upon their own departmental intelligence capabilities. Indeed, Congress ultimately added language to the Truman proposal making clear that other departments and agencies could "continue to collect, evaluate, correlate, and disseminate departmental intelligence."[8]

Congress also made other changes to the bill submitted by the Truman administration, although none altered the original proposal significantly.

The Truman proposal had provided that the DCI could be appointed from the civilian or military sectors. Congress agreed with this but provided that the appointment be made with the "advice and consent" of the Senate. It also provided that any DCI selected from the military would have to sever all ties to the military, albeit without giving up commission, rank, or benefits.[9]

In the interest of minimizing controversy about the functions of the new agency, the Truman proposal had simply incorporated by reference the functions ascribed for CIG as they had been printed in the Federal Register of 22 January 1946. This prompted a specific objection, as well as more generalized concern, from various members. The specific objection involved the new agency's domestic activities. The CIG directive had prohibited it from exercising "police, law enforcement, or internal security powers," and certain members, some fearing the creation of "an American Gestapo," believed it was important to spell out this restriction into the statute rather than leaving it to an executive directive that might later be changed. Vandenberg readily agreed, and the House added language to the administration's proposal providing that "the Agency shall have no policy, subpoena, law-enforcement powers, or internal security functions."

---

[6] Ibid., 12.

[7] Ibid; Barrett, *CIA and Congress*, 10–19.

[8] Ibid., 14.

[9] Ibid., 16.

Congress throughout the deliberation continued to raise general concerns about relying on executive directive to spell out CIA's functions. "It should not be necessary," as one senator argued, "to go to an Executive order to interpret a statute." Another congressman warned that it would be dangerous to create an organization like the CIA on the basis of an executive directive "which could be changed, amended, or revoked or anything else at any time."[10] In the end, Congress set out the functions of the CIA within the statute itself, albeit without significantly altering the wording of the Truman directive.

The Agency would be charged by the law with advising the National Security Council (established pursuant to the Act) on intelligence matters and making recommendations with respect to the coordination of national intelligence activities. It would "correlate and evaluate" intelligence and ensure its "appropriate dissemination" within the government. The DCI would also be responsible for "protecting intelligence sources and methods from unauthorized disclosure."

Furthermore, the law authorized CIA to perform "such additional services of common concern as the National Security Council determines can be more efficiently accomplished centrally." At least the committees that handled the legislation understood this to mean that the CIA was authorized to engage in espionage activity abroad pursuant to extant NSC directives. CIA legislative liaison, Walter Pforzheimer later explained that the committees

> *didn't want the word "espionage" or "spy" or something on that order to appear in the law. They wanted us to do it quietly. They expected it to be done. . . . But they didn't want it in the law, or mentioned, or even breathed, in public. That's the way the atmosphere was then.*[11]

In other words, expressly authorizing CIA to conduct espionage was considered too impolitic at the time to place in a public statute.

The last function listed in the law gave CIA authority "to perform such other functions and duties related to intelligence affecting the national security as the National Security Council may from time to time direct." While there is no indication in the records of the Agency or from the proceedings in Congress that this language, at the time it was adopted, was intended to authorize what became known as "covert action," it later became the statutory basis for the Agency's undertaking such activity (see chapter 9).

---

[10] Ibid., 18.
[11] Pforzheimer interview, 9 July 1996, 117–18.

Congress ultimately enacted section 202 as part of the National Security Act of 1947 by voice vote, and President Truman delayed a trip to Missouri to visit his dying mother in order to sign it into law on 26 July 1947.[12]

The CIA Act of 1949

Almost immediately after passage of the law, CIA began seeking the "enabling" legislation that had earlier been put off to avoid controversy. In the fall of 1947, it presented the proposal to the Bureau of the Budget, which coordinated the administration's position on proposed legislation.[13]

Getting administration approval, however, took several months and thus limited the time for the bill's consideration during the next session of Congress. The Agency was able to get the SASC and HASC to hold closed hearings on the bill in the spring of 1948, where DCI Hillenkoetter, who had replaced Vandenberg, explained the need for the legislation:

> *It was thought, when we started back in 1946, that at least we would have time to develop this mature service over a period of years. . . . Unfortunately, the international situation has not allowed us the breathing space we might have liked, and, so, we present this bill, we find ourselves in operations up to our necks, and we need the authorities contained herein as a matter of urgency. . . . It is necessary to use funds for various covert or semi-covert operations and other purposes where it is impossible to conform with existing government procedures and regulations. . . . In many instances, it is necessary to make specific payments or reimbursements on a project basis where the background information is of such a sensitive nature from a security standpoint that only a general certificate, signed by the Director of the CIA, should be processed through even restricted channels.[14]*

The authority Hillenkoetter described as "urgent" was, in fact, the key feature of the proposed bill: the Agency would be able to expend funds without regard to the laws and regulations that governed the expenditure of government funds and, indeed, could account for those funds based solely on the certificate of the DCI. The administration's proposal would also allow the DCI,

---

[12] Barrett, *CIA and Congress*, 24. For a detailed account of the legislative process that led to the enactment of the CIA provisions of the National Security Act of 1947, see Troy, *Donovan and the CIA*, 365–402.

[13] CIA draft study, Vol. I, 20.

[14] Quoted in Barrett, *CIA and Congress*, 41.

"in furtherance of the national intelligence mission," to bring up to 50 aliens into the country and provide them with permanent resident status, as well as provide CIA with a number of other significant administrative authorities.

While CIA was able to get approval from the HASC for the bill in May 1948 and a favorable vote in the Senate in June, Congress adjourned for the political conventions in August without a vote in the full House. [15]

Determined to obtain the authority he deemed crucial to the Agency's operations, Hillenkoetter resubmitted the bill to Congress in February 1949. This time, the Agency prepared a detailed justification for each provision in the bill for its SASC and HASC subcommittees and was prepared to go into such detail as might be necessary to obtain their approval. Its concern proved unfounded, however, as the bill received prompt and favorable consideration from both committees. Indeed, CIA records do not indicate that either committee added amendments to the bill. Moreover, because the justification for the bill necessarily involved discussion of the Agency's operational needs, floor debate on the measure was minimal. While the chairmen of both the House and Senate Judiciary Committees raised an objection on the floor of each house, questioning the provision allowing the DCI to bring (now up to a 100) aliens into the country for permanent residence, neither of their objections proved decisive. [16] The Senate passed the bill unanimously; the House passed it 348–4.

Despite the limited consideration Congress gave to what became known as the CIA Act of 1949, it provided the Agency with significant authority to execute and protect its activities. In addition to the authority to bring up to 100 aliens into the country each year, the Agency was authorized to expend appropriated funds "for purposes necessary to carry out its functions . . . notwithstanding any other provision of law." This provision essentially exempted CIA from compliance with the myriad of "housekeeping" statutes that applied to other departments and agencies of the federal government and allowed it to establish its own personnel and pay systems. CIA could also now expend funds "for objects of a confidential, extraordinary, or emergency nature . . . solely on the certificate of the Director," allowing it to use its funds for espionage operations and covert action without having to account (to external auditors) for the expenditure of such funds other than having the DCI certify to their use for such purposes—again, authority not available to other departments and agencies. The Agency was also authorized to transfer and receive funds from other government agencies, allowing it, among other things, to hide its annual appropriation in the appropriations of other agencies. It was

---

[15] CIA draft study, Vol. I, 21–23.
[16] Ibid, 23–26; Barrett, *CIA and Congress*, 40–48.

also granted special procurement authority and exempted from laws that might require the disclosure of its organization, functions, or personnel. [17]

Additional Legislation: 1949–64

Not all of CIA's administrative needs were apparent at the time Congress considered the 1949 Act. In 1953, the Agency persuaded Congress to amend the 1947 statute to establish the post of deputy director of central intelligence and repeal a provision of the 1949 Act that had hindered its ability to pay salaries high enough to attract scientists to its employ. [18]

Then, in 1964, the Agency sought congressional approval for a special retirement system for employees with at least five years of service in overseas posts where their duties were considered hazardous. This initiative grew out of an Agency-conducted career development study, which had concluded CIA employees serving in such circumstances deserved at least the same benefits as their colleagues in the Foreign Service. Working virtually on his own, CIA legislative counsel John S. Warner managed to overcome the administration's resistance to the proposal and offered it to the CIA subcommittees of the SASC and HASC. After receiving a negative reaction by the SASC staffer assigned the legislation, Warner elevated the matter to DCI McCone, who met personally with the staffer to convince him of its importance to the Agency. This alone proved enough to overcome the staffer's opposition. On the HASC, the staff worried that Agency officers could qualify for the additional benefits, having served only in "plush" assignments, but Warner assured them this was not what was intended. To obtain their agreement, he offered to share with them the Agency's implementing regulations. On this basis, the proposal went through, without hearings or debate in either house. "It was trust," Warner later explained. "I really don't think [the committees] understood it, but they believed in us." [19] The law became known as the CIA Retirement Act of 1964, and authorized the creation of the CIA Retirement and Disability System (CIARDS).

The Foreign Intelligence Surveillance Act of 1978

Soon after its creation in 1976, the SSCI began developing detailed legislation to implement the Church Committee's recommendations to set forth for

---

[17] See 50 U.S.C. 403a *et seq.*
[18] CIA draft study, Vol. I, 39.
[19] Warner interviews, 2 November 1999, 83-87, and 9 October 1987, 5.

the first time in law what, in the words of a White House press release, intelligence agencies "may do and what they may not do."[20] Initially, CIA, as well as the newly installed Carter administration, endorsed the committee's effort and worked with it to develop a bill that both branches could support. In time, however, as the legislation became increasingly restrictive and burdensome to implement, CIA's concerns grew and the administration withdrew its support for key sections of the bill. By 1980, it was clear that the committee's effort to enact statutory "charters" for the intelligence agencies, including CIA, had failed.[21]

Earlier in the course of this three-year process, however, the SSCI and the Carter administration were able to reach agreement in principle on a particular aspect of the committee's legislative agenda: legislation to deal with the practice of warrantless electronic surveillances undertaken within the United States for foreign intelligence purposes. Rather than waiting for the denouement of the "charters" bill, the committee introduced the legislation in 1977 (largely developed by the Carter Justice Department) that embodied this agreement. Although responsibility for handling the bill in Congress ultimately passed to the Judiciary Committees on both sides (which had jurisdiction over wiretapping, as well as criminal statutes generally), what became the Foreign Intelligence Surveillance Act of 1978, or FISA, passed both houses with ease.

The new law purported to provide the exclusive procedure for conducting electronic surveillance within the United States for foreign intelligence purposes. It established a special court located at the Department of Justice, whose proceedings would be secret, to hear applications for warrants in such cases and established standards and criteria upon which such applications would be granted.

The law did not mention CIA per se and, given the limitations upon its activities within the United States, did not directly affect its activities. There was, however, an indirect effect. If the Agency wanted electronic surveillances to be carried out in the United States for foreign intelligence purposes—which it typically requested the FBI to conduct—from here on, any such request would have to meet the standards and criteria of the FISA. Notwithstanding, Agency records reflect its contentment with, and support for, the new law.[22]

---

[20] CIA draft study, Vol. II, 167.
[21] Ibid, 164–78; Smist, *Congress Oversees*, 123–27.
[22] CIA draft study, Vol. II. 168.

The Classified Information Procedures Act of 1980

The SSCI also developed legislation in conjunction with the Carter administration to address the problem the government had often encountered in prosecuting espionage cases. In dealing with what was known as the "graymail" problem, the government occasionally had to forgo prosecution of an espionage case because it did not want to reveal in open court the classified information that had allegedly been passed to an unauthorized person. The legislation Congress passed in 1980 provided a statutory procedure to govern the use of classified information by courts that were considering such prosecutions. From here on, the government would have the option of redacting sensitive information and/or substituting new characterizations of the information of concern, so long as the court agreed that a defendant's rights were sufficiently protected by the process.[23]

While the CIA was not specifically mentioned in this statute, it benefited from the legislation. From time to time the Agency had not prosecuted an employee under the espionage laws because of the "graymail" problem. Accordingly, it supported the committee's bill.

The Intelligence Identities Protection Act of 1982

More directly tied to the Agency's operations was the legislation passed in 1982 to make it a crime to expose its covert agents. In 1975, Richard Welch, the Agency's chief of station in Athens, was assassinated, his identity having been revealed by a former Agency officer, Philip Agee, in his magazine, *Counter Spy*. In the ensuring years, the Agency estimated that Agee and Louis Wolf, editor of a publication called the *Covert Action Information Bulletin*, had revealed the identity of more than a thousand CIA officers, endangering their lives and severely hampering Agency operations. Then-presidential candidate Ronald Reagan had made passage of legislation to deal with this intolerable situation a priority before his election. Once Reagan was elected, his choice for DCI, William Casey, worked with both intelligence committees to develop and pass such legislation.[24]

The new law made it a crime for persons having authorized access to information identifying a covert agent to deliberately disclose such information to an unauthorized person, if the person making the disclosure knew that the US government had taken "affirmative measures" to protect the identity of such

---

[23] *Classified Information Procedures Act*, Public Law 96-456, 15 October 1980.
[24] CIA draft study, Vol. III, 18–21.

covert agents. Persons violating the law were made subject to fines and/or imprisonment up to 10 years. [25]

Although some in the media criticized the legislation as violating the First Amendment guarantee of a free press, the bill passed both houses of Congress by overwhelming majorities. Agency records reflect that a ceremony was held at CIA Headquarters on 23 June 1982, where President Reagan signed the bill into law. [26]

Exemption from the Freedom of Information Act for CIA: 1984

In 1974, Congress had passed amendments to the Freedom of Information Act (FOIA) of 1967 that required agencies to search their records in response to a request from a member of the public, to identify such documents as may be responsive to the request and to provide such documents to the requestor so long as they did not fall into one of the nine categories exempted from disclosure. Although "properly classified" documents was one of the exemption categories, intelligence agencies, including the CIA, were not exempt from the Act per se and thus had to search their records, identify relevant documents, and determine whether they were "properly classified." Only then could they be withheld from the requestor. [27] President Ford vetoed these amendments at the urging of CIA and other agencies on the grounds that they interfered with his constitutional responsibilities, but Congress overrode his veto.

The Reagan administration, as part of its efforts to rebuild the Intelligence Community, had made relief from the FOIA a priority. In 1981, DDCI Bobby Inman appealed to Congress for a total exemption for the Agency. Casey went even further and asked for an exemption for all US intelligence agencies, noting that there was an inherent contradiction involved in applying a law designed to ensure openness to agencies whose work was necessarily secret. He went on to tell senators that CIA officers spent as much as 5 percent of their day on FOIA requests, often more time than they spent on any other single problem central to the Agency's mission. [28]

Both intelligence committees were receptive to providing the Agency with relief from the FOIA, but the idea of exempting it altogether drew severe opposition from historians, journalists, and the ACLU. This caused the Agency's legislative staff to begin looking, along with the staffs of the two committees, at

---

[25] See §601 of the *National Security Act of 1947*, as amended.

[26] CIA draft study, Vol. III, 21.

[27] See 5 U.S.C. 552.

[28] CIA draft study, Vol. III, 21–22.

ways acceptable legislation might be structured. Casey, however, continued to hold out for a total exemption for all intelligence agencies, contending the Act had harmed their relations with foreign intelligence services.[29]

By 1983, the likelihood of Casey getting the total exemption he sought for the CIA and other intelligence agencies appeared dim. To obtain something out of the long negotiations, CIA lawyers attempted to work out a compromise. Arguing that its operational records were rarely released because they were almost always found to be "properly classified" after review, the Agency's lawyers convinced the committees, as well as the ACLU, that if such records were exempt from review altogether, it would speed the processing of other, "nonoperational" records, such as analytical products, that were more likely to be disclosed in response to a request from the public. The elements of this compromise were incorporated into a bill that SSCI Chairman Goldwater introduced in June 1983 and ultimately became the basis for the CIA Information Act that was passed the following year, albeit after several bumps along the way.[30]

The CIA Inspector General Act of 1989

CIA, since 1952, had had an inspector general (IG) who was appointed by the DCI and served under his direction and supervision. When Congress passed the Inspector General Act of 1978 creating "independent" inspectors general in most departments and agencies, appointed by the president with special reporting obligations vis-à-vis the Congress, CIA had been exempted from the law.

Although the Church and Pike Committees, as well as the Rockefeller Commission, criticized the investigative competence of the Agency's IG in the mid-1970s, it was not until the 1987 report of the congressional committees investigating the Iran-contra affair that Congress was motivated to take up the issue. Noting that the CIA IG "did not appear to have the manpower, resources or tenacity to acquire key facts uncovered by other investigations," the Iran-contra committees recommended that CIA have an "independent," statutory IG like other departments and agencies of the executive branch.[31]

---

[29] Ibid.

[30] The House Government Operations Committee held up the bill for several months in the spring of 1984. The bill also encountered delays because of problems the Department of Justice and the Senate Judiciary Committee raised.

[31] *Report of the Congressional Committees Investigating the Iran-Contra Affair*, 425.

Although the leadership of both oversight committees (who were also members of the Iran-contra committee) had endorsed the IG recommendation as part of the Iran-contra committee's final report, none immediately moved to legislate on the subject. A member of the SSCI at the time, however, Arlen Specter introduced legislation calling for a statutory IG at the CIA and pressed for its consideration by the committee.

The DCI at the time, William Webster, adamantly opposed the idea, believing that an IG operating outside his control had the potential for wrecking the Agency. To head off possible legislation, Webster appointed a senior steering group to find ways to strengthen the capabilities of the existing IG. Later, in what was subsequently described as an effort to hold Senator Specter "at bay," the SSCI imposed a requirement that the IG provide semiannual reports of its activities to the committees in order that they might better evaluate the need for a "statutory" IG.[32]

In the fall of 1988, however, the chairman of the Senate Governmental Affairs Committee, John Glenn (D-OH), indicated he planned to offer legislation during the next session of Congress to bring the CIA IG under the Inspector General Act of 1978. If enacted, it would not only create greater independence from the DCI, it would also make the IG responsible to the governmental affairs committees of the Congress rather than the intelligence committees.

Fearing that such legislation would easily pass, the chairman of the SSCI, David L. Boren, offered legislation of his own in the spring of 1989. Under the Boren proposal, the Agency's "statutory" IG would have less independence from the DCI than IGs appointed under the 1978 Act had vis-à-vis their agency heads. Moreover, Boren's IG would report to the intelligence committees, not the governmental affairs committees in each house.

Glenn decided to support the Boren proposal rather than introduce his own on the condition that Boren would in good faith move the bill through the legislative process. Boren agreed and garnered enough support within the committee to report his legislation. On the Senate floor, it survived a motion to table it by a vote of 64 to 34.[33]

Obtaining the support of the HPSCI for the IG legislation in conference, however, was contingent upon obtaining assurance from the administration that the president would not veto the bill. This reportedly came in the form of

---

[32] For a detailed description of the background of this legislation, see Snider, "Creating a Statutory Inspector General at the CIA," 15–21.
[33] Ibid.

a telephone call from President Bush to Boren.[34] Although Webster had urged Bush to veto the bill, the president chose to sign the legislation.

The CIA would now have an IG appointed by the president and confirmed by the Senate, and who could only be removed by the president. The IG would report to, and be under the "general supervision" of, the DCI but would have authority to carry out investigations, audits, and inspections of his or her choosing. While the DCI, in order to "protect vital security interests of the United States," could stop the IG from undertaking any of these activities, the intelligence committees would be advised when this occurred. Moreover, the IG would make semiannual reports of his or her activities to the two committees and provide copies of other IG reports to the committees upon request.[35]

From the creation of the "statutory IG" in 1989 until 2004, on no occasion did a DCI block the IG from undertaking a proposed activity, thus triggering notice to the committees. The committees, however, often conducted follow-up inquiries into the reports they received from the IG and, on occasion, would request the IG to undertake investigations that exceeded their own capabilites.

The Intelligence Reorganization Act of 1992

With the Cold War drawing to a close and some in Congress—notably, former SSCI Vice Chairman Daniel P. Moynihan (D-NY)—suggesting that the Agency may no longer be needed, Boren believed the time was ripe for Congress to review the organization of the Intelligence Community in terms of meeting the demands of the post–Cold War environment. After an extended staff study in 1990–91, Boren and new HPSCI Chairman Dave McCurdy (D-OK) jointly offered a bill in early 1992 that, among other things, would have created a director of national intelligence (DNI), who would be separate from the director of the CIA and would have program and budget authority over the entire Intelligence Community. Analysis at the national level would be centralized in the National Intelligence Center under the DNI and would also have responsibility for coordinating intelligence-gathering across the board. Under the bill, CIA would have been confined to human intelligence-gathering and covert action.[36] In introducing the legislation, Boren acknowledged that the bill was meant to provoke discussion and that he was prepared to modify it in response to administration concerns.

---

[34] Smist, *Congress Oversees*, 277.

[35] §17 of the *CIA Act of 1949*.

[36] Smist, *Congress Oversees*, 286.

In April 1992, DCI Gates testified that the Bush administration could not support the Boren-McCurdy bill but was willing to work with the committees in terms of revising existing law (essentially the National Security Act of 1947) to reflect changes that had been made within the Intelligence Community.

Responding to this invitation, the SSCI dropped the more controversial, far-reaching elements of the original bill and produced a revised bill that set forth not only the responsibilities and authorities of the DCI vis-à-vis the rest of the Intelligence Community but also did the same for individual agencies within the Community, including the CIA. While the revised bill, for the most part, only reflected the organizational arrangements that had been instituted pursuant to executive orders and other executive branch policy, it nonetheless amplified and clarified these arrangements in far greater detail than existing law. The mission of the CIA, for example, would at last explicitly include gathering human intelligence and coordinating such collection within the executive branch. The DCI would also be responsible by law for foreign liaison in the intelligence area. Covert action would also be defined for the first time, and CIA's preeminent role in this area recognized. The DCI would also be given enhanced authority over the Community in the program and budget area, and the existence and functions of the National Reconnaissance Office (NRO) would, for the first time ever, be disclosed.

In late summer 1992, Gates advised the committees that with minor changes, the revised bill was acceptable to the Bush administration. Agreement was reached on these changes, and the Intelligence Reorganization Act of 1992 was enacted as part of the FY 1993 Intelligence Authorization Act without significant challenge in either house. In its report accompanying the bill, the SSCI described the new legislation as "providing, for the first time in law, a comprehensive statement of the responsibilities and authorities of the agencies and officials of the US Intelligence Community."[37]

Naming of the Headquarters Compound: 1998

In August 1998, the House passed freestanding legislation introduced by a congressman from Ohio who was not a member of the HPSCI, Rob Portman, to name the CIA headquarters compound after former President George H.W. Bush. The SSCI, in turn, incorporated a slightly modified version of the House bill into its mark-up of the Intelligence Authorization Act for Fiscal Year 1999, which was subsequently agreed to in conference with the HPSCI. Officially, the Agency took no position with respect to the proposal, leaving it

---

[37] See Title VII of the *Intelligence Authorization Act for Fiscal Year 1993*.

to Congress to decide. While several Democratic senators on the SSCI questioned the propriety of naming a nonpartisan institution after a politician (albeit a former DCI), their objections did not carry the day. With the enactment of the authorization bill, the Headquarters compound officially became known as the George Bush Center for Intelligence.[38] In a ceremony held at Agency Headquarters on 26 April 1999, with the former president in attendance, the compound was formally dedicated.

The Intelligence Reform and Terrorism Prevention Act of 2004

While Congress enacted minor changes to the CIA's mission and authorities in the aftermath of the 9/11 terrorist attacks,[39] it was not until 2004 that significant legislative change came about in response to the recommendations of the National Commission on Terrorist Attacks Upon the United States (the 9/11 Commission).

In its final report, issued in July 2004, the 9/11 Commission had made more than 40 recommendations to strengthen the ability of the United States to prevent future terrorist attacks. Principal among them were recommendations to reorganize the US Intelligence Community by creating a director of national intelligence (DNI) with expanded authority over the Community and a national counterterrorism center that would operate under his control. The DNI would assume two of the DCI's three functions under existing law: (1) head of the Intelligence Community (overseeing and directing the implementation of the National Intelligence Program) and (2) principal intelligence adviser to the president.[40]

The Agency, like the Bush administration itself, initially opposed these recommendations but soon found itself caught up in a fast-moving political process. The presidential election campaign of 2004 was in high gear. The Democratic nominee, Senator John Kerry of Massachusetts, had endorsed the 9/11 Commission's recommendations in toto and made them a key issue in the campaign. Families of the victims of 9/11 were pressing the administration and Congress to act on the commission's recommendations as a tribute to their loved ones.

---

[38] §309 of the *Intelligence Authorization Act for Fiscal Year 1999*.

[39] In 2002, for example, Congress mandated the creation of the Foreign Terrorist Asset Tracking Center within CIA to conduct all-source analysis relating to the financial capabilities, resources, and activities of international terrorists, as well as the creation of a master list of known or suspected terrorists for use within the Intelligence Community.

[40] 9/11 Commission Report, 399–413.

To inflame the political situation further, reports criticizing the Agency's performance with respect to the prewar intelligence assessments on Iraq emerged at roughly the same time as the 9/11 Commission report (see chapter 7). Cop ing with these criticisms (and demands for reform) was made doubly difficult for the Agency because its leadership was in flux at the time. DCI Tenet had resigned on 11 July; his replacement, Porter Goss, was not confirmed until 24 September 2004. As chairman of the HPSCI, in fact, Goss had previously been on record as supporting the creation of a DNI.[41]

In any event, the congressional leadership responded to the mounting pressure for intelligence reform by instituting a process in the fall of 2004 designed to develop legislation to implement the 9/11 Commission's recommendations. While the leaders of both intelligence committees had offered their own reform bills, the House and Senate leadership gave responsibility for developing this legislation to their respective governmental affairs committees. Even though the resolutions creating the intelligence committees specifically gave them jurisdiction over intelligence reorganizations[42] and both committees had exercised this role over their history, when it came time to produce a bill to implement the 9/11 Commission's recommendations, both committees were so torn by partisanship that it seemed doubtful they could work together to accomplish the objective (see the author's commentary at the end of chapter 2). The leadership in each house thus turned to other committees to produce the bill.[43] While the leaders of the HPSCI did eventually play instrumental roles, ultimately control of the House process rested with Speaker Dennis Hastert (R-IL). On the Senate side, the leaders of the SSCI offered suggestions to their colleagues on governmental affairs, but were relegated to minor roles in the legislative process.

Within the Bush administration, the White House itself served as focal point for dealing with the committees developing the legislation. "It soon became clear where things were going," former OCA deputy director, George Jameson, later recalled. "Our objective changed from trying to stop it [the reform bill] from happening to trying to salvage what we could get from the process."[44] While the Agency was able to obtain language in the bill preserving its key functional responsibilities, the political momentum for creating a director of national intelligence was not to be overcome. With its oversight committees in political disarray and disillusioned with the CIA's performance

---

[41] See the Report of the Joint Inquiry into the Terrorist Attacks of September 11, 2001, By the House Permanent Select Committee on Intelligence and the Senate Select Committee on Intelligence, 2002.

[42] See §11(b)(1) of Rule XXV of the House of Representatives and §3(a)(3) of S. Res. 400.

[43] Snider, "Congressional Oversight of Intelligence after September 11."

[44] Jameson interview, 28 December 2006.

on Iraq, the Agency lacked an effective defender—or even a sympathetic ear—in the congressional process. After Bush won a second term in November 2004, pundits speculated that he might have second thoughts about the intelligence reorganization bill, but several weeks after the election he intervened to break the congressional stalemate over the bill[45] and, in the waning days of 2004, signed into law what became known as the Intelligence Reform and Terrorism Prevention Act.

With its enactment, the position of DCI, established 58 years earlier, ceased to exist. The director of the Agency would now report to the DNI rather than the president. As far as the Agency's mission was concerned, the changes were minor. The new law carried over the language from existing law that pertained to its analytical and collection functions. The only substantive change was to combine the two general provisions pertaining to the Agency's functions into a single provision. Thus, the provisions in prior law authorizing the CIA "to perform such additional services . . . of common concern" as the DCI may determine, and "to perform such other functions and duties . . . as the President or National Security Council may direct" were replaced by a single provision authorizing the CIA to "perform such other functions and duties related to intelligence affecting the national security as the President or the Director of National Intelligence may direct."[46] The new law made no change to the CIA Act of 1949 or the Agency's other statutory authorities.

AUTHOR'S COMMENTARY

Legislating Missions and Authorities for the CIA

At the time CIA was created, members of Congress never seriously questioned the need for it or the need to set forth its missions and authorities in law. Except during the American Revolution, when the Continental Congress established three committees that ran intelligence operations, this had never happened before. Intelligence services of this and other countries had been creatures of their respective executive authorities, never their legislatures.

One of the difficulties in legislating the mission and authorities of an intelligence agency is, first of all, acknowledging to the rest of the world that your government is engaging in these kinds of activities. Hence, Congress was reluctant to acknowledge in 1947 that the CIA was being established to carry

---

[45] Sheenon, "Bush Says He'll Seek to Revive Intelligence Bill House Blocked."

[46] §104A(c) (4) of the *National Security Act of 1947*, as amended.

out espionage operations abroad. Rather it was authorized to perform "such services of common concern" as the National Security Council may direct. No mention at all was made in the law of CIA's covert action function until 1992, 44 years after the Agency undertook its first one.

Because it is difficult for Congress to deal with the missions and authorities of the Agency in public, historically it has been left to the committees that oversee the Agency to sort out behind closed doors what authorities it needs to carry out its functions. Moreover, when such authorities are agreed to, they are often expressed in such broad legislative language that their effect is unclear. Section 8 of the CIA Act of 1949, for example, authorized the Agency to spend its appropriated funds "for purposes necessary to carry out its functions . . . notwithstanding any other provision of law." Any member of Congress who read this language before his or her vote could only have wondered what this was meant to do. The accompanying reports rarely offered much clarification, nor could members expect to learn more in the floor debate. Typically, if such bills were debated at all, debate was limited to procedural points or "nonsensitive" aspects of the legislation. If members were truly concerned and intent upon knowing the reasons for the legislation, they might try confronting the sponsors of the bill off the floor, but in all likelihood, they would not be told a great deal, unless their support were crucial to passage of the bill.

This is why, from the Agency's standpoint, it is important that the parent bodies of the Congress—the House and Senate—have confidence in the Agency's oversight committees. If there is trust in the committees, their legislative recommendations will usually be supported when they are brought to the floor, regardless of the limited justification that usually can be provided

During the early period, from 1947 until the creation of the select committees, only the Agency's charter, embodied in a short section of the National Security Act of 1947, received much attention. Even here the principal interest was not so much in defining in law what the Agency was meant to do but in defining what it was not meant to do: engaging in domestic activities, usurping the departmental roles of other intelligence agencies, and so on. The legislation pertaining to the Agency that followed, including the CIA Act of 1949, passed virtually unnoticed by most of Congress and the public. It was handled in the CIA subcommittees, sometimes only by their staffs. While both sides were willing to make adjustments to the law to facilitate the Agency's work, neither side embarked on such a course without assessing the risks as well as the potential gains.

When the select committees were created in the mid-1970s, this dynamic changed somewhat. Both committees were given authority to report bills to the floor, and both were prepared to exercise this authority, not only to demonstrate to the intelligence agencies what they were capable of achieving but also to show they were reliable partners in the oversight process. Moreover, the annual intelligence authorization bills being developed and reported each year provided vehicles for legislative proposals that had not been there before. Getting free-standing bills through the congressional process was uncertain at best. Authorization bills, on the other hand, had to be put through. Not only did the bill give the committees an opportunity to legislate each year, it gave intelligence agencies an opportunity to request legislation if they chose to do so.

As the oversight committees began to mature in the early 1980s, the Agency, under DCI Casey, took advantage of these opportunities by persuading the committees to put through bills to protect the identity of its covert agents and provide relief from the FOIA. At the same time, the committees, with greater frequency, began legislating restrictions the Agency did not want, for example the two Boland amendments (see chapter 9).

As more legislation involving the Agency was put through, other lessons were learned. First, it may not be possible to control legislation once it is introduced and referred to committee. Deals may have to be struck and more may have to be said to explain the reasons for the bill than the Agency or the committees were prepared to offer, and at some juncture, it may not be worth the price. Both sides need to be prepared for such contingencies.

Second, if special treatment is sought for the CIA, such as perquisites and benefits not available to other departments and agencies, more objection is likely to be heard. Congress does not favor such proposals. Similarly, if other committees object to the bill, the harder it will be to put through the congressional mill. On the other hand, in following what Congress is doing for other departments and agencies, the Agency may sometimes see an opportunity to tack something on for itself. After 30 years of experience with the legislative process, the level of sophistication in the Agency as well as the oversight committees has grown. Both appreciate its opportunities and its pitfalls and adapt their strategies accordingly.

The President and Intelligence Legislation

The president occupies a unique position where intelligence legislation is concerned. Because intelligence lies so close to the exercise of the president's constitutional authorities as commander-in-chief and executor of US foreign policy, it is unlikely that there would ever be a two-thirds majority in both houses of Congress, necessary under the Constitution to override a presidential veto of an intelligence bill.

Over the 58-year period covered by this study, the president has vetoed an intelligence bill only twice and neither time was his veto overridden. The first occurred in 1991 when President Bush "pocket vetoed" the annual authorization bill because he became concerned that lawyers might read the bill's definition of "covert action" as precluding legitimate diplomatic activity, specifically, efforts to have other countries undertake actions in secret on behalf of the United States. The second occurred in 1998 when President Clinton, largely responding to press criticism, vetoed the intelligence authorization bill because it incorporated a provision criminalizing leaks of classified information whether or not intent to damage the national security could be proved.

In both cases, the intelligence committees had been assured before the bills were passed that the president would sign them. The reservations surfaced only after the bills were enacted. In neither case did the committees choose to bring the bills up for a vote to override the veto. In the case of the Bush veto, the committees modified the bill to remove the offending language and passed it the following year. In the case of the Clinton veto, there was still time in the session for the committees to drop the offending provision and put the authorization bill back through both houses.

The intelligence committees recognize, as a political fact of life, that no intelligence bill is apt to become law if the president objects. Thus, they do not normally include proposals in the annual authorization bill or attempt to move freestanding legislation that they know the president objects to. Occasionally, they might report such legislation to send a message to the administration, knowing that the provision is not likely to survive in conference. At other times they might be tempted to bundle what they know is an objectionable proposal with things they know a particular president wants, in order to make the veto decision more difficult. This has rarely been a compelling strategy, however, since there is usually little in intelligence bills that a president really wants.

Thus, for the Agency, the president has always represented something of a safety valve, where legislation is concerned. It knows the committees are reluctant to add provisions to their bills that the president objects to, and if such a thing does happen, there is always the possibility of a veto. But what the Agency cannot be sure of is whether a president's position necessarily will coincide with its own.

In the two cases mentioned above, when presidents exercised their veto power over intelligence legislation, it was not the Agency's objections that motivated them to act, but rather concerns raised in the White House after a bill was passed or outside the government.

There have also been at least three occasions when presidents signed legislation that the Agency objected to. In 1974, in order to obtain the financial assistance he wanted for Greece and Turkey, President Ford signed legislation containing the Hughes-Ryan Amendment, despite the Agency's strenuous objection to it.[47] In 1989, President Bush also signed legislation creating a statutory inspector general for the CIA over the Agency's objection. In 2004, the second President Bush signed the Intelligence Reform and Terrorism Prevention Act, also over the Agency's objection.

So, history shows that, depending upon the circumstances, intelligence legislation that the Agency does not object to can be vetoed and legislation that it does object to can be passed. The position of the president will always be pivotal.

What Never Made It Through the Congressional Mill

As far as the Agency is concerned, what never made it through the congressional mill may be just as important as what did make it through.

Over the years both the Agency and its congressional overseers—members and staff—have made a significant but largely unappreciated effort to keep legislation harmful to the Agency's interests from becoming law. Although both sides are mindful of the problem, the oversight committees have historically relied upon the Agency itself—whatever office is charged with handling congressional affairs—to monitor the legislation in both houses and alert the committees to bills, or amendments, that pose potential problems.

Once the Agency has identified a problem, a decision must be made on how it will be handled. If the oversight committee concerned is sympathetic, its staff (usually its legal counsel) will go the committee or member sponsoring the legislation, explain the problem, and request relief for the Agency in some form. This might entail specifically exempting the Agency from the reach of the legislation or modifying it to cure the problem of concern. Not infrequently, however, the Agency will find the oversight committees unsympathetic and unwilling to "use up their chips" with other committees or members, especially if they think the Agency is overreacting. If this happens, the Agency must decide whether to approach the other committee, or member, on its own or enlist the support of friendly members to take up its cause. Obviously, the Agency's case is stronger if one of its oversight committees vouches for it, but even in the absence of such support, it may see little downside in trying to deal with the problem, especially if it perceives that the legislation's sponsor did not intend the legislation to harm the Agency's interests.

---

[47] Cary interview, 24 November 1987, 34.

Whether it is the Agency or one of the oversight committees that takes the initiative, one or the other must decide what the sponsoring committee or member can be told. Inevitably, they will want to know why their proposal is a problem. Sometimes this can be easily explained but, on other occasions, may involve disclosing highly classified information. While sensitive details are avoided where they can be, if the committee or member refuses to accommodate, the Agency may be faced with revealing more information to get what it wants. Typically such issues are resolved at Agency headquarters, or, if one of the oversight committees is involved, in discussions between the Agency and the staff handling the issue.

If, in the end, the other committee, or individual member, refuses to provide the requested relief, the issue then becomes whether the Agency and/or the oversight committee should elevate. Informal means, such as talking to the leadership of the committee involved, would ordinarily be the first option. Failing that, formal amendments might be drawn up or offered, either in committee or on the floor, to take care of the problem.

Occasionally, the Agency and/or the intelligence committees learn of a troublesome amendment only as it is being offered or about to be offered on the floor. At this stage, members must be consulted, and, if they agree, primed to do battle against the proposal. There is often very little time to mount such a challenge.

If the offending language survives debate on the floor, as sometimes happens, the Agency and/or committee involved can try to have the problem resolved in conference. This would be attempted first at the staff level and, it that fails, at the conferee level. If this does not resolve the problem and it is truly serious, a presidential veto might be sought.

Although this informal, convoluted process has not always been able to prevent objectionable legislation from being enacted, hundreds, if not thousands, of legislative proposals that would have caused problems for the Agency, have been modified or shelved because of it.

CHAPTER 6

PROGRAM AND BUDGET

This chapter describes the interaction that has taken place between the CIA and Congress with respect to the Agency's program and budget during the period covered by this study.

The Agency continues to regard the amount of its prior-year appropriations (and related amounts), as well as the number of its employees at any point in time, as classified information. While figures purporting to represent these amounts or numbers have been published elsewhere, in the interest of maintaining this study at an unclassified level, figures are not used or even cited here. Rather, congressional actions on the Agency's budget and personnel are described in relative terms (as providing either more or less than they had before). The intent is not to describe all such fluctuations over the period but rather to highlight significant change and explain why it occurred.

The purpose of the chapter is to give the reader a sense of how Congress and the Agency have interacted with each other over the years with respect to the program and budget of the Agency, an area Congress, no matter what oversight arrangements were in place, had to act upon in order to provide funding for the Agency's ongoing operations.

The Transition from CIG to CIA: 1946–47

After being created by presidential directive in 1946, the CIG found itself (as an agency expected to last more than a year) obligated by law to seek its own appropriation from Congress. While the Truman administration had agreed to include provisions establishing it as the "Central Intelligence Agency" in drafts of what became the National Security Act of 1947, the CIG could not know for certain that such legislation would be adopted. Thus, to cover itself, in the spring of 1947 CIG sought and obtained its own appropriation from the Congress. Although its funding, per the Truman directive, was to come from the Departments of State, War, and the Navy, CIG had to identify the amounts involved in each departmental budget to the congressional appropriations committees.

According to CIA records, DCI Vandenberg worried at the time that the newly elected 80th Congress, now under the control of a Republican Party touting fiscal restraint, might choose to cut the CIG budget. To prevent this and to reduce the number of members given access to CIG budget information, he approached the chairmen of both appropriations committees—Representative John Tabor (R-NY) and Senator Styles Bridges (R-NH)—and requested they set up small, ad hoc subcommittees to handle the CIG's budget. Both did so. In the HAC, at least one member complained about the CIG's funds being spread over three agencies, believing they should be "in one lump sum in one place in the budget," but nothing appears to have come of this complaint. In the SAC, the eight-member subcommittee created to hear the CIG's request posed no questions concerning its funding and, according to a CIG memorandum for the record, registered its "general approval of the activities of the Group."[1]

What was then appropriated for the CIG in 1947 (for FY 1948) became the first appropriation for the newly created CIA. Section 102(f) (2) of the National Security Act of 1947 provided that "any unexpended balances of appropriations [for the CIG] . . . shall be available and shall be authorized to be made available in like manner for expenditure by the [Central Intelligence] Agency."

Section 307 of the 1947 Act also provided a continuing authorization for the appropriation of "such sums as may be necessary and appropriate to carry out the provisions and purposes of the Act." This was interpreted as obviating the need for an annual authorization for the CIA, requiring it to get from Congress each year only an appropriation.[2]

The process that was instituted to secure that appropriation began each year with a classified letter from the Bureau of the Budget (predecessor of the Office of Management and Budget) to the two appropriations committees, with a copy going to the CIA, setting forth the administration's appropriations request for the Agency for the year. The letter would state that so much money for the Agency had been set aside within particular accounts within the budget requests of the department or agency where the Agency's funding was "hidden." At the end of the appropriations process, the appropriations committees would send a letter back to the Bureau of the Budget setting forth how much had actually been appropriated for the CIA in the budgetary accounts of other agencies. From time to time, the letter might also include restrictions on the use of such funds. "That letter [from the appropriations committees to the

---

[1] CIA draft study, Vol. I, 7.
[2] Cary interview, 30 September 1983, 10.

Bureau of the Budget], in essence, was the appropriations act as far as the CIA was concerned," according to a one-time legislative counsel.[3] This procedure lasted until creation of the two select committees in the mid-1970s.

Covert Action: Funding a New Mission for the Agency

Less than a year after the National Security Act of 1947 was enacted, the Truman administration, confronted with the threat of communists coming to power in the Italian elections, decided to use the CIA to channel support to the noncommunist parties opposing them. The CIA general counsel at the time, Lawrence Houston, had opined several months earlier that the appropriations committees had not had this kind of activity in mind when they approved the Agency's appropriation and thus would need to be informed of and approve the expenditure of appropriated funds for such purposes.[4] There was also realization within the administration that Congress would have to be approached with respect to this new kind of activity.[5]

Although personally unenthusiastic about this new mission on the grounds it would detract from the Agency's other functions, DCI Hillenkoetter appeared in April 1948 before the HASC subcommittee to describe what would be necessary to support "any possible action in connection with the Italian election."[6] In all likelihood, he made the same presentation to the leaders of the SASC, HAC and SAC.

Several weeks later, in mid-June 1948, Truman signed National Security Council Directive 10/2, authorizing a program of "covert operations" by the US government. It provided that such operations would be carried out so that if they were uncovered

> *the US government can plausibly disclaim any responsibility for them. Specifically, such operations shall include any covert activities related to propaganda; preventive direct action, including sabotage, anti-sabotage, demolition and evacuation measures; subversion against hostile states, including assistance to underground resistance movements, guerrillas and refugee liberation groups, and support of indigenous anti-communist elements in threatened countries of the free world.[7]*

---

[3] Warner interview, 27 September 1996, 30.
[4] Barrett, *CIA and Congress*, 29; see also Braden, "The Birth of the CIA."
[5] Barrett, *CIA and Congress*, 28–29.
[6] Ibid., 30.
[7] Ibid., 32.

The directive created an Office of Policy Coordination (OPC) that would have primary responsibility for carrying out these operations and assigned it to the CIA for administrative purposes. OPC would report, however, to the Secretaries of State and Defense, as well as to the DCI. The directive also provided that a supplemental appropriation would be "immediately requested" from the Congress to fund the activities of OPC.[8]

There are no records indicating what happened in response to this direction from the president as far as the Congress was concerned, but it can be presumed that at least the leaders of the HAC and SAC were made aware of NSC 10/2 and that they provided the wherewithal for OPC to begin operations, either by providing a supplemental appropriation or by approving the use of already appropriated funds for this purpose. As described by Professor Barrett, there was, in fact, increasing and widespread support in Congress at the time to do something to counter what was perceived as growing Soviet influence around the world.[9] NSC 10/2 authorized precisely this kind of response by the United States. The fact that this kind of activity had not been envisioned a year earlier when CIA was created seems not to have mattered to the Congress. The new mission fit with the Agency's other operational responsibilities. The State Department was the only other department or agency that conceivably might have offered a platform for such activities, but they were seen at odds with its diplomatic responsibilities.

Interaction in the Early Years: 1948–52

According to Barrett, the Agency received a 25-percent increase for FY 1949—its second year of operation and its first appropriation as the CIA.[10] This trend was to continue for its first four years of operation. Indeed, the Agency experienced exponential growth during this period. Barrett notes that the budget requested for the Agency in 1952 (for FY 1953) was 14 times the size of its budget for FY 1948. To a large extent, these increases were the result of the war in the Korea. Covert action, both in support of the war effort and in other places, was also burgeoning during this period (see chapter 9). According to Barrett, 74 percent of the Agency's budget for FY 1953 was devoted to operational activities, and the lion's share of that (75 percent) went to covert action.[11]

---

[8] Ibid.
[9] Ibid, 30–32.
[10] Ibid., 120.
[11] Ibid., 92, 102.

Knowledge of the Agency's budget within Congress was extremely limited during this early period. Only the HAC chairman knew what the CIA's budget actually was and where it was located in the budgets of other agencies. Moreover, only three staffers, one in the House and one each on the SASC and SAC, were privy to this information.[12] These staffers ensured that the funding requested each year for the Agency was included in nondescript line-items within the appropriations of the Defense and State Departments.

Agency records do reflect that in 1950 it faced the possibility of a cut to its budget as part of government-wide cutbacks. In fact, its legislative counsel, Walter L. Pforzheimer, made sure the HAC knew where CIA funding was hidden in the State and Defense Departments budgets so the committee would not inadvertently cut it when it took action on those budgets. While the Agency did experience a token cut that year, notwithstanding Pforzheimer's efforts, it managed to have the funds restored as part of a supplemental appropriation to fund the Korean War effort.[13]

Having its funds hidden within the appropriations of other agencies, in particular the appropriation of the State Department, was not without its complications. In 1951, for example, CIA received a request to testify before the SAC subcommittee that handled State Department appropriations to defend the amount being requested for Agency activities. Concerned that the Agency might have to open its operations to a wider audience (than its SAC subcommittee), Pforzheimer managed to convince the subcommittee chairman to withdraw his request in return for a briefing from DCI Smith.[14] What happened instead was that Smith met with two senators on the SAC, who, in turn, convinced the SAC chairman that hearings on the CIA's budget request were undesirable because of the security risks. Indeed, CIA records reflect the full committee ultimately approved the State Department appropriation (with CIA's appropriation buried within) without pressing for a formal hearing with the DCI.[15]

Afterwards, a senator on the SAC suggested to Pforzheimer that having part of the Agency's funding in the State Department appropriation might not be such a good idea inasmuch as the State appropriation was more susceptible to being cut (in response to Senator McCarthy's tirades and for other reasons) than the defense budget. He suggested that CIA ought to look at locating all of its funding within the Defense Department budget to guard against the possibility that its own budget might be inadvertently cut, requiring it to come back

---

[12] Ibid., 27, 119.
[13] CIA draft study, Vol. I, 71–72.
[14] Ibid.
[15] Ibid.

to the State appropriations subcommittee again for relief. Pforzheimer took the advice to heart and began working with the Bureau of the Budget to put all of the Agency's budget within the DoD budget. This new practice was instituted, in fact, the following year.[16]

Also in 1951, as part of their action on the Agency's FY 1952 budget request, the appropriations committees for the first time created as part of the Agency's annual appropriation an "unvouchered Contingency Reserve Fund," intended to allow the DCI to address "unforeseen emergencies" around the world. While this fund was intended principally to fund covert action, allowing the Agency to take advantage of opportunities to thwart communism around the world without the necessity of coming back to Congress for a new appropriation, it was also available to fund unforeseen opportunities on the collection side. Initial funding for the development of the U-2 reconnaissance aircraft, for example, came from the reserve fund.[17] The appropriations committees would establish each year the amount to be appropriated for the reserve. Approval was required from the Bureau of the Budget in order to withdraw money from it, and the committees expected the DCI to advise them when large amounts were withdrawn. If the money allocated to the reserve was not spent, it would be carried over to the next year's budget. Within a very short time, the reserve fund became a significant part of the Agency's annual appropriation. Indeed, according to Barrett, DCI Smith requested an increase in the reserve fund for FY 1953 that he said would be three times what the Agency was spending for its intelligence-gathering activities.[18]

Also, late in the summer of 1951, wholly apart from what the CIA subcommittees were doing, Congress adopted an amendment to the Mutual Security Act, which authorized up to $100 million appropriated by the Act to be used for what was essentially covert action. The amendment was offered by a Republican congressman from Milwaukee, Charles Kersten, who was on neither the HAC nor the HASC but was concerned that the United States was not doing enough to subvert the Soviet Union and its East European allies.[19] The Act itself authorized $7.5 billion in foreign economic and military aid. Kersten's amendment allowed up to $100 million of this to be allocated to "underground liberation groups in communist countries." The adoption of the amendment by Congress immediately brought on protests in the United Nations from the Soviet foreign minister and other communist bloc officials.[20]

---

[16] Barrett, *CIA and Congress*, 120.
[17] CIA draft study, Vol. II, 18.
[18] Barrett, *CIA and Congress*, 121.
[19] Ibid., 103–12.
[20] Ibid.

The matter did not end there, however. In March 1952, then-DDCI Dulles was summoned before the HFAC to explain how much, if any, of the $100 million had been spent. He told the committee that none had been spent and, moreover, that CIA itself did not need any of it. Instead, he proposed that $4.3 million of the $100 million be given to the State Department to construct "reception facilities" to take care of defectors from the Soviet Union and Eastern Europe, which he said would serve the Agency's interests in important ways, whatever use might be ultimately made of these people. Kersten himself agreed with Dulles's suggestion, believing such facilities could be used to build "an army of liberation." These comments, which the Soviets saw as an attempt to create military forces to invade and overthrow communist countries, brought on renewed criticism from the Soviet bloc as well as from some in Congress. The committee ultimately approved use of the $4.3 million for "refugee handling," but it is unclear whether such funds were ever expended for this purpose.[21]

Interaction during the Eisenhower Years: 1953–60

The Eisenhower administration came to office in 1953, demanding fiscal discipline from federal agencies. CIA was not exempt from this policy; indeed, when Eisenhower took control of the White House he personally emphasized to DCI Dulles his determination on this point.[22]

Republicans also took control of the Congress in 1953, and CIA came under the first serious budget oversight from any of its subcommittees up to that point. The HAC subcommittee—now made up of the five most senior members of the full committee and chaired by John Tabor of New York—held five meetings with CIA officials in early 1953 and 10 in first half of 1954. Tabor also expanded his staff to include five professionals, which for the first time gave the subcommittee an ability to do its own independent review of the Agency's budget.[23] They demanded not only that the Agency provide a detailed justification for the budget but also that they be allowed to keep it until they were done with it.[24] At other times HAC staff members were allowed to review budget books at the Agency itself.[25]

Tabor's counterpart on the SAC subcommittee, Styles Bridges, also took a hard line on government spending. His committee imposed an across-the-

[21] Ibid.
[22] Ibid., 149.
[23] Ibid., 150–51.
[24] Ibid., 152.
[25] Warner interview, 2 November 1997, 71.

board cut of 27 percent for FY 1954 on all government agencies, including the CIA. It was only after extensive lobbying by DCI Smith after the SAC had acted, that the HAC agreed to hold the Agency's cut to 15 percent. (The SAC went along in conference.)[26]

The cuts taken by the appropriators and their increased level of budget oversight worried the SASC subcommittee. Its members expressed "grave concern" to the SAC in 1954 over the amount of detail the HAC was demanding from the CIA and urged the SAC to designate "as small a group as possible" to review the CIA's budget request for FY 1955.[27] As it happened, the SAC subcommittee was already composed of just five members, two of whom (Russell and Saltonstall) were also members of the SASC subcommittee, so it was hardly necessary to suggest that the number be kept small. More likely, the SASC members were concerned about SAC Chairman Bridges, who had not shown himself to be particularly accommodating to the Agency's interests.

Apparently, their intervention had an impact. When the SAC subcommittee met on the Agency's FY 1955 budget request, according to a CIA memorandum of the meeting, it was approved with very little discussion. Dulles had brought detailed budget data with him, the memo noted, but never had to refer to it: "Most of the session was devoted to questions and answers on matters that appeared to be of particular interest to the senators, many of which had no particular relation to the CIA budget."[28]

The Tabor subcommittee, however, continued to take a tough line where the Agency was concerned. For the first time, the HAC imposed a personnel ceiling on CIA, holding it to the number of employees it had on 30 June 1954. Moreover, it refused to go along with the "plus up" agreed to by the SAC, to make up for the 15-percent cut taken the year before. According to notes of the legislators involved, the budget at that point was allocated as follows:

intelligence	29 percent
Cold War activities (covert action)	40 percent
Contingency Reserve	26 percent
administration	6 percent[29]

In 1955, Democrats regained control of both houses of Congress, which they would retain for the remainder of the Eisenhower presidency. While the new chairmen of the SAC and HAC—Carl Hayden and Clarence Cannon,

---

[26] CIA draft study, Vol. I, 72–73.

[27] Ibid., 73.

[28] Ibid.

[29] Barrett, *CIA and Congress*, 154–55.

respectively—were far less interested in holding down the Agency's spending than their predecessors, the Agency often found it exasperatingly difficult to engage with them.

Although its FY 1956 appropriation remained relatively flat, for the first time it had 20 percent of the Agency's funding going to "science," reflecting the new responsibilities the administration had given it, among them the development and construction of the U-2 reconnaissance aircraft, as well as the growth of its in-house technical capabilities (see chapter 8).[30] Although few members of Congress were aware of the Agency's new responsibilities in this area, the leaders of the CIA subcommittees and their respective staffs, made certain the money was appropriated for them. The Agency's FY 1957 budget grew overall by 20 percent, albeit with a significant decline in "Cold War activities."

Senator Carl Hayden, chairman of the Senate Appropriations Committee.

(US Senate Historical Collection)

In 1957, SAC Chairman Hayden told the Agency he was too busy to hear its FY 1958 budget request, leaving it to his staff instead. According to an Agency memo of the staff briefing, "there were no questions raised of any substance."[31] After the committee had reported the bill that contained the Agency's funding, Dulles again sought to have Hayden hold a hearing before the floor vote, but Hayden told him he was "not at all enthusiastic about a meeting, [and] inasmuch as we had our money, there wasn't any need to get together."[32] Dulles fared no better in the House. The HAC also held no hearings before it acted. Dulles gave George Mahon (chairman of the defense appropriations subcommittee) information to use in case he got a question about CIA's funding on the floor, but he got none. After the House vote, Dulles did manage to get Mahon to hold an "after-the-fact" hearing, but

---

[30] Ibid, 219–20.

[31] CIA draft study, Vol. I, 74.

[32] Ibid.

according to a CIA memorandum of the hearing, the session was "devoted mainly to . . . our substantive operations around the world. . . . There was little detailed discussion of the items in our budget."[33]

In 1958, Dulles was accorded an early hearing with the HAC subcommittee, but according to his memo of the meeting, the only question he received regarding the budget was an inquiry from the chairman whether he had enough money.[34] CIA Legislative Counsel John Warner's account was considerably more descriptive:

> *I was called by* [HAC chairman] *Clarence Cannon's staffer and advised that Cannon wanted to have a budget hearing with the DCI on a Sunday afternoon in a special room in the Longworth Building. . . . It was a crowded room, and Clarence Cannon greets Dulles, "Oh, it's good to see you, Mr. Secretary." He thinks it's* [Secretary of State John] *Foster Dulles . . . or else mistakes his name..*

> *They swap stores for two hours, and in the end,* [Cannon asks] *"Well, Mr. Secretary, have you got enough money in your budget for . . . the coming year?"*

> *"Well, I think we'll be all right, Mr. Chairman. Thank you very much."*

> *That was the budget hearing.* [The other congressmen present] *were visibly disturbed by this. . . . So I pulled the three of them aside and I said, "Gentlemen, would you like me to arrange a briefing . . . for you on our budget?" They all thanked me. And we did it, obviously without telling the Chairman.*[35]

Cannon was also fond of calling his subcommittee together on the spur of the moment. Former Executive Director "Red" White recalled one such meeting:

> *Dulles called me on Sunday morning and said he just got a call from Clarence Cannon, "He wants to have a budget hearing at 2:00 this afternoon. Can we do that?"*

> *And I said, "Mr. Dulles, if that's what Mr. Cannon wants, we can do it."*

> *That was his* [Cannon's] *idea. . . . He'd call the rest of the committee members and say, "Come off the golf course." . . . And they'd be there.*

---

[33] Ibid.
[34] Ibid, 75.
[35] Warner interview, 27 September 1996, 22.

He'd say [to Dulles], *"I don't want you taking up my time with a lot of stuff I'm going to read in the newspaper tomorrow, but I don't want you holding out anything on me, either."*

We'd tell him anything he wanted to know. He wouldn't give us a rough time, but he didn't give us carte blanche [either]. . . . *Year after year* [though] *we got just about what we asked for.*[36]

Notwithstanding Cannon's support for the Agency's annual budget request, when Dulles broached with him in late 1958 the idea of building a residence for the DCI along the banks of the Potomac, Cannon reacted negatively, causing Dulles to give up the idea.[37] Cannon's staff also told the Agency's liaison later in the year that Cannon thought at times that the Agency was "hiding behind a cloak of secrecy and [he] was getting tired of it." When Dulles followed up with Cannon personally, Cannon raised the possibility of putting a member of the HAC staff inside CIA, having CIA provide weekly written briefings, and having it regularly brief the full committee. Dulles was reluctant to agree to any of these ideas but told Cannon that he was prepared to brief the CIA subcommittee whenever Cannon wanted it and later made the same offer to the HASC, SASC, and SAC subcommittee chairmen.[38]

The Agency had a similar experience in the Senate that year. There was but one meeting of its subcommittees, a joint meeting of the SAC and SASC subcommittees that occurred in Russell's office in August. According to a CIA memorandum, the meeting was "completely off the record. No transcript . . . covered the world situation in considerable detail. . . . The Senators appeared to be impressed with the informa-

Representative Clarence Cannon, chairman of the House Appropriations Committee.

(Portrait by Charles J. Fox, Collection of the US House of Representatives.)

---

[36] White interview, 7 January 1998, 37.

[37] Barrett, *CIA and Congress*, 317.

[38] CIA draft study, Vol. I, 68–69.

tion given them." There were no questions about CIA operations, tactics, or finances.[39]

Despite the senators' seeming lack of interest in probing Agency operations, word filtered down from Senate staff that there was discontent among its members. In September 1958, an aide to Senator Bridges, now a member of the SAC subcommittee, reported there was considerable criticism of the CIA within Congress that was fueling "a serious move" to cut its appropriations in the next session. Alarmed by this report, Dulles appealed to the leaders of the SASC (Russell) and SAC (Hayden) when Congress reconvened in January 1959 to hold an early joint hearing on the Agency's FY 1960 budget request. Hayden bluntly refused, explaining that he was too occupied with other business. He also pointed out to Dulles that he had met with him about it the year before.[40] Dulles then turned to the ranking member of the SAC, Senator Saltonstall, appealing for "just five minutes before the budget bill [containing the funding for CIA] was marked up," but Saltonstall was unwilling to broach the issue with Hayden.[41] In September, Dulles tried again, this time with SASC Chairman Russell, to schedule a joint meeting on the Agency's budget, but Russell told him that he was "so tied up with other matters" that it would be impossible to schedule during the balance of the year. When CIA Legislative Counsel Warner later lamented to Senator Stennis how much difficulty the Agency was having in scheduling a hearing on its budget, Stennis expressed surprise that the SASC even had a subcommittee on the CIA.[42]

Ultimately that year, despite the lack of substantive consideration on either side, the subcommittees put through an appropriation for FY 1960 that called for limited personnel cuts, consistent with what the parent committees did generally that year vis-à-vis federal agencies.

The Agency Headquarters Building: 1951–56

Four years after its creation, the Agency's headquarters was located in several antiquated buildings at 2430 E Street in Washington DC and its employees scattered among a dozen or more other buildings in the area. This situation concerned DCI Smith, who in 1951 won administration approval to request $38 million from Congress for a new headquarters building. Smith, however, failed to advise the chairman of the HAC's defense subcommittee, George Mahon, in advance of the request, and Mahon demonstrated his displeasure by failing to

---

[39] Ibid., 63.
[40] Ibid., 76.
[41] Ibid. 77.
[42] Ibid, 69.

act on it. While the SAC approved the proposal, without HAC concurrence, it did not go through. Smith tried again the following year, this time requesting $42 million, but Mahon persuaded him not to pursue it on the grounds that the political climate in Congress was not ripe for its consideration.[43]

When the Democrats (who were seen as less concerned with fiscal restraint) regained control of the Congress in 1955, the time appeared ripe to Dulles to raise the issue once again. By this point, Agency employees were scattered among 34 separate locations in the Washington area. The fact that the request was large (now $50 million) as well as extraordinary, however, dictated its being handled by the military construction subcommittees of the Armed Services and Appropriations Committees rather than the CIA subcommittees, and this brought many more members of both houses into the picture. In a 17 June hearing before the full SASC, several senators who were not on the CIA subcommittee expressed shock at how large the Agency had grown. "The number is fantastic," Senator Margaret Chase Smith commented. "I believe those fellows must be getting in each other's way."[44]

At the comparable hearing before the HASC, Chairman Carl Vinson began by announcing his support for the building but did not quite seem to understand the scale of the project. Addressing Dulles, he said, "Doctor, you are here to ask for a new building, and I think you ought to have a new building. . . . You probably are going to ask us for about $25 million." Dulles replied that, no, he was going to ask for $50 million, prompting Vinson to respond, "My, my, that is going to be a nice building."[45]

Ultimately, Dulles managed to get the HASC and SASC to authorize $46 million for the building, but the appropriators would approve only $5.5 million for planning purposes. Thus, Dulles had to go back again the following year. This time, he requested an additional $56 million to complete the project, which would include not only the purchase of land and the construction of a headquarters building but also the extension of the George Washington Memorial Parkway to reach the entrance to the property. The HAC ultimately went along with $50 million and the SAC, with $46 million, albeit with a limitation that all CIA employees had to be housed there. In conference, the committees appropriated $46 million, and CIA pledged to make "a good faith effort" to house as many of its employees there as possible.[46]

---

[43] Barrett, *CIA and Congress*, 122.
[44] Ibid., 217.
[45] Ibid., 216.
[46] Ibid., 217–19.

Work on the project began in October 1957 and was not entirely completed until November 1963, although Agency employees had begun to occupy parts of the building as early as September 1961.[47]

Developments in the 1960s and Early 1970s

The CIA subcommittees remained generally friendly to the Agency during the 1960s and early 1970s, often supporting its annual budget requests without change, but their review of the budget, especially on the House side, became increasingly thorough and more contentious.

In early 1960, the HAC subcommittee, chaired by Clarence Cannon, in particular, began subjecting the Agency to a far more rigorous budget examination than it had experienced to that point. When Cannon summoned DCI Dulles to appear before the subcommittee to discuss the budget, he told him not to bother with "fancy briefing charts," but to come prepared to "get down to discussing sensitive facts and matters," warning him that he would "catch hell" if he tried to withhold pertinent information. Dulles, in fact, appeared before the HAC subcommittee for seven hours on 28 March 1960; he provided details on the Agency's budget, discussed how the Agency's expenditures were justified by its operations around the world, and fielded probing questions about the Agency's personnel strengths. According to CIA records, it was the most thorough exploration of the Agency's budget request that one of its subcommittees had ever conducted.[48] CIA General Counsel Lawrence Houston later described the briefing:

> *Our appropriations were gone over as thoroughly as any appropriation. Cannon established that we would bring to him any detail and he would question or have the committee question us. They knew our appropriations, line by line. Sure, they were hidden in the defense budget, but to get in there they had to pass the committee.*[49]

Dulles, in his 1963 book on intelligence, also commented on Cannon's tenacity, writing that "a more careful watchdog of the public treasury can hardly be found." Calling the public perception that Congress exercised no control of the Agency "quite mistaken," Dulles said Congress's power of the purse effectively gave it "control over [Agency] operations—how many people CIA can employ, how much it can do and to some extent what it can do."[50]

---

[47] Knapp, *The First Thirty Years*, 133–45.
[48] CIA draft study, Vol. I, 111.
[49] Ranelagh, *The Agency*, 282–83.
[50] Dulles, *The Craft of Intelligence*, 261.

However tenacious Cannon may have been as a budget overseer, he was still a strong defender of the Agency in public. Speaking several weeks later on the House floor, after the shoot-down of the U-2 over the Soviet Union on 1 May 1960, Cannon defended not only the Agency's operation, but his subcommittee's role in funding it:

> *The [U-2] was on an espionage mission authorized and supported by money provided under an appropriation recommended by the House Committee on Appropriations and passed by the Congress. Although the members of the House have not generally been informed on the subject, the mission was one of a series and part of an established program with which the subcommittee in charge of the appropriation was familiar, and of which it has been fully apprised during this and previous sessions. . . . The question immediately arises as to the authority of the subcommittee to recommend an appropriation for such purposes, and especially the failure of the subcommittee to divulge to the House and the country, the justifications warranting the expenditure . . . at the time it was under consideration on the floor. The answer of the subcommittee [to that question] is: absolute and unavoidable military necessity, fundamental national defense.*[51]

At the end of Cannon's speech, members on both sides of the aisle rose to their feet to give him a standing ovation. It was the first time that a chair of one of the House subcommittees had ever defended the funding arrangements for the CIA's activities on the House floor.

The following year the HAC subcommittee conducted another rigorous review of Agency's FY 1962 budget request, but in the end, as it had done the year before, the subcommittee approved what the Agency had requested, even asking DCI Dulles (as it was wont to do) if the amount being requested was enough. It also authorized the Agency, at Dulles's request, to carry over unused amounts in the Contingency Reserve to the next fiscal year without securing congressional approval.[52]

It is clear, though, that even though the HAC ended up supporting its budget requests, the Agency did not take Cannon's support for granted. When John McCone became DCI in 1962, Legislative Counsel Warner wrote him on the need to deal with Cannon:

> *There would be serious disadvantages if the DCI were not to appear before him and the subcommittee in connection with our*

---

[51] Barrett, *CIA and Congress*, 395.
[52] CIA draft study, Vol. I, 112.

> *budget presentation. . . . Mr. Cannon has been heard to say in effect, "If an agency head is not sufficiently interested in his appropriation to appear personally to defend it, maybe he does not need an appropriation."* [53]

McCone obliged, and the Cannon subcommittee once again supported the administration's request without change.

While budget oversight was less rigorous on the Senate side, there were joint hearings in 1961 and 1962 before the SAC and SASC subcommittees during which the members, according to CIA records, asked probing questions. At this juncture, however, Senator Russell chaired both subcommittees, and the total number of senators on both committees was only six. Moreover, two of them—Carl Hayden (D-AZ) and Harry F. Byrd (D-VA)—rarely attended. Like the HAC, the two subcommittees supported the budget requests during these years without change. [54]

In 1963, a funding issue arose with the Defense Department. The Pentagon wanted the Agency to assume responsibility for funding a program in Southeast Asia that DoD had been funding at a cost of $75 million. To accomplish this, CIA requested, with administration approval, that $75 million be added to its budget for FY 1964, in effect having it transferred out of the DoD budget. The Pentagon, however, asked that Congress provide an additional $75 million to its budget to make up for the amount transferred to the CIA. While the conferees on the defense appropriations bill added $13.3 million to the defense budget to help absorb the loss, Congress adjourned without actually appropriating the additional $75 million to the Agency. [55]

In January 1964, DCI McCone appealed to a joint meeting of the SAC and SASC subcommittees to resolve the issue. The fiscal year was half over, he noted, and the Agency still did not know how much money it had to spend. According to CIA records, Senator Russell replied that since it had gotten by for that long, perhaps the Agency could handle some type of budget cut. Bothered that the Agency had "hypnotized" HAC Chairman Cannon into always giving it "everything it wanted," Russell opined that perhaps it was time for the Agency to take a budget cut "just to let you know that Congress is around." [56] Although the Agency later tried to get Cannon to object, he refused to do battle with the Senate. A cut of $25 million subsequently was imposed (albeit a cut in what had been added the year before). [57]

---

[53] Ibid.
[54] Ibid., 105.
[55] Ibid., 114–15.
[56] Ibid., 115.
[57] Ibid.

In part to recoup from this setback, the budget request for FY 1965 was $35 million higher than in the previous year. Cannon's subcommittee readily approved it, but Russell would not go along. After turning down McCone's request for a hearing, Russell got the SAC subcommittee to approve a $20 million cut in the budget request (still increasing it by $10 million over the previous year). Although the DCI bitterly protested this action and attempted to have the new HAC Chairman George Mahon (Cannon died on 12 May 1964) resist it in conference, Mahon, too, was unwilling to take on Russell.[58]

In 1965, SAC Chairman Hayden requested that the Agency advise the CIA subcommittees within 48 hours of getting approval from the Bureau of the Budget to withdraw funds from the Contingency Reserve. Although this went beyond existing practice of giving "timely" notice of significant withdrawals, DCI Raborn agreed to the request since the Senate was not asking for prior approval for such releases. As the Contingency Reserve was frequently used to fund covert actions that had not been anticipated when the budget was prepared, however, it gave the subcommittees a clearer, more timely indication of CIA ventures in this area than they had had before.[59] The same year, members of the SASC who were not on its CIA subcommittee insisted on knowing where the Agency's money was hidden in the overall defense budget. While CIA subcommittee took note of their discontent, it did nothing about it.[60]

On the HAC subcommittee, other complaints were heard that year. One congressman told the CIA's liaison he was "uncomfortable about the paucity of congressional knowledge regarding Agency programs." Another said it was time to "get into the nuts and bolts of the Agency's budget."[61] This led to increased involvement by the HAC subcommittee staff members, who began demanding greater detail on the budget and more documentation to justify the funds being requested. Moreover, the complaining congressmen themselves took the occasion to study the budget request in detail, something that had never happened heretofore. One of the complaining congressmen told the Agency's liaison "that the CIA budget has been examined by the [HAC] subcommittee more thoroughly than the DoD budget or any other budget." In the end, however, this increased scrutiny did not lead the subcommittee to make cuts to the budget request; in fact, it approved a budget that was almost 4 percent higher than the year before.[62] While this increase was reduced somewhat in conference with the Senate, the Agency had nonetheless made a convincing

---

[58] Ibid., 117.
[59] Ibid., Vol. II, 19.
[60] Ibid., Vol. I, 118.
[61] Ibid.
[62] Ibid., 119.

case when one of its oversight subcommittees decided to plumb the intricacies of its budget.

In 1966, however, when the Agency went back to the HAC and SAC for a supplemental appropriation to fund its operations in South Vietnam and the Dominican Republic, both subcommittees reacted negatively and approved only half the amount requested. Nevertheless, the Agency was pleased with the result. The CIA subcommittees are "better informed today on the Agency and its budget needs than ever before," wrote CIA Legislative Counsel Warner. Not only did Warner believe this would help stem congressional criticism of the Agency but would also promote support for its future budget requests.[63]

In early 1967, Warner's confidence was essentially borne out by the subcommittees' reaction to the *Ramparts* episode (see chapter 9). While some in Congress were critical of the Agency's activities, Russell and HASC subcommittee chairman Mendel Rivers (D-SC) publicly defended the Agency. Moreover, when the Agency later found itself struggling to comply with President Johnson's direction to federal agencies to terminate all covert funding of US educational or private voluntary organizations operating overseas, DCI Helms sought help from the subcommittees to find a new source of funding for Radio Free Europe and Radio Liberty, which he argued were "valuable instruments and extremely effective." Both the SAC and HAC proved receptive.[64]

In 1969, CIA heard Stuart Symington (D-MO), a staunch supporter of the Agency for many years, muse at a hearing of his SASC subcommittee that it might be time to make the CIA budget public. Contending that the public had a seriously exaggerated concept of the Agency's budget as well as the relative amount of its appropriation compared with that of other elements of the Intelligence Community, Symington thought the image of the Agency would be improved if the truth were known. With Senator Russell still firmly in command (and firmly opposed to the idea of disclosing the budget figure), however, Symington did not pursue the idea.[65]

The Agency did hear in late 1969 that Russell had problems with the CIA subcommittees merely being "informed" of withdrawals from the Contingency Reserve. He thought there should be an opportunity for the committees to object. Recognizing that they had acquiesced in this practice for several years, however, Russell did not challenge the existing procedures.[66]

---

[63] Ibid., 121.
[64] Ibid., Vol. II, 29–31.
[65] Ibid., 41.
[66] Ibid.

Two years later, Senator George McGovern (D-ND) offered a bill requiring that CIA's budget be publicly appropriated as a single line item. With the "old guard" who controlled the SASC subcommittee still firmly opposed, however, the bill did not receive serious consideration.[67]

Nevertheless, when William Colby returned to the Agency in 1971 after 10 years in the field, he found a "dramatic change" had taken place in the way Congress handled the Agency's budget.

> *It was no longer quite the loose and friendly process it once had been. Now we were required to present a detailed breakdown of our funds and personnel, showing the totals of each by organizational component, by activities conducted, and by the targets sought. . . . Congressional staff experts reviewed all these in detail and came up with sharp questions about, and exceptions to, the Agency's proposals. . . . It was plain to anyone. . . . that our budget received every bit as detailed a review as that given any other department or agency by a congressional committee.*

As Colby saw it, the "new toughness" on the part of Congress had begun after the Bay of Pigs and grown during the Vietnam era as the "credibility gap" between the Congress and Johnson/Nixon administrations had grown. And CIA was especially vulnerable to this growing sense of congressional mistrust because of the secrecy that surrounded its activities.[68]

Consideration of the Budget Process by the Church and Pike Committees

The Church and Pike Committees, created by the Senate and House, respectively, in 1975, were investigative committees. Neither was charged with responsibility for authorizing or appropriating funds, either for the CIA or the Intelligence Community as a whole. These functions remained for the time being with the existing CIA subcommittee structure. Both committees, however, did extensive reviews of the budget process, focusing in particular on what Congress was being provided each year in the way of explanation and justification for the funds being requested.

The Church Committee prepared two detailed staff studies: one dealt exclusively with the CIA budget and the other with spending for intelligence generally. Because of classification concerns, neither was published as part of the committee's final report. The staff study of CIA's budget submissions, however, was critical. While noting that progress had been made to strengthen the

---

[67] Ibid., 41–42.
[68] Colby, *Honorable Men*, 308–9.

process, it faulted the Agency for omitting information with respect to the choices that had been made in course of the budget process within the executive branch; for failing to provide Congress with program performance data, especially with respect to covert action programs; and for failing to have an independent audit capability that could provide greater assurance to management and Congress on how appropriated funds were actually spent. The study found that Congress did not obtain sufficient information to make accurate or timely judgments concerning CIA funding. [69]

The staff study also examined the issue of whether the CIA budget total should be disclosed but recommended against it on the grounds it would be more misleading to the public than informative. Nevertheless, the Church Committee later proposed publishing the total budget figure for the Intelligence Community for FY 1976 as part of its final report. After pleas from then-DCI George Bush, however, the committee voted to defer the matter to the full Senate. The number was never published. [70]

The Pike Committee actually made the intelligence budget the initial focus of its activities, not merely at the staff level but at hearings before the committee. On 5 August 1975, in executive session, DCI Colby argued that disclosing the CIA's budget total would do substantial harm to the US intelligence effort. Moreover, without more detail, he said, it would be impossible for the public to make judgments or reach conclusions about CIA's activities. Colby also defended the existing budget process, arguing that the four CIA subcommittees were fully informed on the missions, programs, and projects being funded within the Agency's budget and could obtain whatever information they desired about the budget. [71]

Although the final report of the Pike Committee never achieved formal status as a House report, it was leaked to the press and contained a number of criticisms of the budget process, most of which dealt with intelligence funding generally rather than the CIA's budget. Describing congressional and executive branch scrutiny of the intelligence budget as ranging between "cursory and nonexistent," the report said that because intelligence funding was hidden throughout the federal budget, Congress had no idea as to what was actually being appropriated, which the report estimated to be three to four times what Congress was being told. The report also criticized the lack of an independent audit capability where intelligence expenditures were concerned. [72]

---

[69] CIA draft study, Vol. II, 90–91.
[70] Ibid., 98–99.
[71] Ibid., 127.
[72] Ibid., 128.

Among other things, the Pike Committee recommended that Congress prohibit significant reprogrammings of funds, or withdrawals from the Contingency Reserve, unless Congress specifically approved them. With respect to the issue of budget disclosure, the committee recommended that all intelligence-related items be identified in the president's budget and that there be disclosure each year of a single sum being spent on intelligence by any agency involved in such activities.[73]

While the Church and Pike Committees had no authority over the Agency's budget, they created an adverse climate insofar as congressional consideration of its budget was concerned during this period. Indeed, the HAC and SAC imposed cuts that carried over to the Carter administration's initial actions on the intelligence budget once it assumed office in 1977.[74]

Budget Oversight by the Select Committees on Intelligence: 1977–81

When the Senate, and later the House, created new select oversight committees in 1976 and 1977, respectively, each committee was given authority to authorize appropriations for the agencies under its purview. Until this time, no separate authorization had been required for the Agency's appropriation; rather the National Security Act of 1947 itself was seen as providing ongoing authorization. From here on, however, there would be two bills, rather than one, for the Agency to see through Congress each year before its funding could be finalized. While new for the Agency, this was no different than what most other federal agencies had to do. Oversight responsibility usually rested with authorizing committees, where most of the substantive expertise resided, with the cognizant appropriations subcommittee handling the appropriation itself. In theory, an authorizing committee would act first, deciding how large the appropriation should be for the forthcoming fiscal year, and the appropriators would act later, able to decrease, but not exceed, the level established by the authorizing committee.

With the establishment of the two select committees, the CIA subcommittees of the two armed services committees were eliminated. On the appropriations committees, the defense appropriations subcommittees subsumed the budget responsibilities of the CIA subcommittees; in practice, they created small staffs within the larger subcommittee staff to handle the appropriations of the CIA and DoD elements of the Intelligence Community. From time to time, even after the select committees were created, appropriations staffs

---

[73] Ibid., 130.
[74] CIA draft study, Vol. III, 11.

would play dominant roles. One of these HAC defense subcommittee staffers, Chuck Snodgrass, by force of his personality and capacity for work, came to exert inordinate influence over the intelligence budget from 1975 to 1979 even after the HPSCI was created.[75]

Established 13 months before its House counterpart, the SSCI rapidly moved to effect its budget responsibilities. In the fall of 1976, it created a sub-committee on budget authorization, with a small dedicated staff, to do over-sight of the intelligence budget and develop the committee's annual authorization bill. In early 1977, the subcommittee held 40 hours of hearings on the budget, including testimony from DCI Turner; examined 11 volumes of budget justification materials submitted by the Agency (including a project-by-project review of covert action operations); and conducted staff interviews with numerous Agency officials. Its new chairman, Daniel Inouye (D-HI) pro-claimed to his colleagues that the CIA budget was now getting "the same degree of scrutiny as other Government programs."[76]

The first authorization bill the SSCI produced as a result of this process (for FY 1978) had to grapple with how to address the amounts being authorized — which were classified. To accomplish this, the committee adopted a novel approach that would become the pattern for how subsequent authorization and appropriations bills dealt with the same issue: the authorization bill would give the effect of law to a classified annex to its report, and subsequently to the conference report, on the bill. If senators wanted to know what was in the annex before voting on the bill, they could come to the committee and read it. Under the old system, members had had no way of knowing what they were voting on in terms of intelligence funding. In fact, the only place this was offi-cially set forth had been a classified letter sent by the appropriations commit-tees to the Agency at the end of the process, telling it what its appropriation was for the next fiscal year. Now, this would be set out in a classified annex to the conference report on the authorization bill that would be available to mem-bers generally (few actually availed themselves of the opportunity) prior to their being asked to vote on the bill.

The first authorization bill was reported to the full Senate in 1977 but was never considered there, largely because it had no place to be referred in the House, which at that point had not created a counterpart committee. Neverthe-less, both House and Senate Appropriations Committees considered the bill in their action on the CIA appropriation. Overall, in its first action on the CIA's budget, the SSCI took a modest cut, but it happened to eliminate the funds for two small covert action programs, both of which the president had approved

---

[75] Smist, *Congress Oversees*, 242–46.
[76] Ibid., 116–19; CIA draft study, Vol. II, 195.

and duly reported to Congress under the Hughes-Ryan Amendment. According to Agency records, the committee's action shocked Agency officials, who complained not only to the committee leadership but to the White House as well. Later the Agency worked with the staff of the appropriations committees to restore the funds for the two programs that had been cut , but the appropriators reduced the amount appropriated for the Contingency Reserve by the same amount. [77]

Acting over the objection of DCI Turner and the Carter White House, the SSCI also recommended as part of the FY 1978 authorization bill that the amount of funds appropriated for national foreign intelligence activities be publicly disclosed. The full Senate, however, never acted on the bill, and the committee chose not pursue it in succeeding sessions. [78]

The HPSCI, created in July 1977, also moved swiftly to implement its budgetary responsibilities, creating a subcommittee on program and budget authorization in November of that year. Like its Senate counterpart, the subcommittee immediately began getting detailed budget justifications from the Agency and meeting with Agency officials.

The first intelligence authorization bill produced by both committees that became law was the authorization for FY 1979. Each committee made small cuts in the Agency's budget, albeit in different areas, but added resources as part of the DCI's requested realignment of the Intelligence Community Staff. More significantly from the DCI's standpoint, both committees weighed in to prevent the HAC from taking serious cuts in the overhead reconnaissance program. [79] When the HPSCI brought its authorization bill to the floor for the first time, some members complained that they did not know what they were voting on. Chairman Boland explained that the bill contained a classified annex that members of the House could come to the committee and read if they wanted to do so. The bill passed, 323–43. [80]

Having an intelligence authorization bill for the first time also complicated the congressional mechanics for handling of the Agency's budget. In prior years, as previously noted, the Agency's appropriation had been hidden in a nondescript line item in the defense appropriation bill. The appropriators would work with the staffs of the two armed services committees to ensure that a corresponding authorization of the appropriation appeared in the defense authorization bill. The actual classified amount would only appear in

---

[77] Ibid., 197–98.
[78] Ibid., 203.
[79] Ibid., 199–200, 240.
[80] Ibid., 240–41.

a letter from the appropriators to the Bureau of the Budget (later the Office of Management and Budget).

Now the intelligence committees would produce a separate intelligence authorization bill that would constitute the annual authorization of appropriations for the Agency, but the amount being authorized was classified and could not be set forth in the bill itself. To provide an authorization that corresponded to the line item in the public defense appropriation bill that contained the Agency's money, the number the intelligence committees authorized would now have to be plugged into the corresponding line item in the defense authorization bill the armed services committees produced.

The last years of the Carter administration saw a series of profoundly troubling events unfold around the world: the fall of the Shah of Iran, the taking of US hostages in Iran, and the Soviet invasion of Afghanistan. In the midst of such turmoil, neither committee posed serious challenges to the administration's budget requests for the Agency.[81]

Interaction During the Reagan Administration: 1981–89

Ronald Reagan's campaign pledge in 1980 to revive and rebuild the Intelligence Community included significant increases to the budgets of intelligence agencies, including the CIA. His choice for DCI, William Casey, immediately pushed for a 20-percent across-the-board increase in intelligence spending that he argued was necessary to reverse the decline of the 1970s and meet the growing challenge of the Soviet Union.[82]

The leaders of both intelligence committees expressed their support, and, indeed, for the first three years of the Reagan administration, the Agency's funding increased by an average of more than 22 percent a year, and personnel by an average of almost 8 percent a year.[83] To support these increases, however, the committees demanded ever more detailed and comprehensive budget justifications. These were provided in the form of Congressional Budget Justification Books, or CBJBs, that often ran several hundred pages in length. Still more documentation was provided on request. While both committees proved to be supportive during this period, their respective staffs were by this point delving deeply (and, for some, intrusively) into the details of the Agency's operations. One Agency officer described the situation this way:

---

[81] Ibid., 204, 242.
[82] CIA draft study, Vol. III, 11–12.
[83] Ibid., 16.

They tell us where to put people and that sort of thing. They are intruding into the DCI's prerogatives. This is micromanaging at its worst.[84]

In 1982, as the Agency under Casey was turning increasingly to covert action to thwart the spread of communism around the world (see chapter 6), some HPSCI members became concerned about use of the Contingency Reserve Fund to finance these operations without the committee's approval and proposed cuts to, as well as limitations upon, the reserve. In the end, however, they settled for a commitment from Casey that he would give the committees prior notice before making withdrawals from the fund. The committees also continued to allow the Agency to carry over the unused funds in the reserve for use in the next fiscal year.[85]

In 1983, the Agency began providing CBJBs to the appropriations subcommittees as well as the intelligence committees. At the same time, as the appropriators began to appreciate the extent of the intelligence committees' budget oversight, they decided they could get by with doing less themselves. As one senior member of the HAC defense subcommittee explained:

Our subcommittee has backed off and done less as the [HPSCI] has become more important. My own view, if you've got a committee dealing day in and day out with intelligence, that's the way it should be.[86]

During the latter part of Casey's tenure, government-wide reductions pursuant to the Gramm-Rudman-Hollings deficit reduction legislation threatened a serious decline in the Agency's budget, causing DDCI Robert Gates to suggest that the National Foreign Intelligence Program budget, which contained the Agency's funding, be moved out of the Defense budget (where it was apt to be cut) to a "fenced" account controlled by the Office of Management and Budget, where it could not be touched. The administration, however, did not support the idea. Casey then appealed to the leaders of the intelligence committees for help to stave off the potential cuts. SSCI Chairman David Durenberger (R-MN) agreed that the Agency should be protected from arbitrary, across-the-board cuts, but his HPSCI counterpart, Lee Hamilton (D-IN), wondered why CIA should not undergo reductions comparable to those imposed on the Defense Department (8–12 percent). Casey responded that any reduction beyond 2 or 3 percent would do serious damage to the Agency and, with the backing of the SSCI, actually succeeded in getting the committees to sup-

---

[84] Quoted in Smist, *Congress Oversees*, 246.
[85] CIA draft study, Vol. III, 17–18..
[86] Ibid., 13; Smist, *Congress Oversees*, 244–45.

port a small increase for the year. Indeed, the Agency experienced small increases in its funding and personnel for the last three years of Casey's tenure (FY 1985–87).[87]

Apart from their action on the Agency's budget in 1986, the committees took significant steps to tighten their control of intelligence funding (see chapter 1 for more details). Agencies could now spend appropriated funds only if Congress had "specifically authorized" them. The law also provided standards and criteria for "reprogramming" of appropriated funds for purposes different from what Congress had been told. While the amendments the committees put through did not depart significantly from existing practice, for the first time they were made a matter of law.

In each of the remaining years of the Reagan administration, the Agency's funding and personnel levels continued to grow modestly, save for a slight decline in funding in 1987, the year of the Iran-contra investigations.[88] And although it did not always receive the increases requested in its budget submission, in all, at the end of the Reagan years, the Agency's budget was more than twice as large as it had been when Reagan took office; its personnel level, larger by a third.[89]

The End of the Cold War and Its Effect on the Budget: 1989–95

In 1989, the Berlin Wall fell, as did communist regimes in a number of East European countries. While the fate of the Soviet Union was not altogether clear at that point, dramatic change was obviously taking place and the oversight committees were quick to recognize that the Agency (and Intelligence Community as a whole) would likely change their focus in the years to come.

The HPSCI, under its new chairman, Anthony Beilenson (D-CA), responded by instituting "zero-based" budget reviews in 1989 and 1990 of each agency within the Intelligence Community.[90] These were intended to assess the continued value of everything that was currently being done.

In 1992, after the Soviet Union had formally ceased to exist, the pressures grew even stronger in Congress for reducing intelligence expenditures, including those of the Agency. In one especially telling episode, when the SSCI brought its authorization bill to the floor in September, Senator Dale Bumpers (D-AK), who was not a member of the committee, offered an amendment to

---

[87] CIA draft study, Vol. III, 83–86.
[88] Ibid., 205.
[89] Ibid., 16, 205.
[90] Smist, *Congress Oversees*, 262.

cut $1 billion from the intelligence budget. Where the cut would be taken was not specified. The chairman of the SSCI at the time, Senator Boren, noted in response to the amendment that the SSCI had already cut a billion dollars from the overall budget request for FY 1993. He warned against deeper, precipitate cuts, arguing they should be done carefully and gradually.[91]

On the HPSCI, the new chairman, Dave McCurdy (D-OK), instituted a budget review process based upon function rather than agency. He believed it would provide a clearer picture how the Intelligence Community was responding to the realities of the post–Cold War world. At the end of this process, the committee concluded that the funding requests of the agencies were not being prioritized to reflect the new geopolitical and fiscal realities that the United States now confronted. The HPSCI, too, supported cuts.

When the two committees conferenced on the FY 1993 bill, they emerged with the largest cuts in intelligence spending that Congress had made in 40 years. Overall, Intelligence Community funding was reduced by 6 percent over the previous year's total. Perhaps more significant for the long run, the committees also directed that agencies within the Intelligence Community reduce their personnel levels by 17.5 percent over the next five years.[92]

More cuts were taken the following year. President Clinton had promised during his presidential campaign to cut $7.5 billion from intelligence spending over a five-year period, but the budget submitted to Congress for FY 1994 actually called for a small increase in intelligence spending. The new chairmen of the oversight committees, Senator Dennis DeConcini (D-AZ) and Congressman Dan Glickman (D-KS), initially sought to keep the intelligence budget at the previous year's level, but in the end—under pressure from their respective caucuses—both agreed to cuts ($1.3 billion and $1.1 billion, respectively) over and above those taken the previous year. Even this did not satisfy some members. When the HPSCI took its bill to the floor, for example, it was forced to defeat an amendment calling for an overall 10-percent reduction in intelligence spending and another calling for a $500 million reduction beyond what the committee was itself proposing.[93]

As far as the Agency itself was concerned, the cuts taken in the overall intelligence budget translated into a reduction of roughly 5 percent spread over a three-year period (FY 1993–95). Of greater consequence to operations, however, was the 17.5-percent reduction in the Agency's authorized personnel level, most of which was taken in the first two years following the congres-

---

[91] Ibid., 287.
[92] Ibid., 293.
[93] Ibid., 311.

sionally-imposed mandate and remained in effect (albeit with small fluctuations) for the rest of the decade.[94]

Return to Relative Stability and Modest Increases: 1995–2000

The last half of the 1990s saw a return to relative stability in terms of fluctuations in the Agency's funding. In every year but one, Congress appropriated more money for the Agency than the administration had requested, coming either as a result of its action on the annual intelligence authorization bill or as part of a supplemental appropriations bill enacted during the year.

At the same time, the increases being proposed by the administration and approved by Congress during this period remained small. "The fact is," DCI Tenet later wrote, "by the mid-to-late 1990s, American intelligence was in Chapter 11 [i.e. bankruptcy] and neither Congress nor the Executive branch did much about it. . . . They provided neither the sustained funding required to deal with terrorism nor the resources needed to enable the recovery of U.S. intelligence with the speed required."[95]

The most substantial increase during the period came in a supplemental appropriations bill for FY 1999 that was pushed through by House Speaker Newt Gingrich, working informally with Tenet. The DCI later admitted:

> My "off-the-books" alliance with [Gingrich] alienated some members of President Clinton's team [but] resources simply were not forthcoming [out of the administration]. My only regret is that much of the money in the 1999 supplemental was for one year only, and was not continued in the years immediately following.[96]

A more consequential problem for the Agency was the impact of congressional restrictions on its ability to hire new employees. While funding for the Agency increased by modest amounts, the authorized personnel levels established by the Congress remained low for the balance of the decade. Again Tenet described the situation in his memoir:

> Our workforce was slashed by almost 25% [during the mid-1990s]. There is no good way to cut an organization's staff by that amount. But there is one incredibly bad way to do it — and that was precisely the method the intelligence community used. They simply stopped recruiting new people. As a result there was half a decade or so

---

[94] Based upon the author's review of pertinent Agency records.
[95] Tenet, *At the Center of the Storm*, 108.
[96] Ibid., 21.

where hardly any new talent was coming in and many, many experienced hands were going out the door.[97]

The Impact of the 9/11 Attacks: 2001–2004

The 9/11 attacks prompted a flurry of activity by the US government designed to go after al-Qa'ida and deal with the terrorist threat to the United States. To fund these activities, Congress passed a series of supplemental appropriations bills in the fall of 2001, five of which provided funding for the Agency over and above what had been appropriated in the annual intelligence bill. In all, they represented a 35-percent increase in the Agency's appropriation for the year.

2002 saw further increases in the Agency's appropriation as the country not only continued the war on terrorism, but seemed to be moving steadily towards possible military action in Iraq. Two supplemental appropriations bills were enacted that year, providing a 15-percent increase over and above what had been appropriated for the Agency as part of the intelligence authorization.

After this, funding for the Agency began to level off, albeit at a significantly higher level than before the 9/11 attacks. While Congress did not appropriate all that the Bush administration had requested for FY 2003 and FY 2004, it did provide substantial increases each year over the previous year's appropriation.[98]

AUTHOR'S COMMENTARY

Exercising Power of the Purse

As far as agencies of the executive branch are concerned, there is no more important power conferred upon the Congress than the power of the purse. The Constitution forbids agencies from spending money that has not been appropriated by the legislative branch. This simple requirement provides the foundation for nearly all the interaction that occurs between the two branches. Intelligence agencies, moreover, despite the inherent secrecy of their activities, are not exempt from this requirement. They need congressional approval each year—formal approval from both the House and the Senate—if they are to exist and operate.

---

[97] Ibid, 14.
[98] Ibid.

At the same time, Congress cannot exercise the power of the purse with respect to intelligence agencies like the CIA in exactly the same way as it does with other departments and agencies. Since the appropriation for the CIA is classified, it cannot be the subject of public hearings or public mark-ups nor can it be openly debated on the floor of either House like the appropriations of other government agencies. in theory any member could ask for a closed session to discuss the appropriation for CIA, but none has ever done so, nor is it likely that the leadership of either chamber would allow it. Indeed, in the history of the Agency, never once has the full House or Senate debated its appropriation. There have been debates on amendments offered on intelligence spending generally or on specific Agency programs, but not one has focused on the CIA's overall budget specifically. Prior to the creation of the select intelligence committees in the mid-1970s, in fact, there was no opportunity for members not on the CIA subcommittees to learn what the appropriation was for the Agency before they were asked to vote on it. Even after this option later became available (by allowing members to review the classified annex to the annual intelligence authorization in secure spaces), few of them chose to do so.

Rather, members relied upon their committees to sort things out. What these committees have come up with over the years in order to address CIA's needs has constituted, in effect, the action of Congress as a whole. It is here, with the committees charged with fiscal responsibility for the CIA, that the power of the purse has effectively rested, not with the parent bodies themselves.

Every DCI has recognized this and made satisfying committee leaders involved in the Agency's funding a priority insofar as relations with Congress were concerned. Throughout its history, the Agency has been willing (if not eager) to provide whatever information these members required to ensure that the Agency's needs were ultimately satisfied. While some of its overseers have had neither the time nor the interest to delve into the Agency's programs and budget, neither have they wanted to be ignored, deceived, or surprised. Any DCI who allows this to happen, risks the fall of the budget ax, for the congressional power of the purse is, for all practical purposes, theirs to wield.

Hiding within the Defense Budget

The CIA appropriation was originally hidden in the budgets of the State and Defense Departments, and later Defense alone, for security reasons. But this funding "contrivance" has had, over the long term, vastly more important consequences for the Agency than merely preventing the disclosure of its funding level. It is doubtful, for example, that the exponential growth that the Agency experienced in the first four years of its existence (and at other times) could have happened if its funding had not been part of the much larger defense budget. There simply would not have been the latitude in the budgets of smaller departments and agencies to accommodate such significant increases.

The Defense budget over the years has also been subject to fewer cuts than the budgets of most departments and agencies. Indeed, the long-term trend of the defense budget has been one of gradual rise, allowing CIA, for the most part, to rise along with it. There are also practical advantages to being in the DoD bills. These are bills that Congress will put through every year, and they are handled by the most powerful members of Congress and, thus, are less often challenged by the congressional rank and file.

While some at CIA would undoubtedly prefer, as a matter of institutional pride, having an independent appropriation (as opposed to having the Agency's money appropriated to the secretary of defense), it is doubtful that the Agency would have fared so well so often from a fiscal standpoint if it had had to face the vagaries of the congressional appropriations process from its own isolated perch.

The Quality of Budget Oversight

From the creation of the Agency in 1947 until the select committees were created in the mid-1970s, budget oversight by the Congress was cursory at best. While there were periods when the CIA subcommittee of the HAC instituted a more rigorous budget process, such oversight did not approach the level of detail and intrusiveness that came to the process after the select committees were created.

In large part, the quality of budget oversight was poor during the early period because the leaders of the CIA subcommittees were too busy taking care of their principal responsibility—the Department of Defense. Similarly, their professional staffs were used, for the most part, to sort out DoD issues. Tending to the relatively small CIA budget was not a priority for them. A former CIA legislative counsel described the situation in the 1950s:

> [A] *national intelligence service in those days was more or less part and parcel of our overall defense establishment. Therefore, as our defense budget went sailing through Congress . . . the relatively modest CIA budget in effect got a free ride. . . . When Directors appeared before Congress, which they did only rarely, the main concern of Members was often to make sure that we* [the CIA] *had what we needed to do our job."* [99]

---

[99] Karalekas, *History*, 52.

When the responsibility for oversight of the CIA budget was split off from those with responsibility for DoD in the mid-1970s, the quality of such oversight immediately improved. And not surprisingly, the committees with the most staff resources to devote to budget analysis—the select committees—gradually gained dominance in this area.

In-depth budget oversight has always been hampered, though, simply by the mundane nature of much of it. Although the Agency had been given exotic, intriguing missions, compared to other federal agencies, its budgetary needs every year come down mostly to personnel costs and operating expenses. Only covert action expenditures have raised much controversy, and, at least during the early period, the CIA subcommittees were not formally briefed on these kinds of operations. They knew the sorts of things the Agency was doing in general terms and did not seek to know more. For example, getting the chairman of the CIA subcommittee of the SAC, who was also chairman of the full committee, to sit still for a discussion of people and numbers often proved impossible.

Even after the select committees were created and far more documentation began to be provided in support of the annual budget request, it was often still difficult to get members themselves to focus on the Agency's budget needs. The committee staffs would prepare analyses of the issues each year, but only budgets for the Agency's covert action programs continued to draw much attention from the members themselves. They might inquire whether the Agency was getting more or less than the year before, but rarely would they go beyond this. As a result, oversight of the Agency's budget since the mid-1970s has been left largely in the hands of the committees' professional staffs. They are guided by the direction they receive from the leaders and staff directors of the committees but have considerable latitude, nonetheless.

Whatever the personal involvement of members in the budget process, the leaders of the responsible committees in Congress nonetheless faithfully put the Agency's funding through the legislative mill each year, becoming staunch defenders for it once their respective committees settled on a number.

The Impact of Budget Oversight

In the first 57 years of the Agency's existence, there were only a few years, most of them after the end of the Cold War, when Congress did not provide more money for the Agency than had been appropriated the year before. In most years, Congress either accepted the administration's budget request for the Agency or reduced it by a modest amount, still leaving an increase over the previous year's appropriation. Occasionally, particularly in times of crisis or national emergency, money would be added over and above what the administration had requested.

Even in the years when Congress cut the Agency's budget, the cuts usually did not have a significant impact on CIA operations. Cuts taken in one budget cycle—as a result of a government-wide reduction, for example—were made up for in the next. The place where most cuts occurred—covert action programs—usually did not result in personnel cuts or reduce the Agency operating budget. Only at the end of the Cold War, when Congress believed that the nation's principal adversary was no longer a threat, did it mandate consequential reductions in the personnel and operating expenses of the Intelligence Community, including the CIA, forcing it to reduce its workforce and shut down certain operational capabilities. Unfortunately, these cutbacks also came at a time when the revolution in information technology was burgeoning, making it difficult for the Agency's hiring and procurements to keep pace with the technological developments taking place in the private sector.

It did not take long, however, for the intelligence committees to appreciate the problem and begin taking action to rectify it. For five years in a row, during the last half of the 1990s, the appropriation for the Agency was larger than it had been the year before, and after the attacks of 9/11, there was exponential growth. So, Congress has, for virtually all of the Agency's history, been a steady and reliable partner in terms of providing the wherewithal for its activities.

It would be a mistake, however, to look at the impact of the Congress on CIA's budget solely in terms of its action on the "bottom line." Indeed, the fact that Congress had fully funded the Agency's budget request in a particular year would provide little comfort to an Agency manager whose program the committees had "zeroed out" in the process. As the committees' oversight of the budget became more detailed over time, its ability (and penchant) for effecting minor change (some might call it micromanagement") has also grown.

Still, for all of the criticism heard from Congress over the years, for all the consternation and anxiety generated each year by the need to secure funding, in the end, Congress has done well by the Agency. Walter L. Pforzheimer, the Agency's first legislative liaison, attributed this to the fact that most in Congress supported its mission. While this undoubtedly continues to be true, it is also true that the congressional committees that have overseen the Agency have understood that stability is key to the accomplishment of its mission. Operational capabilities as well as analytical capabilities take years to develop. Resources and personnel cannot be ratcheted up one year and ratched down the next without doing harm. Congress, over the years, has understood this and kept the Agency, by and large, on an even keel.

CHAPTER 7

OVERSIGHT OF ANALYSIS

As we have seen, Congress envisioned the CIA as the place in the US government where all intelligence would come together and be analyzed in a timely and objective manner for the president and other policymakers. Ideally, the Agency would provide warning of significant events around the world in order to give policymakers time to formulate and execute adequate responses. When it was apparent this had not happened, or the Agency's analysis had simply been wrong, Congress often wanted to know why.

This chapter deals with cases in which Congress chose to exercise oversight of intelligence analysis during the period covered by the study. It does not attempt to describe every episode in which Congress criticized the Agency's analysis (or lack thereof), but it does attempt to identify the key ones. It also describes the relatively few occasions when Congress was moved to examine the process by which intelligence analysis had been produced.

The Early Years: 1947–74

As noted in chapter 3, Congress was not routinely given analytic products until the mid-1970s. From the very beginning, however, CIA regarded Congress as an appropriate consumer of its substantive analysis. Committees with a need to see such analysis might be permitted to read it, but for the most part, it was briefed to them by the DCI and other senior Agency officials.

Generally speaking, these briefings received positive responses from the members who heard them. Indeed, the Agency's briefings on the Korean War during the early 1950s helped solidify its reputation with the Congress as an independent, authoritative voice on national security issues. Where the Soviet Union was concerned, the Agency represented virtually the only source of information members of Congress had. Little trust could be placed in what the Soviet government said publicly, and apart from US intelligence, there were few sources of reliable information. Members were glad to have it. More often, what provoked challenges and criticism was not what had been briefed on the Hill but what members read in the newspapers indicating to them an apparent failure to predict an event that was important to US interests.

This happened for the first time, in fact, less than a year after CIA was created. During an official visit to Bogota, Colombia, in April 1948, a US delegation led by Secretary of State George Marshall encountered widespread rioting following the assassination of a prominent opposition leader. The riots at times appeared to threaten the safety of the delegation, and the under secretary of state at the time said the Department had not had advance notice of the unrest. President Truman admitted he had been "as surprised as anyone."[1] New York Governor Thomas E. Dewey, then campaigning for president, lambasted the administration in general—and the CIA in particular—for its failure to warn Marshall of the potential dangers. This led the House Committee on Expenditures, which had handled the legislation creating the CIA, to form a small subcommittee to look into the Agency's performance. After clearing his appearance with Truman, DCI Hillenkoetter appeared before the subcommittee in closed session and read from several intelligence reports describing the possibility of unrest during the Marshall visit. The direst of these warned that communist agitators planned to humiliate Marshall, and the Agency had passed it to the US ambassador in Bogota. The ambassador, not wanting to "unduly alarm" Marshall before his visit, decided not to send it to Washington. The chairman of the subcommittee was so incensed that he apologized to Hillenkoetter and dragged him out of the hearing room to repeat the same story to the press.[2]

A year later, Hillenkoetter faced hostile congressional reaction to another perceived failure but on this occasion did not fare as well. On 23 September 1949, President Truman announced that the Air Force had detected that the Soviet Union had conducted its first successful test of an atomic bomb several weeks earlier. A few weeks after this stunning announcement, the JAEC summoned Hillenkoetter to appear before it to explain his earlier assessments to the committee. In March, he had told them that the Soviets were "at least a few years" from completing work on an atomic bomb. Then on 20 September, only days before the Agency learned of the test itself, it had issued a formal estimate predicting that the earliest the Soviets could have an atomic bomb was mid-1950 but most probably not until mid-1953. In the Agency's defense, Hillenkoetter pointed out that it knew the Soviets were working on a bomb and that its estimate of a possible completion date was "not that far off." Under questioning, however, he conceded the Agency had not had enough information to make an accurate assessment.[3]

---

[1] Barrett, *CIA and Congress*, 34–35
[2] Ibid., 33–39; DIA draft study, Vol. I, 29–31.
[3] Barrett, *CIA and Congress*, 51–63.

On 23 June 1950, Hillenkoetter testified before a closed session of the House Foreign Affairs Committee. Among the topics the committee asked him about was what was taking place on the Korean peninsula. He said nothing to indicate that a crisis was at hand, but two days later North Korea invaded the South. Two days after that, the secretaries of state and defense told the SAC that the invasion had come as a complete surprise to them, prompting the committee to summon Hillenkoetter to appear later the same day. Bringing several of the Agency's estimates with him, the DCI noted that the Agency had issued numerous reports over the preceding year with respect to the North's military capabilities and had warned several times that the North might well use them against the South.[4] Indeed, the Agency had reported several days before the invasion that North Korean troops were being deployed north of the 38th parallel that divided the North from the South.[5] Hillenkoetter argued that while it was not able to predict the precise time the invasion occurred, the Agency had given policymakers adequate warning.

In the spring of 1951, Senator Russell, then chairman of the SASC, asked DCI Walter Bedell Smith to send him anything CIA might have on the possible entry of Communist China into the war. Smith demurred, fearful that providing such documents to the Hill might result in a security compromise while the war was ongoing. Russell withdrew his request.[6]

In June 1956, the issue of whether the Soviet Union was ahead of the United States in the production of strategic bombers was before the Congress. While the Eisenhower White House did not like the idea of DCI Dulles testifying on this subject before a "non-oversight" committee, it permitted him to appear before the SASC's military preparedness subcommittee, chaired by Stuart Symington (D-MO), that was seized with the issue. During a closed hearing before the subcommittee in June 1956, Dulles refused to draw comparisons between US strength and Soviet strength. His job as DCI, he told the Symington, was limited to providing an assessment of the Soviet side. In an interview with a Republican congressman that was broadcast several days later, however, Dulles opined that "overall, in the atomic field, I feel quite sure they [the Soviets] aren't ahead of us"—precisely the kind of comparison he had refused to make in response to Symington's questioning. For Symington and other Democrats on the subcommittee, who wanted more money for strategic bombers in the defense budget than the Eisenhower administration had requested, Dulles was playing politics. To make matters worse, a few weeks later, new intelligence came in that resulted in a downward revision in the

---

[4] Ibid., 82–89.
[5] CIA draft study, Vol. I, 35.
[6] Ibid.

Agency's assessment of the number of Soviet strategic bombers. Again, Symington thought Dulles was playing politics.[7]

In November 1956, the SFRC invited Dulles to appear to explain why the CIA had not predicted either the Soviet military intervention in Hungary or the British-French attack on Egypt after it had nationalized the Suez Canal. Dulles struggled to put the best face possible on the Agency's foreknowledge of these overlapping events—which occurred almost simultaneously in late October and early November—but did not satisfy some on the committee. The CIA subcommittee of the HAC held a hearing on the same topics a few months afterwards.[8]

The Sputnik launch in October 1957 produced mild hysteria among the American public and prompted more congressional questioning of Dulles, not only with respect to whether CIA had predicted the launch, but, more importantly—given the USSR's obvious ability to propel a satellite into earth orbit—what CIA knew of its capabilities to launch ballistic missiles. Dulles was able to point to a CIA estimate done the previous March that had said the Soviets were capable of putting a satellite into earth orbit. He also provided a detailed description of Soviet capabilities to deliver nuclear weapons that shocked many on the committees. Although he assured the committees that the Agency did not believe Soviet leaders were contemplating war with the United States in the near future, in all, six committees—Symington's military preparedness subcommittee, the CIA subcommittees of the HAC, SAC, and SASC, the JAEC, and the SFRC—asked for Dulles's testimony on these subjects.[9]

A few months later, in May 1958, Dulles was back on the congressional hot seat, this time responding to charges that the CIA had failed to provide warning of the rioting and violence in Venezuela that had threatened the safety of Vice President Nixon and his wife during an official visit. Nixon's motorcade had been attacked, his limousine badly damaged, and personal indignities inflicted upon him. Dulles explained that the Agency had provided warnings of demonstrations, and even rumors of a plot to assassinate Nixon, but had thought Venezuelan security authorities could handle them. "I cannot always predict when there will be a riot," he told the SFRC, "or what a riot is going to do."[10]

A few weeks later Dulles was back before Congress yet again. On 14 July 1958, the army in Iraq had overthrown the pro-Western monarchy of King Faisal in a bloody coup. Fearing this would inspire a similar coup in Lebanon, whose pro-Western government was struggling to put down anti-American

---

[7] Barrett, *CIA and Congress*, 246–49.
[8] Ibid., 251–61.
[9] Ibid., 261–79.
[10] Ibid., 286.

unrest, the Eisenhower administration consulted with key members on whether the United States should introduce American troops into Lebanon to help its government survive. In the meantime, CIA came under public attack from congressman after congressman for its apparent failure to anticipate the Iraqi coup. To elicit CIA's response to these charges, the CIA subcommittees of the HASC and SASC as well as the two foreign relations committees held hearings. Dulles reportedly attempted to get Senator Russell to protect him from the SFRC inquiry, but Russell would not do so. The DCI conceded that the Agency had relied too much upon the assessments provided by the Iraqi government before the coup and believed the security service to be more competent than it proved to be. Still, he said, the timing of the coup "could probably not have been predicted."[11]

Despite his earlier conflicts with Symington, Dulles recognized that the senator expected the DCI to keep him informed with respect to any developments regarding the Soviet ballistic missile capability. So when a new NIE was issued in July 1958 that contained more ominous judgments in terms of the Soviets' ability to launch nuclear-armed missiles against the United States in the near term, Dulles invited Symington to come to his office for a briefing.[12] Already alarmed by what Dulles had told him, Symington was subsequently told by a friend (a former assistant secretary of the air force) that the situation was actually much worse than Dulles had described. The Soviets were doing more missile testing than the CIA was willing to acknowledge, the friend asserted, and were therefore closer to an operational capability. Dulles agreed to meet with Symington to discuss the evidence, but refused to change the conclusions reached in the NIE. Failing to get satisfaction from Dulles, Symington requested a meeting with Eisenhower in August. At the meeting he told the president he did not trust the CIA estimate and gave him a six-page letter setting forth his position. Eisenhower gave the letter to Dulles to evaluate, and Dulles commissioned a formal review of the points in the letter by the Intelligence Community. In December 1958, the White House told Symington that its review had not resulted in a change to its position. Dulles had Symington to his office again to brief him in private on the results of the review. All of this was done at a personal level, outside the official congressional process.[13]

When Congress reconvened in January 1959, however, the dispute with Symington boiled over into the public. Reacting to testimony by Secretary of Defense Neil McElroy that there was still "no positive evidence" that the Soviets had an operational long-range missile capable of delivering a nuclear

---

[11] Ibid., 290–300.
[12] Ibid., 302–3.
[13] Ibid., 306–13.

warhead, Symington publicly charged that intelligence evaluation was being "subordinated" to the budget priorities of the administration; in other words, CIA was "cooking the books." In subsequent testimony, Dulles was indignant:

> *The implication that there has been any change* [in the estimate] . . . *out of budgetary or . . . other considerations . . .* [is] *an insult to the Agency. . . . The integrity of the Agency has to be preserved. . . . Changing estimates for budgetary, political, or any other consideration would be ruinous to the Agency, and I consider a mere question as to whether that has been done to be a very, very serious matter and I hope the Senator would be willing to withdraw* [his allegation].[14]

The dispute with Symington continued to simmer, until the publication of a new NIE in January 1960. The NIE, using a change in analytical methodology, revised even further downward the Soviet advantage in ballistic missile capabilities. Based on the new estimate, Secretary of Defense Thomas Gates made public statements minimizing the missile gap, while Dulles himself was crediting the Soviets with having greater capability in his closed session testimony. This disparity led Symington to charge the Eisenhower administration with "using intelligence information in such a manner that the American people

have been given an inaccurate picture of what is necessary for our national defense."[15] While Symington said he blamed the administration rather than Dulles for the impression the public was being given, Dulles himself acknowledged the change in analytical methodology used in the NIE had not been explained to Pentagon officials and was largely responsible for the confusion that ensued.[16]

For the remainder of the decade, Agency records reflect no significant oversight by Congress of its analytical work. Apart from an appearance by DCI McCone before the SFRC in 1963 to explain the

Senator Stuart Symington.

(US Senate Historical Collection)

---

14 Ibid., 323–30.
15 Ibid., 363.
16 Ibid., 365–74.

Agency's perceived failure to predict political unrest in several Latin American countries, there is no record of a congressional challenge to the Agency's analysis.

Colby did recount in his memoir an episode that took place in 1974 when he testified in closed session before the SASC regarding the Soviet naval presence in the Indian Ocean. The issue before the committee was whether to approve the Nixon administration's request to improve the facilities at Diego Garcia to support US Navy operations in the area. Colby writes that the first part of his testimony, based upon earlier NIEs, was that Soviet naval activity there had grown and would continue to grow. The second part of his statement, however, said that improvements made to the US facilities on Diego Garcia would likely stimulate increased superpower rivalry in the area. After getting Colby's agreement to declassify these judgments, Symington used the latter one publicly to justify his opposition to the administration's request. This, in turn, led the administration to have Colby make it clear that his earlier testimony should not be taken as an indication he opposed the improvements at Diego Garcia. Symington responded by publicly criticizing Colby for "waffling" in the face of administration pressure.[17]

The Church and Pike Committees

The Senate's Church Committee (see chapter 1) devoted very little of its investigative effort to analysis and held no hearings on the subject. Its staff did attempt to evaluate the quality of certain NIEs that it had requested to determine whether any appeared to have been distorted by political bias. Its initial effort focused on a 1970 NIE on Cambodia and the likely effects of US intervention there. DCI Helms, aware that the Nixon administration had already decided to intervene in Cambodia, did not forward the NIE to the White House. Church Committee staff members initially interpreted this as an effort to suppress views the administration did not want to hear. But after they discussed the issue with the senior analysts involved, one of whom told them it would have been "most counterproductive" if Helms had forwarded the estimate, they decided to drop the matter. In its final report, the committee found the quality, timeliness, and utility of finished analysis to be "adequate" but thought it could be substantially improved.[18]

The Pike Committee of the House, in part because of a desire to distinguish itself from its Senate counterpart, did make intelligence analysis a focus of its

---

[17] Colby, *Honorable Men*, 358–59.
[18] CIA draft study, Vol. II, 104–6.

efforts. Advising the Agency that it intended to assess how well it had predicted world events over the previous 10 years, the committee initially
requested "all CIA estimates, current intelligence reports and summaries, situation reports, and other pertinent documents" regarding

- the Middle East war (1973)

- the overthrow of Makarios in Greece and the Cyprus crisis (1974)

- the coup in Portugal (1974)

- the nuclear explosion by India (1974)

- the Tet offensive in Vietnam (1968)

- declarations of martial law in the Philippines and South Korea (1972)

- the Soviet invasion of Czechoslovakia (1968).[19]

On 11 September 1975, two days after sending this request to the Agency,
the Pike Committee held its first public hearing on the Agency's performance
in the analytical area by looking at the 1973 Middle East war. In the course of
this hearing, Chairman Pike, asserting unilateral authority to release information classified by the executive branch, released a portion of a classified report
provided by the Agency that indicated it had obviously misjudged Egyptian
and Arab intentions insofar as their attack on Israel was concerned. The White
House and Agency believed the disclosure seriously compromised US SIGINT
capabilities.

The following day, the committee subpoenaed records on the 1968 Tet
offensive, which it had earlier requested by letter. While the Agency gathered
together documents in response to the subpoena, President Ford advised the
committee on 18 September that the executive branch would no longer provide classified materials, testimony, or interviews to the committee until it had
satisfactorily altered its position.[20] Pike proposed to resolve the issue by giving the White House 24 hours' notice of his intent to release classified information, but this was immediately rejected. On 26 September, however, at a
White House meeting with Pike and the leadership of the House, Ford agreed
to lift his embargo on providing classified information to the committee, in
return for the committee's agreement that he would be the final arbiter in
terms of deciding what the committee would make public in the future.[21]

---

[19] Ibid., 131.
[20] Ibid., 133.
[21] Ibid., 135.

Over time, Pike Committee held public hearings on Cyprus, the Tet offensive, the coup in Portugal, and the 1973 Middle East war. According to one observer, none of them was "well-documented, complete, or effective."[22] Nonetheless, after the hearings, on the basis of its review of the finished intelligence the Agency provided, the committee found the Agency's performance to have been seriously deficient in terms of predicting each of the six events the committee ultimately looked into: the 1973 Middle East war, the 1968 Tet offensive, the 1974 coup in Cyprus, the 1974 coup in Portugal, the 1974 Indian nuclear test, and the 1968 Soviet invasion of Czechoslovakia. In some cases, the committee found that analysts had not been able to digest all the information available to them. In other cases, they asserted, communications between analysts and collectors had been poor.[23]

While the Agency vigorously protested the committee's selective use of data to justify these findings, its protests had no effect on the committee's final report. The committee also rejected the Agency's proposal to publish the criticism of its analytical performance in a classified annex. Although Pike had agreed earlier that the president would be the final arbiter of what would be released to the public, he contended his agreement did not extend to the committee's final report.[24] To strengthen analysis, the committee proposed that a separate office be established outside the CIA itself to support the DCI in his role as chief foreign intelligence officer for the US government.[25]

Early Interaction with the Select Committees: 1976–80

With the establishment of the SSCI in 1976 and the HPSCI the following year, each with approved facilities for the storage of classified information, the principal practical obstacle to sharing finished intelligence with Congress was removed.

In 1976, the Agency decided that several of its regular publications (the *National Intelligence Daily*, the *Economic Intelligence Weekly*, the *Weapons Intelligence Summary*, and the *Scientific Intelligence Digest*) could be shared with the SSCI. Only publications classified at the SECRET level or below, however, would be left with the committee, a limitation that the SSCI initially agreed to.[26] The Agency also considered creating a publication specifically

---

[22] Smist, *Congress Oversees*, 195.
[23] Ibid., 210.
[24] CIA draft study, Vol. II, 136–38.
[25] Ibid., 145.
[26] Ibid., 179.

designed for congressional readers but rejected the idea, fearing it would divert too many resources from its responsibilities toward the executive branch.[27]

For its part, the SSCI created a subcommittee on collection, production, and quality to oversee intelligence analysis, the first time this function had been "institutionalized" by a committee of Congress. Supported by its own staff, the subcommittee provided Congress for the first time with a capability to conduct independent examinations of the Agency's analytical performance. It would no longer need to rely solely on briefings by the DCI.

The subcommittee's first initiative was to assess the so-called Team A / Team B process instituted in 1976 to evaluate the quality of analysis on Soviet strategic capabilities and intentions. DCI Bush had appointed a team of outside experts (Team B) to review and assess the most recent NIEs on this subject prepared by the Community's senior analysts (Team A). After its review, Team B concluded that the NIEs published through 1975 had "substantially misperceived the motivations behind Soviet strategic programs, and thereby tended consistently to underestimate their intensity, scope and implicit threat." The NIE issued in 1976, on the other hand, had been more cautious in assessing Soviet intentions.[28] The SSCI did not attempt to decide whether Team B's evaluation was correct but, rather, focused on the process itself; ultimately it issued a report that criticized the ideological composition of Team B and raised questions about its objectivity. While a majority of the subcommittee believed that having a more broadly based group of outside experts critique NIEs was legitimate, one senator declared that the exercise had seriously compromised the objectivity of the analytical process.[29]

In 1977, the SSCI subcommittee looked into another set of issues. At a televised news conference, President Carter had referred to a classified CIA analysis that the world energy situation was far more pessimistic than generally believed, arguing that the administration's energy program was needed to cope with the deteriorating situation. After a *New York Times* editorial criticized Carter for misusing CIA analysis and criticized the Agency for "cooking" the facts to suit the president's agenda, the SSCI undertook to examine these charges. In a subsequent staff report, it found that the analysis in question had been issued before Carter had taken office and thus could not have been "cooked" to fit the administration's program. With regard to the substance of the analysis (specifically how much oil the Soviets would need to import over the succeeding 10 years to make up for the expected shortfall in domestic production), the SSCI accepted the conclusions of a panel of outside

---

[27] Ibid., 180.
[28] Ibid., 186.
[29] Ibid., 187.

experts who believed the Agency had overestimated the anticipated shortfall. Agency records reflect, however, that overall DCI Turner was pleased with the committee's report.[30]

The HPSCI also created a subcommittee to do oversight of intelligence analysis—the Subcommittee on Evaluation—that was initially subject to the same limitations as the SSCI in terms of what could be left and stored with the committee. The first area the subcommittee tackled was warning intelligence. After reviewing the performance of the Intelligence Community during past crises, including Pearl Harbor, the Korean War, the Cuban missile crisis, the Soviet invasion of Czechoslovakia, Vietnam, and the 1973 Middle East war, the subcommittee found the performance of intelligence agencies to have been spotty at best. It particularly faulted analysts and policymakers for failing, at times, to challenge their own presumptions that had led to the errors in judgment. Among other things, it recommended creating the position of national intelligence officer for warning, a recommendation the Agency adopted.[31]

In later studies, the subcommittee issued a lengthy report criticizing the failure of the Intelligence Community to predict the fall of the Shah of Iran. It noted, among other things, that an NIE being written at the time had found that Iran was "not in a pre-revolutionary state." It found fault with both collectors and analysts for failing to see the vulnerability of the Shah until it was too late and blamed policymakers for restricting collection, as well as taking other actions that had the effect of "skewing" the analysis of the Shah's regime.[32]

The subcommittee also looked into whether the Community had provided adequate warning of China's invasion of Vietnam in February 1979. It found, by and large, the Community had performed well. The invasion—undertaken by the Chinese ostensibly because of Vietnamese mistreatment of its ethnic Chinese minority and its occupation of the Spratley Islands, which China held claim to—lasted only a month before the Chinese withdrew. While the subcommittee acknowledged that Chinese leaders had rather clearly indicated their intent to the rest of the world two days before the invasion, they also found that the Intelligence Community, relying primarily on imagery, had given notice to policymakers severals weeks beforehand.

For the most part, the HPSCI subcommittee found the Agency cooperative in providing access to the documentation needed for these inquiries. Indeed, in the case of Iran, CIA turned over its entire production to the subcommittee. In turn, the subcommittee allowed the Agency to review and comment upon its

---

[30] Ibid., 188–89.

[31] Ibid., 235–36.

[32] House Permanent Select Committee on Intelligence, *Iran: Evaluation of U.S. Intelligence Performance Prior to November, 1978.*

draft reports, often modifying them in response to the Agency's criticism. In late 1979, however, when the subcommittee requested the entire list of "National Intelligence Topics," a formal compilation of consumer priorities to guide intelligence collection and analysis, the Agency, supported by the White House, balked, ultimately agreeing only to show the list to the committee's staff director.[33]

In late 1979, the HPSCI subcommittee conducted a different kind of assessment, evaluating the operation of the National Foreign Assessment Center, which DCI Turner had created to serve as the focal point for intelligence production at the national level.[34]

Later Interaction Regarding Analytical Issues: 1980–90

With the passage of the Intelligence Oversight Act in 1980 the two intelligence committees were by law given access to all information or material they needed to carry out their responsibilities. By this point, the committees and the Agency had been interacting with each other for almost four years. Sensitive information had been shared with both committees, and for the most part, both had demonstrated their intent and capability to protect such information. The comfort level, while far from absolute, had undeniably grown. The Agency now allowed the committees to store finished intelligence analysis classified above the SECRET level. Copies of the daily/weekly publications continued to be furnished, left with the committees, and returned later. Other publications, including NIEs and SNIEs, could be requested from lists provided to the committees. Indeed, the Agency (with apparent acquiescence from the committees) continued treat as off limits only the *President's Daily Brief* and other daily intelligence summaries tailored for cabinet officials. By the beginning of the Reagan administration, the committees had, or could obtain, access to virtually all finished intelligence the Intelligence Community produced.

From 1980 through 1984, the oversight committees initiated few formal inquiries into the Agency's performance in the analytical area. The SSCI subcommittee that dealt with analysis was eliminated in 1981; its HPSCI counterpart was merged with the existing oversight subcommittee to form the Subcommittee on Oversight and Evaluation. In 1982, this subcommittee produced a report on intelligence performance in Central America during the Carter and Reagan administrations, looking specifically at the issue of whether intelligence analysis had been slanted or skewed to support the poli-

---

[33] Ibid., 231.
[34] Ibid., 237–38.

cies of the incumbent administration. In fact, both committees during this period regularly examined whether the Agency's substantive analysis was being slanted to have it appear that the covert action programs in Central America were succeeding (see chapter 9). The HPSCI subcommittee also undertook an evaluation in 1984 of the intelligence performance prior to the bombing of the Marine barracks in Beirut.

For the most part, however, what oversight occurred in the analytical area during this period took place within the context of the committees' consideration of the Agency's annual budget. DCI Casey had come into office intent upon rebuilding the analytic capabilities of the Agency. To do this, he wanted a larger, more capable analytical corps. He also wanted more NIEs and SNIEs produced on topics important to policymakers.[35] Casey himself appointed a "senior review panel" in 1984 to review how well the Agency had done in these areas and provided a copy of the panel's generally favorable report to both committees. Apart from provoking questions in the course of the annual budget process, however, neither committee was immediately moved to initiate its own inquiry.

In 1985, however, the new SSCI chairman, David Durenberger (R-MN), decided to undertake an in-depth review of the analytical process. In a series of closed hearings, the SSCI explored the process by which requirements for analysis were generated, the relationship between analysts and consumers, how analysis was tasked within the Intelligence Community, the process for developing terms of reference for analytical studies, and the degree to which competitive analysis and outside experts were used to improve the intelligence product. The SSCI also looked at five recent intelligence products in an effort to determine whether they had met the needs of consumers.[36]

In the middle of this review, Durenberger, in an interview with the *Washington Post*, chose to criticize several of the products the committee was looking into. CIA had missed the crisis in the Philippines, he said, did not understand the rise of Muslim fundamentalism, and failed to comprehend the changes taking place in the Soviet Union. These off-hand comments angered Casey, who wrote a public rebuttal to Durenberger's charges, taking him to task for conducting oversight in an "off-the-cuff" manner through the news media and making unsubstantiated appraisals of the intelligence products he had criticized. Casey went on to say, "It was time to acknowledge that the oversight process has gone seriously awry." Durenberger countered with his own letter to the *Post*, saying that Casey's view was that "the public has no right to know how effectively the CIA does its job."[37]

---

[35] CIA draft study, Vol. III, 28–30.
[36] Ibid., 89.

Despite this acrimonious public exchange, the SSCI produced a draft report of its inquiry in September 1986 that was generally favorable, offering recommendations to improve "what was already an excellent system."[38] It also included five case studies of finished intelligence products that it said were "not entirely successful in achieving the goal of timely and relevant intelligence." These included

- an NIE on the Philippines that the SSCI concluded had "missed the point";

- an SNIE on Nicaragua that the SSCI thought showed signs of political bias;

- an SNIE on the Arabs and Israelis that the committee said was "a product in search of a consumer";

- an intelligence analysis of the likely Soviet response to the US Strategic Defense Initiative that the committee found unresponsive to the requirement that had prompted it.

On the whole, however, the report concluded "the finished intelligence produced for US policymakers is astonishingly good."[39] Because of classification concerns, the five case studies were dropped from the committee's report prior to its publication.

Developments taking place in the Soviet Union during this period also prompted an unusual degree of involvement by the committees in the analytical process, especially the SSCI. Mikhail Gorbachev had come to power in March 1985 and had quickly established himself as a new kind of Soviet leader. Open and willing to debate, he had shown himself willing to negotiate arms control treaties with the United States and had taken dramatic steps to rejuvenate the Soviet economy.

The issue for US intelligence (and for the Congress) at this point was whether Gorbachev was "for real" or was only appearing to be different to win concessions from the United States. At a closed hearing in August 1986, several senators on the SSCI expressed the view that CIA's analysis appeared to lack insight on this key issue. Following up on this session, the committee added provisions to the intelligence authorization bill for fiscal year 1987 requiring that estimates be prepared on the Soviet situation that made use of outside experts and competitive analysis and dealt with all of the factors bearing upon the issue of Gorbachev's intentions.[40]

---

[37] Ibid., 90–91.

[38] Ibid., 91.

[39] Ibid.

In fact, CIA officials continued to testify frequently before the intelligence committees—and periodically before other committees of Congress—well into 1991 as the Gorbachev era played out. The SSCI went so far as to establish an ad hoc task force in 1988 for the sole purpose of staying abreast of the fast-moving developments in the Soviet Union and Eastern Europe and regularly obtaining the insights of Agency analysts (see chapter 3).

The Iraqi Invasion of Kuwait and the Persian Gulf War: 1990–91

In the aftermath of Iraq's invasion and annexation of Kuwait in early August 1990, both intelligence committees wanted to know precisely what the Intelligence Community had done to provide warning of the Iraqi attack to US policymakers. DCI Webster and other Intelligence Community officials were immediately summoned to testify. Although records of their testimony remain classified, neither of the chairmen of the committees chose to criticize the Community's performance after the briefings.[41]

But a more complex issue remained for the Congress: what the United States should now do. The Bush administration had organized a multinational coalition to prevent an Iraqi attack on Saudi Arabia and to persuade Saddam Hussein to order his forces out of Kuwait. Many saw the principal means of persuasion to be the UN-mandated economic sanctions imposed immediately after the invasion. The issue for Congress and the administration was whether Saddam could be induced to leave Kuwait without a war.

On 8 November 1990, President Bush announced he was doubling the size of the US military deployment in the Gulf, in what appeared to be preparation for military action. Bush also indicated his intent to seek congressional endorsement for the use of military force if that became necessary.

With votes on this issue looming before them, the armed services and intelligence committees in both houses held multiple hearings in November and December 1990, both to assess Iraqi military strength and the damage being caused by the UN-mandated economic sanctions. With respect to Iraqi military strength, one staffer who heard the briefings recalled the committees being told:

> *The Iraqi military was the most advanced in that part of the world, battle-tested by eight years of war with Iran. . . . [It] would use*

---

[40] Ibid., 92–93.

[41] For a detailed description of the events leading up to the Iraqi invasion of Kuwait, see May and Zelikow, *Prelude to War: US Policy Toward Iraq 1988–1990*; Gordon and Trainor, *The General's War*, 1–30.

chemical and biological weapons against the coalition forces. . . . In
all likelihood, the United States was in for a prolonged conflict of at
least six months duration involving many casualties." [42]

On the issue of whether UN sanctions would force Saddam out of Kuwait, the assessments coming out of the Intelligence Community were initially ambivalent. In early December, however, DCI Webster appeared in open session before the HASC on the sanctions issue, and the Community's assessment at that point had become more definite. While the UN sanctions had damaged the Iraqi economy, Webster said, they had left Saddam's military and vital industries "virtually unscathed." He could offer "no assurance or guarantee that economic hardships [would] compel Saddam to leave Kuwait." [43]

In a meeting with editors of the *Washington Post* on 15 December 1990, Webster predicted that Saddam would only quit Kuwait if he were convinced he were "in peril of imminent military attack. [44] Subsequent news stories interpreted Webster's comment as saying that Saddam would quit Kuwait if he thought he were in imminent peril of an attack. This prompted a strong reaction from intelligence analysts at the Pentagon who told reporters they saw no signs of Saddam's willingness to withdraw under any circumstances. [45]

On 8 January 1991, President Bush submitted his request to the House and Senate formally asking them for a resolution authorizing him to use military force to compel Iraq to leave Kuwait if it had not done so by the 15 January deadline established by the UN. In preparation for the vote in the House, HASC Chairman Les Aspin (D-WI) asked DCI Webster to provide a letter setting forth what the Agency's position now was on the issue of sanctions. On 10 January, Aspin made the letter public. In it, Webster stated that it was "unlikely" that UN sanctions had "substantially eroded" Iraq's military capability to defend Kuwait. "Even if the sanctions continue to be enforced for another six to 12 months, economic hardship alone is unlikely to compel Saddam Husayn to retreat from Kuwait or cause regime-threatening popular discontent in Iraq." [46]

The letter angered Senate Democrats, who wanted to give sanctions more time and they publicly accused the DCI of trimming the Agency's analysis to fit the Bush administration's plan for war. SSCI Chairman Boren said the Agency appeared to be trying its best not to "undermine" the administration's policy. Majority Leader George Mitchell (D-ME) said the Webster letter "ran

---

[42] Quoted in Snider, *Sharing Secrets with Lawmakers*, 49.

[43] Webster, "Crisis in the Persian Gulf: Sanctions, Diplomacy, and War, 112–15.

[44] Lardner, "No Iraq Move Seen Until Attack Near."

[45] Cassidy and Colvin, "Accusations Fly as Iraq Cancels White House Meeting with Bush."

[46] William Webster, Letter to Rep. Les Aspin, 10 January 1991.

directly contrary to the facts [he] had presented [earlier]."[47] On 15 January 1991, both houses passed resolutions authorizing the administration to use military force to oust Iraqi forces from Kuwait, albeit over the dissent of prominent Democratic senators, including Boren and SASC Chairman Sam Nunn (D-GA).

Two days later, the air war against Iraq began. For five weeks, coalition aircraft pounded Iraqi forces and strategic installations in preparation for the ground assault that would liberate Kuwait. In mid-February, as the ground war loomed, the issue for US military commanders was how much damage the air assault had inflicted upon Iraqi forces. The Community was divided, however. CENTCOM imagery analysts were more positive about the air war's effectiveness than were their Agency counterparts. The internal debate over these estimates was leaked to the press, prompting both intelligence committees to hold closed hearings on the damage assessment issue.[48]

When the ground war did begin, it lasted but a few days. No chemical or biological weapons were used, and the Iraqi army was routed within hours of the initial assaults. American casualties were few. According to his staff, Boren was "livid," believing the Intelligence Community had deliberately "sandbagged" him by overplaying Iraq's military capabilities. He was, after all, chairman of the SSCI, supposedly someone "in the know," and yet had obviously misread the situation. He vowed to his staff he would never be so trusting of intelligence analysts again.[49] Senator Nunn, for his part, later told the *Washington Post* that his negative vote on the Iraq resolution — also based on the intelligence assessments — had significantly impaired his credibility as chairman of the SASC and had removed any thought he might have had for running for president the following year.[50]

After the war, both intelligence committees conducted postmortems of the performance of the Intelligence Community, as did the two armed services committees. The HASC study covering both phases of the war is, in fact, unclassified.[51] It focused primarily on the difficulties in assissing the results of US air strikes on Iraqi forces.

---

[47] Meddis, "Critics Charge CIA Analysis is Politically Biased."

[48] Royce, "Damage Reports That Don't Add Up"; Gordon and Trainor, *The Generals' War*, 334–35.

[49] Snider, *Sharing Secrets with Lawmakers*, 49.

[50] *Washington Post,* "Nunn Regrets Vote on Gulf War.."

[51] House Committee on Armed Services, *Intelligence Successes and Failures in Operations Desert Shield/Desert Storm*.

The Gates Confirmation Hearings: 1991

Robert M. Gates, who had served as deputy director for intelligence and DDCI under DCI Casey, was himself nominated to be DCI on 24 June 1991 (see chapter 11 for a detailed description of the confirmation process). Within weeks of the nomination, several former CIA analysts who had served under Gates during the Casey era contacted the SSCI, alleging that analysis produced under Gates had been politicized to fit the policy predilections of Casey and/or the Reagan administration.

SSCI contacted other Agency analysts, both present and former, to obtain corroboration of the allegations it had received. These interviews surfaced still more allegations. In all, according to its report on the nomination, the committee interviewed approximately 80 analysts and reviewed "several hundred documents" as part of its investigation of the politicization issue.[52]

The SSCI asked six present and former analysts to testify about these allegations: three opposed to the nomination and three in favor. The initial testimony took place in closed session as the analysis at issue was still classified. Having decided, however, that the testimony adverse to Gates had to be made a matter of public record, the committee had the six analysts return on 1 and 2 October 1991 in open session. Gates was afforded an opportunity to respond to their testimony, also in open session, a day later.[53]

The details of these hearings, as well as how the committee dealt with the specific allegations against Gates, are set forth in chapter 11. Suffice it to say, however, for purposes of this chapter, these three days of hearings were the first and only time in the Agency's history that a committee of the Congress subjected its analytical process to searching public scrutiny.

In order to understand the nature of the allegations being made against Gates, the committee first sought to understand the "ethos" that governs intelligence analysis. One of the analysts who testified said there had been

> *a strong tradition among older CIA officers, one* [that stressed] *the need for integrity of judgment and action, a generation of officers raised on the need to tell it like it is, of going where the evidence takes one and then candidly so telling senior policymakers, whether they find such judgments congenial or not—the aim being to enlighten them about the true shape of the world, not to please them or cater to their preconceptions.*[54]

---

[52] Senate Select Committee on Intelligence, *Nomination of Robert M. Gates to be Director of Central Intelligence*, 4.

[53] Ibid., 2.

[54] Ibid., 100.

Others noted that politicization could take many forms. Judgments might be reached that are not supported by the available evidence. Evidence that does not support the desired judgment might be ignored. The review process that finished analysis goes through might be skewed to produce a desired result. Personnel assigned to produce analysis might be known to favor the desired result. Managers might, by their actions, create a "politically charged" atmosphere—"a fog," as one analyst testified—that permeates the entire workplace. "You cannot hold it in your hand or nail it to the wall," the analyst said, "[but] it is real. It does exist. And it does affect people's behavior."[55]

Still others pointed out that the impetus to skew analysis might come as a result of discussions with fellow analysts concerned that policymakers do not like (or read) the analysis the office has been producing.[56] Another argued that more tangible evidence was needed and that politicization had to involve more than simply creating an atmosphere but also deliberate efforts to produce the desired political outcome in a particular case.

All agreed that politicization destroyed the integrity of the analytical process, but that it was difficult to prove. Rarely are intelligence analysts told what to write or directed to change their conclusions, one noted. When they see their analysis changed, some naturally leap to the conclusion that it is being changed for political reasons. This is especially apt to happen, one testified, when analysts know that their boss—in this instance, DCI Casey—has strong political views. At the same time, there is a great deal of subjectivity involved in deciding what goes into intelligence analysis, the analysts acknowledged, on the part of both the drafter and the reviewer. And no matter what judgments are ultimately reached, one testified, they are not going to please everyone.[57]

Ultimately, the committee's investigation did not produce evidence of a "smoking gun" that Gates had directly and personally intervened to make an analytical product come out a certain way. The SSCI voted 11 to 4 in favor of his nomination. The committee's inquiry nonetheless had a profound effect, not only on the Agency itself, but on the public, who, for the first time, received an education in what intelligence analysts actually do.

---

[55] Ibid., 101.
[56] Ibid., 103.
[57] Ibid., 202.

Interaction with the Select Committees 1991– 2000

While there were no comparable examinations of the analytical process by either intelligence committee during the rest of the 1990s, there were certain analytical products that generated controversy on the Hill.

The Haiti Imbroglio: 1993

In February 1991, Jean-Bertrand Aristide had been elected president of Haiti in what had been a relatively open and free election. In September of the same year, he had been overthrown in a coup undertaken by Haitian security forces and had fled the country, first to Venezuela and then to Washington DC. It had been the policy, first of the Bush administration and then the Clinton administration, to return Aristide to power.

By the time the Clinton administration took office, the situation in Haiti was claiming widespread public attention, largely because of the huge number of Haitian refugees who were attempting to leave Haiti for the United States to escape the increasing violence. A new NIE was produced in January 1993 entitled *Haiti Over the Next Few Months*. Among other things, it judged that Aristide suffered from a serious psychiatric disorder and predicted that his return to power would spur greater violence and instability.[58]

Nevertheless, in March 1993 Aristide and the military leader who controlled Haiti accepted an UN-brokered agreement setting 30 October as the date Aristide would return to Haiti to assume the presidency. Several weeks before the transfer of power was to have taken place, the United States sent a transport ship, the USS Harlan County, to Haiti, carrying lightly armed troops and police to begin training Haitian police prior to Aristide's arrival. The ship had to turn back, however, when confronted with angry mobs on the dock.

Republican members of Congress seized on this episode as a sign of the new administration's weakness and incompetence. The NIE that had been issued in January and subsequently shared with the intelligence committees then became the focus of the administration's critics. The NIO responsible for the assessment was hauled up to the Hill for repeated briefings, not only before the intelligence committees but before other committees and individual members. Jesse Helms (R-NC), who led the attack on the administration in the Senate, claimed on the floor that CIA had confirmed his own assessment that Aristide was "a killer" and "a psychopath."[59] A few weeks later, when DCI Woolsey appeared before the SFRC, he was taken to task by Senate Demo-

---

[58] *New York Times*, "Administration is Fighting Itself on Haiti Policy."
[59] See Remarks of Senator Jesse Helms, *Congressional Record*, 21 October 1993.

crats, who were sure the Agency had deliberately leaked the analysis on Aristide to undermine the administration.[60]

While both intelligence committees conducted detailed inquiries into the evidence underlying the judgments contained in the January NIE, neither issued a public report of their findings. A year later, in October 1994, Aristide was reinstalled as president of Haiti after US military elements had deployed to the island to ensure his safe return.

Analyses of the Ballistic Missile Threat to the United States: 1995–99

During the last half of the 1990s, the intelligence committees, especially the SSCI, focused several times on the analysis done of the ballistic missile threat to the United States.

In 1995, the Intelligence Community produced an NIE whose purpose was to look at the long-range missile threat to the United States over the ensuing 15 years. The conclusions of this NIE essentially downplayed such a threat, judging that, with the possible exception of North Korea, no country other than a declared nuclear power would be capable of developing or acquiring a ballistic missile that could reach the continental United States or Canada by 2010. Two years earlier, the Community had judged such a threat as "low" or "quite low" but still possible.

In early 1996, some in Congress, including two members of the SSCI, were publicly attacking the judgments of this NIE as too benign and politically motivated. At the time, the Clinton administration had been arguing against the need and legitimacy (under the 1972 ABM Treaty) to build a new missile defense system against such threats, a system being urged on the Congress by Republicans, who now controlled both houses. The SSCI directed its staff to look into how the 1995 NIE had been put together. At the same time, the two armed services committees, in their action on the FY 1996 defense authorization bill, directed DCI Deutch to commission a panel of independent experts to review and evaluate the 1995 NIE.

In December 1996, the panel Deutch commissioned, led by former DCI Robert Gates, presented its report in public session to the SSCI.[61] While it found no evidence that the analysts involved had been influenced by policymakers in the Clinton administration, it found a number of shortcomings in how the NIE had been assembled and how it presented the available evidence. With regard to the ICBM threat, the panel found that the NIE had not used all the available evi-

---

[60] Center for the Study of Intelligence monograph.

[61] Senate Select Committee on Intelligence, *Intelligence Analysis of the Long-Range Missile Threat to the United States* .

dence to make its case. On the other hand, it found the NIE had failed to give sufficient attention to the threat posed by cruise missiles or sea-launched ballistic missiles.[62] The vice chairman of the National Intelligence Council, which was responsible for the NIE, defended it to the committee. He argued that NIEs, generally, are never the last word and frequently provoke controversy and that in the end such debate is healthy for democratic governance.[63]

The SSCI staff inquiry into the production of the NIE also found no basis for the charge that analysts had been pressured to reach the conclusions they did,[64] but the committee decided not to publish its results inasmuch as the Gates panel (whose report was published in sanitized form) had reached the same conclusion.

Although the findings of the Gates panel were critical of the methodology used in producing the 1995 NIE, they did not go far enough, in the view of some Republican members, in providing an alternative view of the ICBM threat to the United States. To provide such a view, the armed services committees included a provision in the FY 1997 defense authorization bill creating a new commission to consider the issue. Its charter went well beyond examining the earlier intelligence judgments to examining any information bearing upon the issue. Chaired by former Secretary of Defense Donald Rumsfeld, the commission reported to Congress in July 1998 that the threat was more immediate and more uncertain than the 1995 NIE had portrayed. In addition to the existing threat posed by the nuclear capabilities of China and Russia, the commission judged that countries like North Korea, Iran, and Iraq could develop a ballistic missile capable of threatening the United States within five years of a decision to acquire such a capability and the United States may not know that such a decision had been made.[65]

Less than two months after the Rumsfeld Commission issued its report, North Korea, in an attempt to put its first satellite into space, conducted a launch using what had been regarded as its intermediate-range ballistic missile (the Taepo Dong-1). The launch surprised US intelligence analysts, however, because instead of launching a two-stage missile, North Korea had launched a three-stage missile. Not only did this indicate technological sophistication exceeding US estimates, it also made the threat posed to the United States by North Korea's ICBM (the Taepo Dong-2) even more ominous than the Rums feld Commission had believed.

---

[62] Ibid., 16–18.

[63] Ibid., 10.

[64] Ibid., 5 (statement of Senator Kerrey).

[65] Commission to Assess the Ballistic Missile Threat to the United States, "Executive Summary."

Responding to this and other developments, the Intelligence Community issued a new NIE in September 1999, forecasting the ballistic missile threat to the United States. through 2015, rather than 2010. Not only did it use certain methodologies the Rumsfeld Commission recommended, it provided a far more alarming assessment of the threat.

> *Most analysts believe that North Korea probably will test a Taepo-Dong 2 this year. . . . A two-stage Taepo Dong-2 could deliver a several-hundred-kiloton payload to the western half of the United States. A three-stage Taepo Dong-2 could deliver a several-hundred-kiloton payload anywhere in the United States."* [66]

Given the controversy produced by the 1995 NIE, the SSCI held a closed hearing on the 1999 NIE to explore how it had been put together, reporting favorably afterwards that it incorporated a number of the improvements the Rumsfeld Commission recommended. [67]

Indian Nuclear Test: May 1998

The Intelligence Community had for decades been concerned about the possibility of a nuclear conflict between India and Pakistan, intently tracking any development that might indicate progress on the part of either country toward developing a nuclear weapon. In fact, the Community had been able to provide President Clinton with sufficient warning of an impending nuclear test in1995 that he had been able to intervene with the government of India to stop it. On 11 May 1998, however, the Indian government conducted an underground nuclear test, which US policymakers learned of on CNN. More tests were conducted two days later.

A media frenzy followed. Upon hearing the news, Senator Shelby, chairman of the SSCI at the time, put in a call to DCI Tenet. Tenet describes the conversation.

> *Not surprisingly, he asked me what had happened. One of my habits is to be plainspoken, maybe too much. "Senator, . . .we didn't have a clue." . . . Within minutes, Shelby was on CNN, calling the miss a "colossal" intelligence failure. Was it a failure? No doubt. [But] "colossal" is in the eye of the beholder.* [68]

In fact, Shelby told CNN he regarded it "a colossal failure of our nation's intelligence gathering, possibly the greatest failure for more than a decade,"

---

[66] National Intelligence Council, *Foreign Missile Development and the Ballistic Missile Threat through 2015"* (unclassified summary).

[67] Senate Select Committee on Intelligence, *Committee Activities*, 11.

[68] Tenet, *Center of the Storm*, 44.

and warned that it could "set off a nuclear arms race in Southeast Asia."[69] Within hours of Shelby's statement, Tenet announced that he was commissioning a "blue ribbon" assessment of the Intelligence Community's performance, to be headed by retired ADM David Jeremiah. Jeremiah, Tenet said, would file his report within 10 days.

Neither intelligence committee was prepared to wait even that long and summoned Tenet to appear before them in closed session later the same week. According to press reports, Tenet explained the Indian government had taken quite elaborate steps to conceal the tests. This was confirmed by an Indian nuclear researcher who told the press, "It's not a failure of the CIA. It's a matter of their intelligence being good [but] our deception being better."[70]

Jeremiah made a preliminary report to both committees within Tenet's 10-day timeline but did not issue his final report until 2 June 1998, when he provided closed briefings to each intelligence committee. While his report was classified, Jeremiah held a press conference at the CIA to explain his findings in general terms. Confirming the earlier reports of the elaborate efforts the Indian government had made to conceal the tests, Jeremiah also faulted the "mind-set" of US intelligence analysts who failed to appreciate what was going on within the Indian government as well as the "disconnects" that were apparent between analysts and collectors and among collectors themselves.[71]

The day after Jeremiah's briefing, the leaders of the SSCI went on a nightly news program to say that in their judgment Jeremiah had "gotten it right." While there was a need for follow-up to ensure this kind of failure does not happen in the future and to ensure that US intelligence agencies do not become "complacent" again, they did not indicate the need for more investigation.[72] Indeed, neither the SSCI nor the HPSCI undertook their own assessments of the Intelligence Community's performance regarding the Indian nuclear tests despite the calamitous characterizations that were issued when the tests were reported by CNN.

Warning of the Attacks of 9/11: 2002

The 9/11 terrorist attacks prompted the two intelligence committees to undertake, for the first time in their history, a joint investigation into the activities of the Intelligence Community before and after the attacks. While CIA was but one of a number of agencies whose activities the investigation encompassed, all three of the Agency's mission areas—analysis, collection, and

---

[69] CNN, "CIA Caught Off Guard on India Nuclear Test, Hearings, Inquiry Planned."

[70] Associated Press, "CIA Searching for Answers behind its India-nuclear failure."

[71] Central Intelligence Agency, "Jeremiah News Conference," 2 June 1998.

[72] PBS. *The Online News Hour with Jim Lehrer*, 3 June 3 1998.

covert action—were examined in the course of the joint inquiry. Here, the findings and recommendations with respect to CIA analysis are summarized.

The overriding issue for the committees was why the Intelligence Community had failed to learn of the attacks before they took place, and what warnings, if any, had the IC provided policymakers to prepare them for such a contingency. To answer these questions, the committee staff sought and received access to all of the intelligence analysis produced on terrorism generally, and al-Qa'ida in particular, from 1994 until the attacks of 2001.

While the committees ultimately found that the Intelligence Community did not have information specifically identifying the time, place, and nature of the attacks, it had warned of the possibility of such attacks for a long while. Beginning in 1998, the committees found, there had been a "modest but relatively steady stream" of intelligence reporting warning of terrorist attacks within the United States. In the spring and summer of 2001, moreover, there had been a "significant increase" in intelligence reports indicating that al-Qa'ida planned to strike against US interests in the near future. The potential use of airplanes as weapons had also been raised years before but had never prompted a formal intelligence assessment.[73]

In fact, the central problem the committees identified with regard to analysis was that there had been very little of it. While intelligence reporting on terrorist threats like al-Qa'ida had been voluminous, rarely had the Intelligence Community assessed what it meant. No NIE was ever done on the threat to the United States posed by al-Qa'ida. As the committee pointed out:

> *Active analytic efforts to identify the scope and nature of the threat, particularly in the domestic United States, were clearly inadequate. . . . The quality of counterterrorism analysis was inconsistent, and many analysts were inexperienced, unqualified, under-trained, and without access to critical information. As a result, there was a dearth of creative, aggressive analysis targeting Bin Ladin and a persistent inability to comprehend the collective significance of individual pieces of intelligence. These analytic deficiencies seriously undercut the ability of US policymakers to understand the full nature of the threat and to make fully informed decisions.[74]*

As far as the Agency itself was concerned, the committees faulted the relative paucity of analysts assigned to Bin Ladin and al-Qa'ida in the years prior to the attacks.

---

[73] *Report of the Joint Inquiry Into the Terrorist Attacks of September 11, 2001*, 7-10.
[74] Ibid., 59–60.

To address these problems, the committees recommended the creation of a National Intelligence Officer (NIO) for Terrorism, who would ensure and oversee the development of strategic analysis on terrorist topics. They also recommended the establishment of an "all-source terrorism information fusion center" within the Department of Homeland Security to improve the focus and quality of counterterrorism analysis and to ensure its distribution within the Intelligence Community and to other appropriate recipients.[75] The first recommendation was not acted upon. The second was, but in a different way: with the creation of the TTIC (Terrorist Threat Integration Center) in 2003, which reported to the DCI, and the creation of the NCTC (National Counterterrorism Center) in 2004, which was placed under the DNI in 2005.

The Prewar Intelligence Assessments of Iraqi WMD: 2003–2004

By June 2003, it was increasingly apparent that the intelligence assessments on Iraqi weapons of mass destruction done before the United States invaded Iraq in March 2003 had been wrong. Although US military personnel and civilian specialists were still trying to find such weapons, their initial efforts targeting the most likely locations where such weapons would be produced or stored had failed to produce the expected results.

Reacting to these developments, the SSCI announced on 20 June 2003, it intended to review the intelligence assessments that had formed the basis for the US intervention in Iraq: the assessments regarding Iraqi WMD programs, Iraq's ties to terrorist groups, the threat Iraq posed to stability and security in the region, and Iraq's repression of its own people.

Over the next 12 months, the committee sought and received access not only to the assessments themselves but also to the intelligence underlying them. In all, it reviewed more than 45,000 pages of documents, and its staff interviewed more than 200 witnesses. The committee also held four closed hearings on aspects of the inquiry, but its staff carried out the bulk of the investigation.

The 422-page report of the committee's inquiry was published on 9 July 2004. The first 303 pages dealt with the intelligence assessments on Iraqi WMD capabilities, and, in particular, the NIE that the committee itself had requested in early September 2002 in order to prepare its members as well as the Senate as a whole for the upcoming vote on the proposed resolution authorizing the use of military force in Iraq.

Although time was short and DCI Tenet questioned the need for such an estimate in light of the assessments already available, he had authorized prep-

---

[75] Ibid., appendix, 5–6.

aration of the NIE, which was published on 1 October 2002, a little less than three weeks after it had been commissioned. It was 90 pages long, including a five-page summary of its key judgments that addressed each major aspect of Iraq's WMD activities: nuclear, chemical, biological, and delivery systems.

In its 2004 report, the SSCI painstakingly examined each area addressed in the NIE, noting first the key judgments made in each area and then looking at the quality and quantity of the evidence underlying each of these judgments.[76]

While the committee found "significant shortcomings" in collection on all aspects of the WMD program, it reserved its most scathing criticism for the quality of the analysis. Most of the key judgments in the NIE, the committee found, "either overstated, or were not supported by, the underlying intelligence reporting." The evidence was simply "mischaracterized." The "uncertainties" behind the key judgments were not "accurately or adequately explained to policymakers." Ambiguous evidence was given more weight than it deserved, and evidence that indicated Iraq did not have "active and expanding" WMD programs was "ignored or minimized." Overall, the committee said, there had been a serious failure of leadership and management. Analysts had not been encouraged "to challenge their assumptions, fully consider alternative arguments, [or] accurately characterize the intelligence reporting," nor were they counseled once it became evident they had "lost their objectivity."[77] With regard to the CIA itself, the committee found it had "abused its unique position in the Intelligence Community" by failing to share information on Iraqi WMD programs with analysts in other intelligence agencies.[78]

Intelligence assessments on Iraq's links to terrorists, including its relationship with al-Qa'ida, received higher marks. The committee found the Agency had "reasonably assessed" Iraq's contacts with al-Qa'ida and confirmed that no evidence had been found to link Iraq with the attacks of 9/11 or any other al-Qa'ida attacks. Moreover, the committee said, CIA's analysis of Iraq's support to terrorist groups had been "reasonable and objective."[79]

With regard to past intelligence assessments of Iraq as a threat to regional security and stability, the committee generally found such assessments to have been "reasonable and balanced" but faulted the Intelligence Community for not having produced NIEs and other community-wide assessments of Iraqi capabilities before the war and early enough to alert policymakers when it had become evident that these capabilities had significantly changed.[80] Finally, the

---

[76] Senate Select Committee on Intelligence, *U.S. Intelligence Community's Pre-War Intelligence Assessments on Iraq.*

[77] Ibid., 14–23.

[78] Ibid. 27.

[79] Ibid., 346–47.

committee found the body of analysis on Saddam Hussein's human rights record was limited but "an accurate depiction of the scope of abuses under this regime."[81]

Without question, the SSCI report represented the most thorough dissection of a body of intelligence analysis that Congress had ever done. While the Agency initially took issue with some of its findings and contended that shortcomings found with respect to a single NIE should not be taken as an indictment of intelligence analysis generally, it also acknowledged there were serious flaws in some of the prewar intelligence on Iraq and steps had already been taken to assure they are not repeated.[82]

AUTHOR'S COMMENTARY

The Nature of the Interaction over Analysis

Where analysis is concerned, most of the Agency's interaction with Congress has involved failures (perceived and real) to predict significant events. Before the select committees were created, this was almost the exclusive focus of congressional oversight. The issue was simply whether the Agency had predicted an event that had had consequences for US interests. Congress had created the CIA to provide warning of such events, and when this did not appear to have happened, Congress wanted to know why. Typically, the DCI was summoned to explain and defend the Agency's performance, and at times he was more persuasive than at others. There was no independent effort by the Congress to look behind what he was telling them.

This changed once the select committees came along. With their own professional staffs, the committees now had a capability to look more thoroughly at the Agency's performance, not only to determine why it had failed to predict a particular event but also to look at how it arrived at its analytical judgments on a range of topics. Over time, several inquiries were undertaken into the analytical process itself. There were also occasional "deep dives" into particular assessments to determine whether the analytical judgments rendered

---

[80] Ibid., 393.

[81] Ibid., 402.

[82] McLaughlin press conference, 9 July 2004. In his memoir, DCI Tenet also acknowledged the validity of many of the committee's criticisms but pointed out that most of the shortcomings lay in the presentation of the "key judgments" rather than in the body of the estimate itself (*In the Center of the Storm*, 321–39).

were adequately supported by the underlying intelligence (the SSCI's review of the prewar assessments of Iraqi WMD).

Looking behind intelligence analysis has proven difficult for the committees to do and do well, however, even with professional staffs. Intelligence analysis is inherently subjective: analysts must weigh the evidence based upon their knowledge and experience, separate the wheat from the chaff, and characterize their conclusions in a way that neither understates nor overstates what they believe the evidence means. Beyond this, there are several layers of reviewers and supervisors who have the opportunity to change it in the course of the analytical process. Congress knows this. It also knows that intelligence analysts are expert in their respective fields, usually more knowledgeable than members of Congress or their staffs. Thus, for an oversight committee to mount an independent challenge to an analytical assessment requires a great deal of time and effort on the part of its professional staff. For this reason alone, the committees shy away from doing them.

Even if an oversight committee knows that the analysis in question proved to be wrong, for its critique to be credible, the analysis must have been "wrong" based upon what was known at the time it was published, not what was later found to be the case—unless that lack of information is itself the result of a serious inadequacy. The committee might spend considerable time ascertaining what was known at the time a judgment was rendered, only to decide that the judgment that proved to be erroneous was reasonable under the circumstances. Further complicating the committee's task is the fact that intelligence analysts commonly caveat and condition their judgments or set them out in terms of "alternative scenarios." Analysts resort to such techniques especially when significant gaps remain in their knowledge. So while the judgments they ultimately reach may be way off the mark, they have left in enough "weasel words" or "alternative scenarios" that the committees may be hard pressed to find them unambiguously "wrong."

This is not to say the select committees cannot do independent evaluations of intelligence analysis or do them well. The HPSCI's 1979 report on the fall of the Shah of Iran and the SSCI's 2004 evaluation of the prewar assessments on Iraq are cases in point. The considerable effort required to mount such inquiries and the difficulties inherent in arriving at a crisp, objective results tend to limit the amount of serious effort that is done in this area. Indeed, the committees are often content to rely on panels of outside experts, or perhaps the Agency's inspector general, to evaluate suspect analytical work rather than tackling it themselves.

The Implications of Sharing Intelligence for Oversight

When substantive intelligence analysis is briefed to members of Congress, it is normally because they want the benefit of such analysis, not because they want to criticize the analyst doing the briefing or the agency responsible for producing it. Yet, not infrequently, criticism results. Impressions are inevitably created in the minds of the members who hear them. Does the analyst appear to have command of the subject matter? Do his or her conclusions, based upon the available evidence, appear justified?

Most of the time, members come away satisfied. Even if they do not agree with the analysis, they will credit the analyst with making a persuasive case for his or her position. After all, most members have nowhere near the background that analysts have with respect to the subjects being briefed.

On occasion, though, what was meant to be an "informational" briefing can turn hostile. Members will not be satisfied with what they hear and will want to know more about how and why analysts arrived at particular conclusions. They may question the reliability and accuracy of the intelligence that underlies their judgments. They may be looking for "ammunition" to use against the administration or to promote their own agendas. This can pose a delicate problem for the analyst, especially if the member being briefed is not on one of the oversight committees. Normally, their parent agencies instruct analysts to avoid discussing sources and methods with anyone other than members of their oversight committees. But not all members understand that distinction and may take umbrage at an analyst for refusing to answer their questions. If the analyst cannot come up with a way to satisfy the member, he or she may become the target of a complaint to his parent agency. Even if the member is on one of the intelligence committees—allowing analysts to go into greater detail to explain their position—the member may still not be satisfied. The member might urge the committee to launch a full-scale inquiry in terms of how this particular analysis was put together or may see it as a sign of a larger, more pervasive problem the committee should look into.

The same thing can happen with respect to written analysis that is made available to the Hill. While this happens less often, finished intelligence can also provoke hostile reaction and lead to oversight inquiries, to wit, the 1993 NIE on Haiti and the 1995 NIE on the ballistic missile threat, described earlier in this chapter.

Thus, the sharing of intelligence with Congress, either as in the form of briefings or documentary material, can lead to oversight inquiries. While the analysis may have been provided to inform Congress—or otherwise support its institutional functions—it might also spark questions from the members who receive it.

CHAPTER 8

OVERSIGHT OF COLLECTION

As noted in chapter 1, the Agency's original statutory charter made no mention of espionage, but Congress clearly understood that one of its principal functions would be to mount such operations to collect foreign intelligence. Over time, presidents have authorized the Agency to undertake other kinds of collection.

This chapter describes the extent to which Congress was aware of, and has been involved in overseeing, the Agency's collection activities. It does not go into these activities in detail but only to the extent necessary for the reader to understand the issues and concerns that have prompted Congress to become involved in them over the years. This chapter does not cover congressional action on the Agency's budget, described in chapter 6, nor does it include Congress's involvement in covert action, described in chapter 9, or counterintelligence and security matters, described in chapter 10.

Early Congressional Awareness of Espionage Operations: 1947–60

It is true that many, if not most, of the Agency's early overseers in Congress were reluctant to be given information of a sensitive nature, including information about the Agency's operational activities. For them, it was enough to know that the Agency was conducting espionage around the world to collect foreign intelligence; they did not need the details.

It would be a mistake to conclude, however, that they never received such information. While the documentary record is sparse, there are scattered, sometimes oblique, references (noted below) indicating that Congress was given information from time to time about the Agency's operations, even during the early years of its existence. Specific ongoing operations were rarely, if ever, discussed—the names or identities of agents would have been considered off-limits even by the committees themselves—but, as former Legislative Counsel Walter Pforzheimer recalled, early DCIs would "talk broad programs . . . occasionally talk generally in the field of techniques."[1] They would also let their subcommittees know about notable successes and failures. From time to time, they would explain the difficulties inherent in carrying out espionage operations in denied areas, and, at times, even provide nonspecific information on the Agency's extant capabilities in a particular country.

More often than not, this kind of information was imparted at a personal level to the leaders of the CIA subcommittees. Occasionally it would be provided at formal meetings of the subcommittees—either to justify the Agency's annual budget request or to justify other legislation the Agency was seeking—but testimony pertaining to such topics would typically be off-the-record. On rare occasions, non-CIA committees might be given a glimpse of the Agency's operational capabilities, either to explain why the Agency had failed to predict a particular event (see chapter 7) or to respond to other kinds of criticism. Typically, though, congressional access to information concerning operations—sources and methods—was limited at best and confined to the CIA subcommittees, none of which had the capability or the interest in probing into them, apart from pressing the DCI for answers as the situation might require.

In 1948, when DCI Hillenkoetter was preparing to testify before the HASC subcommittee on what eventually became the CIA Act of 1949, his legislative counsel advised him to show off "two or three obsolete gadgets in the nature of trick fountain pens, trick cameras, or other 'toys' which would be effective as exhibits indicating the specialized nature of certain of our procurements."[2] Later, during the Senate's consideration of the bill's provision authorizing the DCI to bring 100 aliens into the United States each year, one senator explained, apparently reflecting the justification provided the Agency, that the provision was essential to provide protection for individuals engaged in the "most dangerous work of espionage."[3]

In October 1949, after the Soviet Union had exploded its first atomic bomb, a senator on the JAEC took Hillenkoetter to task for misleading the committee when he previously told it that the CIA "actually had agents in Russia; that it had gotten some of its agents out of Russia with information; that it was screening people leaving and escaping Russia; and [implied] that it possessed much factual data upon which the previously estimated date of completion of the first weapon by Russia had been arrived at."[4] The senator went on to tell Hillenkoetter that he thought the Agency had "muffed it for a year and a half, maybe longer." When the discussion apparently turned to what the CIA needed to obtain this kind of information, Hillenkoetter angrily replied,

> *We could put 10,000 people in Russia, and there is no assurance that we would have all the information that we have . . . you can*

---

[1] Pforzheimer interview, 7 March 1983, 20.

[2] CIA draft study, Vol. I, 20.

[3] Ibid., 25.

[4] Barrett, *CIA and Congress*, 55–56.

give us 100,000, and . . . [not] *know definitely what they were going to do and when they would produce a bomb. This thing doesn't work that way.* [5]

In 1950, Congressman John Tabor, the ranking Republican on the HAC, was frank to note, "Off-the-record testimony indicates that we have no real penetration behind Iron Curtain countries."[6]

DCI Smith told a class of young CIA officers in 1952 that the CIA could not "get the money we need if we didn't tell [Congress] a good deal about our operations."[7] At the same time, he was wary of getting into too much detail. When members' questioning became uncomfortably pointed, former CIA liaison Pforzheimer later recalled, Smith would sometimes attempt to divert attention by saying, "Now, as I recall, Marshal Stalin once told me" . . . and this [according to Pforzheimer] would always make an impression."[8] Having served as US ambassador to the Soviet Union following World War II, Smith was one of the few people in Washington who had actually met with the "archenemy."

In 1953, after DCI Dulles learned that Polish intelligence had penetrated one of the Agency's espionage networks, he reportedly commented to his aides, "Well, I guess I'll have to fudge a little. I'll tell the truth to Dick [Senator Russell]. I always do. That is, if Dick wants to know."[9]

In 1954, Dulles appeared before the HAC subcommittee, now chaired by Congressman Tabor, where he was told to be prepared to provide "details" with respect to the Agency's operations. Dulles took with him a book describing espionage successes as well as failures and, according to one account of the meeting, spoke candidly about the problems posed by clandestine collection inside the Soviet Union.[10] (The fact that the HAC subcommittee had asked for such sensitive information later provoked complaints from the CIA subcommittees in the Senate.)

Prior to this hearing, Tabor spoke with Dulles about information the congressman had received indicating that the CIA was involved in SIGINT activities and wanted to know whether they were duplicating NSA's efforts. Dulles explained that "through our relations with foreign intelligence services" the

---

[5] Ibid., 61–62.
[6] Ibid., 96.
[7] Ibid., 136.
[8] Montague, *Walter Bedell Smith*, 256.
[9] Ambrose, *Ike's Spies*, 177.
[10] Barrett, *CIA and Congress*, 155–59.

CIA "did obtain NSA-type of information of great value that we turn over to [NSA]." There was no duplication, though, he contended.[11]

In 1956, Senator Russell, in a floor speech defending the existing oversight arrangements, told his colleagues that he had been told of activities, which "almost chills the marrow of a man to hear about."[12]

In early 1959, in response to a specific request from Congressman Cannon, who then chaired the HAC, Dulles provided a briefing on "the Agency, its operations, and accomplishments."[13] CIA records do not indicate what he actually briefed. Dulles also appeared four times before the HASC subcommittee in early 1959, discussing world events during his first appearance and "Agency activities" during the latter three.[14]

Later the same year, after Soviet leader Nikita Khrushchev boasted to local officials during a visit to Los Angeles that his government had intercepted US diplomatic communications and that certain CIA agents were "double agents," working for the Soviet Union, Dulles wrote to the chairman of the HASC subcommittee, Congressman Paul Kilday (D-TX), to condemn Khrushchev's remarks as "part of a deliberate campaign to discredit US intelligence." He went on to explain it further:

> *From time to time, [CIA] agents are exposed and apprehended. This often happens to Soviet agents. These agents sometimes carry both money and ciphers known as one-time pads. These pads are useful solely for communications between the agent and his home base, and do not affect any other communication system. As far we are concerned, Khrushchev has not got much comfort out of us in this respect; in fact, nothing comparable to what we have gained from Soviet defectors and agents.[15]*

In January 1960, before a closed session of the SFRC, Dulles, as part of a survey of world events, described the number of defectors the CIA had handled the previous year and specifically mentioned the value of a particular Soviet defector.[16]

Writing of his experience as DCI, Dulles noted that the CIA "reports its current operations to the extent and in the detail the [HASC and SASC subcommittees] desire . . . dealing here not so much with the financial aspects of

---

[11] Ibid., 156–57.
[12] Ibid., 231.
[13] CIA draft study, Vol. I, 69.
[14] Ibid., 333.
[15] Ibid., 342.
[16] Ibid. 360.

operations but with all the other elements of the CIA's work." He also defended their ability to keep secrets:

> *From almost ten years of experience in dealing with the Congress*
> *. . . I have found that secrets can be kept and the needs of our legis-*
> *lative bodies met. In fact, I do not know of a single case of indiscre-*
> *tion that resulted from telling these committees the most intimate*
> *details of CIA activities.[17]*

Early Technical Collection: The U-2 and CORONA Programs

In late 1954, President Eisenhower approved a program to build a high-altitude reconnaissance aircraft, the U-2, principally to photograph military installations within the Soviet Union. CIA and the Air Force would have joint responsibility for the project, and the funds used to build and test the aircraft would be channeled through the Agency's Contingency Reserve Fund to provide better security and simplify the procurement process.[18]

Although this decision involved the Agency in a new kind of collection activity and the use of the Contingency Reserve Fund as a funding mechanism, because of the extreme secrecy surrounding the project at the time, no one in Congress was told of it until early 1956, after the U-2 was built, tested, and in production—but before any missions had been flown. Dulles initially briefed Senators Saltonstall and Russell in February and, on their recommendation, Cannon and Tabor of the HAC subcommittee. The DCI had planned to brief others in Congress, but in early July the president directed him not to discuss the U-2 program outside the executive branch.[19] Although Dulles had his staff prepare a briefing for selected members of Congress in 1958, in the event the president's embargo should be lifted, no formal briefings occurred until a U-2, piloted by Francis Gary Powers, was shot down over the Soviet Union on 1 May 1960.[20]

It is possible, if not probable, however, that a few other members of Congress were told of the U-2 program before 1 May. Although CIA records reflect that only the four were briefed, two other senators said, after the shootdown, that Dulles had informally told them about the program. Cannon even went so far as to say his entire HAC subcommittee had been briefed as part of its annual consideration of the Agency's budget. Answering the question he

---

[17] Dulles, *Craft of Intelligence*, 241, 262–63.

[18] For a detailed description of the origin, purpose, and operation of the U-2 program, see Pedlow and Welzenbach, *CIA and the U-2 Program*.

[19] Ibid., 88; CIA draft study, Vol. I, 80.

[20] The congressional reaction following the shootdown is described in detail in Barrett, 375–422.

assumed was on the minds of his colleagues, Cannon explained that out of "absolute and unavoidable military necessity," other members of the House could not be told of the U-2.[21]

Dulles did apologize to the chairman of the HASC CIA subcommittee, Paul Kilday, for failing to apprise him of the U-2, but Kilday said he understood the Agency's security concerns. Dulles received a different reaction from Speaker of the House Sam Rayburn (D-TX), however, who expressed anger, first to Dulles, then to President Eisenhower, about the Agency's failure to bring him into the matter.[22]

In any event, CIA records do not reflect any congressional scrutiny of the U-2 program from the time Dulles briefed the four members in early 1956 until Powers was shot down. Funding for the U-2 had to be provided each year (in either the CIA or Air Force budget allocations), but whether the administration identified these funds to the subcommittees as such is not clear. There is no indication in Agency records that any of its subcommittees ever raised questions about the program.

After the shootdown, however, a flurry of congressional inquiries ensued. Dulles appeared first on 9 May 1960 before a select group of 18 congressmen. During this briefing, he was questioned about the U-2 program in general and the Powers flight in particular; members seemed particularly concerned about the timing of the flight (less than two weeks before a scheduled Eisenhower-Khrushchev summit meeting in Paris) and with the clumsy cover stories the administration had been put out after Khrushchev had announced that a U-2 had been shot down over Soviet territory. The initial explanation offered by a spokesman of the National Aeronautics and Space Administration—that a U-2 based in Turkey might have accidentally violated Soviet airspace while doing meteorological research—had, in fact, been picked up and defended by members of Congress after it was issued. When Khrushchev announced on 7 May that the U-2 pilot had survived the crash of his plane, other members, ignorant of the true purpose of flight, had taken the floor to condemn the Soviets. Eisenhower, for his part, approved a public statement on 7 May, saying that Washington had not authorized the flight and suggesting it might have been on a reconnaissance mission along the border and strayed off course. This led others in Congress to complain about "rogue" intelligence operations and the need for greater control by the White House.

In fact, when Dulles made his first appearance before the select group of 18 congressmen on 9 May, he was continually pressed to say who had authorized

---

[21] Ibid., 395.
[22] Ibid., 390, 392.

the ill-fated flight but managed to evade answering the question directly. At a news conference two days later, Eisenhower, without discussing the flight per se (other than to say the emphasis given it by the Soviets "can only reflect a fetish for secrecy"), attempted to take responsibility generally for US intelligence-gathering activities that he said were necessary to prevent surprise attack and to make effective preparations for the country's defense. [23]

On 25 May, after the Paris summit had collapsed in the wake of Khrushchev's vehement attack on the U-2 flights, Eisenhower went on television to again take responsibility for "approving all the various programs undertaken by our government to secure and evaluate military intelligence." At the same time, he said that, while US aircraft were no longer being permitted to fly over the Soviet Union, "new techniques, other than aircraft, are constantly being developed." [24] A congressman from Pennsylvania, presumably reflecting information he had received from the administration, had already announced "that, in a few short months, we will have in orbit observer satellites that can collect all the information to be gleaned by the U-2 plane." [25]

After his televised address, Eisenhower expressly rescinded his earlier order and allowed Dulles and other administration officials to testify at congressional hearings on the U-2 program, albeit with certain limitations. The president did not want Congress to be told that he had approved specific missions or what the purpose of those missions had been. [26]

Subsequently, Dulles testified in closed session before four committees: the Senate Foreign Relations Committee, the House Foreign Affairs Committee, and the CIA subcommittees of the SASC and HASC. In his opening statement before the SFRC, Dulles said it was appropriate for the president to have taken responsibility for the U-2 program, although he admitted he had been prepared "to assume the full measure of responsibility," if necessary. When pressed by certain senators on whether the CIA had other operations that were equally as hazardous, Dulles replied there were "some," but only "one or two" that required the president's knowledge prior to undertaking them. Asked whether any CIA agents had been caught before, Dulles replied, "Oh, yes," but told the committee that the United States never acknowledged this had occurred. [27] The same issue arose before the HFAC, where Dulles expanded upon what he had said earlier:

---

[23] Ibid., 399.
[24] Ibid., 406.
[25] Ibid.
[26] Ibid., 410–11.
[27] Ibid., 415.

I don't think the President should be drawn into the ordinary espionage situation. In fact, I would not think of going to consult the President as to whether I should send an agent to [a particular country]. [Most operations] *are "disavowable. You send in an agent. You have an operation of this or that kind. Disavow it. Forget it. The President doesn't have to know anything about it.*[28]

In August 1960, as the U-2 controversy was dying down, the United States successfully launched its first reconnaissance satellite. Named CORONA, the project had begun in early 1958 under the joint auspices of the Air Force (principally responsible for the launch of the satellite) and the CIA (principally responsible for development of the on-board camera). It was envisioned that a capsule containing the exposed film would be ejected over the ocean where it would be retrieved before landing. Like the development of the U-2, the funds used to develop the on-board camera came from the Agency's Contingency Reserve Fund, but it is unclear from CIA records whether its subcommittees in Congress were advised of this. While it is likely, after Eisenhower's decision in May, 1960 to terminate U-2 flights over the Soviet Union, that the CIA subcommittees were told what was envisioned to take its place, CIA's own historical account of the CORONA program makes no mention whatsoever of congressional involvement.

The Cuban Missile Crisis: 1962–63

After President Kennedy announced to the world the presence of Soviet offensive missiles in Cuba on 22 October 1962, DCI McCone was summoned to appear twice before joint meeting of the SASC and SFRC and once before a joint meeting the HASC and HAC as the crisis played out over the next six days. In addition the Agency provided individual briefings to 15 members.

While the world breathed a sigh of relief once the Kremlin announced it would dismantle the missiles and return them to the Soviet Union, a few weeks later questions began to be raised about the timing of the president's initial announcement. After the November midterm elections—won by the Democrats—the chairman of the Republican National Committee charged that Kennedy had delayed releasing evidence showing the missiles in Cuba until just before the election in an effort to bring American voters to his side. As many as 20 Republican seats had been lost as a result, he contended. McCone flatly rejected the accusation in appearances before the SAC and HASC subcommittees, saying that intelligence on Cuba "could not have been

---

[28] Ibid., 418.

handled in any way which would have altered the final timing of the policy decision."[29] To provide further assurance, McCone also provided the committees with copies of the internal executive branch report on the crisis.

No sooner had McCone put out that particular fire than he had to contend with charges that CIA had blundered by suspending overhead reconnaissance of Cuba in August 1962, precisely when the first missiles were arriving on the island. A Republican member of the HASC publicly attributed this failure to a rivalry between the Air Force and CIA over control of the U-2 flights and went on to allege that CIA had ignored human intelligence reports indicating something unusual was taking place on the island.[30]

Although President Kennedy was reluctant to have him do so, McCone testified twice before Congress on this subject: first to the Senate Preparedness Investigating Committee and later to the HASC. In his two-hour briefing to the HASC in late March 1963, McCone denied there had been any dispute with the Air Force, explaining that the delays in U-2 coverage of the island had resulted from bad weather and the administration's desire to avoid another incident involving the U-2. (A U-2 flight that had strayed over the Sakhalin Islands on 30 August 1962 had drawn protests from the Soviet Union; another had crashed in China on 8 September 1962). The HUMINT reporting, McCone went on to say, was sketchy and often unreliable, and it had constituted but a small fraction of the intelligence weighing on the decision to reinstitute reconnaissance operations. Although neither committee issued a public report on the Agency's performance, McCone noted after the HASC hearing that the Republican congressman who had made the original allegations "seemed reasonably satisfied" with his explanation.[31]

Contact with Respect to the Nosenko Case: 1967

In December 1961, a KGB officer, Anatoly Golitsyn, defected to the United States. In addition to providing the Agency with a wealth of information about KGB operations, Golitsyn contended that most Soviet defectors were, in fact, agents of the KGB sent to the United States to provide disinformation. In 1964, when another KGB officer, Yuri Nosenko, defected after having cooperated with the Agency for almost two years, Golitsyn claimed that Nosenko was still working for the KGB. This led to a prolonged period, lasting several years, where the Agency attempted to resolve the issue of Nosenko's bona fides. Nosenko was held in solitary confinement during much of this period

---

[29] Robarge, *John McCone,* 132.
[30] CIA draft study, Vol. I, 102–3.
[31] Ibid; Robarge, *John McCone*, 133.

and occasionally subjected to hostile interrogation, in an effort to break him. By mid-1967, the issue had yet to be resolved, and because of the attention the case had drawn within the Agency itself, Legislative Counsel John Maury believed that the CIA subcommittees should be told about it rather than hear of it in some other way.

On August 5, 1967, after obtaining the approval of DCI Helms, Maury briefed one staff member from each of the four CIA subcommittees on the case. According to Maury's memo of the meeting, none showed interest in pursuing it.[32]

Nosenko was released from detention in 1968 after the Agency concluded that there was insufficient evidence to show that he was not bona fide.

Helms and the Leaders of the CIA Subcommittees: 1966–73

Helms later acknowledged he had routinely discussed operational matters with the leaders of the CIA subcommittees, albeit on a limited, one-on-one basis. The way he characterized his approach to Senator Russell on such matters was typical.

> I would go down with all the documents and I would say, "Senator, we are contemplating such and such a thing," and I wouldn't get very far into it and he'd say, "Dick, do you really think we ought to do this?" And I would say, "Yes, Senator, I do." And the Senator would say, "Well, that's good enough for me."[33]

Helms said he was prepared to tell his overseers what they wanted to know, assuming it was relevant to their responsibilities, but would not volunteer information that they did not want to know. He also said there were times — when an operation was "dicey, tricky, or might fail" — that he, as DCI, wanted to "hold hands" with the Congress. Helms put it this way:

> Despite all those who say, "Well, you shouldn't talk about secret matters with congressional committees," and all the pomposity that follows this, in our kind of democracy, a [DCI] does need guidance from time to time from people in Congress as to how far he may go in certain kinds of activity. At least he would like to have some advice. When this is not available . . . it makes it slightly difficult for him. In fact, it makes it very lonely indeed. Not that I was unwilling to take on the onus of responsibility. . . . It was simply that I thought

---

[32] CIA draft study, Vol. II, 20.
[33] Ibid., 9.

a better system of relationships between the Agency and Congress should have been arranged." [34]

In May 1968, Helms requested that the Agency's operations directorate set up a system for identifying "nuggets"—examples of operational achievements—suitable for briefing to the CIA subcommittees as part of his annual budget presentation. In fact, Helms used the first two such "nuggets" in his budget presentation to the HAC subcommittee that year. One involved a technical monitoring system in use in South Vietnam; the other, the Agency's acquisition and exploitation of a Soviet fighter aircraft. [35]

The practice that Helms began expanded dramatically after the two select committees were established in the mid-1970s and began demanding more detailed budget justifications. Significant operational successes were routinely touted in these annual submissions and, on occasion, would lead to follow-up inquiries by the committees. Given that most of these "success stories" remain classified, however, no further effort is made to identify or describe them here. Suffice it to say, the practice begun by Helms has continued to the present.

The Church Committee's Investigation of CIA Domestic Activities: 1975–76

During the summer of 1967, at a time when racial unrest and antiwar sentiment were escalating around the country, President Johnson ordered DCI Helms to ascertain whether foreign agents, principally communists, were fomenting such unrest. (Johnson clearly believed they were.) To accomplish this task, Helms established a special unit within the Agency's Counterintelligence Staff that began collecting and analyzing information about individuals and groups involved in such activities. Although the special unit never found credible evidence of foreign involvement, at the insistence of the White House, it kept looking. [36] Indeed, this effort steadily intensified and, with the backing of Helms, lasted for almost seven years, terminated by DCI Colby in March 1974. By that point, the program had accumulated files on more than 7,000 American citizens and 6,000 political groups. [37] Most of this information had come from the FBI, but the Agency had also recruited agents to infiltrate a number of domestic organizations. [38]

---

[34] Helms interview, 3 June 1982.
[35] CIA draft study, Vol. II, 24.
[36] Hathaway and Smith, *Richard Helms*, 16–21.
[37] Ford, *William E. Colby,* 85
[38] Hathaway and Smith, *Richard Helms,* 18.

The program had been controversial within the Agency from its inception, and to ensure it was not disclosed, the Agency created a special compartment (MHCHAOS) to protect its operations and analytical products.[39] In May 1973, in response to DCI Schlesinger's direction that CIA employees identify any activity undertaken by the Agency that might arguably violate its charter (see chapter 1), the CHAOS program figured prominently in employees' responses.

But it was not the only questionable activity CIA employees cited in the 793-page compilation that became known as the "Family Jewels." Also identified were CIA surveillance and bugging of US journalists to discover who was leaking sensitive information to them; a mail-opening program undertaken for the same purpose; drug experiments on unwitting subjects; assistance to local law enforcement; and involvement in assassination plots against Fidel Castro, Patrice Lumumba in the Congo, and Rafael Trujillo in the Dominican Republic.[40]

On 22 December 1974, a year and a half after the "Family Jewels" were compiled, they formed the principal basis for a front-page story in the *New York Times* charging that the Agency had engaged in a massive program of domestic spying.[41] The article stunned members of Congress, leading both houses to create special investigating committees (the relationship between the Agency and these committees is covered in chapter 1).

The Senate acted first, creating a committee chaired by Frank Church (D-ID) to investigate any "illegal, improper, or unethical" activities of the US Intelligence Community, including "the conduct of domestic intelligence or counterintelligence operations against US citizens."[42] Indeed, a major part of the committee's effort was devoted to investigating the Agency's domestic activities identified in the "Family Jewels" report: the MHCHAOS program, drug testing on unwitting subjects in the United States, and mail-opening and electronic surveillance to determine the source of leaks. The committee also explored the extent of the Agency's involvement in the formulation and execution of the so-called Huston Plan, an effort mounted by the Nixon administration in 1970 to mobilize intelligence agencies to collect on US citizens opposed to the administration's policies.[43]

---

[39] Ibid., 18–21.

[40] On 26 June 2007 the CIA released a 700-page collection of documents known as the "Family Jewels," which are available at the FOIA electronic reading room at www.foia.cia.gov. For further insider comments on the Family Jewels see Dujmovic, "Reflections of DCIs Colby and Helms," *Studies in Intelligence,* Vol. 51, no. 3.

[41] Hersh, "Huge CIA Operation Reported in US Against Anti-War Forces."

[42] CIA draft study, Vol. II, 63, 82.

[43] Ibid., 84.

While the Agency attempted to cooperate with the Church Committee's investigation of its domestic activities, it nevertheless drew a line at the outset, according to former legislative liaison, John Warner, at providing specific operational data.

> *At one point, we were asked* [by the Church Committee] *for a list of all real estate* [the Agency] *owned or leased. Well, that's a list of safe houses* [and] *we said, "You're not going to get it" . . . and we explained it to them and they seemed to understand. . . . Plus we were not going to give them names of any agents. That's basic.*[44]

In its final report, the Church Committee recommended that the Agency's statutory charter be revised to make clear that its activities were confined to the gathering and analysis of foreign intelligence. While the committee recognized that the Agency had to carry out certain activities within the United States, they must be in furtherance of its foreign intelligence mission.[45]

The Church Committee's Look at Liaison Relationships: 1976

The Church Committee also looked into intelligence liaison relationships, the first time that a committee of Congress had ever done so. The specific issue that prompted this review was whether CIA was complying with the Case Act, a law that required the Congress be notified of international agreements. DCI Colby had issued a blanket statement in 1974 that the Agency was not party to any international agreement that needed to be reported to Congress under the statute. The Church Committee did not take issue with this opinion per se but found that the Agency had no process for systematically reviewing its agreements with foreign intelligence services for this purpose. While the committee found liaison relationships critical to the Agency's operational mission, it recommended that CIA be prohibited by statute from using foreign intelligence services to undertake actions that were forbidden to the Agency itself. It also recommended, whether or not the Case Act was applicable, that the oversight committees of the Congress be kept fully informed of agreements being negotiated with other governments using intelligence channels.[46]

---

[44] Warner interview, 9 October 1987, 2.
[45] CIA draft study, Vol. II, 101–2.
[46] Ibid., 103.

The Pike Committee's Treatment of Operational Issues: 1975–76

While covert action received considerable attention (see chapter 9), relatively little of the House of Representatives' counterpart investigation—the Pike Committee—concerned the Agency's collection operations. The committee left the investigation of the "Family Jewels" to the Senate. In fact, some on its staff believed the Agency was deliberately trying to get them to focus on the same set of allegations as the Church Committee, to keep them out of other areas.[47] The former counsel for the Pike Committee later said the Agency had tried to divert them from their purpose by exposing them to the more exotic aspects of espionage operations. "They wanted to put on shows for us," he recalled. "This was to distract us. They wanted to fly us down . . . to see how CIA people are trained. . . . They offered to let us see secret movies of foreign officials in compromising circumstances. We could have had that forever."[48]

The Pike Committee ultimately held four days of hearings on domestic intelligence-gathering, none of which directly involved the CIA. The committee did look superficially into the Agency's procurement practices—its members were upset that the Agency had purchased limousines, golf hats, golf stroke counters, and putters. The committee also raised concern about detailing CIA employees to other agencies, a practice it perceived as infiltrating "spies throughout the government," and recommended against the Agency's use of journalists to provide operational cover.[49] Congress took no action with respect to these recommendations.

Early Involvement of the SSCI in Operational Matters: 1976–80

In July 1976, a few weeks after the SSCI was created, its staff leaders met with Agency representatives to discuss the committee's access to Agency information. Among other things, according to an Agency memorandum of the meeting, the committee staff agreed that the Agency should "protect fully" the identities of its human assets.[50] Apparently, the staff agreed that this was not the kind of information it would need to conduct oversight.

Later the same year, the requirements of the Case Act again became an issue. In response to a query from the chairman of a Senate judiciary subcommittee, a State Department lawyer had stated that, in his opinion, two international agreements involving the Agency and a foreign intelligence service

---

[47] Smist, *Congress Oversees*, 176.

[48] Ibid., 177.

[49] Ibid., 200; CIA draft study, Vol. II, 150.

[50] CIA draft study, Vol. II, 178.

required reporting to Congress. Although the Agency objected to this opinion and sought support from the White House to quash it, Agency representatives subsequently agreed that the leaders of the SFRC and HFAC would be advised of the agreements in question, which would then be stored at the intelligence committees where access would be severely limited.[51] Insofar as future agreements were concerned, it was agreed the SSCI could receive oral, off-the-record briefings that would identify the country involved, summarize the US involvement, and where necessary, describe the results of such cooperation. It is not clear, however, whether such briefings were actually provided.[52]

While the committee apparently stood by its earlier agreement that the identities of the Agency's human sources be protected, in 1978 it requested that the Agency provide "voluminous and detailed" information on its clandestine collection activities. This provoked considerable concern within the Agency. One Agency officer argued that if the request were accommodated, it would give the SSCI an ability to "micromanage" and "second-guess" the Agency's overseas operations that it did not now have. Conceding that the committee's understanding of its operations was "murky," he recommended that the Agency attempt to explain its internal decisionmaking process to the committee rather than "laying bare our entire covert collection apparatus." In fact, after its concerns were raised with the committee's staff director, the SSCI backed off its initial request and established a three-member subcommittee, assisted by two senior staff members, to do oversight of clandestine collection.[53]

The first significant test of the committee's ability and intent to protect operational information came in 1979–80 as part of the Senate's consideration of the Strategic Arms Limitation Treaty II (SALT II) that, among other things, set numerical limits on the number of long-range bombers and missiles the United States and Soviet Union could maintain and limited each country to one land-based missile system. While the treaty had formally been referred to the SFRC for consideration, that committee asked the SSCI to assess whether the Intelligence Community had sufficient capabilities to monitor Soviet activities under the treaty and to make these findings available to the full Senate. The SSCI had, in turn, requested detailed information about all of the collection capabilities of the Intelligence Community, including the CIA's human and technical capabilities, that could contribute to treaty verification. According to CIA records, DCI Turner was initially "terrified" about the prospect of putting such information together in one place, but in the end he arranged for the SSCI to have access to the information it required to make its assessment.

---

[51] Ibid., 183.
[52] Ibid., 246.
[53] Ibid., 180–81.

The committee, in turn, protected the information it was given and produced a short, unclassified report of its findings for the Senate that confirmed the Intelligence Community's capabilities were adequate to verify the treaty. At the same time, the leaders of the committee wrote to President Carter, encouraging him to fully fund the DCI's requested enhancements to these capabilities in the forthcoming budget submission.[54]

Senate consideration of SALT II was halted in December 1979 as a result of the Soviet invasion of Afghanistan, but what the SSCI had been able to achieve stood as a watershed to many in the Congress as well as the Agency. For the first time, the committee had been given access to and allowed to store highly classified information that it had not only managed to protect but had competently analyzed and presented to the Senate as a whole.

Early HPSCI Involvement in Operational Matters: 1977–80

Coming along 14 months after the SSCI, the HPSCI, as a practical matter, found itself contending with what its Senate counterpart had earlier agreed to. Documents classified above the secret level were to be stored at the Agency. The Agency also contended, as it had with the SSCI, that some information, such as the identities of human agents, was so sensitive it could not be shared with the committee. In November 1977, the new chairman of the HPSCI, Edward Boland (D-MA), wrote to DCI Turner challenging the notion that there was any information that, as a matter of principle, should be considered off-limits to the committee. When Turner responded in a letter to Boland that there were certain sensitive details that, as a result of "statutory responsibilities and conscience," he could not share with the committee, other HPSCI members took issue. Rather than continuing to assert his previous position, Turner agreed to brief Boland and senior staff of the HPSCI on especially sensitive matters that might arise in the future, implying they would then decide how such information would be treated within the committee as a whole.[55]

In his letter to Turner, Boland also made clear that he expected the committee to be informed of "sensitive intelligence collection operations" and to receive detailed written summaries of all intelligence agreements with foreign nations, written or oral, whether they were covered by the Case Act or not. While Turner responded that he was committed to serving the committee's needs, he was vague in terms of how these requirements would be met.

---

[54] Ibid., 190–94.
[55] CIA draft study, Vol. II, 228–31.

Indeed, he ignored altogether Boland's request for summaries of intelligence agreements.[56]

In July 1978, however, the HPSCI staff director reiterated the committee's request for detailed briefings on written intelligence agreements with other governments that entailed a substantial commitment on the part of the United States. Of particular concern to the committee was whether the Agency was doing things through its liaison relationships that it would not otherwise be entitled to do, such as providing training or technical advice to foreign services engaged in monitoring or stifling internal dissent or committing human rights abuses.

The Agency, nevertheless, strongly resisted the committee's request, arguing that it could "very possibly lose the cooperation of foreign intelligence services if they found out we were briefing Congress on those relationships." Asserting that specific information concerning these relationships was not necessary for Congress to perform its oversight function, Agency representatives said the most they could provide were generic descriptions of what these relationships involved and what they produced, without identifying specific services or, indeed, the country involved. Liaison relationships were themselves "sources and methods," they contended, that would not ordinarily be briefed in detail to the committees.[57]

Although the disagreement took several months to work out, the HPSCI ultimately agreed in October 1978 to accept generic briefings concerning liaison relationships that did not specify either the service involved or the nature of the cooperation.[58]

Executive Order 12333 and Limits on Domestic Activities: 1981

The Carter administration had issued an executive order in the wake of the Church and Pike Committee investigations that, among other things, required the domestic activities of US intelligence agencies, including the CIA, to be carried out in accordance with procedures approved by the attorney general. By the time the Reagan administration took office in 1981, these procedures had been in place for several years, and copies had been provided the two intelligence committees.

As one of its first orders of business, the Reagan administration set about to issue its own executive order on intelligence, ostensibly to loosen the restric-

---

[56] Ibid., 245.
[57] Ibid., 247–48.
[58] Ibid., 248.

tions on domestic intelligence-gathering that had been put in place. Although there was no legal requirement to do so, DCI Casey shared drafts of the proposed order with each intelligence committee in an effort to ensure they did not react negatively when the new order was issued. Each had concerns with the draft that were addressed in the executive branch process. The HPSCI also insisted that the new implementing procedures each intelligence agency was required to promulgate be shared with it and asked Casey to provide a semi-annual report on the use of "special collection techniques" within the United States, for example, electronic surveillance and infiltration of domestic groups.[59] Neither committee, however, launched a major protest when the new order — Executive Order 12333 — was issued.

SSCI Inquiry into "Death Squads" in El Salvador: 1984

In 1980, right-wing elements of the Salvadoran National Guard murdered four Roman Catholic nuns. These killings were followed by the murders of a Salvadoran land reform leader and two US agricultural advisers, apparently the work of the same right-wing elements.

In 1984, press stories appeared in the United States alleging that the CIA had been involved in supporting these right-wing "death squads," and in an effort to head off legislation cutting off US assistance to El Salvador, SSCI Chairman Barry Goldwater announced the committee would investigate. It held several closed hearings on the matter, and its staff was given access to pertinent operational files of the Agency. In October, the committee released a summary of its findings to the public. It found that the Agency worked regularly with both the intelligence service and national police of El Salvador and that the Agency had had contact with certain of the Salvadorans thought to have been involved in the violence. But it found "no evidence to support the allegation that elements of the US government have deliberately supported, encouraged, or acquiesced in acts of political violence in El Salvador, including extreme right-wing death squad activity." Indeed, the committee said it had found "substantial material" indicating the CIA had attempted to ameliorate the political violence in El Salvador.[60]

---

[59] CIA draft study, Vol. III, 10.
[60] Ibid., 49–50.

HPSCI Inquiry into Cuban Operations: 1987

In September, 1987, a Cuban intelligence officer who had defected to the United States told the Agency that virtually all of its Cuban operations over the preceding 15–20 years had been controlled by Cuban intelligence. After evaluating this report and concluding it was probably correct, the Agency notified both intelligence committees.

The news stunned the HPSCI in particular, which immediately held a closed hearing to find out how this could have happened. What followed was a painstaking review by the committee of the Agency's operations in Cuba and, in particular, measures the Agency used to vet its sources there. After its review, the committee told DCI Webster that the Agency needed to revamp its entire procedure for vetting human sources, something Webster promised to personally follow up on.[61]

HPSCI Inquiry into the Agency's Relationship with Manuel Noriega: 1988

Both intelligence committees were aware that CIA had had a relationship with Panamanian strongman Manuel Noriega for many years. He had been an anticommunist and a supporter of the Reagan administration's efforts to oust the Sandinistas in Nicaragua. Indeed, DCI Casey had met openly with him on three occasions between 1983 and 1986. In the late 1980s, however, Noriega's connection with international drug rings had been the subject of a Senate investigation as well as several press exposes. In February 1988, the US Justice Department indicted him in Florida on drug-trafficking charges. This, in turn, prompted the HPSCI to inquire into precisely what the Agency's relationship with Noriega had been and, in particular, the extent of its knowledge or awareness of his drug-trafficking activities. While no public report was made of this inquiry, the Agency made available the records documenting its prior relationship.[62]

The SSCI's Consideration of Arms Control Treaties: 1987–92

As the SSCI had done earlier with respect to SALT II, it undertook in 1987 a comprehensive review of the Intelligence Community's capabilities to monitor the provisions of the INF treaty the Reagan administration had negotiated with the Soviet Union and referred to the Senate for ratification. Like the ear-

---

[61] Ibid., 181–82.
[62] Ibid., 195–96.

lier effort, this involved a review of the Agency's technical and human source capabilities to collect pertinent information, as part of the Community's broader capability.

In this case, however, the committee produced a 350-page classified report that raised concerns about the Community's ability to monitor certain aspects of the treaty. As a result, the administration renegotiated portions of the treaty, including a clarification of the US rights to conduct on-site inspections. With such clarifications, the Senate ratified the treaty, and the Reagan administration committed to fund additional collection capabilities.[63]

During the next Congress, the SSCI considered two other arms control treaties being negotiated with the Soviets: the Threshold Test Ban Treaty and the Treaty on Peaceful Nuclear Explosions. In 1991, the Strategic Arms Reduction Treaty (START) was before the Senate. On each of these occasions, the issue for the committee was again whether the treaties at issue could be adequately monitored by US intelligence.[64]

The SSCI's Reviews of CIA Support to Military Operations: 1990–91

In early 1990, in the wake of the military operation known as JUST CAUSE, undertaken by the Bush administration to capture Panamanian strongman Manuel Noriega after his indictment on drug trafficking charges and free a CIA employee being held in a Panamanian jail, the SSCI conducted a review of the intelligence support CIA had rendered to the operation in advance of its execution. This entailed looking at not only the assets the Agency had in Panama but also the quantity and quality of their reporting bearing upon the anticipated operation. Responding to what it saw as a serious disconnect between the Agency and the military commands responsible for planning and carrying out JUST CAUSE, the SSCI placed language in the FY 1991 Intelligence Authorization Bill requiring that the DCI create a new position within his staff, to be filled by a general or flag officer, to improve the flow of information between the Agency and military commands around the world. With the support of the Armed Services Committees in each house, the provision became law in November 1990.[65]

Several months later, Operation DESERT STORM to oust Iraqi forces from Kuwait began (see chapter 7 for a discussion of the intelligence assessments prior to and during the war). The operation took 42 days, 38 of which were

---

[63] Smist, *Congress Oversees*, 272.
[64] Ibid., 274, 289.
[65] Ibid., 285.

consumed by airstrikes. When the land war was launched, Iraqi forces were sent into a hasty retreat by the invading coalition forces, which suffered a minimum number of casualties. In the aftermath of the operation, the CENTCOM commander in charge of the operation, GEN Norman Schwarzkopf, publicly criticized the intelligence support he had received from the CIA during the operation.[66] This criticism, in turn, prompted the SSCI to investigate precisely what CIA's role had been. No public report of its findings, however, was ever issued.

The SSCI's Banca Nazionale del Lavoro Investigation: 1992–93

In June 1992, an employee of the Atlanta branch of an Italian bank, Banca Nazionale del Lavoro (BNL), pled guilty to a 347-count federal indictment charging him with an elaborate scheme to defraud the parent bank as well as the US government by arranging for more than $4 billion in unauthorized loans to the Iraqi government.

At the sentencing hearing in September 1992, the bank employee's attorney alleged that he was merely a pawn in an operation that senior officials of the parent bank in Rome had been aware of. He further alleged that the CIA had information that would confirm this allegation, citing statements to this effect that had been made on the floor of the House of Representatives by the chairman of the House Banking Committee. This, in turn, prompted the SSCI to explore the situation.

The ensuing investigation did identify several CIA reports that seemed to show that BNL officials in Rome had known of the fraud. Some, in fact, had been written after the federal criminal investigation of the Atlanta branch bank had begun. This raised several issues for the committee: (1) the propriety of using intelligence sources to collect law enforcement information for an ongoing criminal investigation; (2) whether the Agency had adequately informed, or misled, the Justice Department regarding the information in its possession; and (3) whether the Agency and/or the Department of Justice had adequately informed, or misled, the federal court in Atlanta, as well as the defendant himself, of the information that was known to them.

After a lengthy investigation, involving a complex set of facts, the committee concluded there had been no intentional malfeasance on the part of the Agency officers involved; however, the need for better guidance to govern such situations as well as closer coordination with the Department of Justice was apparent.[67]

---

[66] Moore, "Schwarzkopf: War Intelligence Flawed."

The Guatemala Inquiries and their Aftermath: 1995–96

In January 1995, the Agency told the staff of the intelligence committees for the first time that it had received an intelligence report in October 1991 alleging that one of its assets within the Guatemalan Army, a Colonel Alpirez, had been present at the June 1990 murder of an American expatriate living in Guatemala, Michael DeVine.[68] The Agency had reported this allegation to the Department of Justice when it first received it in 1991 but not to the committees. Nor did the Agency make it available anytime during the intervening four years, despite several opportunities to do so when Agency representatives had met with the committees or their staffs to discuss its operational activities in Guatemala. Initially, both committees perceived a deliberate effort to withhold pertinent information from them. Indeed, the SSCI took the unusual step of holding a public hearing on the matter to demonstrate its displeasure with the Agency's performance and cast doubt on its explanation to the committee. Acting DCI William O. Studeman said he regretted the committees had not been told of the 1991 report but that it had not been deliberately withheld.[69] The committee subsequently held two closed sessions to explore the matter.

The Agency did not contest the committees' contention that the 1991 intelligence report was something that should have been briefed to them pursuant to the "fully and currently informed" language in the 1980 Intelligence Oversight Act; in fact, it was able to point to briefing notes that had been prepared at the time indicating it intended to do so. Why the briefer had omitted this from his oral presentation was not clear. Moreover, it was unclear why the matter had not surfaced at subsequent meetings with the committee staff, at least one of which specifically concerned the Agency's knowledge of Guatemala's human rights record.

While subsequent investigation—by the committees, the CIA Inspector General, and the Intelligence Oversight Board at the White House—did not conclusively establish a deliberate intent on the part of the CIA employees involved to withhold information from the committees, they were found derelict insofar as they had allowed this to happen. DCI Deutch disciplined 12 CIA officers for this failure, forcing two to retire.

After the initial flurry of activity regarding the DeVine case, the committees also wanted to know what the Agency may have known about the alleged

---

[67] Senate Select Committee on Intelligence, *The Intelligence Community's Involvement in the Banca Nazionale del Lavoro (BNL) Affair.*

[68] For a detailed description of the matter, see the public report of the Intelligence Oversight Board, *Report on the Guatemalan Review,* 28 June 1996.

[69] Studeman, Statement before the Senate Select Committee on Intelligence, Subject: Guatemala, 4 April 1995.

murders, torture, or disappearances since 1984 of nine other Americans who had lived in Guatemala. In addition, the SSCI asked the CIA inspector general to review all of the Agency's operational assets in Guatemala since 1984 to ascertain the extent to which the Agency was aware of their possible involvement in human rights abuses. This investigation took several years to complete and was ultimately shared with the committees.

CIA Use of Journalists, Clergy, and Peace Corps Volunteers: 1996

Responding to a recommendation of a task force of the Council on Foreign Relations that the Agency's policy on the operational use of journalists, clergy, and Peace Corps volunteers should be re-examined, the SSCI held a public hearing in February 1996, on this issue.[70] DCI Deutch testified that although it had not been the Agency's policy or practice for many years to use the affected groups for operational purposes, it would be unwise to foreclose such use altogether.[71] After hearing from representatives of the groups involved, the committee inserted language in the FY 1997 intelligence authorization bill stating that it was the "policy of the United States" that journalists would not be used for "purposes of collecting intelligence." However, the new law provided that the president or the DCI could waive this policy, so long as the two intelligence committees were advised. The law also said it should not be construed to prohibit "the voluntary cooperation of any person.[72] This action essentially left in place the existing policy with respect to operational use of clergy and Peace Corps volunteers.

Alleged Involvement in Crack Cocaine Sales in Los Angeles: 1996–2000

In August 1996, a California newspaper, the San Jose *Mercury News*, ran a three-day series entitled "Dark Alliance: The Story behind the Crack Explosion" that purported to trace the origins of the crack cocaine epidemic in Los Angeles in the early 1980s to a pair of Nicaraguan drug dealers who had connections with the US-backed "contras." The articles alleged, in fact, that the two Nicaraguans had sold cocaine to a drug dealer in south Los Angeles as a way of raising money for the contras. The dealer then allegedly turned the powder into "crack cocaine" and sold it in predominantly African-American

---

[70] Since the mid-1970s, use of these groups for operational purposes had required the approval of the DCI.

[71] Senate Select Committee on Intelligence, *CIA's Use of Journalists and Clergy in Intelligence Operations*, 6–7.

[72] §309 of Public Law 104-293.

neighborhoods. The articles did not specifically allege that CIA was involved in, or even knew of, the alleged sales, but they did contend that the ability of local law enforcement authorities to investigate the drug dealers involved had been "hampered by the CIA or unnamed national security interests."

The Agency's role in supporting the contras in Nicaragua during the early 1980s was, at this juncture, well known. Thus, the possibility that an agency of the federal government might have somehow been complicit in, or bear responsibility for, sales of crack cocaine within the United States created an immediate sensation. And even though other newspapers immediately began to raise doubts about the allegations and the Agency's initial efforts to find information bearing on the allegations turned up nothing, both the SSCI and the HPSCI launched investigations, as did the inspectors general at CIA and the Department of Justice.

Indeed, the investigations carried out by the HPSCI as well as the CIA inspector general far exceeded the questions raised in the original newspaper series. The Agency's relationship with each of the contras they had worked with during the 1980s was examined to ascertain whether they were involved in drug-trafficking and, if so, whether the Agency had been aware of and/or abetted such activities. After reviewing "tens of thousands of pages" of documents and interviewing "hundreds" of officials, the HPSCI concluded in May 2000, that the allegations raised by the *Mercury News* were false. Rather than hamper the investigation of drug traffickers within the United States, they noted, CIA had routinely assisted such investigations.[73]

Although the Agency was ultimately vindicated, it had taken almost four years for the HPSCI to determine that the allegations were false. By this point, many in the public had long since accepted them as true.

CIA's Role in the Accidental Bombing of the Chinese Embassy in Belgrade: 1999

In May 1999, as part of the NATO air campaign against Serbia, US military aircraft accidentally bombed the Chinese embassy in Belgrade. The building was severely damaged, and three Chinese nationals were killed. The incident provoked a formal protest from the Chinese government and led to violent demonstrations at US diplomatic facilities in China.

In the aftermath of the bombing, it was ascertained that the embassy had been mistakenly targeted by the CIA. Given the opportunity by the Pentagon

---

[73] See Press release, House Permanent Select Committee on Intelligence, "Evidence Does Not Support Allegations of CIA Participation in Drug Trafficking," 11 May 2000.

to recommend targets for the bombing campaign, CIA had nominated what it thought was a supply and procurement agency for the Yugoslav military. While the CIA had the correct street address for the agency, one of its contract officers had mislocated it on the map he was using and provided the wrong geographical coordinates to the military. As it turned out, the coordinates identified not the Yugoslav procurement agency but the Chinese embassy, which was located several blocks away on the same street. Despite elaborate target validation procedures in place at both the Pentagon and in Europe at the time, the error was not caught.

In July, after an internal investigation by the CIA inspector general, DCI Tenet was summoned to testify in closed session before the HPSCI, assuring it that the Agency's procedures had been tightened to prevent a similar mistake in the future. He also indicated he was considering disciplinary action against those employees whose performance had been deficient.[74] He provided similar assurances to members of the SSCI. The contract officer was fired. Neither committee pursued the matter further.

SSCI Inquiry into the Shootdown of a Civilian Aircraft in Peru: 2001

During the latter half of the 1990s, both committees regularly reviewed the assistance CIA was providing to certain South American governments to help them counter the production of narcotic drugs in their respective countries and prevent them from reaching the United States. For the most part, the committees were interested in the type of assistance being provided, the extent to which Agency personnel were being put at risk by such activities, and how successful such joint efforts had been.

In April 2001, however, the focus of the SSCI shifted to the shootdown of a civilian aircraft in Peru. A Peruvian fighter plane had fired on and disabled a small airplane that the pilot believed to be involved in drug trafficking operations. It turned out that the aircraft was owned by the Association of Baptists for World Evangelism and was returning missionaries to their home base. The gunfire killed one of the missionaries and her infant daughter and wounded a third. CIA officers, participating in the bilateral drug interdiction program, had been tracking the missionaries' plane from their own small aircraft (with a Peruvian government rider aboard) and had called in the Peruvian military fighter that ultimately launched the attack. As a result of the incident, the air interdiction program in Peru was suspended indefinitely.

---

[74] Tenet, "Statement on the Belgrade Chinese Embassy Bombing."

The SSCI held two closed hearings on the Peruvian matter and had its staff conduct an independent follow-up investigation. In October 2001, it issued a detailed report of its findings. It found that the CIA-operated aircraft had tried to make contact with the missionary airplane and that the CIA personnel aboard had tried to dissuade the Peruvian rider aboard from seeking authority for the Peruvian fighter to attack the missionary plane; it also found that relatively poor language skills of the CIA personnel involved contributed to the confusion that occurred. And it found a lack of awareness and involvement on the part of US officials with respect to the air-interdiction operation as well as a failure to appreciate and address the risks involved. Among other things, the committee recommended that the executive branch reassess whether CIA's responsibility for this kind of assistance be transferred to other agencies of the US government.[75]

Operational Issues in the Joint Report on 9/11: 2002

As discussed in chapter 2, the terrorist attacks of 9/11 prompted the two intelligence committees to undertake, for the first time in their history, a joint investigation into the activities of the Intelligence Community. Although CIA was but one of a number of intelligence agencies whose activities before and after the attacks were subject to investigation, all three of its mission areas—analysis, collection, and covert action—were examined in the course of the inquiry. In this chapter, the findings and recommendations of the committees with respect to operational matters are summarized.

The joint inquiry focused specifically on what CIA had known about the 19 hijackers who had carried out the attacks and, more generally, on the Agency's efforts to collect against al-Qa'ida.[76]

With regard to the hijackers, the joint inquiry found that CIA, in early January 2000, had learned that two men thought to be connected with the embassy bombings in Kenya and Tanzania that had occurred in August 1998—Khalid al-Mihdhar and Nawaf al-Hazmi—were traveling to Malaysia for a meeting. A third individual, thought to be al-Hazmi's younger brother, Salem, was traveling to the same meeting. (All three turned out to be future hijackers.) Once the three men arrived in Malaysia, CIA was able to photograph them, as well as other participants at the meeting. The Agency was also able to obtain a photocopy of al-Mihdhar's Saudi passport, showing that he had obtained a visa to the United States that would expire four months later.

---

[75] Senate Select Committee on Intelligence, *Review of United States Assistance to Peruvian Counter-Drug Air Interdiction Efforts and the Shootdown of a Civilian Aircraft on April 20, 2001*.
[76] *Joint Inquiry into the Terrorist Attacks of September 11, 2001*, 128–67.

Although this information was passed to Agency Headquarters, no one placed al-Mihdhar's name, or the names of the other participants at the Malaysia meeting, on the State Department's visa watchlist, which might have prevented them from entering the United States. In fact, on 15 January 2000 al-Mihdhar and Nawaf al-Hazmi flew to Los Angeles, where they entered the United States with tourist visas and rented an apartment in San Diego. The Agency learned in early March that al-Hazmi had entered the country, but again his name was not added to the State visa watchlist, nor was any effort made to locate him. The Agency did not know the whereabouts of al-Mihdhar at that point.

In October 2000, a US warship, the USS Cole, was bombed in the port of Aden, South Yemen, by terrorists who pulled alongside the ship with a boatload of explosives. In December 2000, after several months of investigation, the FBI developed information that a key planner of the attack had been at the January meeting in Malaysia. This brought renewed attention on the other participants at the earlier meeting, including al-Mihdhar and the al-Hazmi brothers, but again the Agency failed to place their names on the State Department's visa watchlist. In fact, in June 2000, unbeknownst to the Agency, al-Mihdhar had left the country and his visa had expired, forcing him to obtain a new one before he returned to the United States, which he did on 4 July 2001.

Finally, in August 2001, three weeks before the attacks in New York and Washington, an FBI analyst detailed to CIA put the earlier information together and was able to confirm that al-Mihdhar and al-Hazmi had entered the country together in January 2000 and that all-Mihdhar had left in June 2000 and returned in July 2001. There was no record of al-Hazmi leaving the country. On the basis of this information, their names were at last placed on the State Department's visa watchlist, and at the end of August the FBI began searching for them. "The CIA's failure to watchlist [these] suspected terrorists aggressively," the joint inquiry later concluded, "reflected a lack of emphasis on a process designed to protect the homeland from terrorist attack."[77]

With regard to the Agency's efforts to collect against al-Qa'ida prior to 9/11, the joint inquiry explored a wide range of issues: whether adequate resources had been sought and dedicated to such collection; whether the Agency had relied too heavily upon foreign liaison services; whether its unilateral efforts to recruit assets targeted against al-Qa'ida were adequate; and whether its technical collection efforts against al-Qa'ida had been effective.

---

[77] Ibid., 33.

In each area, deficiencies were identified. Resources put against the target had been insufficient, the committees found, and the Agency had relied too heavily upon supplemental appropriations to fund its counterterrorism activities (making it difficult to plan for them). There was too much reliance on liaison services, especially prior to 1999. Even though the Agency had managed to recruit several unilateral sources within al-Qa'ida prior to 9/11 and a number of sources within Afghanistan who reported on the movements of Usama bin Ladin and other al-Qa'ida leaders, it was never able to penetrate bin Ladin's inner circle. The Agency had mounted technical collection against bin Ladin, but these efforts had produced relatively little.[78]

Inquiries into Counterterrorism Activities: 2003–2004

After issuing their joint report on the 9/11 attacks, both committees continued to make the Intelligence Community's counterterrorist activities a principal focus. The HPSCI, in particular, held hearings on collection against the terrorist threat in 2003, which were followed up a year later with hearings on the importance of interrogation in obtaining information from terrorists.

According to former OCA Director Moseman, however, neither committee showed much interest in pursuing the issues associated with the capture and handling of detainees either before or after 9/11 — renditions, abusive interrogations, or the treatment of detainees. "They were briefed on these things," Moseman recalled, "but there was very little follow-up. . . . There just didn't seem to be much interest up there." Whether their reluctance was politically motivated (the desire not to embarrass the incumbent Bush administration) or stemmed from the committees' distaste for involving themselves in such issues (raising concern for the treatment of terrorists), Moseman said he did not know.[79]

Operational Issues in the SSCI's Inquiry into the Prewar Intelligence Assessments on Iraq: 2004

Although the SSCI's in-depth inquiry into the prewar intelligence assessments on Iraq dealt primarily with the Agency's analytic performance (see chapter 7), the committee also examined the Agency's collection effort in prewar Iraq. Collection on each of the two main issues considered in the committee's report—Iraqi WMD programs and Iraqi links to terrorist groups—was separately evaluated.

---

[78] Ibid, 250–307.
[79] Moseman interview, 28 December 2006.

In the case of collection on Iraqi WMD programs, the committee explored (1) the nature and extent of the Agency's capabilities while UN weapons inspectors had been stationed within the country (1991–98), (2) the actions the Agency had taken to improve its collection on Iraqi WMD after the inspectors had left, and (3) the actions the Agency had been taken in 2002 and 2003, once it was apparent the United States was moving toward war with Iraq. To assess these issues, the committee requested and was provided information concerning the Agency's unilateral assets as well as information it was receiving from foreign liaison.

In its final report, the committee found that the Intelligence Community had relied too heavily upon the UN inspectors between 1991 and 1998 for information on Iraqi WMD programs, failed to mount sufficient unilateral operations while the inspectors were there, and failed to give sufficient priority to recruiting new assets after they had left. Instead, the committee found, the Community relied too heavily on defectors being handled by foreign liaison services, which made source credibility difficult to evaluate. While the Agency "dramatically picked up the pace" of HUMINT collection in the summer of 2002 once it became clear that war with Iraq was in the offing, it was never able to recruit sources with personal knowledge of Iraq's WMD programs. While the committee recognized that the lack of an official US presence inside Iraq and the heavy Iraqi security presence made operational activity difficult to mount and sustain, it believed a more aggressive effort should have been made.[80]

With respect to Iraqi links to terrorist groups — in particular, al-Qa'ida — the committee examined the relevant HUMINT reporting that had come in during the years preceding the war. Virtually all of it, they found, had come from detainees, defectors, opposition groups, and foreign intelligence services, not the Agency's own targeted collection effort. While this reporting provided historical context of the Iraqi regime's contacts with known or suspected terrorist groups, it provided little evidence of an operational relationship with such groups. It was only in the summer of 2002, the committee found, that the Agency designed and carried out a focused collection strategy to develop information on this issue.[81]

---

[80] Senate Select Committee on Intelligence, *US Intelligence Community's Pre-War Intelligence Assessments on Iraq*, 258–71.

[81] Ibid., 350–55.

HPSCI Criticism of the DO: 2004

The shortcomings that were evident to the SSCI in terms of collection on Iraq also motivated the HPSCI to use uncharacteristically harsh language in the public report accompanying its markup of the Intelligence Authorization Act for Fiscal Year 2005 to lambaste the Directorate of Operations (DO) for its "mismanagement of the HUMINT mission." Noting that it had for years offered criticism of the DO in its classified reports, based upon "hundreds of meetings and continuous dialogue with CIA field operatives," the committee said the DO had long ignored its "core mission activities" and was in "dysfunctional denial" with respect to the corrective actions that were needed. Citing damage done through its "misallocation and redirection of resources, poor prioritization of objectives, micromanagement of field operations, and a continued political aversion to operational risk," the committee said the CIA "continues down a road leading over a proverbial cliff."[82]

Provided with this assessment in advance of its being approved, DCI Tenet wrote a blunt letter to the committee, saying he objected to the "tone and content" of the report, and called some of its conclusions "frankly absurd."[83] Yet the committee stood by its criticism.

The US cannot afford to be in the position again that the DO and other collectors within the Intelligence Community have not provided analysts with sufficient information upon which to base their assessments.[84]

In subsequent testimony to the HPSCI, Tenet defended the Agency's performance. In his memoir, he recounts what he told the committee:

That year we were graduating the largest class of clandestine officers in our history. Since 1997, we had deployed a thousand operations officers in the field. The numbers were great, I said, but nonetheless it would take another five years before our clandestine service was near where it needed to be. This shouldn't have been a surprise. When you have a decade of neglect, it takes you at least that long to recover.[85]

---

[82] House Permanent Select Committee on Intelligence, *Report to Accompany the Intelligence Authorization Act for Fiscal Year 2005*, 23–24.

[83] Quoted in Jehl, "House Committee Says CIA Is Courting Disaster by Mismanaging Its Human Spying."

[84] House Permanent Select Committee on Intelligence, *Report to Accompany the Intelligence Authorization Act for Fiscal Year 2005*, 23.

[85] Tenet, *At the Center of the Storm*, 24.

AUTHOR'S COMMENTARY

Collection in General

Congress charged the Agency with collecting foreign intelligence around the world and expects it to be out there doing it, or at least trying to do it. In fact, more often than not, Congress's principal complaint has been with the lack of collection, not with operational failure itself. Problematic as it might be, collecting foreign intelligence, in principle, has never been particularly controversial on the Hill. There are places and things, members recognize, that the US government cannot know about in any other way. Other countries do it against us, they reason, so why shouldn't we do it against them? Even when the Agency moved to new forms of technical collection in the mid-1950s—something Congress had little role in—few eyebrows were raised. If the Agency were able to do it, the prevailing sentiment seems to have been, more power to it. While a few in Congress wondered at the end of the Cold War whether the Agency needed to do quite so much of it, this sentiment proved short-lived and never compelling.

Having said this, the historical record clearly shows that, however well accepted the Agency's intelligence-gathering efforts may be, Congress is still likely to intervene, either before or after the fact, when members perceive problems with them. If Congress thinks such activities have caused or may cause undue embarrassment for the country if disclosed, or if they will adversely affect US relations with other countries, it may ask what the justification is. If it perceives that the Agency is collecting against inappropriate targets (US citizens, friendly foreign countries) or is using dubious means to acquire information (unwitting Americans, people with records of human rights abuse, blackmail, or torture), it is also apt to inquire. Before the two intelligence committees were created, Congress rarely became aware of such problems. Now, and especially after the new notification procedures were put in place in 1996, such awareness is commonplace.

Congress and Espionage

No area of governmental activity is more secretive than espionage operations. The identities of clandestine agents the Agency recruits and the details of their activities on behalf of the United States are typically not shared with the outside world at all. Even within the Agency, access to such information is limited to a relative few. While information produced by such operations is shared on a limited basis outside the Agency, access to it is tightly controlled.

The reason for such secrecy is obvious: the more who are exposed to such information, the greater the risk of disclosure and harm to those who have put their lives on the line.

Consider, on the other hand, the Congress, for the most part an open institution whose members are accustomed to making political "hay" out of the information that comes their way. Moreover, most would not be where they are if they did not like to talk. Entrusting them, no matter how well-intentioned they might be, with the most sensitive information held by the federal government would seem, to some, a bad idea.

In fact, it has also seemed that way to the Congress. The committees that have overseen the Agency have not demanded to know the identities of its clandestine agents, nor have they demanded to know where they are or what they are doing. They have not routinely asked to be consulted with respect to ongoing operations, nor have they routinely demanded to see the intelligence being produced by such operations. They assert the right to know such things if they should become necessary to the execution of their institutional responsibilities, but rarely have they found this to be the case. Instead, Congress has found it can ordinarily exercise its responsibilities over the Agency, even in the problematic area of espionage, without knowing the identities of its agents or the details of its operations.

Until the intelligence committees were created in the mid-1970s, Congress's understanding of the Agency's clandestine operations was, in the words of one CIA officer, "murky at best." Its overseers may have had a general idea about how the Agency went about recruiting and handling clandestine agents, based upon the occasional briefings they received, but without documentation to refer to, the perceptions created by such briefings could only have been sketchy and fleeting.

The select intelligence committees that superseded them also did not get the details of ongoing operations, but over time—through briefings, budget presentations, trips to the Agency, visits to overseas stations, and investigative activity—they were able to gain a far clearer, far more sophisticated understanding of the Agency's clandestine tradecraft than their predecessors. Certainly by the early 1980s, the intelligence committees had come to understand how the Agency identified potential assets and how it vetted, recruited, and handled them. They also had a pretty clear idea how well the Agency was doing at it. They saw how difficult it was to mount such operations—especially to recruit assets with access to information that mattered to US policymakers—and control assets once recruited.

All of this helped them to assess the Agency's annual budget requests. It also helped them understand why it was sometimes necessary for the Agency to work with "bad" people in order to obtain crucial information and not fore-close potential avenues of collection that might someday be critical to US interests. On the investigative side, it helped the committees understand why things sometimes went wrong and assess the complaints and allegations they periodically received about the Agency (some coming from assets them-selves). To be sure, a great deal of operational information was still withheld from the committees—for example, neither was officially told about the com-promise of many of the Agency's assets in the Soviet Union that occurred as a result of Aldrich Ames's treachery (see chapter 10). Nevertheless, they had learned enough by this point to develop a relatively sophisticated frame of ref-erence in which to carry out their responsibilities.

In the mid-1990s, as described in the text, the Agency took the additional step of formalizing and regularizing the notification of its operational activi-ties to the two committees. The Agency would continue to withhold opera-tional details that were not needed to understand the situation, but a great deal more information began to be provided.

Perhaps nothing better illustrates how far things had come in an oversight sense than the two major inquiries the committees conducted at the end of the period covered by this study: the joint inquiry into 9/11 in 2002 and the SSCI's investigation of the prewar intelligence assessments on Iraq in 2004. In both cases, the committees wanted the details of all the Agency's collection activities (either against al-Qa'ida or the Iraqi regime of Saddam Hussein)— unilateral operations, liaison activities, and technical collection. And in both instances, the Agency gave them what they needed to know, all without a great deal of argument or controversy. This is not to say that the Agency made no effort to protect sensitive operational details but only that the relationship with the oversight committees had progressed so far by this point that both sides understood and accepted the needs of the other. Access by the Congress to operational information that might have dogged such investigations in the past did not generate significant controversy.

Congress and the Agency's Technical Collection

The CIA subcommittees had limited awareness of, and almost no involve-ment in, the early technical collection programs that the Agency managed or participated in: the U-2 and A-12 reconnaissance aircraft and the early recon-naissance satellites. In part, this was due to the extreme secrecy surrounding these programs and, in part, to the inability of the subcommittees themselves to contribute meaningfully to the direction and execution of these efforts. While their approval was needed each year to fund these programs, it appears this was usually accomplished by the leaders of the subcommittees whose trusted staff aides made sure the administration's requests were plugged into the appropriate funding bills. Agency records, in fact, do not reflect any substantive discussion of any of these programs with the Congress.

Still, it was the shootdown of the U-2 over the Soviet Union in May 1960 that provoked the biggest reaction Congress had had to any CIA activity to that point. For the most part, the reaction was favorable. Although the existence of the U-2 came as a surprise to all but a few members in each chamber, most seemed impressed that the Agency had managed to develop and fly such an aircraft. Their main gripes were with the Eisenhower administration over the timing of the ill-fated flight and the clumsy cover stories that had been put forth after the shoot-down. Hardly anyone in Congress seemed worried, as Eisenhower was, that the overflights might be seen as violating Soviet sovereignty.

Neither the reconnaissance satellites that came along later nor the high-altitude, supersonic A-12 posed the same danger of being shot down, but they did pose issues with respect to their costs and capabilities. While Agency records do not reflect what Congress was told about them, it is likely that DCIs broached these programs with at least the leaders of the CIA subcommittees in the course of the annual budget process. Apparently, however, they were not motivated to inquire beyond what they were told.

Like so much of the Agency's relationship with Congress, this changed after the creation of the select committees in the mid-1970s. Both committees began to demand voluminous documentation from CIA about its technical collection programs and, over time, developed professional staffs with detailed knowledge of them. Indeed, because the subject matter was technical and arcane as far as members were concerned, the staff that monitored these programs came to have considerable influence over them. Typically, the issues involved were sorted out each year in the course of the budget process. But on occasion, notably in the course of the SSCI's inquiries into the ability of the Intelligence Community to monitor various arms control treaties, the committee, independent of the annual budget reviews, would assess the capabilities and/or performance of the Agency's technical systems against particular targets.

The committees would also look from time to time at other kinds of technical collection the Agency engaged in. For example, they would look at signals-intelligence-gathering that was sometimes done as part of clandestine operations, or perhaps, they would look at the Agency's efforts to acquire and analyze Soviet military equipment. Occasionally the committees would be concerned about the reaction of foreign governments if such activities were disclosed, but more often they simply wondered whether the Agency's activities were duplicating those of other intelligence agencies.

Historically, though, because the Agency's technical collection activities were relatively passive and the issues associated with them were considered in the context of the budget process, they have had a lower profile than other Agency activities. Still, programs with large price tags will always produce controversy with the Congress, and these programs were no exception.

CHAPTER 9

OVERSIGHT OF COVERT ACTION

This chapter covers Congress's awareness of, and involvement in, the third of the Agency's functional areas: what has come to be called "covert action." Generally speaking, covert actions are activities that the CIA might undertake in other countries to accomplish a US foreign policy objective without the hand of the US government becoming known or apparent to the outside world. Thus, it is something different from "collection": it is doing something in another country beyond merely gathering information. The Agency might use the same people for both kinds of activity, but functionally, the Agency and the Congress have treated these roles differently.

As noted earlier in this study, covert action was not a role that Congress specifically contemplated for the Agency when it was created. But it came along soon thereafter and, judging from the resources Congress made available for it in the early years of the Agency's existence (see chapter 6), was wholeheartedly embraced by the Agency's overseers on Capitol Hill. That history will not be repeated here; instead this chapter will focus on what happened afterwards.

Like the two previous chapters, this chapter will identify the issues and concerns that have motivated Congress to engage with the Agency over this particular function, apart from the necessity to appropriate resources for it each year. To illustrate these issues and concerns, only covert actions that have been previously disclosed to the public will be cited. Lest readers think they are being shortchanged, however, these include the operations that, from an historical perspective, have been the largest and arguably the most significant of those undertaken during the period covered by the study.

Congressional Awareness and Involvement from 1948 until the Bay of Pigs

Documentation bearing upon Congress's awareness of covert action during the early period of CIA's existence is extremely sparse, both at the Agency itself and, judging from Barrett's book, in the records of the legislators involved in the Agency's affairs. As noted in chapter 6, several of the leaders of the CIA subcommittees were briefed in 1948 in advance of the Agency's initial foray into covert action: support for the noncommunist parties vying for electoral office in Italy.[1] From 1948 until the spring of 1961, when the Bay of Pigs operation was in the offing, no documentary evidence has thus far been found that establishes beyond doubt that the CIA subcommittees were formally briefed on specific operations, either in advance or after the fact.

Yet, from what is known about the way the system operated during these early years, one can reasonably assume this happened informally with some regularity. Certainly the CIA subcommittees were aware of the kinds of things the Agency was doing around the world, and it is probable that DCIs advised at least their leaders of specific operations, especially if they had attracted public attention.

It is instructive to note that during this early period Congress identified covert action in its own budget documents under the rubric "Cold War activities." Clearly, covert action was viewed as part of the nation's Cold War arsenal to do battle against the forces of communism. Congress was fully aware that the Soviet Union, as a matter of doctrine and practice, was aggressively trying to establish and promote communist regimes around the globe using overt as well as covert means. The United States needed a means of countering these efforts—beyond diplomacy but short of military action—and the CIA, given its clandestine mode of operating abroad, seemed to Congress to be the natural candidate for such a mission. Indeed, as Barrett later found, senior members repeatedly implored early DCIs to do more of it. [2]

Many of the covert actions in the early period were efforts to get the US message across in places it was not being heard. Often the aim was simply to tout US foreign policy or the virtues of democratic societies; at other times it was to criticize communist regimes or organizations in order to create internal problems for them or stir international sentiment against them. Getting articles or political commentary placed in the news media of particular countries was a staple of the effort, as was assisting with the publication abroad of books, periodicals, and brochures favorable to the US point of view. The Agency was also behind the broadcasts into denied areas carried out by Radio Free Europe and Radio Liberty. In fact, Barrett, citing an interview with Walter Pforzheimer, leaves no doubt that the CIA subcommittees received accounts of such programs.[3]

---

[1] Barrett, *CIA and Congress*, 29–31.
[2] Ibid, 96–99
[3] Ibid., 99–103

In various places, the Agency would also see opportunities to keep communists from coming to power or ways to undermine them where they already held power. This might take the form of providing money or other assistance to noncommunists in democratic countries who were vying for power or trying to cling to power against communist opponents. Or it might entail helping dissidents in communist countries resist or stir up problems for the regime in power. It might also involve struggles for the control of international organizations aimed at keeping communists on the sidelines. The CIA subcommittees also knew the Agency was involved in this kind of thing.[4]

They were also aware that the Agency undertook covert action of various kinds in support of US military deployments overseas, notably in Korea in the early 1950s.[5]

On occasion, though, during the Eisenhower administration, the Agency was directed to undertake something qualitatively different: a clandestine effort to overthrow—by force or by inciting popular resistance against—a communist government or a government (even one that had been popularly elected) that was perceived as falling to the communists. Obviously such operations raised more serious political and ethical issues and usually required different, more substantial forms of assistance. They might require significant outlays of cash, the provision of military equipment; the training of paramilitary forces, or acts of sabotage and physical violence, perhaps even leading to the death of a foreign leader. The extent to which the CIA subcommittees perceived the Agency was being directed to undertake this kind of operation is less clear.

Several such operations were mounted during the Eisenhower administration: in Iran in 1953, in Guatemala in 1954, and in Indonesia in 1957. But there is no documentary evidence showing that any of the CIA subcommittees were consulted about these operations, either before or after they occurred. Given the circumstances surrounding them, however, one might reasonably conclude that at least the leaders of the Agency's subcommittees were told about them after-the-fact.

The operation in Iran, codenamed TPAJAX, was prompted largely by British concerns conveyed to President Eisenhower soon after he took office in 1953, that Iran soon might fall into communist hands.[6] Two years earlier In 1951, the Iranian government, led by its 69-year-old nationalist prime minister, Mohammed Mossadegh, had nationalized the Anglo-Iranian Oil Company,

---

[4] Ibid.

[5] Ibid.

[6] For a detailed account of the background and conduct of the operation, see Kinzer, *All the Shah's Men.*

which was supplying 90 percent of Europe's petroleum. The British government, a majority shareholder in the company, was infuriated and began looking at ways, including military action, to topple the Mossadegh government. Mossadegh got wind of the plotting, however, and closed the British embassy and expelled British citizens from the country. Without a base of operations in Iran, the British turned to President Truman. Although worried about Iran falling into Soviet hands, Truman vetoed the idea of military action against Iran and was unsympathetic to the idea of a coup. CIA had never overthrown a government, he reportedly told the British, and he did not want to establish such a precedent here.[7] Truman had met Mossadegh when he visited Washington in 1951—Mossadegh had been named *Time* magazine's Man of the Year that year—and was not unsympathetic to the nationalist movement he led in Iran.

When the Eisenhower came to office, however, the British found a more sympathetic ear. By this point, there was growing dissatisfaction with Mossadegh inside Iran among those who wished to return control of the country to the monarch. Moreover, his relationship with the Soviet Union seemed to be growing closer, and the communist Tudeh party had gained strength and had largely aligned itself with Mossadegh. DCI Dulles and others warned Eisenhower in the spring of 1953 that the Iranian government was in danger of collapse, potentially giving the Soviets an opportunity to seize control. On the basis of these concerns, Eisenhower approved, with apparent reluctance, a covert effort to overthrow Mossadegh.

This came about a few months later, in August 1953, after further US diplomatic efforts to compromise the oil issue with the British government had failed. The operation was orchestrated largely by a single CIA officer sent to the scene—Kermit Roosevelt, grandson of Theodore Roosevelt. After securing the approval of the Shah of Iran, Mohammed Reza Pahlavi, for the coup—the Shah also agreed to sign a decree dismissing Mossadegh that was to provide it legitimacy—Roosevelt set about to create a situation in which the coup could occur. Using a network of contacts left behind by British intelligence and the Agency's own assets, he mounted an intensive propaganda campaign against Mossadegh, spurring demonstrations and protests across the country. When the time came to oust the prime minister, however, the effort faltered. Mossadegh had gotten wind of the coup and had the Iranian military officer who was to deliver the decree dismissing him arrested. The shah fled the country, fearing for his safety, and Mossadegh thought he had put at end to the coup.

Roosevelt tried again a few days later, however, first organizing violent "fake" demonstrations against the monarchy, which were in fact, joined by

---

[7] Ibid., 3, 209.

members of the Tudeh party; then organizing "backlash" demonstrations in support of the Shah. As these played out, the Iranian military units, police, and rural tribesmen under Roosevelt's control were able to overcome the limited military forces that Mossadegh could muster. Mossadegh was arrested, and the Shah returned to Teheran to take control.

The *New York Times* portrayed the coup as an effort by Iranians loyal to the Shah to return him to power. The role of the CIA was not mentioned.[8] In another article published the same day, however, the *Times* reported that the Soviet newspaper, *Pravda*, had charged that American agents operating inside Iran had engineered the coup.[9] This might well have prompted the Agency's overseers in Congress to follow up with DCI Dulles, but there is no evidence that they did. In all likelihood, the charge, coming as it did from the Soviets, was not seen as credible. There were no follow-up stories that immediately appeared in the American press, nor were there any formal congressional inquiries.

Still, the upper reaches of the US security establishment were aware of what CIA had managed to pull off—Roosevelt himself had briefed them upon his return. One of them, perhaps Dulles himself, might well have confided the story to members of his choosing. Moreover, as time passed, the US role in the Iranian coup became something of an open secret in Washington. Eisenhower himself noted with satisfaction what had taken place in Iran in his 1954 State of the Union address, referring to it as one of several "heartening political victories [of his administration]...won by the forces of stability and freedom."

In any event, the perceived success of the operation in Iran undoubtedly contributed to the administration's decision later in the year to begin planning a similar kind of operation in Guatemala. The popularly elected president of the country, Jacobo Arbenz, had expropriated the property of several large US corporations and had allowed the communist party to gain a substantial foothold within the country. An NIE published in April 1954 had, in fact, warned that "communists now effectively control the political life of Guatemala." When CIA learned in May that Arbenz had obtained Soviet-made military equipment from Czechoslovakia, it proved too much for Eisenhower, who directed CIA to mount an operation to overthrow him.[10]

To carry out the coup, the Agency trained a small group of Guatemalan exiles in Honduras, under the leadership of former Guatemalan army colonel, Carlos Castillo Armas, and provided them with several aircraft, flown by CIA

---

[8] *New York Times* "Royalists Oust Mossadegh; Army Seizes Helm."
[9] *New York Times* "Moscow Says US Aided Shah's Coup"
[10] Barrett, *CIA and Congress*, 160.

pilots. When the operation began in June 1954, the small exile force entered Guatemala and set up camp near the border. The CIA-provided aircraft carried out limited bombing runs and "buzzed" a number of Guatemalan towns and cities. At the same time, the Agency began an elaborate deception operation with the support of other US entities in Guatemala, using what appeared to be radio broadcasts between rebel forces to make it seem that a large invasion force was moving toward the capital. On 27 June 1954, the chief of the Guatemalan armed forces, COL Carlos Enrique Diaz, met with US Ambassador John Peurifoy to plead that it be stopped. In return for the ambassador's assurance that it would be, Diaz agreed to lead a coup against Arbenz. Upon learning this later the same day, Arbenz himself stepped aside, and in the ensuring deliberations, the Guatemalan army agreed to accept Armas as the country's new president.

The news accounts of the coup did not mention the Agency's role, although it was later alluded to in a column written by James Reston of the *New York Times*.[11] Even without confirmation in the press, however, it is likely that many in Congress suspected CIA's involvement and that its subcommittees were told. Although he did not have a specific recollection, CIA Legislative Counsel Pforzheimer said years later he was "sure the committees were informed [of the Guatemalan operation]" and there would have been "no holding back on details."[12]

DCI Dulles had earlier informed key members that Arbenz had purchased Soviet-made military equipment from Czechoslovakia. This had led to resolutions being passed overwhelmingly in each House condemning the action and urging action by the administration to deal with it. In private channels, the pressure coming from key legislators to do something about Arbenz was even stronger.[13]

Thus, when the coup actually occurred, it would have been natural for the Agency to tell its subcommittees what had happened, but no documentary evidence of such briefings exists. Barrett writes, however, that he finds it "thoroughly implausible" that the subcommittees did not know something about what was happening there, given the congressional interest in Guatemala at the time.[14]

In 1957, perceiving that Indonesian President Achmed Sukarno's policy of "nonalignment" was, in fact, moving the country toward communism, the Eisenhower administration authorized the Agency to provide arms and other

---

[11] Ibid., 165–67.
[12] Ibid., 168.
[13] Ibid.
[14] Ibid., 162.

assistance in response to a request from a group of Indonesian dissidents — anticommunists, principally former Army colonels, located on the island of Sumatra — who were in open rebellion against the Sukarno government. When the group proclaimed its independence in February 1958, however, the central government responded with a blockade of the rebel-controlled area and later with military force. The Agency continued to provide assistance during this period to counter the government's offensive, but by April 1958 the dissidents on Sumatra were no longer a viable political or military force.

Another group of dissidents on the island of Sulawesi, however, continued to receive Agency support. This group controlled its own airfield, from which CIA-supplied aircraft carried out bombing and strafing runs against the government forces that had massed against the dissidents. It was during one of these runs, on 17 May 1958, that government forces shot down an aircraft piloted by an American, Allen L. Pope. Pope survived the crash and later contended that he was merely a private citizen, an American "soldier of fortune," but among his effects discovered in the crash was evidence linking him to the CIA. An Indonesian military tribunal convicted Pope and sentenced him to death, but the sentence was never carried out. He was released to the United States in 1962. In the aftermath of the shootdown, assistance to the dissidents was halted, as the Eisenhower administration changed course and began providing substantially greater levels of foreign aid to the Sukarno government.[15]

Although there is no documentary evidence that the CIA briefed its subcommittees on these operations, Barrett writes that Dulles "almost certainly" told the heads of the CIA subcommittees about it.[16] Several weeks before Pope's aircraft was shot down, Eisenhower had stated publicly that the United States was staying neutral in the Indonesian rebellion.[17] After the shootdown, it was apparent to the Congress (and the rest of the world) this was not the case. If this were not enough, once the Indonesian government publicly charged Pope with working for the CIA — at a press conference it displayed the document identifying him as an employee of an Agency proprietary — in all likelihood, the leaders of the CIA subcommittees would have been advised.

In April 1959, Dulles appeared in closed session before the SFRC to discuss the escape of the Dalai Lama from Tibet a few weeks earlier. In the course of his testimony, not only did Dulles describe the Agency's role in the escape but with some specificity also made reference to the assistance the Agency had been covertly providing the local Tibetan resistance since the Chinese had occupied the country in 1957.[18] While it was unusual if not

---

[15] See Conboy and Morrison, *Feet to the Fire.*

[16] Barrett, *CIA and Congress*, 315.

[17] Prados, *Presidents' Secret Wars*, 143.

unprecedented for a DCI to provide this kind of information to a "non-CIA committee," there was overwhelming sympathy in Congress at the time for the plight of the Tibetans, and, no doubt, Dulles—so often forced to bear the brunt of criticism from the SFRC—for once was able to relish its praise.

The Bay of Pigs: 1961

As noted earlier, records show that Congress was briefed in advance of the Bay of Pigs operation, the first documented instance of prior notice since the Agency embarked on its covert action mission in 1948.

Planning for the operation had begun in the Eisenhower administration. By the beginning of 1960, the last year of the Eisenhower presidency, it had become clear that Fidel Castro was a committed communist, and Eisenhower feared that he might infect the rest of Latin America. To deal with this perceived threat, the president directed the Agency to come up with a covert plan for getting rid of Castro, which he approved in March 1960. It authorized the Agency to attempt to unify and strengthen the opposition to Castro outside of Cuba, to build a guerrilla organization within the country, to mount a propaganda campaign against Castro, and to train a paramilitary force outside of Cuba to lead an invasion.

In August 1960, after a diplomatic effort failed to get the Organization of American States to intervene in Cuba, the covert action plan took on greater urgency. By the late fall, however, the Agency had achieved mixed results. It had recruited a paramilitary force of Cuban exiles—including Cuban pilots for the aircraft that were to support the ground operation—and trained them in Guatemala, but efforts to build a credible guerrilla force within Cuba itself had produced relatively little.

As Barrett notes, many in Congress at the time were urging Eisenhower to do something about Castro.[19] While there is no documentation to suggest that the administration saw fit to bring Congress into its plans in the fall of 1960, it is possible that it did so if only to answer this mounting concern. Dulles, at this point, was also still embarrassed by his failure to bring congressional leaders into the U-2 program and wanted to avoid repeating this mistake in the future.[20]

By the first of the year, the HAC subcommittee knew or suspected that something was afoot with respect to Cuba. At a meeting of the subcommittee

---

[18] Barrett, CIA and Congress, 346–51. Also see Knaus, *Orphans of the Cold War: America and the Tibetan Struggle for Survival.*

[19] Barrett, *CIA and Congress*, 425–37.

[20] CIA draft study, Vol. I, 83.

on 6 January 1961, Dulles was asked whether the Agency was training Cuban exiles for an invasion. "He gave a fairly detailed picture of CIA action with respect to Cuba," Legislative Counsel John Warner later recalled, "mentioning the two-pronged program of propaganda…and the paramilitary effort, and indicating the number of Cubans being trained and the supply efforts and the bases."[21] Four days later, the rest of Congress learned, courtesy of an article in the *New York Times*, that the United States (CIA was not specifically mentioned) was training anti-Castro guerrillas in Guatemala.

President Kennedy had been briefed on the Agency's plans weeks before he took office and had not raised objection to them. Once he was in office, planning for the invasion continued.

On 10 March 1961, Dulles provided a detailed briefing to the CIA subcommittee of the HASC on the Agency's operational activities against Castro: its efforts to mount a propaganda campaign, organize the Cuban resistance parties, and train a paramilitary force to invade the island. He said the paramilitary force numbered about a thousand Cubans and had its own "air force."[22] Although several members wondered how an army of 1,000 exiles could be expected to defeat a Cuban army of 200,000, Dulles replied that he expected the exiles to "light the fuse" that would spark a general uprising on the island.[23]

Agency records do not reflect that the Agency's other subcommittees were briefed in advance, but Legislative Counsel Warner later told Professor Barrett that the leaders of the CIA subcommittees in the Senate would also have been told.[24] Barrett also writes that Senator Fulbright, the chairman of the SFRC, was brought into the operation by the president. Hearing rumors of the administration's intentions, Fulbright had written Kennedy a personal letter attempting to persuade him not to let the operation go forward. Reacting to the letter, Kennedy invited Fulbright to a meeting at the State Department in early April 1961, where he was allowed to express his misgivings personally.[25]

The operation itself began on 15 April 1961, with airstrikes against Cuban airfields. Two days later, the "Cuban brigade" established a beachhead at the Bay of Pigs. It did not go smoothly. Without air cover, which the administration declined to provide because it still sought to protect the fact that the United States was involved in the operation, the exiles remained pinned down on the beach. They had sparked no uprising inside the country. Two days after

---

[21] Ibid., 84.

[22] Barrett, *CIA and Congress*, 441–42.

[23] Ibid., 443.

[24] Ibid., 445.

[25] Ibid., 447–48.

the landing, the fighting was over. Castro's forces killed 114 of the exiles and took 1,189 prisoners.

In the weeks that followed, the CIA subcommittees of the HAC and HASC held closed hearings on the fiasco. For the most part, their tenor was favorable to the Agency. Taking their cue from Dulles's testimony, members blamed the administration and/or the Pentagon for failing to provide air cover and faulted the administration for not taking stronger action.[26] The SFRC also held closed hearings the first week in May, and these were more contentious. Fulbright complained that the committee should have been forewarned of the invasion; others questioned whether CIA should be charged with undertaking operations of this kind at all. One senator told Dulles that CIA "should go back to its responsibility of being an intelligence agency and gathering information throughout the world." [27]

Apart from these hearings, Congress did no independent investigation of the Bay of Pigs. This was left to a blue ribbon commission appointed by the president and to an internal CIA inquiry conducted by the inspector general.

The Ramparts Affair: 1967

Ramparts magazine, a Catholic leftwing publication published a series of articles in February 1967 disclosing that the Agency since the early 1950s had been covertly funding certain international student groups, notably the US National Student Association (USNSA), in an effort to counter the spread and influence of communist youth groups and front organizations around the world. The program had been instituted, in fact, at the suggestion of a former USNSA activist who had gone to work at the Agency in 1949; it entailed the passage of funds through private US foundations principally to pay the travel expenses of USNSA members to international conferences, annual meetings of foreign student organizations, and the like, as well as to provide college scholarships to students from Third World countries to US educational institutions. In his memoir, DCI Helms said the Eisenhower White House had approved the program and that it was briefed to "appropriate senators" before its inception. It was subsequently approved by Presidents Kennedy and Johnson.[28]

Forewarned of the *Ramparts* articles, DCI Helms, in order to head off an adverse reaction in Congress, led Agency efforts to brief the CIA subcommittees before the articles were published. According to Agency records, Helms

---

[26] CIA draft study, Vol. I, 86.

[27] Ibid., 87.

[28] Helms, *A Look Over My Shoulder*, 348.

appeared before all four subcommittees to assure them that the program's sole purpose had been to counter the influence of international communist youth groups around the world. CIA, he said, had simply given money to the US groups involved; it had not told them how to spend it.[29] While this money might have been channeled through other government agencies, Helms noted, someone in the federal government needed to do it, and CIA, given its unique capabilities and authorities, was best positioned to carry it out.

Although the CIA subcommittees had not previously been advised of the program (Helms said "appropriate senators" had been briefed when the program began in the early 1950s), they generally refrained from citicizing the Agency or attacking Helms publicly after the articles began appearing.

The reaction elsewhere was less benign. *Ramparts,* itself portrayed the program as a "case study in the corruption of youthful idealism" and a threat to academic freedom. Eight Democratic congressmen wrote to President Johnson that the program "represents an unconscionable extension of power by an agency of government over institutions outside its jurisdiction."[30]

President Johnson was sufficiently concerned that he announced two days after the first article appeared that he was appointing a three-person committee— Under Secretary of State Nicholas deB. Katzenbach (chair), HEW Secretary John W. Gardner and Helms himself—to look into the relationship between the Agency and private American organizations operating abroad. In June 1967, the committee recommended, and Johnson approved, a prohibition on covert financial assistance to any US educational institution or private voluntary organization, saying that henceforth such financial assistance in support of overseas activities should be done openly by a "public-private mechanism" when considered essential to the national interest. All such funding activities by the CIA were to be terminated by the end of the year.[31] Before that deadline, the CIA subcommittees of the SASC and HASC had Helms testify in December 1967 with respect to how the Agency planned to implement the recommendations approved by the president.[32]

The "Secret War" in Laos: 1962–71

During the 1960s, the Agency regularly briefed the CIA subcommittees on covert operations as part of the ongoing war effort in Southeast Asia. The sub-

---

[29] CIA draft study, Vol. II, 27; Hathaway and Smith, *Richard Helms,* 170.

[30] Quoted in Glass and Grant, "NSA Officers Describe Aid Given by CIA," *Washington Post,* 15 February 1967.

[31] CIA draft study, Vol. II, 30.

[32] Ibid., 31–32.

committees worried, as did Agency managers, about the demands these operations were placing on the Agency's overall resources. In 1968, for example,
despite the Johnson administration's insistence that the Agency fund an
expansion of its program to improve social, medical, and economic conditions
in the South Vietnamese countryside, the leaders of the SAC and HAC subcommittees cut off Agency funds, leaving continued funding a matter for the
Pentagon to decide.[33]

In Laos, however, US military forces were not involved. In 1962, the
Agency began supplying and directing Laotian government troops and irregular forces that were resisting the advances of the Pathet Lao, the Laotian communist party. By the mid-1960s, this irregular force had grown to
approximately 40,000 Laotian tribesmen.

From the very beginning, the Agency sought to bring Congress into these
activities. Its subcommittees were briefed, and their approval obtained to
finance the paramilitary program. In addition, Agency records reflect that the
SFRC was briefed—in all, more than 50 senators received information about
the Laotian program over the course of its existence. The Agency also went so
far as to arrange several visits to Laos for one supportive senator, Stuart Symington, and in 1967 permitted the head of its Laotian operations to brief the
entire SASC on the status of the program.[34]

By 1970, however, as public support for the Vietnam War waned, congressional backing for the Agency's paramilitary program in Laos also dimin-
ished. At this point, the tide had turned against the Laotian government forces,
and Pathet Lao and North Vietnamese troops controlled much of the country.
To bolster the government forces, the Agency introduced into the country paid
Thai troops that it had trained, supplied, and directed. The additional costs of
introducing these troops worried the leaders of the SAC and HAC subcommittees, not only because of the impact on the Agency's overall budget, but
because they provided ammunition to the antiwar members of Congress, who
were charging that the Nixon administration was financing the war in South
Vietnam through the CIA to avoid public and congressional scrutiny.[35]

In early 1971, South Vietnamese forces invaded Laos for the first time, pre-
cipitating renewed congressional interest in the ongoing CIA role there. At the
end of February, DCI Helms appeared before the SFRC to provide a status
report. Later in the year, Congress approved an amendment establishing a
budgetary ceiling for US expenditures in Laos. CIA was not mentioned per se,

---

[33] Hathaway and Smith, *Richard Helms*, 175–76.
[34] Ibid., 177.
[35] Ibid., 178.

but in August, 1971, the SFRC published a sanitized staff report that acknowledged in so many words the Agency's long involvement in the country.[36] It was at this point that Senator Symington, who had been briefed on the Laotian program for many years, publicly disclosed the program, solemnly labeling it "a secret war."

John Stennis, who now chaired the SASC, reacted to Symington's comment by characterizing the Agency's performance in Laos as "splendid," but he provided ammunition to the Agency's critics when he added, "You have to make up your mind that you are going to have an intelligence agency and protect it as such and shut your eyes some and take what is coming."[37]

Once the Agency's long involvement in Laos had been publicly disclosed, however, the prevailing sentiment on the CIA subcommittees was that it was now time for the Agency to disengage, leading DCI Helms to recommend to the Nixon administration that its involvement be brought to an orderly end.[38] After the 1973 peace agreements were signed, the CIA terminated its operations in Laos.

Chile and the Hughes-Ryan Amendment: 1973–74

In the spring of 1970, the Nixon administration, concerned that Salvador Allende, an avowed Marxist and founder of the Chilean Socialist Party, could well be elected president in the country's upcoming elections, directed the Agency to undertake a covert propaganda campaign against Allende, principally to convey the message that a vote for Allende would be bad for Chilean democracy. There is no indication in Agency records that anyone in Congress was briefed on the operation, but DCI Helms later recalled that soon after the decision was made to undertake the program, he was summoned to the office of SFRC Chairman Fulbright, who appeared to know (and disapprove) of it. "Dick, if I catch you trying to upset the Chilean election," Fulbright reportedly warned Helms, "I will get up on the Senate floor and blow the operation."[39]

Unaware of the administration's covert initiative, certain US companies with business interests in Chile — International Telephone and Telegraph (ITT) among them — had the same concern and approached Helms a few weeks later to help them channel funds to anti-Allende forces with Chile. Ultimately, CIA

---

[36] Ibid., 179.

[37] CIA draft study, Vol. II, 37.

[38] Hathaway and Smith, *Richard Helms*, 180.

[39] Helms, *A Look Over My Shoulder*, 399.

representatives provided advice to ITT on making contacts within Chile but left it to the company to arrange for any donations on its own.

When the election occurred on 4 September 1970, Allende won a small plurality, and under Chilean law, the Chilean National Congress would choose between the top two vote-getters when it reconvened on 24 October. When this had happened in the past, the legislature had chosen the candidate who had garnered the most votes in the popular election.

At this point Nixon directed the Agency to intensify its covert efforts to keep Allende from being chosen. In one series of actions that came to be known as Track I, additional funds were authorized for anti-Allende propaganda and political support to his principal challenger. Agency representatives also actively sought to persuade influential groups and individuals, both within and outside Chile, to oppose or undermine Allende's election. These included some of the US companies that had earlier been concerned with Allende's election, but at this juncture none was interested in active intervention. In a separate action that came to be known as Track II, which came about as a result of a personal meeting between Nixon and Helms, the Agency was directed to arrange a military coup before Allende could be chosen president. Again, there is no indication in Agency records that it advised any of its congressional subcommittees of either Track I or Track II. Helms also confirms this in his memoir.[40]

Ultimately the Agency's efforts failed. Although CIA did establish contact with, and provide assistance to, certain Chilean military officers prepared to undertake a coup, it never materialized because of the lack of support from the incumbent Chilean president as well as the Chilean military. Two days before the Chilean legislature was to vote, a group of the coup plotters (without the Agency's direct support) unsuccessfully attempted to abduct the Chilean chief of staff, BG Rene Schneider—regarded as the most formidable obstacle to their plans—mortally wounding him in the process. As a result, whatever impetus remained for a coup quickly evaporated.[41]

Twice in early 1973, Helms appeared before "non-CIA committees" where the issue of the Agency's involvement in the 1970 Chilean elections was posed. The first came in February before the SFRC, which was considering Helms's nomination as US ambassador to Iran. In closed session, in response to questions from Senator Symington, Helms denied that the Agency had tried to "overthrow the government of Chile" or "passed money to the opponents of Allende."[42] A few weeks later, at an open hearing of an SFRC subcommittee

---

[40] Ibid. 405.

[41] For a detailed description of the Chilean operation, see the Church Committee hearings on covert action (vol. 7); also, Helms, *A Look Over my Shoulder*, 393–408.

[42] Hathaway and Smith, *Richard Helms*, 100.

investigating the role of multinational corporations in Latin America, Helms denied having contacts with the Chilean military during his tenure as DCI.[43] He later maintained he had not intended to mislead these committees, noting, in particular, that Symington had previously been briefed on the Track I activities in Chile (though not Track II). In other words, as Helms wrote, the senator "knew the answers" to the questions he was asking.[44] Helms went on to assert that since these committees had no authority over the Agency's affairs, he was not obliged to divulge highly classified information in contravention of an order he received from the president.[45]

In September 1973, Allende was overthrown and committed suicide during a military coup. Allegations soon appeared in the US press that CIA had been involved. At the urging of the principal source of these allegations, Congressman Michael Harrington (D-MA), a subcommittee of the House Foreign Affairs Committee held a closed hearing to obtain the response of new DCI William Colby to the allegations, but Colby demurred, asserting that such testimony could only be provided to the CIA subcommittees.

This testimony did not come about until April 1974, when Colby appeared in closed session before the CIA subcommittee of the HASC, which had been recently renamed the Special Subcommittee on Intelligence, chaired by Lucien Nedzi (D-MI). Colby denied that the Agency had been involved in the 1973 coup that had led to Allende's death but revealed the Agency's earlier activities in 1970 which had been part of Track I. With regard to Track II, however, he chose to reveal CIA's effort to mount a military coup only to Nedzi.[46]

What had occurred under Track I, however, would prove controversial enough. Citing House rules entitling him to read hearing transcripts, Congressman Harrington was allowed by Nedzi to read Colby's classified testimony. In turn, Harrington went to the press with the substance of what Colby had said, asserting that CIA had admitted having tried to "destabilize" the Allende candidacy in 1970. In other words, the Agency had covertly intervened in the electoral process of another democratic country.

Coming as it did in the final stages of the Watergate scandal, this disclosure provoked a firestorm of criticism. In Congress, a number of bills were introduced to drastically curtail, or eliminate altogether, covert action in the future. As noted in chapter 1, a more modest proposal, offered by Senator Harold Hughes (D-IA) as an amendment to the Foreign Assistance Act, called for a significant change to the congressional oversight arrangements where covert

---

[43] Helms, *A Look Over My Shoulder*, 415.
[44] Ibid., 414.
[45] Ibid., 415.
[46] Ford, *William E. Colby*, 70; CIA draft study, Vol. II, 46.

action was concerned. This proposal, which became known as the Hughes-Ryan Amendment, was signed into law in December 1974. From that point on, the president would have to personally approve such operations by signing a written "finding" that the operation was important to the national security and provide "timely notice" of such operations to the "appropriate committees" of the Congress. This was interpreted to include not only the armed services and appropriations committees but also the foreign affairs committees on each side.

Angola: 1975–76

The first repercussion of the Hughes-Ryan Amendment came less than a year later, when members of the SFRC raised concerns about a covert action program on which they had been given "timely notice"—Angola.[47] In May 1975, Portugal announced it would grant independence to its colony of Angola on 11 November 1975. During the interim period, three political groups struggled for power. All were tribally based and nationalistic, but the strongest one (the MPLA) was avowedly communist while the other two (the FNLA and UNITA) were not. Not surprisingly, Angola became the next battleground in the Cold War. The USSR and Cuba supported the MPLA; the United States supported the FNLA and UNITA. Other countries were involved, notably South Africa, which was heavily engaged in funneling military supplies and other assistance to UNITA.

When the Soviet Union began increasing its support to the MPLA, the Ford administration countered by authorizing an increase in US support for the two noncommunist groups. This entailed a "finding" being signed by the president in July 1975 pursuant to the Hughes-Ryan Amendment, enacted six months before, as well as briefings of the six congressional committees entitled to receive "timely notice."

One of the SFRC senators briefed on the operation, Dick Clark (D-IA), traveled to Africa in August 1975. In the course of his travels, he learned of the South African support for UNITA and became concerned that the United States had aligned itself with the apartheid government there. A month after Clark's return, several press stories revealed the South African involvement with UNITA (and indirectly with the United States), forcing Colby to deny publicly that the United States was directly providing weapons to the Angolan groups or that Americans were involved in the fighting taking place.

In November, however, Colby acknowledged during a closed session of the SFRC that the United States was providing arms to the noncommunist forces

---

[47] Gates, *From the Shadows*, 65–69; Prados, *Presidents' Secret Wars*, 338–47.

in Angola and, in some cases, was doing so through other governments. Testimony from this session leaked the following day to the *New York Times*, causing Senator Clark, among others, to wonder if the Agency was more directly involved than he had been led to believe, especially with the apartheid government in Pretoria. In December 1975, after his SFRC subcommittee had held yet another session with Colby to explore the Agency's role, Clark introduced an amendment prohibiting the expenditure of CIA funds in Angola—except for intelligence gathering—and the use of any DoD funds to continue the operation. The amendment passed the Senate and House within a matter of weeks and President Ford signed it into law on 9 February 1976, the first time that Congress had ever ended a covert action by denying the funds for it.

The Church Committee and Alleged Assassination Plots: 1975

As noted earlier, the Church Committee was originally established to look into allegations of domestic abuses by the Agency. But within weeks of its creation, an off-the-record remark that President Ford had made to journalists and publishers became public and caused it to shift its original focus. "President Ford has reportedly warned associates," CBS News reported on 28 February 1975, "that if the current investigations go too far they could uncover several assassinations of foreign officials involving the CIA."

Assassination plots had been mentioned several times in the "Family Jewels," to which the committee already had access, but the uproar that ensued once these charges became public dictated they be addressed as a matter of priority. In the spring and summer of 1975, the committee held 60 days of closed hearings involving 75 witnesses.[48] Of perhaps greater long-term significance for the Agency, the committee made assassination the first issue to examine when it held its first public hearing on 16 September 1975. By this point, Senator Church had already compared the Agency to a "rogue elephant rampaging out of control," and by making the Agency's efforts to develop exotic weapons to carry out political assassinations the first issue put before the public, the committee appeared intent on making the charge stick. Indeed, the sight of members passing among themselves an electronic pistol designed by the Agency to deliver poison darts created a lasting impression in the minds of the public. Colby attempted to make clear the pistol had never been used, but his message was lost in the blinding flash of press photography that accompanied the pistol's display.

---

[48] Smist, *Congress Oversees*, 69.

Senator Goldwater examines CIA dart gun as Senator Charles "Mac" Mathias (R-MD) looks on.

(© Bettman/Corbis)

The committee's investigation of the assassinations issue lasted six months. In December 1975, the committee issued an "interim report" containing its findings. Even though the Ford administration objected to the release of the report on security grounds, the committee—after presenting the issue to a secret session of the full Senate and noting an "absence of disapproval"— went ahead with its publication.[49] It was the first time in the history of executive-legislative relations that a committee of the Congress, with the putative support of its parent body, asserted the right to release a report a president contended was classified.

The committee found that US officials had initiated plots to assassinate Fidel Castro in Cuba and Patrice Lumumba in the Congo. The efforts against Castro had gone on for some time and involved bizarre techniques (putting an exploding seashell where he went snorkeling, recruiting a mistress to put poison into his drinks) as well as questionable means of implementing them (use of the Mafia). But none of these plans came to fruition. Lumumba had been overthrown in a coup in September 1960, involving people with whom the Agency had been working, who later handed him over to a group that murdered him on 17 January 1961. The committee found no evidence directly linking CIA with the coup or the subsequent murder, however. The report also found that US officials had encouraged, or were privy to, coup plots that had

---

[49] Church Committee, *Alleged Assassination Plots*; Smist, *Congress Oversees*, 52.

resulted in the deaths of certain foreign officials—Rafael Trujillo in the Dominican Republic, BG Rene Schneider in Chile, and Ngo Dihn Diem in South Vietnam—but the committee found no evidence the Agency had been directly involved in any of these deaths.[50]

On the issue of presidential responsibility, although the committee found no "paper trail" indicating Presidents Eisenhower or Kennedy had specifically authorized the assassination of any foreign official, it found that CIA understood itself to be acting in response to the wishes of "the highest levels of the US government."[51]

In addition to its findings with respect to plots involving particular foreign officials, the report found that the CIA had instituted a project in the early 1960s to create a standby capability to incapacitate, eliminate the effectiveness of, and, if necessary, perform assassinations of foreign officials.[52] The project involved researching various techniques for accomplishing these objectives (the poison dart gun, for example) but according to the committee, none of the devices or techniques was actually ever used. By the time the committee issued its report, the Ford administration had already promulgated an executive order prohibiting the assassination of foreign officials or the planning of such activities. The committee, for its part, recommended that these prohibitions be made a matter of federal criminal law.

Other Covert Action Investigated by the Church Committee: 1975–76

Initially, the Church Committee asked the Agency to provide data on "all its covert action activities."[53] In June 1975, however, the committee scaled back its request to data on five specific programs, including the Agency's prior activities in Chile, as well as an overview of all covert action programs since World War II.[54]

In the end, the committee produced six staff reports on covert action programs, only one of which (on Chile) was made public. It was here that the Agency's activities pursuant to Track II—the fruitless effort to mount a military coup to prevent Allende from coming to power—were made public and developed in considerable detail for the first time. But the committee was unable to conclude, despite exhaustive efforts to prove otherwise, that the Agency had been involved in the overthrow and murder of Allende three years later.

---

[50] CIA draft study, Vol. II, 77.

[51] Ibid.

[52] Ibid., 78.

[53] Ford, *William E. Colby*, 147.

[54] CIA draft study, Vol. II, 58.

In its final report of April 1976, however, the Church Committee gave the world (and the rest of Congress) a glimpse of covert action it had never had before. Between 1961 and 1975, the committee reported, the Agency had conducted more than 900 "major" projects and "several thousand" smaller ones, three-quarters of which had never been reviewed outside the Agency. Instead of being an extraordinary tool to use when vital US interests were at stake, the committee found, covert action had become part of the routine with its own bureaucratic momentum. Not only had such programs often failed to achieve their objectives, they had at times been self-defeating. Providing assistance to foreign parties, leaders, the press, and labor unions, the committee explained, often created a dependence upon the Agency that kept the recipients from doing more for themselves. The committee also believed intelligence analysis had been skewed to have it appear to policymakers that the Agency's covert action programs were succeeding.[55]

Looking at the cumulative effect of covert action, the committee questioned whether the gains for the United States outweighed the costs, especially the damage done to its reputation around the world. But it did not recommend doing away with it. Rather, the committee concluded that covert action should be employed only in exceptional cases where vital security interests of the United States were at stake.[56]

Covert Action and the Pike Committee: 1975–76

Covert action played a more limited role in the Pike Committee's inquiry. The committee initially told the Agency it wanted information on covert actions generally over the previous 10 years and planned to look specifically at three recent ones: assistance to certain political parties in the Italian elections of 1972, assistance to the Kurds in northern Iraq from 1972 to 1975, and ongoing activities in Angola (see above).[57]

At first, the committee insisted on discussing these programs in open hearings, but when it met resistance from the Agency, it agreed to have its staff delve into them instead. At its public hearings on covert action, the committee confined itself to examining the public policy issues such programs raised and to looking at the process within the executive branch for approving them.[58]

---

[55] Ibid., 88.
[56] Ibid.
[57] Ibid., 138.
[58] Ibid., 138–40.

In its final report, the committee concluded, "All evidence in hand suggests that the CIA, far from being out of control, has been utterly responsive to the instructions of the President and the Assistant to the President for National Security Affairs."[59] While Agency officials welcomed this conclusion—which appeared intended to offset Senator Church's earlier characterization—they objected to the committee including within its final report, its findings with respect to the three covert action programs it had looked into. The committee refused to take the references to the programs out of its final report, however, and ultimately they were made public as part of the material that was leaked to journalist Daniel Schorr.

Overall, based on its inquiry, the committee concluded that covert actions "were irregularly approved, sloppily implemented, and, at times, forced on a reluctant CIA by the president and his national security advisors."[60] But, apart from assassination attempts, it did not recommend abolishing them altogether. It did recommend that DCIs notify the committees in Congress responsible for the CIA of all covert actions within 48 hours of their implementation.[61]

The Select Committees and How "Findings" Were Handled: 1976–80

After the two select committees were created in the mid-1970s, they were naturally considered "appropriate committees" to receive "timely notice" of covert actions under the Hughes-Ryan Amendment, thus increasing the number of committees entitled to receive such notice to eight. From the Agency's standpoint, this was patently unworkable. Almost immediately, therefore, Agency officials began urging the select committees to repeal Hughes-Ryan and make themselves—their parent bodies had now given them exclusive jurisdiction over the Agency—the sole committees to receive notice of covert actions.

Until this issue could be resolved, however, there were practical questions that had to be answered, which, until the select committees were created, the Agency had not tried to sort out with the other committees involved. Instead, the notifications made under Hughes-Ryan had been largely ad hoc, both in terms of what was notified and how it was done.

How notice would be provided was the first issue DCI Turner addressed with the new committees, first with the SSCI and later with the HPSCI, and the issue was resolved with little controversy. The DCI would advise the com-

---

[59] Ibid., 141.
[60] Ibid., 140.
[61] Ibid.

mittees as soon as possible after a presidential finding had been signed. Subsequently he would brief the program to the full committee with representatives of the State Department and/or DoD present to answer questions. The committees would then be free to express their concerns to the DCI or the president with respect to the program but would not have a veto over it. In other words, the administration was free to move ahead regardless of the concerns expressed. Both committees emphasized, however, the importance of being notified *before* implementation of the program—or as SSCI Chairman Inouye put it, "before irrevocable actions are taken"—otherwise, their concerns may have little practical effect.[62]

What was to be notified to the committees proved a more difficult problem. As the Church Committee's report had suggested, in years past the Agency had conducted hundreds of covert actions, most of which did not rise to the level of presidential approval or congressional consideration. Yet, under Hughes-Ryan, all covert actions were made subject to a presidential finding and reporting to Congress. Resolution of this issue did not occur until late 1978, however, after the two committees had come to appreciate the situation the law had created. As DDCI Frank Carlucci bluntly told the HPSCI in September, "As a practical matter, the CIA covert action capability was moribund as a consequence of Hughes-Ryan."[63]

To resolve this dilemma, both committees agreed to the concept of "general," omnibus findings signed by the president to authorize routine, ongoing, low-risk activities undertaken for such broad, noncontroversial purposes as counterterrorism assistance to other governments or propaganda and political action activities to thwart the spread of communism.[64] These kinds of findings would be accompanied by "Perspectives" that would set forth in detail the kinds of activities being authorized. Other kinds of covert action—involving high-risk, large-resource commitments or the possibility of harm to the participants or embarrassment to the United States—would be the subject of "specific" findings.

Although many on the select committees agreed with the Agency that the list of committees receiving notice under Hughes-Ryan needed to be pared down, this was a delicate proposition for the committees, still in their infancy, to take on. In 1980, however, an opportunity presented itself. While the SSCI's effort to enact "charters" legislation for the Intelligence Community had come to naught (see chapter 3), one part of the proposed bill, establishing the obligations of intelligence agencies toward the two oversight committees,

---

[62] Ibid., 206, 244–45.
[63] Ibid., 250
[64] Ibid., 211, 249–51.

was still under discussion with the Carter administration. In return for the administration's agreement to support the oversight provisions, the SSCI inserted into the new oversight bill essentially the same obligations created by the Hughes-Ryan Amendment: the requirement for the president to approve and give "timely notice" of covert actions to the Congress. But here the obligation to provide "timely notice" ran only to the two intelligence committees. Thus, while the new legislation did not repeal Hughes-Ryan per se (this was done eight years later without fanfare), it was regarded as "superseding" Hughes-Ryan because it was subsequent legislation.

Interestingly, none of the six committees that had been getting "timely notice" of covert actions publicly objected to the change. In part, this may have been because they recognized the existing system did not allow for meaningful oversight. According to a former staff director of the SFRC, briefings under Hughes-Ryan were oral and often cursory. They were limited to the chairman, the ranking member, and one or two staff members, all of whom were prohibited from saying anything to the others. In other words, there was no opportunity for follow-up. "We were 'established eunuchs,'" he later recalled.[65]

Initial Oversight Efforts of the Committees: 1977–79

In their early years both committees undertook inquiries of covert action programs (beyond what occurred in the course of the notification process itself). In May 1977, the SSCI announced that it would investigate allegations appearing in the Australian press that the Agency had secretly intervened in the early 1970s to undermine and bring about the dismissal of its leftist-leaning government headed by Labor Party leader, Gough Whitlam. Although the committee's report of its inquiry was never made public, it was the first time that an oversight committee had indicated its intent to explore the propriety of the Agency's operational activities in a friendly country.[66]

In early 1978, the HPSCI reviewed the Agency's use of foreign journalists, not only to assess the continued value of this practice but also to consider problems that it posed, the "blowback" of propaganda to the United States, for example. Although no report came out of the inquiry, the committee held several hearings on the subject, and committee staff was given extensive access to Agency records. The committee ultimately "accepted . . . that the CIA needed foreign media assets to counter the Soviet Union's massive program in this area."[67]

---

[65] Smist, *Congress Oversees*, 119.
[66] CIA draft study, Vol. II, 207–10.
[67] Ibid., 254–59.

In late 1978, as a result of allegations made in *In Search of Enemies: CIA Story* by former CIA employee John Stockwell, the SSCI opened an investigation of the Angola covert action program that had been terminated two years before. As a result of this investigation, the committee drafted a highly critical report asserting that the Agency had been responsible for "misinforming and misleading the Congress." The adversarial tone of the report so upset DCI Turner that he wrote SSCI Chairman Birch Bayh (D-IN) to complain there had been a breakdown in the oversight relationship.[68]

The Iranian Rescue Operations: 1979–80

On 4 November 1979, a group of Iranian "students" overran the US embassy in Tehran and captured 66 American hostages. Unbeknownst to the Iranians at the time, six Americans working at the embassy had managed to avoid capture and took refuge in the residences of the Canadian ambassador and deputy chief of mission.

The Pentagon immediately began planning an operation to rescue the 66 hostages; President Carter gave DCI Turner the mission of rescuing the six being sheltered by the Canadians. CIA was, in fact, heavily involved in both operations.

To extricate the six being sheltered by the Canadians, the Agency sent a team to Tehran, disguised as a Hollywood film crew. The team brought disguises and passports for the embassy employees in hiding. On 28 January 1980, after satisfying Iranian immigration authorities, the six flew out of Tehran for Zurich.[69] The operation to rescue the rest of the hostages took place in April 1980. It was to use helicopters to ferry a commando force into Tehran to storm the embassy and rescue the hostages. Because of the distances involved, the helicopters would have to be refueled before they made the flight to Tehran. The plan was to have refueling aircraft land in a remote part of the Iranian desert and wait for the helicopters to arrive. CIA sent operatives into Iran several months before the rescue to scout the embassy and purchase trucks to transport the rescue force during the operation. The Agency also secretly landed a light plane on the desert refueling site to take soil samples to ensure the landing area would support the refueling aircraft.[70]

Unfortunately, the operation had to be aborted when three of the helicopters had mechanical problems, leaving insufficient capability to transport the res-

---

[68] CIA draft study, Vol. II, 207.
[69] Turner, *Burn Before Reading*, 173–76; Mendez, *Master of Disguise*, 267–305.
[70] Turner, *Burn Before Reading*, 177–79

cue force. As the aircraft involved were preparing to leave the landing area, one of the helicopters collided with one of the refueling aircraft, resulting in the deaths of seven Americans.

At the time these operations occurred, Hughes-Ryan was still the law, and the DCI was required to provide "timely notice" of all covert actions; both operations qualified as such—neither was undertaken for intelligence-gathering purposes. Because of the risks involved if either operation were disclosed, the Carter administration decided not to brief any congressional committee until after they were over. "In both instances," DCI Turner later wrote, "I informed the intelligence committees as soon as I could afterward. They were not happy, but were understanding."[71]

In fact, most committee members indicated afterwards that they understood why they had not been told, but not SSCI Chairman Bayh. He saw it as a sign that the administration did not trust the committee and suggested that in the future, a smaller group might be told, "so at least somebody in the oversight mechanism" would know. Bayh went on to note, "If oversight is to function better, you first need it to function [at all]."[72]

Later the same year, when the Intelligence Oversight Act of 1980 passed the Senate, it gave the president the option of providing "timely notice" to a "gang of eight"—the majority and minority leaders in each chamber and the leaders of the two intelligence committees—rather than the full committees, when it was "essential . . . to meet extraordinary circumstances affecting vital interests of the United States." Although the "gang of eight" provision could not be justified publicly by pointing to the Iranian rescue operations—the CIA role was still secret—those operations clearly formed the backdrop for its consideration and adoption.

Afghanistan: 1979–87

In December 1979, only a few weeks after the US embassy in Tehran was overrun, Soviet troops intervened in Afghanistan. The Marxist leader of the country, Hafizullah Amin, was killed in a shootout with the invading forces and replaced by another communist leader, Babrak Karmal, who "invited" the Soviets in, in force, to stabilize the country. By the end of the month, 8,000–10,000 Soviet troops were inside the country.

The Carter administration and other governments around the world immediately denounced the intervention, and United States took various diplomatic

---

[71] Ibid., 179.
[72] Smist, *Congress Oversees*, 121.

steps to "punish" the Soviets for their adventurism. The administration also turned to covert action. Tribal resistance forces, collectively known as the mujahedin, already existed in Afghanistan, and Carter signed a finding in January 1980 authorizing the CIA to equip them with weapons. To keep US involvement secret, the operation would acquire Soviet weapons through countries like China and Egypt and transport them to the resistance forces through Pakistan. Both intelligence committees supported the program.[73]

In 1981 the new Reagan administration, with the backing of the committees, began to increase the funding of the Afghan program significantly and to provide the mujahedin with more sophisticated weapons and other forms of assistance. By 1984, the funding had reached $60 million a year, an amount the Saudi government matched.[74]

Even at that, one flamboyant congressman, Charles Wilson (D-TX), was not satisfied. After several trips to Pakistan to assess the progress of the war, he concluded that the Afghan program was vastly underfunded. What the mujahedin really needed, he believed, was a high-tech, rapid-fire antiaircraft gun known as the Oerlikon to use against Soviet helicopters and other aircraft.

Although Wilson was not a member of the HPSCI, he was a member of the defense subcommittee of the HAC that had jurisdiction over CIA funding. While the intelligence committees had already approved the amount the administration requested for the program—and technically the appropriators could not appropriate more than had been authorized—Wilson managed to have the HAC subcommittee add $40 million for the program—most of which would go for the Oerlikon guns. Because this additional money had to come from somewhere in the DoD budget, the Pentagon initially objected to the subcommittee's action. Wilson threatened DoD with additional cuts, and it backed off.

This still left a problem with the intelligence committees, however, which had to go back and authorize the additional funds. Although CIA, like DoD, initially argued that the Oerlikon guns were in no way what the mujahedin needed—among other things, they were too difficult to transport and maintain in the Afghan environment—in the end, the Agency went along as well. After all, it was nonetheless funding they had not counted upon.[75]

DCI Casey thought the time was right for a quantum leap to extend the program's objectives and resources even further. In the fall of 1984, after consulting with the committees, he told the Saudis the United States would raise its

---

[73] For detailed accounts, see Lundberg, *Politics of a Covert Action: The US, the Mujahideen, and the Stinger Missile;* Bearden and Risen, *The Main Enemy;* and Crile, *Charlie Wilson's War.*

[74] Gates, *From the Shadows,* 251.

[75] CIA draft study, Vol. III, 42; Gates, *From the Shadows,* 319–21; Woodward, *Veil,* 316–18.

contribution to $250 million in 1985, increasing it several times over in a single year. From here on, the aim would be to push the Soviets out of Afghanistan.[76]

Although both committees supported these initiatives, members of the SSCI became concerned in the summer of 1984 that arms being furnished under the program were being siphoned off along the way and never reaching the mujahedin. To ascertain whether this was occurring, a staff member made a trip to Pakistan in the summer of 1984 to trace and examine the supply line. Agency officers strenuously objected to such an examination, believing it could harm the program, but in the end the staffer was permitted to conduct his inquiry.[77]

In 1985, the administration began exploring with the committees the idea of providing the mujahedin a more effective antiaircraft capability, namely, US Stinger ground-to-air missiles, which at that point were far from being integrated with US forces. Initially, the Agency objected to providing the Stinger because, among other reasons, it would no longer be possible to "plausibly deny" US involvement and might prompt retaliatory action by the Soviets. In March 1986, however, President Reagan, on Casey's recommendation, approved providing Stingers to the mujahedin, pursuant to the original program finding signed by President Carter. Although both committees had considered the Stinger issue throughout the preceding year, Casey chose to brief only the leaders and staff directors of the two committees, two days after Reagan's decision. According to CIA records, neither committee held follow-up hearings, their leaders apparently agreeing with the president's action.[78]

Both committees continued to receive briefings on the Stinger issue over the next two years. While concern arose for the number of Stingers reportedly lost, it was also clear the missiles were having a decided impact on the war, prompting the committees to approve the provision to the mujahedin of other advanced weaponry (as well as thousands of mules to transport it across the rugged Afghan terrain).[79] Even after the Soviets announced in April 1988 their intention to withdraw from Afghanistan, the committees insisted that US support continue so long as the Soviets were supplying aid to the Afghan government.[80]

---

[76] Gates, *From the Shadows*, 321, 349.
[77] CIA draft study, Vol. III, 42.
[78] Ibid., 110–11.
[79] Gates, *From the Shadows*, 349.
[80] CIA draft study, Vol. III, 186.

Angola and South Africa: 1985–88

As described earlier in this chapter, in 1976 Congress had enacted the Clark Amendment prohibiting covert assistance to the two noncommunist parties in Angola, UNITA and MFLN. By 1985, after 10 years of fighting, UNITA had emerged as the principal resistance force, but it had been barely kept alive, principally by the efforts of the government of South Africa. Meanwhile Soviet and Cuban assistance to the MPLA-controlled Angolan government had steadily increased. In the summer of 1985, yet another infusion of men and material was provided the MPLA, which prompted the South African government to increase its support for UNITA. Concerned with these developments, Congress repealed the Clark Amendment on 8 August 1985, allowing covert US assistance to UNITA for the first time in 10 years.

In November, President Reagan signed a new finding on Angola, which, because of objections from Secretary of State Shultz, was initially limited to nonlethal assistance to UNITA. Even so, at the insistence of the White House, it was briefed to the congressional leadership—the "gang of eight"—rather than the full committees.[81]

Casey kept working for a finding that authorized lethal aid to UNITA. To garner congressional support, he had the leader of UNITA, Jonas Savimbi, come to the US in early 1986 to make his case before the intelligence committees and the congressional leadership.[82] After the visit, congressional leaders implored Secretary Shultz to drop his opposition to lethal aid, and Reagan issued a new finding in March, allowing for such aid. This time briefings were provided to the full committees.[83]

The chairman of the HPSCI at the time, Lee Hamilton (D-IN), strongly opposed the new finding, which he believed represented a major escalation of US activity in Angola without the benefit of adequate public or congressional debate. In a letter to the *Washington Post* on 20 March 1986, Hamilton asserted that covert action should be seen as a means of supporting a policy that was open and understood by the public, not as a means of changing that policy in secret. To prevent this from happening, he introduced an amendment, reported by the committee, barring all assistance to UNITA unless and until Congress had publicly debated and approved such assistance. When the amendment came to a vote on the House floor in September, however, it was defeated, 229–186, largely in response to concerns that the vote would hand the Soviets a victory in Angola.

---

[81] Ibid., 112.
[82] Ibid., 113.
[83] Ibid.

The committees, in fact, approved a covert program for Angola that began in 1986 and significantly expanded it over the next two years. It included lethal as well as nonlethal assistance for UNITA. In 1987, the assistance appeared to pay dividends as UNITA won an important victory over the Angolan government in the largest battle of the long war. Despite this success, the new HPSCI chairman, Louis Stokes (D-OH), became concerned that because of the Angola program, the United States was becoming increasingly tied to the apartheid regime in South Africa. Although Agency officers attempted to assure him that their interaction was limited and appropriate, Stokes proposed an amendment to the intelligence authorization bill in April 1988, barring all military and intelligence relationships with South Africa. The amendment itself did not pass (broader legislation was pending in the parent body), but the HPSCI did "zero out" the funding of all liaison activities for FY 1989 as a demonstration of its concern. Although this action did not survive conference with the Senate, it did cause concern among Agency officials.[84]

Central America: 1979–86

In July 1979, the Somoza family that had ruled Nicaragua for 35 years was thrown out of office by a political group commonly known as the Sandinistas. The new government pledged to hold free elections, end oppression, and introduce other trappings of democracy, but its actions—shutting down hostile newspapers, pressuring opposition parties, and expropriating private property—belied these promises. While the Carter administration initially responded with emergency food aid and economic assistance, it also issued a covert action finding in the fall of 1979 to help moderate elements in Nicaragua resist attempts by Marxist groups to consolidate power in the country.[85] The following year, as the Sandinistas appeared to be consolidating their own control, funding for the program was doubled.[86]

Even though the oversight committees were briefed on the 1979 finding, their requests for subsequent briefings on the activities being taken pursuant to the finding were initially turned down because of what they were told was a "presidential embargo." This prompted a furious letter from HPSCI Chairman Boland to DCI Turner, saying the embargo raised "serious concerns for the entire oversight process."[87] Turner, in turn, had the White House lift the embargo.

---

[84] CIA draft study, Vol. III, 190–91.
[85] US Congress, *Report of the Committees Investigating the Iran-Contra Affair*, 27.
[86] CIA draft study, Vol. II, 260.
[87] Ibid.

US concerns about what was happening in Nicaragua were also mirrored in the country itself where a new rebel movement—collectively known as the contras—was taking shape to oppose the Sandinista regime.

Another troublesome situation was brewing in nearby El Salvador. In October 1979, a new government headed by Jose Napoleon Duarte was installed following a military coup. While the United States saw the need to encourage Duarte to promote and implement democratic reforms, it also became increasingly concerned that Cuba (and indirectly the Soviet Union) was supporting and training guerrilla elements to subvert his regime. In November 1979, President Carter issued a covert action finding authorizing training and other resources for moderate elements in El Salvador resisting these guerilla elements.[88]

When Reagan took office in January 1981, the situation in both countries had grown more critical. Concerned with Nicaragua's internal repression, its ties to the Soviet bloc, and its support for the guerrilla elements in El Salvador, President Carter suspended US aid to Nicaragua a few weeks before leaving office. Reagan continued this policy, saying assistance would be resumed only when democratic government was established and Nicaragua had ceased its support of the Salvadoran rebels. Within two months of taking office, Reagan also signed a new covert action finding designed to assist the Duarte government in El Salvador with the detection and interdiction of arms and other material destined for the guerilla forces in the countryside.[89] In December 1981, yet another finding was issued, this one authorizing the provision of paramilitary training to Nicaraguan exile groups opposed to the Sandinista regime.[90]

Both intelligence committees were briefed on these findings. The issue that raised the greatest concern in the HPSCI was that these activities would inevitably lead to the insertion of US military force in the region. With regard to the assistance for the Nicaraguan exile groups (the contras), the HPSCI also expressed concern with their limited size, disparate objectives, and lack of a unified command structure. Assuring them he understood their concerns, Casey promised to provide a status report every two months.[91]

In 1982, according to Agency records, Casey made what appears to have been his most convincing presentation to date to both committees that Cuba and Nicaragua were training, financing and arming the insurgents in El Salvador.[92] Soon afterwards, in fact, the HPSCI issued a public report stating

---

[88] CIA draft study, Vol. III, 46.
[89] Ibid., 44.
[90] US Congress, *Report of the Committees Investigating the Iran-Contra Affair,* 32.
[91] CIA draft study, Vol. III, 44, 51.
[92] Ibid., 47.

that the aid being provided the rebels in El Salvador constituted "a clear picture of active promotion for 'revolution without frontiers' throughout Central America."[93]

Both committees continued to fret that they were not getting the full story of the Agency's activities in Central America. For example, in response to press reports in July 1982 that CIA had meddled in the Salvadoran elections, both committees asked the Agency to explain exactly what had been done.

Prompted by press reports, Congress as a whole became increasingly wary about the direction events in Central America were going in the fall of 1982. While the Reagan administration asserted it was not trying to overthrow the Sandinista government in Nicaragua but only to keep it from exporting revolution to El Salvador, the contras themselves seemed clearly bent on overthrowing the Sandinistas, not simply interdicting weapons and supplies for the El Salvadoran guerillas.[94]

In December 1982, a member of the HASC, Thomas Harkin (D-IA), offered an amendment to the FY 1983 Defense Appropriation Bill prohibiting US support for the contras. This prompted HPSCI Chairman Boland to offer a substitute amendment that prohibited support for the contras "for the purpose of overthrowing the government of Nicaragua or provoking a military exchange between Nicaragua and Honduras." Boland's substitute passed the House by a vote of 411 to 0 and was later adopted by the Senate conferees on the bill. Because it allowed assistance to the contras to continue, Reagan signed the "Boland Amendment" into law.[95]

No sooner had the legislation been signed, however, than questions began arising whether the administration in general, and the CIA in particular, was complying with it. Two members of the SSCI, Vice Chairman Daniel Moynihan (D-NY) and Patrick Leahy (D-VT), made separate visits to Central America in early 1983 to review the Agency's operations. Both came back concerned that the Agency was not complying with the new law. In a letter to Casey, Moynihan said it was clear to him that the 3,000–4,000 contras that the Agency was supporting along the Nicaraguan border were intent on overthrowing the Sandinista regime. "We have labored six years to restore the intelligence community to a measure of good spirits and self-confidence," he wrote, "all of which is dissipating in another half-ass jungle war."[96]

---

[93] Ibid.
[94] US Congress, *Report of the Committees Investigating the Iran-Contra Affair*, 32.
[95] Ibid., 33.
[96] CIA draft study, Vol. III, 53.

Notwithstanding the growing chorus of doubt both in Congress and in the press, the administration continued to assert that it was complying with the Boland Amendment: it was not trying to overthrow the government of Nicaragua. Addressing a joint session of Congress on 27 April 1983, Reagan said,

> *Our interest is to ensure that* [the Nicaraguan government] *does not infect its neighbors through the export of subversion and violence. Our purpose . . . is to prevent the flow of arms to El Salvador, Honduras, Guatemala, and Costa Rica.*[97]

Both intelligence committees reacted to the speech, albeit in different ways. The HPSCI approved legislation cutting off covert assistance for "support of military and paramilitary activities in Nicaragua," but approved $80 million for Central American governments to interdict the flow of arms to rebel groups operating in their respective countries. Despite the administration's efforts, it passed the House on 28 July 1983 by a vote of 228 to 195.[98] The SSCI, with a Republican majority and more inclined to support the administration, wanted a clearer statement of the program's objectives before it would vote for more covert assistance—that is, it wanted a new finding. Reagan issued one on 19 September 1983, after he had discussed it with SSCI Chairman Goldwater and other key senators on the committee.

Under the new finding, the administration agreed that Agency personnel would not be involved in paramilitary activities themselves; rather they would channel assistance to third-country nationals. The primary objective remained the interdiction of Nicaraguan and Cuban support for regional insurgencies, but the overthrow of the Sandinista regime was not mentioned and a new objective—bringing the Sandinistas into meaningful negotiations and treaties with neighboring countries—was added. On the basis of this new finding and the assurances Casey provided, the SSCI voted to continue the covert action program in Nicaragua. Later, in conference on the FY 1984 Intelligence Authorization Bill, the two committees reached a compromise: a cap of $24 million was placed on contra funding and the Agency was prohibited from using its Contingency Reserve Fund to make up any shortfall during the coming year. In other words, if the program required more money, the administration would have to return to Congress to obtain it.[99]

In the early part of 1984, recognizing that its prospects for obtaining future funding from the Congress were uncertain, the administration directed the Agency to intensify its paramilitary operations against the Sandinista regime

---

[97] US Congress, *Report of the Committees Investigating the Iran-Contra Affair*, 33.
[98] Ibid., 34.
[99] Ibid., 35.

in order to bring the situation in Nicaragua to a head.[100] New, more violent attacks were instigated, including the placing of mines in Nicaraguan harbors in an effort to limit or halt shipping into those ports. At the same time, because of these intensified efforts, it was clear the $24 million congressional cap would be reached in a matter of months.

On 6 April 1984, just as the Senate was taking up the administration's request to increase the funding for the Nicaraguan program, the *Wall Street Journal* published an article claiming the CIA was behind the mining of certain Nicaraguan harbors. SSCI Chairman Goldwater, who was caught by surprise by the allegation, fired off a blistering letter to Casey saying he was "pissed off" at Casey's failure to keep him informed. "This is no way to run a railroad," Goldwater concluded.[101]

Four days after the article appeared, the Senate voted 84–12 to condemn the mining, and Goldwater took the floor to denounce the Agency for its failure to keep the committee "fully and currently informed" of its activities, as the law required. Casey initially took issue with Goldwater, pointing out not only that he had mentioned the mining on two occasions during committee hearings but also that he had briefed a member of the committee separately. This did not, however, satisfy the committee, most of whose members saw the mining as a virtual act of war, and as such, something that required far greater highlighting or emphasis to the committee.

To make matters worse, Casey reportedly asked SSCI Vice Chairman Moynihan "what the problem was" with Goldwater: why he was making such a fuss? Moynihan reacted two days later on a Sunday morning talk show by dramatically resigning his committee post, claiming the Agency had undertaken a disinformation campaign to discredit Goldwater.[102] This prompted Casey to offer a formal apology to the committee, conceding that, under the circumstances, notification had been inadequate. While Moynihan agreed to return to the committee, Goldwater's anger still simmered. In late May, he sent Casey a copy of the 1980 oversight legislation, underlining himself the obligation of intelligence agencies to keep the committees fully and currently informed. "I can't emphasize too strongly the necessity of your complying with this law," Goldwater wrote. "Incomplete briefings or even a hint of dishonest briefings can cause you a lot of trouble."[103]

As a result of the harbor mining episode, Casey and the SSCI agreed to new oversight arrangements (see chapter 2). The more immediate effect, however,

---

[100] Ibid., 36.
[101] CIA draft study, Vol. III, 60–61.
[102] Woodward, *Veil*, 332–34.
[103] CIA draft study, Vol. III, 63.

was to diminish the likelihood that the administration would get additional funding for the contra program. Indeed, in August 1984, the House approved another amendment offered by HPSCI Chairman Boland (which became known as "Boland II") to an omnibus appropriation bill. It prohibited the use of funds by CIA, DoD, "or any other agency or entity engaged in intelligence activities . . . for the purpose or which would have the effect" of supporting the contras, directly or indirectly. The Senate agreed to the amendment and President Reagan signed it into law on 12 October 1984.[104]

Three days later, the *New York Times* ran an article accusing CIA of producing an "assassination manual" for the contras. At issue were two manuals used by the contras: one providing instruction on various forms of sabotage; the other, calling for a popular uprising against the Sandinistas and the "neutralization" of certain Nicaraguan officials. Both intelligence committees demanded to know what CIA's role had been in the production of these manuals. The HPSCI went further and opened a formal investigation. Casey acknowledged Agency personnel had been involved in the production of the manuals, but disputed the allegation that they were intended to provoke violence or that the reference to "neutralization" should be read as "assassination."[105] In the end, the HPSCI concluded that there had been no intent by the Agency to violate the assassination prohibition in Executive Order 12333 but that its efforts to oversee the production of the manual were lax and insensitive to the issues involved. The manuals were "stupid," the committee wrote, "not evil."[106]

With US funding for the contras having run out in May 1984—and officially shut off by Boland II in October—the Reagan administration returned to Congress in April 1985 seeking to reestablish the program, including the provision of lethal assistance if the Sandinistas refused to participate in negotiating a peace settlement. While the SSCI was amenable, the HPSCI was not. The full House voted down the proposal on 23 April.

After the vote, Reagan imposed new economic sanctions against Nicaragua and vowed that he would return to Congress "again and again" to obtain funding for the contras. In fact, within two months' time, attitudes in Congress began to shift. Sandinista leader Daniel Ortega had traveled to Moscow and throughout Europe seeking military aid and had thereby stirred members' fears of a formidable communist presence in the Americas. On 12 June 1985, the House passed a bill providing $27 million in humanitarian aid for the contras. The Senate concurred, and the president signed the measure into law on 16 September. The new law prohibited CIA from playing any role in provid-

---

[104] US Congress, *Report of the Committees Investigating the Iran-Contra Affair*, 41.
[105] CIA draft study, Vol. III, 68.
[106] Ibid.

ing the humanitarian assistance being authorized—a new office in the State Department would handle the aid program—and barred all paramilitary assistance to the contras. It did, however, allow CIA to carry out a political action program in support of "democratic forces" in Nicaragua and to share intelligence on the Sandinistas with the contra leadership. The FY 1986 Intelligence Authorization Bill, enacted a few weeks later, took a further step and authorized CIA to provide communications equipment to the contras. To ensure CIA was hewing to these new laws, both committees announced they would require biweekly updates on the Agency's contra operations.[107]

As the committees' oversight intensified (including staff visits by both committees to CIA installations in the affected countries), it became apparent to them that the contras were getting substantial military support from somewhere. As far as Congress was concerned, the US government had been barred from providing paramilitary assistance, yet the contras were showing themselves to be a viable fighting force. Both committees repeatedly asked in 1985 and 1986 whether the United States was behind the lethal assistance the contras were obviously getting. Administration officials continued to deny that it was.[108]

The visits made by the oversight committees to Central America during this period do seem to have had the effect of increasing the sentiment on both committees in favor of support for the contras. It became increasingly clear to them, according to CIA records, that the Sandinistas were being heavily influence by Cuba and the Soviet Union and intent on establishing a Marxist-Leninist government in the country. By early 1986, CIA counted 12 of the 15 members of the SSCI as favorable to establishing a CIA-run lethal assistance program for the contras.[109]

Taking advantage of what it perceived to be the changing sentiment in Congress, in February 1986 the Reagan administration requested $100 million in "covert" aid for the contras, including $70 million in lethal aid. The war was not going well for the contras, and the administration argued that humanitarian aid was not enough. It was time for the United States to provide military support to stop the Sandinistas from consolidating their control over the country. Rather than signing a new covert action finding and requesting the funding through the annual appropriation process, however, Reagan put it in the form of a direct and open request to the Congress for a $100 million "aid package."

---

[107] Ibid, 117–18.
[108] US Congress, *Report of the Committees Investigating the Iran-Contra Affair*, 131.
[109] CIA draft study, Vol. III, 119.

The House initially rejected the request, but after a Senate vote in favor of it on 27 March 1986, the House reversed itself and approved the $100 million "aid package" on 25 June 1986. Because of the time required to iron out differences with the Senate bill and pass the compromise bill back through both Houses, however, the "aid package" did not become law until 25 October.

In the meantime, even as the Agency was endeavoring to explain to the oversight committees how it planned to monitor and account for the funds it expected to receive, on 5 October 1986 the Sandinistas shot down a cargo aircraft in southern Nicaragua carrying ammunition to the contras. Three of its crew were killed, but one, Eugene Hasenfus, survived and was captured. Identification cards were found on all four, identifying them as employees of Southern Air Transport. Hasenfus himself was identified as a former CIA employee and told the Sandinistas he believed himself to be working for the Agency.[110] While the Agency denied any involvement with Hasenfus or the contra supply flight, the incident prompted inquiries by the Congress as well as several federal agencies. Who were these people involved in supplying the contras? How were they being financed? What did the US government know about them? Had it been behind their activities? If so, this would clearly have violated the laws on the books. On 19 October 1986, the House Judiciary Committee sent a letter to Attorney General Edwin Meese, asking that he appoint an independent counsel to investigate the roles of the National Security Council, the NSC staff, and DCI Casey in the contra supply effort.

Several weeks later, on 3 November 1986, what appeared at first to be an unrelated event supplanted the Hasenfus story on the front page of the country's newspapers. A Lebanese newspaper, *Al-Shiraa*, reported that in order to win the release of hostages in the Middle East, the United States had been selling arms to Iran. National Security Advisor Robert McFarlane, it said, had traveled to Tehran to arrange for these sales. The report created an immediate uproar. If true, the administration would appear to have violated not only the US laws pertaining to arms sales but also its own policy for dealing with terrorists and regimes that sponsor terrorism.

On 12 November 1986, President Reagan called the congressional leadership together, including the leaders of the two intelligence committees, to brief them on Iranian arms sales. The following night, in an address to the American people, he declared:

> *The charge . . . that the United States has shipped weapons to Iran as ransom payment for the release of American hostages . . .* [is]

---

[110] Ibid., 121.

utterly false. . . . We did not trade weapons or anything else for hostages.[111]

On 21 November, Casey appeared before both intelligence committees to describe the Agency's role in the arms sales. He admitted the Agency had provided support to the sales but said they had been handled out of the White House, whose goals, at least, he believed to have been laudable.[112] Although members of both committees expressed irritation at not having been provided "timely notice" of CIA's support to the arms sales, Casey argued that the president had to be able to conduct foreign policy in the manner he saw fit.

The following day, Justice Department officials responsible for investigating the NSC staff's involvement in the arms sales, discovered a memorandum that confirmed that proceeds generated from the sales of arms to Iran had been used to purchase supplies for the contras in order to help them "bridge the gap" created by the delays in getting the contra aid package through Congress.[113] On 25 November 1986, Attorney General Meese publicly acknowledged what became known as "the diversion." The president fired those members of the NSC staff chiefly responsible for the operation (LTC Oliver North and RADM John Poindexter).

Both intelligence committees expanded their investigations to encompass the diversion. Casey was invited back to testify, but on 15 December, the day before such testimony was to occur, he had a "cerebral seizure" in his office and was hospitalized, never to return to the job. Both committees proceeded with their inquiries, but it was clear by this point—given the predominant role played by the White House—that they lacked the jurisdiction to conduct a comprehensive probe. Accordingly, both houses created ad hoc select committees that included the leaders of their respective intelligence committees to carry out the investigation (see chapter 1 for a more detailed description). The SSCI issued a "preliminary report" in February 1987, summarizing the results of its investigation to date, while the HPSCI chose not to do so in view of the broader, follow-on investigation.

The Investigation of CIA's Involvement in the Iran-contra Affair: 1987

Within weeks of being established, the two select committees decided to merge their investigations. Ultimately, their staffs reviewed 300,000 documents and interviewed 500 witnesses. They held 40 days of joint public hear-

---

[111] Ibid., 131.
[112] Ibid., 132.
[113] US Congress, *Report of the Committees Investigating the Iran-Contra Affair*, 310.

ings over the spring and summer of 1987, as well as several days of closed hearings. In November, the committees issued a joint public report that totaled 690 pages.[114]

What the investigation found was that the staff of the NSC had, in effect, carried out two "covert actions" without the knowledge of the Congress. The first began in the summer of 1984 and involved soliciting support for the contras from third countries and private donors during the period when such support could not be obtained from Congress The other began in the summer of 1985 and involved sales of arms to Iran in order to obtain the release of American hostages being held by Middle Eastern terrorists. Over time, the two operations merged. Not only did the NSC staff use some of the same private individuals in both operations, but in early 1986 it came to realize the arms sales to Iran could be used to generate excess funds that could be given the contras to supplement what was being provided by the third-party donors.

As far as CIA's involvement was concerned, the investigation produced evidence that DCI Casey had known about both operations. The principal NSC staff member involved in the operations, Oliver North, testified that Casey also had known of the "diversion" of money from the arms sales to the contras. By that point, however, Casey had died, and while the investigation confirmed that CIA officers had raised the possibility of a diversion with the DCI in the fall of 1986, it failed to produce documentary evidence to substantiate North's claim.

Other CIA officers had become aware of the NSC staff's efforts to solicit support for the contras from third parties as well as their subsequent efforts to procure and deliver weapons to the contras. A few Agency officers in Central America, in fact, were later shown to have facilitated these efforts, which raises the issue of why a presidential finding was not in place. The more confounding problem created for the Agency officers witting of the NSC staff's activities, however, involved their dealings with Congress. They were, in fact, the same officers who interacted with the two intelligence committees on CIA's operations in Central America during the period at issue (see the preceding section). On the one hand, they realized the NSC staff's operation was intended to circumvent congressional restrictions and knew the White House was intent on keeping it secret. On the other hand, they were regularly briefing the committees on the Agency's operations in the region and accompanying them on trips there. As one of them later observed, it was like being trapped in a "giant nutcracker."

---

[114] For a detailed account of the events summarized in this subsection, see *Report of the Congressional Committees Investigating the Iran-Contra Affair.*

To deal with the situation, the investigation found, the CIA officers involved adopted a strategy of learning as little as possible about what the NSC staff was doing. But this purposeful avoidance went only so far. At times, in appearances before the intelligence committees and other congressional committees, certain officers responded to direct questions with statements that a court later found to have been false or misleading. The Agency's involvement with the arms sales to Iran was more substantial. Not only was there greater awareness among Agency officials, the Agency was directly involved in supporting the sales.

In August 1985, President Reagan approved an Israeli government request to sell US-made TOW antitank missiles to Iran, and as a result, one of the American hostages was released. North asked a CIA official to monitor what was happening in Iran during the intervening period in an effort to ascertain how its government may be responding.

In November 1985, a second shipment (HAWK antiaircraft missiles) was ready and North sought CIA's help in arranging transport from Israel to Tehran, which it did, using an aircraft owned by one of its proprietaries. When DDCI John McMahon learned of the flight after the fact, he insisted that the Agency's role in the operation and the operation itself be authorized in a presidential finding. President Reagan did this by signing a finding on 5 December 1985 that retroactively approved the sale of the HAWKs and the support the Agency had rendered. At the same time, fearing that if the intelligence committees were told they would object and that the finding would likely be leaked, jeopardizing the release of additional hostages, Reagan specifically directed that the committees not be notified.

Since the arms sales to Iran were expected to continue, the Agency sought a new finding that authorized it to provide operational and logistical support for such sales in the future. The president signed this finding on 17 January 1986. It, too, specifically directed the DCI to refrain from notifying the intelligence committees until the president directed him to do so. (Although Attorney General Meese later testified he interpreted this to mean that Congress would be given notice once the hostages were released, this was not spelled out in the finding per se.) An NSC memorandum that accompanied the finding also called for a change in CIA's role in the sales. No longer would arms be sold to Iran out of Israeli stocks (and then replenished), but rather CIA would purchase the arms out of DoD stocks and transfer them directly to Iran, using the NSC's private operatives to broker the sale.

New sales of arms and spare parts followed in February and May 1986 — each generating profits that were sent to the contras — but no more American hostages were released. Increasingly dissatisfied with the results the sales were producing, North, with CIA's assistance, arranged for National Security Advisor McFarlane to fly to Tehran in May 1986 to meet with Iranian officials in an effort to break the deadlock. No results were immediately forthcoming but a second hostage was set free on 29 July, leading Reagan to approve the sale of additional spare parts. But, again, nothing happened as a result. In September, its frustration increasing, the NSC staff, using the private brokers who had been involved in the sales and with the assistance of CIA officers, began searching for new intermediaries within Iran. Before they could be found, however, the arms sales were disclosed in the Lebanese newspaper. While CIA made an additional shipment of arms after the disclosure, for all practical purposes, the operation had come to an end.

According to the final report of the investigation, North never told the CIA officers involved in the arms sales that he was using the surpluses the sales generated to support the contras. However, in the fall of 1986, two of those involved in the arms sales learned that one of the private individuals working for North suspected it. This information was reported to DCI Casey who took it up with Admiral Poindexter, North's boss,. This would seem to suggest, in fact, that Casey had not had prior knowledge of the diversion, but the investigation was never able to reach this conclusion.

As described in chapter 2, the Iran-contra affair had profound, long-term consequences for the oversight arrangements then in place. The revelations that seemed to come in an endless stream, each more stunning than the last, shattered the trust that had taken so much time and effort to build. The committees had been repeatedly misled and deceived, and at least some in the Agency had been a party to it. While the Agency could point to the fact that it had been acting pursuant to directions from the White House, the committees had expected the Agency not to stand idly by when its political bosses did things that clearly violated and undermined its relationship with the committees. They were wrong. The Agency's commitment to the oversight process had taken a backseat to the demands of the administration. While the committees had no doubt where Casey's loyalties lay, they had expected that the "system" would hold together to overcome the predilections of a particular DCI. It obviously had not, and for the committees this realization was unsettling.

In the aftermath of Iran-contra, not only did the committees seek to change the existing oversight arrangements for covert action (see chapter 2), they began to subject such programs to greater oversight. In the fall of 1987, SSCI Chairman Boren announced the committee would institute quarterly reviews of all covert action programs on the books. The Agency's administration of the $100 million aid package for the contras that Congress had approved shortly before Iran-contra broke received especially close scrutiny from both committees. They also became increasingly skeptical of new proposals and cut off funding for certain of them.[115]

To improve the lines of communication with the committees, new DCI Webster and his deputy, Robert Gates, instituted monthly meetings with the leaders of the intelligence committees in the fall of 1987 to provide regular opportunities not only to apprise them of sensitive operational matters but for the committee leaders to express any misgivings they may have about the Agency. While both committees welcomed the initiative, CIA records reflect that HPSCI Chairman Stokes cautioned that the monthly meetings could not be seen as a substitute for notice to the full committees when that was required.[116]

Noriega and the SSCI: 1988–89

In February 1988, Panamanian strongman, Manuel Noriega, was indicted in a federal court in Florida on drug trafficking charges. In March, a coup attempt against him failed. In April, President Reagan signed a covert action finding authorizing the Agency to provide certain assistance to Panamanian exiles who planned to challenge Noriega in the presidential elections the following year. In May, a second finding was signed authorizing a political action campaign inside Panama that included propaganda and nonlethal support to the opposition forces. The objective was to get Noriega to step down voluntarily and leave Panama. After Noriega adamantly rejected the idea when it was proposed by State Department officials, however, Reagan signed a third finding, this one authorizing CIA to undertake activities to bring about the removal of Noriega from power, including working with disaffected members of the Panamanian Defense Forces (PDF) to bring about his removal by force if necessary. While the finding specifically directed that the Agency not assist in any effort to assassinate Noriega, it recognized that the operation could produce such an outcome.

Although the SSCI had supported the two previous findings, it balked at the third one and, by a vote of 13 to 1, authorized its chairman, David Boren, to send a letter to the president asking that it be withdrawn. Although the administration believed the committee was overreacting, it sent a letter to the committees saying that if it learned that groups the Agency was working with planned to assassinate Noriega, it would inform the Panamanian leader.[117] The administration also increased the amount of nonlethal aid being furnished under the May 1988 finding.[118]

---

[115] CIA draft study, Vol. III, 184.
[116] Ibid., 143.
[117] Webster interview, 21 August 2002, 42.

In May 1989, the Panamanian presidential election took place, and despite widespread reports of fraud and voting irregularities, the opposition party claimed victory. But Noriega remained in control and refused the public demands of President George H.W. Bush and other world leaders to step aside, leading Bush to publicly encourage the PDF to organize a coup.[119]

Noriega's refusal to step down after the election also led the Bush administration to look more closely at identifying elements of the PDF it could work with to remove Noriega from power. Advised by Webster of the Reagan administration's earlier commitment to the SSCI to inform Noriega if it became aware of assassination attempts against him, Bush wrote a letter to the committee saying that, whatever the earlier understandings might have been, they no longer pertained. According to Webster, the SSCI immediately backed off, saying that in any event it had never been its intention to obligate the administration to notify Noriega.[120]

Webster also took the occasion to ask the Office of Legal Counsel at the Department of Justice to provide a legal opinion on the kinds of activities that would violate the ban on assassination contained in E.O. 12333 and those that would not.[121] Although neither intelligence committee gave its unqualified endorsement to the Justice opinion when it was presented to them in the late summer of 1989, it did represent the first authoritative legal interpretation of the assassination ban to that point.

In early October 1989, a group of PDF officers (who had specifically rejected help from CIA) attempted a coup against Noriega.[122] He managed to call for help, however, and was able to escape in the fighting that ensued. In a rage, he ordered the immediate execution of the PDF officers involved.

The ensuing barrage of congressional criticism faulting the administration for its failure to support the coup plotters, prompted National Security Advisor Brent Scowcroft, appearing on a Sunday morning talk show, to point to the SSCI's opposition as a key factor in stopping the administration "from doing what they're now saying we should have done." Appearing separately on the same program, Boren countered that the committee had given the administration "all the money and authority" it had sought for Panama. Scowcroft categorically denied this and shot back that not only the committee's concerns about assassination but also its funding cuts to the covert action program for working with the PDF had hampered the administration's

---

[118] CIA draft study, Vol. III, 199.
[119] *New York Times*, "Bush Urges Effort to Press Noriega to Quit as Leader."
[120] Webster interview, 42.
[121] Ibid.
[122] Ibid.

efforts in Panama.[123] Reportedly, the personal intervention of Bush himself was required to restore calm.[124]

Iranian Arms Shipments to Bosnia: 1996

In April 1996, the *Los Angeles Times* published an article alleging that in 1994 the Clinton administration had given a "green light" to the government of Croatia to allow Iranian arms destined for Bosnian Muslims fighting in the former Yugoslavia to transit its country. At the time, a UN arms embargo was in effect forbidding shipments of arms to the former Yugoslavia, an embargo the United States had pledged to uphold. The press account also speculated the US government was engaged in a covert action, not reported to the congressional oversight committees, to facilitate the flow of arms from Iran to the Muslims in Bosnia.

Both intelligence committees began investigations at the request of their respective leaderships. Ultimately, the committees found that the US ambassador to Croatia, when asked by Croatian government officials whether the United States would object to the transit of Iranian arms through the country, had responded that he had "no instructions" from Washington on the matter. This response, in turn, led the Croatian government to believe that the United States had no objection, and the flow of Iranian arms through its country expanded significantly.

DCI James Woolsey later contended that CIA had not been advised of the ambassador's response or of any change in the US position of support for the embargo. Indeed, as the Agency began to see signs of the expanded arms flow its own officers raised concerns that the United States might be covertly facilitating the flow of such arms, contrary to the UN embargo.

Beyond this, the committees reached somewhat differing conclusions. The HPSCI found that the US government had had no role in facilitating the arms flow, and thus no covert action had taken place. While the failure of the US ambassador to object to the transshipments had encouraged Croatia to allow them, HPSCI saw his conduct as "traditional diplomatic activity" rather than as covert action. The SSCI, on the other hand, was unable to reach agreement on whether a covert action had occurred but specifically rejected the notion that the ambassador's response to the Croatians constituted "traditional diplomatic activity." Both committees lauded the CIA officers for having raised their concerns to higher levels in the US government.[125]

---

[123] *New York Times* "Bush Aide and Senator Clash Over Failed Coup in Panama."
[124] Smist, *Congress Oversees*, 276.

The Gingrich "Add" for Covert Action in Iran: 1995

As an "ex officio" member of the HPSCI, House Speaker Newt Gingrich took an inordinate interest in intelligence activities, occasionally using his position to chide the Clinton administration for its failure to make greater use of covert action to achieve US foreign policy objectives.

In October 1995, for example, Gingrich wrote the first of several articles calling for a covert action program to topple the government of Iran. Not surprisingly, these articles had prompted vehement protests from Tehran. Apparently undaunted, Gingrich, over the initial objection of the Clinton administration, managed to insert $18 million into the classified portion of the annual intelligence authorization for a covert action program designed to "change the behavior" of the Iranian regime rather than to topple it. Word of the provision leaked to the press a few weeks later, before Clinton had even signed the legislation, prompting the Iranian parliament to denounce the United States and establish a $20 million fund to counter the covert action.[126]

Support for the INC and the Iraq Liberation Act of 1998

In the spring of 1991, in the wake of the Persian Gulf War, President Bush approved a covert action finding to encourage and support dissidents both inside and outside Iraq who wished to remove Saddam Hussein from power.[127]

Pursuant to this authorization, CIA began working with Ahmed Chalabi, a leading figure in the Iraqi opposition who lived outside Iraq, to create an organization—the Iraqi National Congress, or INC—to coordinate the activities of the opposition. In 1992, the INC established an office in Kurdish-controlled northern Iraq as well as media outlets to spread its message. While the Agency kept the two intelligence committees apprised of these activities, Chalabi, on his own initiative, began making periodic visits to Washington to lobby Congress to provide support for the INC.

In 1994, the INC helped broker a cease-fire between two warring Kurdish groups in northern Iraq. When the cease-fire began breaking down the following year, the INC, with US involvement, obtained the agreement of the parties to a new understanding that contemplated, among other things, the insertion of

---

[125] House Permanent Select Committee on Intelligence, *Investigation into the Iranian Arms Shipments to Bosnia*; Senate Select Committee on Intelligence, *US Actions Regarding Iranian Arms Shipments to the Bosnian Army*.

[126] *New York Times*, "US Plan to Change Iran Leaders Is an Open Secret Before It Begins."

[127] For a detailed discussion of the program, see Senate Select Committee on Intelligence, *The Use by the Intelligence Community of Information Provided by the Iraqi National Congress*. 5–35.

an INC peace-keeping force between the two groups. The INC force contemplated by the agreement required US funding, however, to be viable.

As the issue of funding the INC force was being sorted out in Washington, the Agency in early February 1995 learned for the first time of an INC plan, to be carried out within several weeks' time with the help of Shi'a elements inside Iraq, to capture Saddam Hussein and overthrow his regime. In meetings Chalabi arranged in early March with Iranian officials to gain their support for the plan, he intimated that the United States would provide military support to the operation, a claim presumably made more credible by the presence of a CIA officer at the meeting site (although not at the meeting itself). When Chalabi's assertions to the Iranians was reported back to Washington, however, it created a furor in the Clinton White House, which had been unaware of the INC's plan. Chalabi was informed that under no circumstances would the United States provide military support for any such operation. Chalabi believed the plan was now too far along to cancel it, however, and opted to proceed without US assistance. The operation ended in disaster. Saddam Hussein was not captured, neither the Iraqi army nor the Iraqi people rose up against him, and the INC's forces were decimated.

While the Agency reduced its support for the INC after this, Chalabi himself continued to make visits to Washington to plead for US support. The fighting between the Kurdish parties continued in northern Iraq, he noted, and the US had never provided funding needed for an INC peace-keeping force.

In August 1996, Saddam Hussein sent military forces into northern Iraq to destroy what they could find of the INC. A hundred INC members were captured and executed; the rest were forced to evacuate the country. In December, with it becoming increasingly evident the INC's ability to be a unifying force for the Iraqi opposition had faded, the Clinton administration determined that the CIA should terminate its funding of the organization. In February 1997, the Agency broke off its relationship with Chalabi and the INC entirely.

Undeterred, Chalabi continued to lobby his contacts in Congress, many of whom openly expressed sympathy with his plight. In 1998, with the support of House Speaker Gingrich, Republican lawmakers proposed what became the Iraq Liberation Act of 1998, a public bill to provide assistance to the Iraqi exile groups then opposing the regime of Saddam Hussein. While the INC was not specifically mentioned, the president was authorized to provide up to $97 million in aid to Iraqi democratic opposition organizations designated by the president. (Ultimately, seven such organizations, including the INC, were designated.) For the first time in a public document, the law provided that the US policy toward Iraq required "regime change." Although the Clinton administration initially resisted the proposal, the president signed the law, pledging to work through the United Nations and with "opposition groups from all sectors of the Iraqi community" to bring about a popularly supported government. The State Department, rather than the CIA, was given responsibility for administering the funds.[128]

In the months that followed, however, a dispute broke out in the Senate over implementing the new law. At first, Republicans complained the administration was taking too long to designate the opposition groups to receive the funding.[129] Once such groups had been designated, SSCI Chairman Richard Shelby demanded that more of the money go to opposition groups headquartered outside Iraq, rather than to those inside the country, and threatened to block any further expenditures that were not consistent with his views.[130]

Covert Action in the Joint Report on 9/11: 2002

As part of their joint inquiry into the performance of intelligence agencies with respect to the terrorist attacks of 9/11, the committees explored the use of covert action by the Clinton and Bush administrations against Usama bin Ladin and al-Qa'ida both before and after the attacks.[131]

Although the heavily redacted report was generally critical of the size and aggressiveness of the Intelligence Community's operational activities against al-Qa'ida before 9/11, covert action was not singled out for particular criticism, at least in the part of the joint report that was made public. Nor did the committees question in the public part of their report the adequacy of the notice provided them during this period. While suggesting that most had been "gang of eight" notifications, there had not, apparently, been an absence of notice.[132]

In the report of the 9/11 Commission, released 17 months after the congressional report, the efforts of the Agency to capture or kill bin Ladin prior to and after the 9/11 attacks—redacted in the congressional report—were described in detail.[133] While the commission's narrative confirms that appropriate findings and memorandums of notification were prepared to authorize the activities being contemplated at the time, there is no indication in its report that

---

[128] Presidential Signing Statement, *The Iraq Liberation Act*, The White House, 31 October 1998.
[129] *New York Times,* "Defining Goal in Iraq."
[130] *Los Angeles Times,* "US Dispute Holds Up Covert Iraq Operation."
[131] Senate Select Committee on Intelligence and House Permanent Select Committee on Intelligence, *Joint Inquiry into Intelligence Community Activities Before and After the Terrorist Attacks of September 11, 2001*, 279–303.
[132] Ibid., 290.
[133] *Final Report of the Commission on Terrorist Attacks upon the United States*, 111–15, 126–34, 137–43, 210–14.

either intelligence committee ever intervened to raise questions about the objectives of the operations or how they would be carried out.

AUTHOR'S COMMENTARY

Why Congress Paid Little Attention At First

Covert action, by definition, involves interference in the internal affairs of other countries. Given our own notions of sovereignty, one would expect that Congress would take a strong interest in overseeing such activities. Indeed, in recent times, it has. Yet, until the Bay of Pigs, the Agency's overseers appeared to exhibit little curiosity with respect to this aspect of its operations. What might account for this?

While covert action has always been cloaked in secrecy, in the beginning it probably did not seem all that controversial. It was, after all, intended to combat the spread of communism around the world. The Soviets were doing these sorts of things to us; we should be doing the same things to them. Although the lack of documentary confirmation is frustrating, one can reasonably assume the CIA subcommittees understood the kinds of things the Agency was doing. From 1948 until 1953, they funded exponential increases in them, something they would not have done without knowing—at least in general terms—what the increases were going for.

Another factor contributing to the committees' lack of curiosity may have that they were used to dealing with the defense budget. The annual appropriation for CIA's "Cold War activities" must have seemed a bargain after dealing with defense expenditures. In addition, these activities were, by their very nature, hard to get a handle on. In any given year, the Agency might be engaged in hundreds of them, many quite small: broadcasts to denied areas, media placements, money for international conferences, money for noncommunists vying in elections, money for dissident groups in communist countries to stir up trouble. It was a menu that CIA could choose from as opportunities presented themselves, all part of a grand plan to weaken communism around the world. The CIA subcommittees undoubtedly regarded these "Cold War activities," taken as a whole, as a key weapon in the country's arsenal but looking at them individually was not something they were either equipped to do or interested in doing.

Even when President Eisenhower began directing the Agency to do things that from a policy standpoint were qualitatively different (and more questionable)—overthrowing popularly elected governments thought to be sliding into communism , for example—it is not clear that the significance of this change registered with the Agency's subcommittees. They probably learned of the operations that occurred in Iran, Guatemala, and Indonesia after the fact, but even so, there is no indication they ever questioned the premises of these operations. In part, this may have been because they were perceived as successes. It may also have been due in part to the perception that many in Congress held of the Agency at the time. As one congressman who served on the HASC subcommittee later recalled:

> *When you think back to the old days* [the Eisenhower years], *it was a different world and a different perception of us and our role in the world. The political zeitgeist at the time was that CIA was wonderful. In politics, anybody who wanted to make trouble for the CIA was seen as a screwball and not to be countenanced.*[134]

It was not until 1961 that a covert action resulted in significant worldwide embarrassment for the United States, and it was only then that CIA's overseers in Congress began asking the kinds of fundamental questions that were to echo down the rest of the Agency's history: Why were we trying to do this? Why did we ever think it would work?

Like other aspects of early oversight, the lack of a professional staff capable of independently probing and assessing what the Agency was being directed to do also hampered the CIA subcommittees. The handful of members who learned of the Agency's covert operations had to rely on what the DCI told them, and since few records were made of these conversations, it is, unfortunately, impossible to know either what they were told or how they reacted.

The Issues Covert Action Raises for Congress

So, historically, what have been the issues Congress cares about? Since the two intelligence committees arrived on the scene and hands-on oversight of covert action was instituted, the issues have fallen into two broad categories: policy issues and issues of implementation.

Under the category of policy issues, the usual question is why the United States needs to do it at all. How is the operation in question consistent with US foreign policy? How does it square with our notions of sovereignty . . . our notions of free and fair elections . . . our sense of propriety and proportion? What do we expect to gain from it? What can we expect to lose if it is disclosed to the rest of the world? Why do we need to do it in secret?

---

[134] Quoted in Smist, *Congress Oversees*, 5.

The committees also want to understand how the Agency plans to carry out the operation in question. What activities does it entail? Does it stand a reasonable chance of success? Are people likely to get hurt or killed as a result? How much will it cost? Are the individuals and groups we are working with reliable and credible partners? What are *they* really trying to achieve? Can they deliver what they promise? If third countries are involved, do we want to align ourselves with them? If US citizens are being used, are they witting of the Agency's purpose?

Generally speaking, the policy issues are for a representative of the incumbent administration (typically, a State Department official) to explain to the committees, while implementation issues are for an Agency representative to explain. Over the years, members are more apt to focus on policy issues, leaving it to the staff to follow up on implementation issues. Although, as the SSCI's reaction to the proposed Noriega finding illustrates, implementation issues sometimes take center stage.

In considering covert action proposals, the oversight committees tend to come at them with a different frame of reference. The executive branch is chiefly concerned with achieving the objectives of the president, whatever they might be. Because of this, it is sometimes tempted to downplay the risk and accentuate the gain. The oversight committees will also want to see the president succeed but not if, in their view, what the president proposes to do carries substantial risks for the country. Members will also have to take into account what the sentiment in their parent body, or in the public, would be if the operation were disclosed. Would they understand and support what the administration is trying to do?

Contrasted with the Agency's other functions—collection and analysis—covert action raises issues that most members can readily sink their teeth into. They do not have to master volumes of technical data to get the picture; they do not have to know enough to challenge the Agency's analytical experts or question its clandestine tradecraft. Whether the United States should undertake a covert action abroad usually boils down to political judgments, and members of Congress, political animals all, see such judgments as things they can understand and contribute to. Covert action involves high-stakes global politics, and as such, it has engaged members of the oversight committees to a far greater degree than any other aspect of their oversight responsibilities.

The committees' involvement in a given program will depend heavily upon their initial reaction to it. If members are satisfied with what they hear from administration witnesses, not only will they acquiesce in the implementation of the operation, they are apt to devote less attention to it down the road. If they are not satisfied, they may recommend to the president that the program be modified to accommodate their concerns or be dropped altogether. If the president fails to take the committee's concerns into account, rest assured, it will review the program more frequently and more carefully as it plays out over time. It may also eliminate funding for the program if it carries over into the next budget cycle (and cannot be funded out of the Contingency Reserve Fund). Needless to say, the Agency appreciates these dynamics and attempts to shape the covert action proposals it develops for an administration in a way that avoid the potential concerns of members. Depending upon what a particular administration wants done, however, this may or may not be possible.

"Overt" Covert Action

The executive branch initiates almost all covert action programs and classifies them to protect the fact of their existence, their funding levels, and the activities undertaken pursuant to them. However, from time to time, as the narrative indicates, the existence of a covert action program, its funding level, and even the activities envisioned for the program will be openly debated on the floor of Congress, and the world is thereby treated to the spectacle of an "overt" covert action.

When this has happened, it has been for one of several reasons. First, the program or policy issues may have already received so much public attention that an administration decides to offer its proposal in public. President Reagan did this in 1986 with respect to his request for assistance to the contras. The money, had it been appropriated, would have gone into the Agency's covert action appropriation and the Agency would have disbursed it. A covert action program can also "go public" when a member decides to offer legislation to do something about one: either to initiate a program that a member thinks is needed (funding the Iraqi opposition in 1998, for example) or to augment, restrict, or end a program a member has heard about. More often than not, these proposals have come from members who are not on one of the oversight committees. Sometimes, members of the oversight committees—who have lost in committee—decide to take their proposal to the floor. Sometimes, the oversight committees themselves will decide to take a covert action to the floor when they know several members of their parent body are planning to offer amendments. By doing so, they may be maneuvering to preempt such amendments and better control the floor debate.

While purists are naturally horrified when this happens, there may be no practical alternative. If members insist on discussing a covert action on the floor, there is not much that can be done to stop them. The "speech and debate" clause of the Constitution protects them with respect to what they might say on the floor, and while they can be encouraged to work through their respective intelligence committee, no one can force them to do so. Besides, the committee may not agree with what the member proposes. How else are they to exercise their prerogative as legislators except by raising questions on the floor or offering amendments to a bill they are concerned about? Each chamber does have procedures for going into closed session to consider classified matters, but secret sessions have never been used to debate public legislation.

In short, having open debates on covert action proposals seems unavoidable under our constitutional system. This is not to say they should be encouraged. Obviously, the target of the operation is put on notice and may take retaliatory action of some kind. Moreover, there is a certain "unseemliness" about debating whether the United States should interfere in the internal affairs of another country in the hallowed halls of the Congress, even if that country is universally despised.

The good news is that the congressional system discourages individual members from freelancing where covert action is concerned. Virtually every amendment to limit, restrict, or end a covert action program has failed without the support of the intelligence committee involved. For members to make a persuasive case for such amendments in the face of intelligence committee objection is difficult, simply because the intelligence committee controls the pertinent information. Accordingly, when it comes to covert action, most members rely on the recommendations of their respective intelligence committee. Proposals to initiate covert actions or augment existing ones have fared somewhat better, especially if the intelligence committee concerned does not object to them. But such initiatives have often prompted negative reactions around the world and have historically never been well received or implemented by the executive branch. All of this, if appreciated by members, would tend to discourage them from striking out on their own, although there will always be some who want to make a public splash regardless of their chances for achieving legislative success.

Covert Action Since the End of the Cold War

From 1948 until the end of the Cold War, covert actions were undertaken primarily to thwart the spread of communism. During the 1980s, they began to be used for other purposes—countering threats to the United States posed by terrorism, drug trafficking, and the proliferation of weapons of mass destruction. When the Cold War ended, these targets came to dominate the covert action agenda. Covert action remained a tool that could be used against the few communist regimes and "rogue states" that remained on the world stage, but the focus of such operations increasingly became groups or individuals, not governments. Rather than containing the spread of a threatening ideology, the objective became preventing harm to the United States.

This shift in objective had significant implications for congressional oversight. Not only were covert actions fewer in number, they were less controversial from a policy standpoint. Between 1991 and 2004, few became public, and those that did raised comparatively minor issues (the Iranian arms shipments to Bosnia, for example). Gone for the most part were the old staples of the program: election support to noncommunist political parties, efforts to unseat governments thought to be coming under communist sway, media placements and the like. Replacing them were programs to help other governments counter the same threats that were of concern to the United States.

The oversight committees readily understood the need for these programs and in general supported them. When more direct US action was contemplated against terrorists or drug-traffickers, the committees supported that as well. Operations of this sort, however, often involve highly sensitive sources and methods and, not infrequently, put lives at risk. So while the goals may not have been controversial, the means of accomplishing them remained highly sensitive, occasioning a proportionally greater use of the limited notice options retained by the executive branch than had been the practice during the Cold War.

The Impact of the Select Committees' Oversight of Covert Action

Where covert action is concerned, the two intelligence committees have, since their inception, provided the only significant check and balance outside the executive branch. The appropriations committees occasionally weigh in on the funding levels for these programs, but the intelligence committees are where the policy issues are weighed and adjudicated.

It is true that the statutory arrangements governing this aspect of congressional oversight pay considerable deference to the president's constitutional responsibilities. The law gives Congress a say in such activities, but it cannot veto them. If especially sensitive operations are contemplated, the president has the options of delaying notice for a short while or of limiting notice to the "gang of eight" rather than the (now 36) members of the two committees. Last but not least, Congress appropriates money each year for a special fund—the Contingency Reserve Fund—which it allows the president to use to carry out covert actions during the year without having to come back to Congress for approval. This can become especially important if a president needs to act quickly.

It would be a mistake to conclude, however, that the committees' role is insignificant. If the committees do not support a particular operation or have concerns about aspects of it, an administration would have to think twice about proceeding with it as planned. If it is disclosed or ends in disaster, the administration will want to have had Congress on board. If it is going to last more than a year, the committees' support will be needed for continued funding. The committees are also likely to be better indicators of how the public would react if the program were disclosed than the administration's in-house pundits.

Obviously, the committees can be wrong. They can see problems that are not there and overreact to what is being proposed. But, at the end of the day, after their concerns have been thrashed out and they still remain opposed, most administrations will back off rather than push ahead. It has not happened very often since the committees were created, but it has happened often enough that the concerns of the committees have to be reckoned with.

CHAPTER 10

OVERSIGHT OF SECURITY AND PERSONNEL MATTERS

This chapter looks at the extent to which the Agency's overseers in Congress have become involved in security and personnel matters over the period covered by the study. At first blush, readers may think such matters "beneath the noise level" of lawmakers. At times, however, they have come to the forefront of the Agency's relationship with Congress. Indeed, the Agency's overseers have always been concerned by the prospect (not to mention, the reality) of a penetration of the Agency by a hostile intelligence service. They have also been concerned about Agency employees thought to be security risks or who had committed serious security violations. On occasion, Congress has also become involved in personnel matters that had nothing to do with security: the competence of a particular employee, whether employees whose performance fell short had been adequately held accountable for their failure, or whether the treatment accorded a particular employee or group of employees had been fair and equitable.

This chapter describes the episodes that have generated the greatest controversy. It does not cover inquiries made with regard to persons whose positions are subject to appointment by the president and confirmation by the Senate, which are discussed in the next chapter.

The Confrontations with Senator Joseph R. McCarthy: 1950–54

On 20 February 1950, Joseph R. McCarthy (R-WI) took the Senate floor and dramatically charged that 81 people, all but one working for the State Department, were communists or communist sympathizers. The one who did not work at the State Department, whom he did not identify by name, worked for the CIA, he said. The Agency immediately sought and was given the employee's name. After an expedited internal investigation, DCI Hillenkoetter wrote McCarthy and told him in no uncertain terms that the charges could not be sustained. In return for the Agency's promise not to make its letter public, McCarthy agreed not to cite the case again in the future.[1]

---

[1] CIA draft study, Vol. I, 40-41; Barrett, *CIA and Congress*, 64–66.

A few weeks later, however, McCarthy rose from his chair on the Senate floor to make a new charge: the CIA had a "notorious homosexual" on its payroll.[2] Although the man (a State Department employee assigned to the CIA) made no effort to conceal his sexual orientation, at the time homosexuals were widely regarded as being vulnerable to blackmail and, therefore, security risks. When other members of Congress also expressed concern, Hillenkoetter, after discussing the matter with the President Truman, allowed the employee in question to resign.[3]

Hoping to prevent additional confrontations, Agency liaison Pforzheimer elicited a commitment from McCarthy in late May 1950 that he would not publicly levy charges about communists in the CIA without at least informing the Agency privately before he did so.[4] In fact, while McCarthy continued his assault on other agencies, he did not engage with the Agency again for three years.

In the meantime, however, DCI Smith found himself embroiled in controversies with other congressional committees created largely as a result of McCarthy's anticommunist crusade. Although it was not made public at the time, the man who had served as British liaison with the Agency for two years, Harold "Kim" Philby, was recalled to London in May 1951, after his housemate in Washington defected to the Soviet Union. Assuming Philby himself was a spy (as he later was shown to be), the compromise of the Agency's information was potentially devastating. Agency records do not reflect whether Smith informed the CIA subcommittees of Philby's suspected treachery, but testifying publicly in September 1952 in a libel suit involving McCarthy and a fellow senator, Smith stated that he believed, although he did not know, that "there were communists in my own organization." He added that he suspected "communists had infiltrated practically every security organization of the government."[5] These statements earned Smith an invitation from the House Un-American Activities Committee (HUAC) a few weeks later to explain himself. While he admitted the Agency had a few suspected communists within it, he said none were Americans "within the scope or interest of this committee."[6]

In July 1953, McCarthy's focus again returned to the Agency. A few weeks earlier, members of his staff had traveled to Europe. In the course of their travels they had asked to interview Agency officers, who declined to meet with

---

[2] See Barrett, *CIA and Congress*, 61–81, for a detailed description of this episode.
[3] Ibid., 7.
[4] CIA draft study, Vol. I, 41.
[5] Barrett, *CIA and Congress*, 129.
[6] Ibid., 132.

them. Miffed, they began to request, upon their return to Washington, CIA records on a wide variety of subjects. The Agency declined these requests as well. On 9 July, McCarthy demanded to question William P. Bundy, assistant to the DDI at the time, about his relationship with Alger Hiss. Hiss, a State Department official, was suspected of working for the Soviet Union and had earlier been convicted of perjury in a federal court. Bundy was a friend and former law partner of Hiss's brother.[7]

The Agency tried to duck the confrontation, first by issuing an internal memorandum reminding employees that only the DCI was authorized to testify before Congress[8] and then by rushing Bundy to an unplanned vacation in New England and having Pforzheimer tell McCarthy that Bundy was on annual leave. Learning from another source that Bundy had, in fact, reported to work on the morning of 9 July, McCarthy accused Pforzheimer of "a barefaced lie" and subpoenaed him to testify the following day regarding Bundy's whereabouts. DCI Dulles ordered Pforzheimer to ignore the subpoena and, asking for assistance from the White House, had Vice President Nixon call McCarthy urging him to drop the Bundy matter.[9]

McCarthy initially appeared ready to do so, meeting with Dulles on 14 July to work out the terms of their future relationship. Within 48 hours, however, angered by criticism in the press and by fellow senators, McCarthy took the offensive again, charging publicly that Bundy had contributed $400 to an Alger Hiss defense fund and had once been active in a communist front organization.[10] This in turn led Dulles to respond that these things were known when Bundy was granted a security clearance and did not prove disloyalty. McCarthy, outraged, demanded to see Bundy's file. Dulles refused. On 3 August, McCarthy expressed shock that Dulles would continue to protect the associate of a "convicted traitor" and vowed to investigate the Bundy case during the next session of Congress.

McCarthy never carried out his threat. By this point, his power was on the wane. Three senators on his committee resigned in July when his staff made sensational charges regarding the involvement of US clergy in communist groups. President Eisenhower also expressed his displeasure, and senators from both sides of the aisle began to openly question allowing McCarthy to continue his investigations.

In June 1954, during the televised Army-McCarthy hearings that were exploring McCarthy's charges that communists had infiltrated the US Army,

---

[7] Ibid., 177–96.
[8] Knapp, *The First Thirty Years*, 155.
[9] CIA draft study, Vol. I, 43.
[10] Ibid., 44.

the senator attacked the Agency again, saying that there was now new evidence showing that communists who had been members of OSS now "blanketed" the Agency.[11] Dulles immediately issued a press statement denying the charges. Although McCarthy later turned over to the Hoover Commission what he said was the "evidence" to support his charges, by this point he lacked the credibility to be taken seriously. In December, the Senate officially censured his conduct, effectively ending his challenge to the CIA.[12]

The Agency's overseers in the Senate left the Agency to deal with McCarthy largely on its own. Indeed, sentiment among them was split. Some expressed sympathy for his objectives, if not his methods. Initially at least, the political furor created by his charges was simply too powerful for them to intervene on the Agency's behalf, asserting what would have been essentially a jurisdictional issue.

The Paisley Matter: 1978

On 1 October 1978, the body of a retired CIA officer, John A. Paisley, was found floating in the Chesapeake Bay with a weighted diver's belt around his waist and a gunshot wound to the back of the head. Paisley had been heavily involved in Soviet operations during his Agency career. Given the bizarre circumstances surrounding his death and amid speculation in the press, the SSCI opened an inquiry in an attempt to determine whether Paisley's death resulted from his activities as an employee of the Agency. After two years and three public statements regarding the case, the committee ultimately reported it had "found no information to support the allegations that Mr. Paisley's death was connected in some way to involvement in foreign intelligence or counterintelligence matters."[13]

Max Hugel and the SSCI's Investigation of DCI Casey's Prior Business Dealings: 1981

When William Casey became DCI in January 1981, he brought with him a brash, hard-driving New Yorker, Max Hugel, with whom he had worked during the Reagan election campaign. Hugel had no experience in intelligence but had impressed Casey during the campaign, and Casey believed he would inject life and imagination into the Agency's operations. In May 1981, after a

---

[11] Barrett, *CIA and Congress*, 194.
[12] Ibid., 196; CIA draft study, Vol. I, 46.
[13] Smist, *Congress Oversees*, 114.

short time as the deputy director for administration, Hugel was named deputy director for operations, putting him in charge of the Agency's clandestine activities. The appointment drew immediate criticism from a number of retired Agency veterans. It was also apparent that SSCI Chairman Goldwater, while not part of the early public criticism, was nonetheless cool toward Hugel's appointment.[14]

In July 1981, after allegations surfaced that he had passed insider information concerning his company seven years earlier in order to improve its stock position, Hugel decided to resign from the Agency. In covering the story the *New York Times* also disclosed for the first time that a federal judge in New Orleans had ruled two months earlier that Casey had knowingly misled investors in a company he had helped to found in 1968.

Three days after this article appeared, the SSCI voted to open a formal investigation regarding the judge's ruling against Casey, as well as the circumstances of Hugel's resignation. Goldwater initially told reporters that until he knew more he saw no reason for Casey to resign, but later at a appearance in the Senate press gallery, he answered a reporter's question as follows:

> *That he appointed an inexperienced man to be, in effect, the nation's top spy was bad enough. I must say that as a person with long involvement in intelligence matters that it was a very bad mistake and I might even say dangerous because he is the man in charge of clandestine activities. This in itself constitutes the worst thing Casey has done. . . .The damage done by Mr. Hugel's appointment to the morale of the CIA, in my opinion, is a sufficient [reason] for either Mr. Casey to decide to retire or for the President to ask him to retire.[15]*

Although Casey subsequently apologized to the SSCI for Hugel's appointment,[16] he did not resign, and the SSCI proceeded with an extensive investigation of his prior business dealings. The investigation lasted from July until October, but the committee did not release a report of its investigation until December, six months after the allegation surfaced.[17] It found that in failing to disclose various investments, debts, liabilities, board memberships, and work done for foreign governments, Casey had been "at a minimum inattentive to detail" in complying with financial disclosure requirements during his confirmation process. But, while the committee said this pattern of omission sug-

---

[14] Woodward, *Veil*, 132, 148.

[15] Ibid., 130.

[16] CIA draft study, Vol. III, 7.

[17] Senate Select Committee on Intelligence, *Report on Casey Inquiry.*

gested an "insufficient appreciation of the obligation to provide complete and accurate information to the oversight committees," a majority concluded that "no basis has been found for concluding that Mr. Casey is unfit to hold office as director of central intelligence."[18]

Casey's Emphasis on Counterintelligence and Security Issues: 1981–84

DCI Casey saw an expanded counterintelligence and security effort as key to his effort to rebuild US intelligence. For the first time, a DCI provided the Agency's congressional overseers with detailed information on hostile intelligence threats, not only to obtain their support for funding activities needed to counter such threats but also to attune them to the growing and pervasive nature of the threats, both in the United States and abroad.

These briefings led both committees to examine what the Intelligence Community and, in particular, the Agency were doing to counter such threats. While both committees were generally supportive of the initiatives Casey had taken within the Agency (an interagency center within CIA to assess US technology transfers to other countries, for example) the SSCI proposed creating an interagency deception analysis unit to analyze efforts by hostile intelligence services to deceive US intelligence-gatherers. Casey argued that such a unit was not needed inasmuch as the Agency was already doing such analysis. While some of its members took issue with Casey's assessment, the SSCI as a whole did not pursue the idea.[19]

Casey was also troubled by leaks of classified intelligence information and in 1983 attempted to get both intelligence committees to enact new criminal legislation to deal with the problem. The SSCI did hold hearings on this subject during the summer, however, it did not produce a consensus for legislation. Casey tried again a year later with both committees, but neither considered the political climate favorable for such an effort.[20]

The "Year of the Spy" and Its Aftermath: 1985–87

In the space of a year's time, six different espionage cases exploded onto the front pages of the country's newspapers, leading editorial writers to dub 1985 the "year of the spy." One case involved a spy ring within the Navy that had passed high-level cryptographic materials to the Soviets; another, an NSA

---

[18] Ibid., 1–2, 38.
[19] CIA draft study, Vol. III, 30–31.
[20] Ibid., 32–33.

communications specialist who had sold signals intelligence information to the Soviets; and a third, a Navy intelligence analyst who had passed classified documents to the Israeli government. The other three cases involved CIA employees.

The first involved an operations support assistant in Ghana, Sharon Scranage, who was convicted of passing classified information identifying certain CIA officers to Ghanaian intelligence officials. The second case involved a translator and foreign media analyst, Larry Wu-tai Chin, who had passed information regarding CIA intelligence assessments to the Chinese government. The most serious, however, involved a former DO case officer, Edward Lee Howard.

Howard, 33, had worked for the Agency from 1981 until 1983 and had been given access to information concerning the Agency's operations in Moscow because he had been slated to go there. In September 1984, after leaving the Agency, Howard mentioned to two of his former Agency coworkers that he had recently spent several hours outside a Soviet Embassy wondering whether he should go in and offer to work with them. (Four days earlier, the investigation later disclosed, Howard had actually met with Soviet intelligence officers in Austria.) His former colleagues reported his unsettling comment to Agency security officers, but the Agency decided to handle it internally rather than report it to the FBI. Howard at that point had left the Agency and was living in New Mexico.

A year later, KGB defector Vitaly S. Yurchenko gave his debriefers sufficient information that the Agency was able to identify Howard as a likely Soviet spy. Howard was put under round-the-clock FBI surveillance in New Mexico. Eluding the surveillance using methods he had learned as a case officer, Howard fled to Finland and later turned up in the Soviet Union. The damage to Agency operations was thought to be significant.

Both intelligence committees announced they would open inquiries into the Howard case, focusing upon the handling of former employees generally, once they leave the Agency; the actions the Agency took in response to Howard's comment to his colleagues; and the failure to bring the FBI into the case when Howard's comment was reported.[21]

Surfacing in the middle of the other spy cases that came to light that year, the Howard case prompted some in Congress to call for a national commission to evaluate the nation's security posture. Neither intelligence committee supported the proposal, believing they could do a better job of it themselves. Both held extensive hearings—the SSCI alone held 16 hearings on counterin-

---

[21] *New York Times*, "Officials Say CIA Did Not Tell FBI of Spy Case Moves."

telligence and security issues during 1985–86—and both produced extensive reports of their inquiries that were published over the objection of DCI Casey, who considered them to be a "roadmap" of US counterintelligence capabilities.[22]

While the committees were in the midst of these investigations, Casey renewed his crusade to stop leaks of intelligence information. In a letter to President Reagan in November 1985, he described leaks as "a cancer which mortally threatened presidential authority to conduct national security policy, the national security process, and US intelligence capabilities."[23] In May 1986, Casey went public with his concerns, noting that because of leaks,

> *every method we have of obtaining intelligence: our agents, our relationships with other intelligence services, our photographic, our electronic, our communications capabilities have all been damaged. Every one of them has been damaged by disclosure of sensitive information.*[24]

At least partly to blame, Casey believed, was the Congress. In September 1986, he instructed the Office of Legislative Liaison to be more circumspect about what was briefed to the committees and to limit such briefings to the chairman and ranking members whenever possible. As far as briefing other committees was concerned, the Agency needed to begin turning them down. "The resource cost [alone] has become enormous," Casey wrote, "and the number of leaks, outrageous."[25] If the risk of disclosure was thought to be too great in a particular case, Casey advised NSC adviser Robert McFarlane at the time, "We will simply decline the [congressional] request."[26]

The Agency continued to quarrel with the intelligence committees over leaks even after Casey had passed from the scene. In March 1987, after a member of the HPSCI revealed the existence of the then-secret National Reconnaissance Office as well as the KEYHOLE satellite program in a speech on the House floor, Acting DCI Robert Gates met with HPSCI Chairman Louis Stokes to discuss what could be done about leaks from the committee. According to CIA records, Gates identified four cases where he believed it was clear that leaks had come from the oversight committees. Stokes responded that it was his view CIA had been "setting the committees up" by leaking information to the press itself and then blaming the committees. Gates

---

[22] Senate Select Committee on Intelligence, *Meeting the Espionage Challenge*; House Permanent Select Committee on Intelligence, *US Counterintelligence and Security Concerns—1986*.
[23] CIA draft study, Vol. III, 93.
[24] Ibid., 97.
[25] Ibid.
[26] Ibid.

did not accept Stokes's assertion but committed to fostering a more responsive attitude within the Agency toward the oversight committees.[27]

While Gates—and later DCI Webster—continued to underscore their concerns to both committees with respect to leaks coming from the legislative branch, the publication of *Veil* in late 1987 effectively put an end to their complaints. Not only did Bob Woodward's book reveal the details of numerous covert action programs and compartmented collection operations, it had obviously been prepared with Casey's cooperation and participation. Incensed, both committees threatened to investigate but ultimately deferred to an internal CIA investigation commissioned by DCI Webster. That investigation confirmed Casey not only met with and spoke to Woodward on numerous occasions but had authorized Agency officers to provide him background briefings.[28]

Concerns over Embassy Security: 1985–88

In 1985, as the "year of the spy" was unfolding, the Agency told both oversight committees that there was strong evidence the Soviets had embedded a complex electronic surveillance system within the new American embassy under construction in Moscow. Work on the building was halted until a decision could be reached on how to proceed, and at the initiative of the SSCI, Congress approved a supplemental appropriation to improve security countermeasures at US diplomatic establishments worldwide.

Embassy security continued to concern both committees in the years that followed. In 1987, the SSCI issued a lengthy report on the Moscow embassy, recommending that it be torn down completely and rebuilt. The committee also recommended that the DCI certify the security conditions at all US diplomatic establishments.

The Agency produced its own study of the new Moscow embassy building, recommending that everything above the fourth floor be demolished and that no classified activities or discussions be held on the floors that remained. DCI Webster also responded to the SSCI's recommendation by creating a Security Evaluation Office to analyze the security vulnerabilities of US missions abroad.[29]

---

[27] Ibid., 176.
[28] Ibid., 179.
[29] Ibid., 178–79.

Providing Authority to Redress Past Injustices: 1988

During the late 1960s and early 1970s, a number of employees were asked to leave the Agency after then–counterintelligence chief, James J. Angleton, had raised questions about their loyalty. In the early 1980s, several of these employees asked DCI Casey to reconsider their cases. At the end of an extensive internal process lasting several years, Casey decided that certain of the individuals involved had, in fact, been unfairly treated, but he lacked the legal authority to provide them monetary compensation.

In 1988, more than a year after Casey's death, DCI Webster broached the matter with both intelligence committees, which agreed to have their respective staffs review the files on each case. Ultimately, the committees agreed with the assessment of the two DCIs and provided a special, one-time authority in the annual intelligence authorization bill for the Agency to pay monetary compensation, as it saw fit, out of its appropriated funds to redress the recognized injustices of the past.[30]

The HPSCI's Inquiry into Sex Discrimination: 1994

In 1994, the Agency found itself a defendant in two widely publicized lawsuits alleging sexual discrimination. One was a class action suit brought by 100 women in the Directorate of Operations; the other, an individual lawsuit over the Agency's promotion practices.

Taking note of these complaints, the HPSCI held open hearings in September 1994 to explore the Agency's personnel policies and practices with respect to the hiring and promotion of women and other minorities. While conceding that "minorities are still underrepresented in the Agency's workforce, and the advancement of women and minorities is still limited," DCI Woolsey said he was intent on breaking down any existing barriers. "The ability to understand a complex, diverse world," he stated, "a world which is far from being all white male—is central to our mission."[31]

The Congressional Reaction to the Aldrich Ames case: 1994

On the morning of 21 February 1994, the FBI arrested a long-time DO employee and his wife on charges of espionage. The affidavit accompanying the arrest warrant alleged that Aldrich H. Ames had begun spying for the

---

[30] §501, Intelligence Authorization Act for FY 1989, PL 100-453, 29 September 1988.
[31] Weiner, "CIA Is Working to Overcome Sex and Race Bias."

Soviet Union in April 1985 and that his activities had continued until the day of his arrest. The damage Ames caused was unclear at the time, but Justice Department officials confirmed that a number of CIA and FBI Soviet sources had been imprisoned or executed as a result of his betrayal. The reaction in Congress was immediate and powerful. Some members called for aid to Russia be curtailed or ended. Others called for the expulsion of suspected Russian intelligence officers from the United States. Still others introduced a flurry of bills to beef up US security programs.[32]

Both intelligence committees received initial briefings and announced their intent to investigate. The leaders of the SSCI also wrote to the CIA inspector general, Frederick P. Hitz, asking that he investigate within the CIA. Initially, though, the requirements of the criminal process restrained both the committees and Hitz. Justice Department prosecutors insisted that the criminal investigation run its course before separate investigations—which had the potential for creating problems for the prosecution—could begin.

Over the ensuing months, however, details of the case began to emerge in the press, raising questions about why the Agency had not identified Ames as a traitor any earlier. He had lived well beyond the means afforded by his Agency salary but apparently had never attracted attention. He had been a mediocre employee with a history of problems with alchol but continued to have access to the Agency's most sensitive information. He had passed all of his security evaluations, including two polygraph examinations. Members of the oversight committees openly began to wonder how this could have happened and what DCI Woolsey planned to do with respect to those who had allowed it to happen. Woolsey responded that he would wait until the IG had completed his investigation—until all the facts were in—before he made any decisions. This did not satisfy his congressional critics. One HPSCI member reacted to the DCI's statement by saying, "If the director's intention is to restore confidence within Congress, I'm still waiting." SSCI Chairman DeConcini added,

> *Woolsey is trying to hunker down and divert all the attention he can. Perhaps it helps morale and increases his following inside the agency, but it doesn't get to the problem.*

Unable to undertake their own investigations immediately, both committees turned to finding legislative remedies to improve the ability of the government to identify potential spies and investigate them. While the Agency supported some of the measures the committees proposed—making the death penalty

---

[32] For a detailed description of the interaction that occurred with Congress as a result of the Ames case, see Kennedy School of Government, "James Woolsey and the CIA: The Aldrich Ames Spy Case." Unless otherwise noted, the quotations in this section are taken from this case study.

available in espionage cases, requiring financial disclosure by federal employees, amending the Foreign Intelligence Surveillance Act (FISA) to include physical searches—others were not. In particular, the proposal requiring the Agency to report to the FBI any employee reasonably believed to have compromised classified information produced violent objection from Woolsey, who believed it would force the Agency to reveal its operational activities to the FBI. Woolsey also objected to the proposal of SSCI Vice Chairman John Warner (R-VA) to create a presidential commission on intelligence needs in the post–Cold War era, in part to restore the public's confidence in the Agency after the Ames case. Both proposals were ultimately enacted over Woolsey's objection and signed into law by President Clinton.

On 28 April 1994, Ames pled guilty to espionage and was sentenced to life in prison without parole. This freed the committees as well as CIA Inspector General Hitz to pursue their independent investigative efforts. While both committees received briefings from the Agency on the Ames case, they decided against initiating independent probes until they had seen what the Hitz investigation produced.

Meanwhile, Woolsey announced at a speech on 18 July a "comprehensive overhaul" of the Agency's counterintelligence and security policies and practices and promised to make changes "in the culture of the CIA itself." But this was "too little, too late," the *New York Times* reported, as far as "senior members" of the intelligence committees were concerned. They were still waiting "for heads to roll." [33]

The IG report was not officially transmitted to Woolsey until late September 1994, although Hitz had earlier provided a draft to the DCI and both intelligence committees. While the broad outline of the case had been in the public domain for several months, the IG report added vivid details that brought home the extent of the damage Ames had caused: 10 Soviet assets, executed; two dozen CIA officers, exposed; and roughly 50 operations, compromised. But Hitz also reported on how bad the Agency had been in tolerating his misconduct and detecting his treachery. Ames had had repeated security violations, including leaving classified material on a subway train. The evidence of his drinking problem included a report that a colleague found him passed out in a gutter in Rome. Even after a fellow employee reported in 1989 that Ames had "unexplained affluence," it took several years for the Agency to link the acquisition of such wealth to his spying activities.

---

[33] Weiner, "Agency Chief Pledges to Overhaul 'Fraternity' Atmosphere at C.I.A.," *New York Times*, 19 July 1994.

In the classified version of his report, which was made available to the two intelligence committees, Hitz named 23 present and former Agency officials who, in his judgment, should be held accountable, including former DCIs Casey, Webster, and Gates. All either had had supervisory responsibility for Ames or had been responsible for the "mole hunt" that had failed to identify Ames for nine years.

To assess Hitz's recommendations, Woolsey convened a group of top CIA officials over the weekend of 24 September 1994 and asked what they thought should be done with respect to each of the 23 individuals named in the report. A few days later, without prior consultation either with the committees or with the White House, Woolsey announced his decisions before the HPSCI. Of the 23 people Hitz identified, Woolsey said he would discipline 11. All 11 would receive reprimands of some kind and four would receive "serious reprimands." But of the four identified for such reprimands, three had already retired and the fourth was due to retire two days later. The remaining seven (three of whom had retired) would receive milder reprimands that would stay in their personnel files for a year's time. In announcing his decisions, Woolsey said he recognized that

> *some have clamored for heads to roll . . . regardless of the particular merits of each case. That is not my way. And, in my judgment, that's not the American way, and it's not the CIA's way.*

Woolsey went on to explain that he had acted "like a judge." He had taken into account the achievements of the employees involved. He had also taken into account how personally and how directly each was responsible for the failures that occurred.

Reacting to the announcement, SSCI Vice Chairman Warner noted that Woolsey was not a judge but a manager and that his disciplinary actions fell well short of what a manager should impose. DeConcini agreed:

> *You don't lose your job* [if you fall short] *and you don't get demoted. There's a huge problem here that you're not going to get at by leaving some of these people in place.*

Several weeks after Woolsey announced his disciplinary actions, two senior DO officials presented to one of the four officers who had received a "serious" reprimand—the one who was about to retire—a plaque in recognition of his service to the DO. Seeing their action as a challenge to his authority, Woolsey immediately ordered the demotion of the two officials involved, who resigned rather than accept demotion. While the Agency workforce was reportedly shocked by this turn of events, the chairmen of both intelligence committees supported Woolsey's decision. HPSCI Chairman Dan Glickman told the

Washington Post that the action by the two officials was either "an unconscionable act of stupidity or a direct challenge to the Director."[34]

As far as the committees were concerned, the severity of the DCI's disciplinary actions in October stood in stark contrast to his actions a few weeks earlier. In its public report on the Ames case, the SSCI unanimously condemned Woolsey for his handling of the disciplinary issues involved.

> *In response to what was arguably the greatest managerial breakdown in the CIA's history, the disciplinary actions taken by the Director do not, in the collective experience and judgment of the Committee, constitute adequate "management accountability." All Committee members believe the Director's disciplinary actions in this case are seriously inadequate and disproportionate to the magnitude of the problems identified in the Inspector General's report.*[35]

The Mishandling of Classified Information by Former DCI Deutch: 2000

John Deutch resigned as DCI on 14 December 1996. Within a few days of his resignation, CIA security personnel went to his residence to retrieve a government-owned computer, configured only for unclassified work, which had been loaned to him during his tenure as DCI. On the hard drive and various storage media at the residence, the security personnel found a substantial number of highly classified documents, including draft memorandums for the president and others involving compartmented covert action programs. This discovery was reported to Agency managers, who directed that a security investigation be initiated.

The investigation that took place during the first half of 1997 confirmed the presence of voluminous classified information on other unclassified computers used by Deutch (17,000 pages of material were ultimately recovered). It could not be determined, however, whether the classified material on the computers or storage media had actually been compromised. CIA management took no action at the end of the security investigation, however, inasmuch as Deutch was no longer an Agency employee. He did, however, retain an Agency security clearance.

In February 1998, one of the security officers involved in the investigation complained to the Agency's Office of the Inspector General (OIG) that the investigation of Deutch had been frustrated by certain of Deutch's staff who

---

[34] Pincus, "2 CIA Officers Choose Retirement over Demotion."
[35] Senate Select Committee on Intelligence, *An Assessment of the Aldrich H. Ames Espionage Case and its Implications for US Intelligence.*

had remained at the Agency while the investigation was under way. There was also a significant disparity in the treatment accorded Deutch and that accorded another senior Agency official who had also been found to have kept classified information on his home computer.

In March 1998, after the OIG had opened a formal investigation of the allegations, a "crimes report" was submitted to the Department of Justice, raising the possibility of appointing a special prosecutor to investigate the case. In May, the Department advised that a special prosecutor was not required, allowing the OIG to proceed with its own investigation. In early June, DCI Tenet verbally notified the leaders of the congressional intelligence committees of the OIG investigation of Deutch. OIG completed a draft of its investigative report in early 1999 and gave a copy to the Department of Justice. In April, Attorney General Janet Reno declined prosecution but suggested a review of Deutch's suitability to retain a security clearance.

In August 1999, copies of the finished OIG report were sent to the two intelligence committees. The report was critical not only of Deutch's behavior but that of Agency management, including DCI Tenet, for failing to ensure the security issue had been handled properly in 1997.[36] Neither committee, however, reacted to the report until February 2000, after the substance of it had been leaked to the *New York Times*. In the public uproar that followed, the attorney general announced she was reopening the issue of possible criminal prosecution, and both committees announced they would hold hearings on the matter. The SSCI, in fact, held three hearings, requiring testimony not only from Tenet but Deutch and his former staff as well. Calling Deutch's behavior "reckless and beyond explanation," SSCI Vice Chairman Richard Bryan (D-AR) also faulted the Agency for having taken too long to inform the oversight committees of the pending investigation.[37]

The Department of Justice never resolved the issue of whether to prosecute Deutch criminally for his behavior. In the waning days of his administration, President Clinton pardoned the former DCI, removing the threat of criminal prosecution.

HPSCI Action on Proposed Compensation Reform: 2003–04

In 2003, DCI Tenet proposed a pay-for-performance (PFP) compensation reform program that would tie the pay of CIA employees more directly to their job performance. While the program was intended to provide financial

---

[36] Office of Inspector General, *Improper Handling of Classified Information by John M. Deutch*.

[37] Press Release of Senator Richard Bryan, 22 February 2000.

incentives for those taking on the most challenging work of the Agency and for those who took time off from their duties to acquire critical skills, it also left greater discretion in the hands of immediate supervisors in determining employees' pay.

Both intelligence committees were briefed on the proposed program, and of the two, HPSCI was the more skeptical. A number of Agency employees had informally made their concerns with the program known to the HPSCI; as a result it was prepared to go along only with a pilot program to test the concept advanced by management. In addition to assessing the effect of PFP on personnel costs, the pilot program also called for a survey of CIA employees to gather data regarding their attitudes toward the program.

A year later, after the pilot program had been implemented, the HPSCI held several contentious hearings, during which Agency managers were challenged both with respect to the veracity of their testimony on the costs of the program and the objectivity of the employee survey. Its members' concerns apparently unmet, the committee in its action on the FY 2005 Intelligence Authorization Bill blocked the expenditure of any funds to implement the PFP program agency-wide until certain (generally onerous) conditions had been met.[38]

In the face of the committee's hostility (it was doubtful that conditions the committee imposed could ever be satisfied) and the fact that the Agency managers who had proposed the program were leaving, Tenet's successor, Porter Goss, chose not to pursue it further. Tenet later wrote,

> I'm convinced that the [PFP] plan could have produced an invaluable boost to morale . . . unfortunately, until the day I retired, Congress refused me the authority to implement it . . . a terrible mistake.[39]

AUTHOR'S COMMENTARY

The Threat and Reality of Espionage

Throughout the Agency's history, its overseers in Congress have been concerned by the prospect of a "mole" in its midst. It has always been recognized that one well-placed spy could do enormous damage to the Agency's operations. Fortunately, relatively few spies have been uncovered over the years,

---

[38] House Permanent Select Committee on Intelligence, *Report to Intelligence Authorization Act for Fiscal Year 2005*, 27–30.
[39] Tenet, *At the Center of the Storm*, 25.

although some—Aldrich Ames and Edward Lee Howard—have been particularly devastating.

Predictably, whenever a spy has been identified, the intelligence committees have wanted to know not only what happened, but how it was allowed to happen. They have wanted to know why the mole was not detected sooner. They have asked to know the extent of the damage and what the Agency is doing to mitigate its effects. And they have wanted to know what the Agency is doing to prevent it from happening again.

Depending upon the circumstances, however, even a serious case may not prompt an independent investigation by one of the committees. The case of Harold J. Nicholson, a 47-year-old case officer employed by the Agency for 16 years, is a case in point. Nicholson admitted that he had given the Russians classified information over a two-year period in return for $300,000. He pled guilty to one charge of espionage in June 1996 and was sentenced to 23 years in prison. While the damage he did was judged to be substantial, there did not appear to be significant shortcomings either in the way the Agency had handled him over his career or in the investigation that led to his arrest. Neither committee saw fit to pursue the case on its own.

In addition to spies at the Agency, the possibility of a mole on the staff of one of the oversight committees has always been a concern for both the committees and the Agency. None has ever been uncovered, but there have been a few cases when the aberrant behavior on the part of a committee staffer has raised suitability issues that led to a dismissal. When this has happened, the Agency typically has been apprised of the circumstances. Committee staff members have also been disciplined, albeit infrequently, for security violations.

Security violations by Agency employees may also raise concern with the committees if they are serious and/or involve senior personnel. The Agency typically notifies the committees, in fact, of such cases.

Personnel Matters

Not infrequently, the oversight committees have received complaints from Agency employees (including former assets and defectors), who believe they have been treated unfairly. Although the staffs will usually hear out such complaints and make a preliminary effort to assess their credibility and seriousness, few are formally investigated, and fewer still are brought to the attention of members. Quite often, the Agency will simply be asked to provide a response to the complaint the committee has received and that will end the matter.

On occasion, however, when a committee has received multiple complaints involving the same issue (the resettlement of defectors), complaints that may indicate a systemic problem (the treatment of minorities), or complaints involving a senior official, it may choose to hold formal hearings or conduct a staff inquiry into such complaints. On occasion this would result in a formal report or recommendations, but most often the issues were addressed by the Agency explaining its actions or policies or by having the committees scrutinze them.

CHAPTER 11

THE SENATE CONFIRMATION PROCESS

By law, certain executive branch positions require appointment by the president and confirmation by the Senate. Once the president announces a choice for a position, the nomination is officially transmitted to the Senate where it is referred to the committee of jurisdiction for consideration. Typically, the nominee is required to provide certain background information to the committee and to appear before it at a confirmation hearing. Afterwards, the committee reports the nomination, usually with its recommendation, to the full Senate which takes final action on the appointment.

From 1947 until 1953, the only Agency position subject to Senate confirmation was that of the DCI. In 1953, the deputy DCI's position was added. It was not until 1989 that a third position—the Agency's inspector general—was made subject to Senate confirmation, and in 1994, Congress added a fourth—the Agency's general counsel. From 1947 until 1976, nominations for the DCI and DDCI positions were referred to the SASC. After 1976, they were referred to the SSCI, as were the nominations for the other Agency positions that came to require Senate confirmation.

This chapter is limited to the Senate's handling of nominees for DCI. While several nominees have received negative votes, never has a majority of the Senate—nor for that matter a majority of the committee responsible for handling the nomination—voted to reject a nominee for the DCI position. Four nominees, however, have withdrawn after their nomination was sent to the Senate: two before confirmation hearings had begun, and two after such hearings had begun. The circumstances of each of these cases are described in what follows.

The Early DCIs: Souers through Dulles

President Truman appointed the first three DCIs—Souers, Vandenberg, and Hillenkoetter—without Senate approval. Prior to the enactment of the National Security Act of 1947, the DCI position was established by executive directive, rather than by law, and did not require Senate confirmation.

This changed in July 1947, with the enactment of the landmark legislation. Those appointed DCI could come from either military or civilian ranks, the new law provided, but a military officer appointed DCI would be required to sever personal ties to the military. Truman's nominee to be the first "statutory" DCI under the new law, Admiral Hillenkoetter, was a military officer, whom he had earlier appointed pursuant to executive authority. The Senate confirmed him by voice vote in December 1947 without a formal hearing.

The first person nominated to the DCI's position to receive a formal (albeit perfunctory) confirmation hearing was Hillenkoetter's successor, LTG Walter Bedell "Beetle" Smith, who had served as Eisenhower's chief of staff during World War II, and as US ambassador to the Soviet Union from 1946 to 1949. At the time Truman nominated him, Smith was serving as commanding general of the 1st Army. Hailed by Republicans and Democrats alike, the appointment sailed through the congressional process in the span of a week. Smith was nominated on 21 August 1950 and testified at a confirmation hearing before the SASC on 24 August. He emphasized his intent to follow the law and comply with congressional intent and was unanimously confirmed four days later.[1]

The nomination of Smith's successor, Allen Dulles, also enjoyed smooth sailing. The first civilian to be nominated for the DCI's position, Dulles had been in OSS during World War II and had continued to serve as a consultant to Vandenberg and Hillenkoetter while practicing law in New York City. In November 1950, Dulles returned to the CIA to serve as a consultant to Smith, went on to become deputy director for plans (the predecessor of the DDO), and later DDCI to Smith.

By the time Dulles was nominated, he had already established himself with the CIA subcommittees and enjoyed broad support within the Congress. Affable and gregarious by nature, his experience and enthusiasm for intelligence work was evident. The fact that President Eisenhower had also nominated his brother, John Foster, to be secretary of state was seen not as a liability by the Congress but an asset. When Dulles appeared at his confirmation hearing before the SASC on 12 February 1953, "all joined in praising the nominee and asking no questions," according to the memorandum commemorating the occasion prepared by the Agency's legislative liaison, Walter Pforzheimer.[2] The hearing lasted 10 minutes. Dulles, too, was confirmed by unanimous vote of the full Senate.

Two months later, in April 1953, Congress amended the National Security Act of 1947 to require presidential appointment and Senate confirmation for

---

[1] Knapp, *The First Thirty Years*, 53; Barrett, *CIA and Congress*, 91.
[2] CIA draft study, Vol. I, 39–40.

the DDCI as well as the DCI. The amendment also prohibited military officers, active duty or retired, from holding both positions at the same time.

John McCone: 1962

In the wake of the fiasco at the Bay of Pigs, President Kennedy decided that the Agency needed a change of leadership. To replace Dulles, he chose John A. McCone, a tough-minded California businessman and lifelong Republican. McCone had held several positions at the Pentagon between 1947 and 1951 and, from July 1958 until the end of the Eisenhower administration, had served as chairman of the Atomic Energy Commission (AEC), where he had made an impression on Kennedy as well as other members of Congress. The chairmanship of the AEC had also exposed him to a considerable degree to the analysis and, to a lesser degree, the operations of the Intelligence Community.

Kennedy announced McCone's appointment on 27 September 1961, and because Congress was out of session, he was sworn in as a recess appointment on 29 November 1961. It was not until Congress reconvened in January 1962 that his confirmation hearings could be held. In the intervening months, McCone came under criticism, both from members of Congress and the press, reflecting to some extent the sudden sensitivity that now attached to the occupant of the DCI's position after the Bay of Pigs. Some critics questioned McCone's qualifications for the job; others worried that his strong anticommunist views would hamper his objectivity as DCI. Muckraking journalist Drew Pearson wrote a series of columns questioning his prior business dealings and suggesting conflicts of interest were likely to arise if he were confirmed as DCI.

All of these concerns were raised at McCone's 18 January 1962 confirmation hearing, the first such hearing for a prospective DCI to involve controversy. In addition to answering his critics, McCone introduced into the record a letter he had requested and received from President Kennedy, in effect, setting forth his charter as DCI. It indicated that McCone would serve as the government's principal intelligence officer, whose functions would include coordination and leadership of the total US foreign intelligence effort.[3]

During the course of the confirmation hearing, SFRC Chairman Fulbright complained that he did not know enough about McCone's foreign policy views to support his nomination and intended to vote against it on the floor to

---

[3] John F. Kennedy, "Memorandum to McCone," 16 January 1962, in *Central Intelligence: Origin and Evolution,* Warner (ed.), 67–68.

protest the relative passivity of the SASC's oversight of the CIA. SASC Chairman Russell immediately challenged this statement.[4]

Notwithstanding Fulbright's criticism, three days after the hearing, the SASC unanimously reported the nomination to the Senate floor. While the Senate confirmed McCone on 31 January, by a vote of 71 to 12, it came only after Fulbright and other senators had reiterated the concerns they had earlier expressed in committee. It was the first time, in fact, that members of the Senate had ever cast negative votes for a person nominated to the DCI's position.

William F. Raborn: 1965

William Raborn was a retired vice admiral, best known for his work on the Navy's Polaris missile program. After his retirement from the Navy in 1963 he had worked in private industry until 12 April 1965, when President Johnson tapped him to replace McCone as DCI.

Although Raborn had no experience in intelligence or foreign affairs, he had earned plaudits from the SASC for his work on the Polaris program—which he had brought in under budget and ahead of schedule—that overshadowed any concerns the committee might otherwise have had about his inexperience in intelligence matters.[5] After a perfunctory hearing before the SASC, Raborn was confirmed by the full Senate by voice vote and sworn in on 28 April 1965, two weeks after his nomination had been submitted.

Richard M. Helms: 1966

At the time President Johnson nominated him to be the next DCI, Richard M. Helms was serving as DDCI to Raborn. Given his own inexperience, Raborn had relied heavily on Helms during his short tenure not simply to run the Agency but to assist him in handling relations with Capitol Hill.[6] Helms had spent virtually his entire professional life in intelligence. After a short stint as a journalist before the war and service in the wartime Navy, Helms had joined OSS in 1943 and had stayed with its successor organizations that were ultimately melded into the CIA in 1947. He spent his entire career at the Agency in operations, ultimately rising to become McCone's deputy director of plans in 1962.

---

[4] Robarge, *John McCone*, 43.
[5] Helms, *A Look Over My Shoulder*, 246.
[6] Ibid., 251.

Johnson announced Helms's appointment on 18 June 1966, and the Senate confirmed him 10 days later. The incumbent DDCI, his appointment came as no surprise to members. Moreover, he had been through the confirmation process a year earlier when nominated to be DDCI and had accompanied Raborn to all of his appearances before the SASC subcommittee. Adding to the appeal of Helms's appointment, Raborn had shown little appreciation of, or aptitude for, intelligence work during his short tenure. He had also antagonized SFRC Chairman Fulbright by refusing to answer questions (on grounds of revealing sources and methods) about the Fulbright scholarship program and whether it was being used as a cover for intelligence activities. Having him bow out as DCI in favor of Helms essentially removed this source of irritation for the SASC.[7]

Thus, the committee greeted Helms's nomination with something of a sigh of relief. While his extensive involvement in the operations of the Agency over a 20-year period might have prompted members to inquire into his role in such activities, especially operational failures like the Bay of Pigs, they did not do so. His confirmation hearing produced no controversy whatsoever.

James R. Schlesinger: 1973

Helms had a difficult relationship with President Nixon that had culminated in his refusal to cooperate in what later became known as the Watergate cover-up.[8] At a November 1972 meeting at Camp David, Nixon told him he would be replaced. A month later, the president announced the appointment of James R. Schlesinger to be DCI.

At the time of his appointment, Schlesinger was serving as chairman of the AEC, a post to which Nixon had appointed him in June 1971. Prior to this, Schlesinger had served as assistant director of the Bureau of the Budget (the predecessor of the Office of Management and Budget), where, at Nixon's behest, he had conducted a study of the Intelligence Community that had led Nixon to strengthen the DCI's fiscal management role over the Community. Prior to his government service, Schlesinger had been an economics professor at the University of Virginia and served two years at a government think tank.

The SASC held a perfunctory hearing in mid-January, clearing the way for Schlesinger's unanimous confirmation by the full Senate on 23 January 1973.

---

[7] Knapp, *The First Thirty Years*, 248–49.
[8] Helms, *A Look Over My Shoulder*, 4–13.

William E. Colby: 1973

In May 1973, less than five months after being confirmed, Schlesinger was nominated to be secretary of defense as part of a cabinet shuffle necessitated by the resignation of certain cabinet officials during the Watergate scandal. To take his place as DCI, Nixon nominated a career CIA officer, William E. Colby, who at the time was serving as the DDP.

Colby had served with the OSS and after the war had gone to work at the New York law firm of William Donovan, the former head of the OSS. With the outbreak of the Korean War in 1950, Colby returned to Washington and joined the CIA. Like Helms, his career was spent in clandestine operations. Before becoming executive director in 1971, his principal preoccupation had been the war in Vietnam. From 1958 until 1962, he served as deputy station chief and station chief in Saigon. This was followed by six years at Headquarters, where he oversaw the Agency's operations in the region during the US military buildup there. In 1968, he went on leave without pay from the Agency to accept a position (with ambassadorial rank) with the Agency for International Development that ultimately made him responsible for the village pacification program in South Vietnam, which included a controversial program known as Phoenix.

The Phoenix program, begun in mid-1968 after the Tet offensive, was created to root out the Viet Cong's secret apparatus from the South Vietnamese countryside. South Vietnamese police and intelligence services worked with local villagers to identify known or suspected infiltrators and then turn that information over to the South Vietnamese military for follow-up action. In some cases, known or suspected Viet Cong were reportedly killed. While the South Vietnamese government had responsibility for carrying out the program, albeit with direction and assistance provided by the US organization headed by Colby, CIA ultimately became identified with the program, in part because of Colby's involvement and in part because of the methods used in the program.

In 1971, a subcommittee of the House Government Operations Committee held public hearings on the conduct of the Vietnam War that focused on the Phoenix program, and Colby was called back to Washington to testify. Although he staunchly denied that Phoenix was "a program of assassination," he admitted that South Vietnamese military officers involved in the program may have carried out isolated assassinations. He assured the committee, however, that the United States had effectively put an end to such abuses.[9]

---

[9] Prados, *Lost Crusader*, 235–36.

When Colby was nominated two years later to be DCI, his involvement in the Phoenix program was again raised as an issue. To make matters worse for him, the country was in the throes of the Watergate scandal, and press articles were appearing alleging CIA's involvement in that and other activities, for example, the 1970 presidential election in Chile (see chapters 1, 8, and 9). For the first time in the Agency's history, the leaders of its subcommittees in the SASC, SAC, and HASC began calling for special investigations of the Agency's activities. The atmosphere had never before been as hostile for a DCI's confirmation, and when the hearings had to be put off to give SASC Chairman Stennis time to recuperate after being shot in a street crime, Colby's critics had more time to prepare themselves.

In the end, the SASC held three days of contentious hearings on Colby's nomination in July 1973, during which time he faced an unprecedented barrage of hostile questioning, both with respect to alleged CIA illegalities and his role in the Phoenix program. The most serious accusation, in fact, came from a Massachusetts congressman, Robert Drinan, who told the committee that Colby had misled him and other members of a congressional delegation about the program during a visit to Saigon in 1969. This testimony later led a member of the SASC to confide to the CIA's legislative liaison that he also felt misled by Colby regarding the Phoenix program.[10] As part of Colby's confirmation process, the SASC also took the occasion, for the first time, to invite witnesses, pro and con, to testify publicly about the workings of the Intelligence Community.

The Senate confirmed Colby on 1 August 1973 by a vote of 83 to 13, but only after he had endured a considerable battering before the committee.

George H.W. Bush: 1976

President Ford dismissed Colby in November 1975, in the midst of the Church and Pike investigations and nominated George H.W. Bush as his successor. Bush was a Navy pilot during World War II. After the war, he completed his education and entered into private business. In 1966, he was elected to Congress and served two terms. At the beginning of the Nixon administration, he was appointed to be US ambassador to the United Nations. He went on to serve as chairman of the Republican National Committee and, at the time of his appointment as DCI, was serving as first chief of the US liaison office in Beijing.

---

[10] Ford, *William E. Colby*, 15.

In announcing the appointment, President Ford said he was putting Bush into the job to restore the public's confidence in the Intelligence Community. He would personally meet with his new DCI each week, Ford said, to ensure that the activities of US intelligence agencies were being properly supervised.

On 30 January 1976, the Senate confirmed Bush by a vote of 64 to 27, and he was sworn in immediately. Although the number of negative votes was the largest ever cast against a nominee for the DCI's position to that point, it had more to do with the disenchantment with the Agency evident within Congress at the time than with the nominee himself. Indeed, Bush's confirmation hearing before the SASC did not produce serious controversy.

President Carter's Appointments: Sorensen and Turner

After the presidential election of 1976, Bush resigned as DCI, and President-elect Jimmy Carter announced that his choice to replace Bush would be Theodore Sorensen, who had been a speechwriter and confidant of President Kennedy. Before his confirmation hearing even began, however, problems developed, primarily in the form of his admission in earlier courtroom testimony that he had used classified White House material in the book he had written about the Kennedy administration. It was also revealed that Sorensen had taken a tax deduction when he donated these materials to the National Archives. Perhaps more troubling to the committee members themselves was the nominee's seemingly cavalier attitude toward them. When SSCI Chairman Inouye asked to see him before the confirmation hearing, Sorensen reportedly told him, "I'm pretty busy. I don't think I have the time." Inouye exploded, and Sorensen managed to find time to see him. But for a committee already troubled by Sorensen's lack of experience in intelligence and foreign affairs, this prelude did not bode well for his nomination. On 17 January 1977, moments before his confirmation hearing was to begin, Sorensen advised the president he was withdrawing his name from consideration.[11]

A few weeks later, on 7 February 1977, Carter announced the appointment of ADM Stansfield Turner to the DCI's position. A former Rhodes scholar, Turner spent 30 years as a naval officer. At the time of his appointment, he was serving as commander-in-chief of Allied Forces in Southern Europe. He would remain on active duty, it was announced, while serving as DCI.

Turner's confirmation hearings were the first to be held before the SSCI. The committee had two days of hearings, including one day hearing testimony of three public witnesses. Not surprisingly, the hearings focused heavily on

---

[11] Smist, *Congress Oversees*, 130.

congressional oversight and the rights of American citizens. Turner promised to cooperate with the committee and said he would resign rather than implement directives that he believed were "unconstitutional, illegal, or in conflict with moral standards."[12]

Turner's nomination was voted out of committee by unanimous vote, and the Senate confirmed him by voice vote. He was sworn in on 7 March 1977.

William J. Casey: 1981

Ronald Reagan was elected president in November 1980, in part based upon his campaign promise to revitalize the Intelligence Community. To help him do this, he nominated a 67-year-old Wall Street lawyer, William J. Casey, to be his DCI. Casey had been Reagan's campaign manager. While his experience in intelligence was dated (he had served in OSS) as well as limited (he had served for a year on the President's Foreign Intelligence Advisory Board), he nonetheless had maintained an interest in foreign affairs over the course of his legal career. In 1969, he served on an advisory council for the Arms Control and Disarmament Agency. From 1973 to 1974, he was chairman of the Securities and Exchange Commission, providing him experience at the helm of a federal agency.

While the incoming SSCI chairman, Barry Goldwater, had pressed the administration to appoint ADM Bobby Ray Inman, the outgoing NSA director, instead of Casey, Reagan stood firm. After initially refusing Casey's offer of the DDCI's position, Inman later accepted the appointment.[13]

Casey's confirmation hearing before the SSCI took place on 13 January 1981, a week before Reagan was inaugurated. The nominee asserted that his goals as DCI would be "rebuilding, performance, and security." When members pressed him on his understanding of, and intent to comply with, the recently enacted oversight statute—establishing his obligations vis-à-vis the committee—Casey replied that he intended to "comply fully with the spirit and letter" of the law. In subsequent questioning, however, he also observed that "rigid accountability . . . can impair performance."[14] Apparently the committee did not find that qualification troubling, however, voting unanimously to report Casey's nomination to the floor. On 27 January 1981, the full Senate approved the nomination by a vote of 95 to 0.[15]

---

[12] Senate Select Committee on Intelligence, *Nomination as Director of Central Intelligence of Adm. Stansfield Turner.*

[13] Woodward, *Veil,* 47.

[14] Ibid., 83–84.

The First Gates Nomination: 1987

Casey suffered a brain seizure on 15 December 1986, just before he was to testify before the SSCI on the Agency's role in the Iran-contra matter (see chapter 9). Incapacitated, he officially resigned as DCI on 28 January 1987. To replace him, President Reagan nominated 43-year-old Robert M. Gates. A career intelligence officer, Gates had risen through the ranks of CIA analysts to become DDI under Casey and then his DDCI in April 1986.

Gates enjoyed good relations with both oversight committees, but it became apparent that his nomination could not move forward until his role in the Iran-contra scandal had been fully explored and any doubts about his conduct removed. Gates had been aware of the administration's arms sales to Iran and was also in a position to have learned of the private network the NSC staff established to support the contras in Nicaragua (see chapter 9). The SSCI attempted to delve into his involvement in these matters during a day-long confirmation hearing and at one point got him to admit that the Agency "actively shunned information" with regard to how the contras were being funded. At the same time, the joint congressional investigation of Iran-contra and the criminal probe by the newly appointed independent counsel, Judge Lawrence Walsh, were only just beginning. Whether any of these investigations would implicate Gates in the scandal could not be known. Needing more time to determine what action the committee should take, Chairman Boren announced a vote on the nomination would be delayed for two weeks. Meanwhile, the Tower Commission investigating the Iran-contra matter for the White House issued a report broadly criticizing the Agency's role in Iran-contra and implying that some of its analysis had crossed the line in terms of advocating policy.[16]

With trouble on the horizon, and no prospect that it could be laid to rest any time soon, Gates asked the White House to withdraw his nomination on 3 March 1987.

William H. Webster: 1987

Shortly after the withdrawal of the Gates nomination, President Reagan nominated the incumbent director of the FBI, William H. Webster, to be the next DCI. While Webster lacked experience in intelligence matters and foreign affairs, he had a reputation for uncompromising integrity. Highly

---

[15] See chapter 10 for an account of the SSCI's investigation of charges against Casey that emerged six months later.

[16] CIA draft study, Vol. III, 141.

regarded for his leadership of the FBI, Webster was also a former federal appellate judge. With the Agency embroiled in the Iran-contra scandal, his nomination immediately gained broad, bipartisan support.

At his confirmation hearing on 8 April 1987, Webster promised to stay out of politics. He would no longer serve as a member of the president's cabinet as Casey had done, he told the committee. He would be forthright with the committees and pledged to keep them "fully informed" of all covert action activities. If he ever found himself in sharp disagreement with the president over such activities as the arms-for-hostages deals with Iran, he would resign rather than carry out the president's orders.[17]

Reassured by these commitments and eager to have a confirmed official at the helm of the CIA as the Iran-contra investigations were playing out, the SSCI unanimously supported Webster's nomination as did the full Senate.

The Second Gates Nomination: 1991

On 24 June 1991, Robert M. Gates was nominated for a second time to be the DCI, this time by President George H.W. Bush. Gates is the only person ever to be nominated twice for the DCI's position and the only person to be nominated by different presidents. After he withdrew his first nomination, Gates remained as Webster's deputy until January 1989, when he moved to the White House to become deputy assistant to the president for national security affairs in the newly elected Bush administration.

The problem that had plagued his first nomination—his knowledge of, and involvement in, the Iran-contra affair—had not entirely gone away, however. Aalthough the congressional investigations had ended in 1987, the criminal investigation of Iran-contra, headed by Independent Counsel Lawrence Walsh, was still ongoing when Gates was nominated a second time. While it appeared unlikely after four years that Gates would be indicted, until Walsh submitted his final report this could not be ruled out.

A few weeks after the Gates nomination went to the Senate, one of the CIA officers involved in the Iran-contra scandal pled guilty to two misdemeanor charges of withholding of information from Congress. At the time his plea was entered, the officer publicly asserted there had been greater knowledge of the Iran-contra affair within CIA than had previously come to light. Although he did not specifically implicate Gates, the committee delayed his confirmation hearings until September when the testimony of the former officer could

---

[17] Ibid., 142.

be arranged. It also voted to give the officer immunity from further prosecution in order to obtain his testimony.

During this interim period, the committee began receiving other allegations regarding the nominee. A number of former CIA analysts who had served under Gates during the Casey period alleged that he had repeatedly slanted or distorted intelligence analysis to suit the political predilections of Casey and the Reagan administration. Another set of allegations, coming from outsiders or raised by the news media, suggested Gates had been involved in a range of other dubious activities during his tenure at the CIA, including withholding information from Congress, illegally sharing arms and intelligence with other governments, and involvement in political activity. The committee staff investigated this latter set of allegations but never held public hearings on them because none of them could be substantiated. The allegations of the former CIA analysts, however, proved more troubling.

The committee staff interviewed the former analysts making the allegations, and these led to interviews of other analysts who had served under Gates and had knowledge of the cases where "politicization" was alleged to have occurred. In all, the staff interviewed 80 current and former analysts and reviewed several hundred documents prior to the hearings.

The confirmation hearings began on 16 September 1991. For the first two days the committee questioned Gates, mostly regarding his views of congressional oversight and his commitment to the oversight process. Two days of hearings on Gates's role in the Iran-contra affair followed, including the testimony of the CIA officer who alleged there had been greater knowledge within the CIA than previously disclosed. His testimony did not prove detrimental where Gates was concerned. The allegations of "politicization" the committee had received were initially considered in closed session since the analytical reports at issue were still classified, but upon hearing testimony adverse to the nominee, the committee decided it had no choice but to air the allegations in public. Witnesses were directed to "sanitize" their statements for public release; members were told by the committee leadership what the appropriate bounds for their questioning would be.

On 1 and 2 October 1991, the committee held public hearings on the issue of "politicization," where six current and former analysts, both for and against the nominee, presented testimony. On 3 and 4 October, Gates returned to testify in response to the allegations that had been made against him. In all, he responded to 20 separate allegations in his rebuttal, ending with a list of actions he planned to take, if confirmed, to deal with the perceived problem of politicization.

On 18 October, by a vote of 11 to 4, the SSCI voted to report the nomination to the full Senate. To accompany the nomination, the committee filed a 225-page report summarizing the results of the committee's exhaustive inquiry.[18] It was by far the longest report on a nominee for the DCI's position ever to be filed. Members were left, however, to draw their own conclusions from the record.

Calling the investigation the most thorough ever conducted for a nominee to the DCI's position, SSCI Chairman Boren explained in detail why he had decided to vote for Gates. On Iran-contra, while he was bothered by Gates "lack of aggressiveness" in responding to the information that had come into his possession, he did not believe Gates had done anything illegal. He was placed in a difficult position, Boren acknowledged, and had learned from his experience.

On the politicization issue, Boren found there was as much in the record to suggest intelligence was not being politicized during Gates's tenure (numerous assessments that ran counter to the Reagan administration's position) as there was to suggest that it was. While he thought Gates had come across at times as abrasive and insensitive to the analysts that worked for him, he also acknowledged the pressures of the position that he held. In an unusual closing to his statement in support of the nomination, Boren saluted the "courageous" CIA analysts who had come forward and said he would be watching to ensure that no adverse action would be taken against them. He did not expect this from Gates, he said, but he would be watching. "This will be a time for healing, not stridency," Boren continued, "for compassion, not vindictiveness. A time to get on with the future."[19]

The full Senate approved the Gates nomination by a vote of 64 to 31—the most negative votes ever cast for a nominee to the DCI's position. Because President Bush was defeated in the 1992 election, however, Gates ended up serving in the position for only a year. None of the analysts who had come forward during the confirmation process subsequently complained to the committee that Gates had taken adverse action against them.

President Clinton's Choices: Woolsey, Carns, Deutch, Lake, and Tenet

President Clinton nominated five men to serve as DCI, the most of any president. Two of his nominees, however—Carns and Lake—withdrew without a vote on their nominations.

---

[18] Senate Select Committee on Intelligence, *Report on the Nomination of Robert M. Gates.*
[19] Ibid., 210.

Clinton's first nominee, R. James Woolsey, was a partner in a Washington DC law firm but had significant experience in government: general counsel of the SASC in the early 1970s, under secretary of the navy during the Carter administration, and a member of two US arms control delegations during the 1980s. Immediately prior to being nominated, he had chaired a task force commissioned by DCI Gates to evaluate US satellite collection programs. While having a limited personal relationship with the president-elect, Woolsey was well known within the national security establishment in Washington.

The nomination hearing held before the SSCI on 2 February 1993, proved noncontroversial, and the committee reported his nomination by unanimous vote. Two days later, the Senate confirmed him by voice vote. A commitment that Woolsey made at the hearing, however, subsequently created a minor problem for the committee. He had owned shares in a privately held corporation that held contracts with the Agency. While his interest was small enough that the Office of Government Ethics had determined that no conflict-of-interest issue was raised under applicable law, one member of the SSCI was bothered by the situation. When he raised the matter with Woolsey at his confirmation hearing, Woolsey promised to sell the shares within a year.[20] When the committee learned that Woolsey had yet to sell the stock after a year had passed, the committee chairman sent the DCI a letter expressing his dissatisfaction.

In December 1994, after a year of sparring with the oversight committees over the Ames case (see chapter 10), Woolsey resigned with less than two years in the job. To replace him, Clinton nominated a recently retired Air Force general, Michael P.C. Carns, who had last served as Air Force's vice chief of staff. A highly decorated fighter pilot during the Vietnam War, Carns had an MBA from Harvard and had served as director of the Joint Staff during the Persian Gulf War. Although he was not an intelligence specialist per se, he had had considerable exposure to the intelligence business over his military career.

After the nomination was announced, however, the SSCI received allegations that Carns had violated US immigration laws when he brought a Filipino servant into the United States from a previous posting in the Philippines. The committee passed these allegations to the FBI. When the ensuing investigation also raised questions about his wife's involvement in the matter and it came to light that his son had previously admitted to having had a peripheral role in a petty theft at Bolling AFB, Carns decided to withdraw his nomination rather than put his family through the ordeal of a public hearing.[21] Citing the "venomous and abusive accusations . . . aimed at smearing my wife and my

---

[20] Senate Select Committee on Intelligence, *Nomination of R. James Woolsey.*

[21] *Washington Post*, "Carns Withdraws as CIA Nominee," 11 March 1993.

children," Carns said they had "killed my willingness . . . to proceed with the confirmation."[22]

The same day Carns withdrew, Clinton announced the nomination of John M. Deutch to be the next DCI. Deutch was then serving as the deputy secretary of defense and reportedly had turned down the DCI's post when it was first offered. However, when Clinton agreed to give the position Cabinet rank as it had had under President Reagan, Deutch agreed to accept it.[23]

A professor of chemistry at MIT, Deutch's résumé reflected considerable government experience as well as work with the Intelligence Community. He had served as director of energy research at DOE in the late 1970s. During the 1980s, he was a paid consultant to the National Intelligence Council and had served on the DCI's Nuclear Intelligence Panel. Initially appointed as under secretary of defense for acquisitions and technology, Clinton later made him deputy secretary.

Capitol Hill welcomed his appointment, especially after Woolsey's rocky tenure and the relatively long interim that had followed his resignation. After a perfunctory confirmation hearing, where he pledged to undertake tough reforms at the Agency in the wake of the Ames case, Deutch was confirmed by the Senate on 9 May 1995, by a vote of 98 to 0 and sworn in the following day. Deutch also stayed in the DCI's job a relatively short time, resigning on 15 December 15 1996.

To succeed Deutch, Clinton nominated his national security adviser, Anthony Lake, also an academic with considerable government experience. A professor at both Amherst and Mount Holyoke Colleges in Massachusetts, Lake had been a foreign service officer early in his professional career and had served as director of policy planning at the State Department during the Carter administration. Mild-mannered and scholarly, he had served four comparatively noncontroversial years as national security adviser.

Lake's nomination was sent to the Senate on 9 January 1997, roughly coinciding with the appointment of a new SSCI chairman, Senator Richard Shelby (R-AL). Twice, Shelby set dates for a confirmation hearing only to postpone them on the grounds that there were "unanswered, perplexing questions" about Lake that the committee needed time to explore.[24] Two weeks later, after two Republican senators on the committee told the press they would probably vote for Lake—giving him a majority on the committee—Shelby announced he would hold no hearing on the nomination at all until the com-

---

[22] Carns, Press Release.
[23] *Washington Post*, "Carns Withdraws."
[24] *New York Times*, "More Delays in Hearings to Confirm CIA Chief."

mittee had been given access to all of the FBI's files on the nominee, including raw data from the files. The SSCI had never asked for this kind of data before, causing one Republican senator who objected to the request to publicly complain, "The whole confirmation process has become more and more outrageous . . . people feel it's their duty to engage in character assassination."[25] While the administration initially objected to the release of these files, Shelby was ultimately allowed to see them.

When the confirmation hearings began in mid-March, Shelby opened the proceedings by announcing that the committee's investigation was still ongoing and that he intended to explore thoroughly "the many issues surrounding this nomination."[26] He went on to say these included Lake's role in the administration's acquiescence in allowing Iranian arms to transit Bosnian territory, an issue the SSCI had previously investigated (see chapter 9); the state and future of the CIA; the NSC's involvement with DNC fundraisers; and settlement of Lake's alleged ethics violations.[27] The Justice Department and Office of Government Ethics had cleared Lake of any ethics violations prior to the hearing.

As Shelby and other Republican senators on the committee read their opening statements, it was apparent they intended to give the nominee a hard time. Shelby began by questioning Lake's management experience and his alleged failure to ensure that information passed to the White House regarding an alleged covert effort by the Chinese government to buy influence during the US election campaign had been adequately disseminated. Other Republicans questioned Lake's objectivity; his failure to notify Congress of the Iranian arms transshipments; his alleged failure to hold his own NSC staff accountable; alleged Clinton administration failures in Somalia, Bosnia, and Haiti; and his role in naming political contributors to the President's Foreign Intelligence Advisory Board. One questioned Lake about a comment he had made during an interview that seemed to indicate he was not sure whether Alger Hiss had been a spy.

At the end of three days of contentious questioning by the Republican members of the committee, Shelby insisted that more information was needed before a vote on the nomination could take place. CIA learned that Shelby staffers had asked NSA if there were any derogatory information on Lake in its database of communications intercepts.[28] Lake also learned that Shelby had

---

[25] *New York Times*, "Leaders in Senate Demand FBI Files on CIA Nominee."
[26] Senate Select Committee on Intelligence, *Nomination of Anthony Lake to be the Director of Central Intelligence.*
[27] Ibid., 3.
[28] Tenet, *In the Center of the Storm*, 7.

insisted that, before they voted, other members of the committee read the raw investigative reports the FBI had prepared.

For Lake, this was the last straw. In a letter to the president dated 18 March 1997, he asked that his nomination be withdrawn. While he believed he would prevail if his nomination ever came to a vote in the full Senate, Lake wrote that he had "finally lost patience" with the process and that, if he continued, he was apt to lose his dignity as well. This is a "nomination process with no end in sight," he told the president, "a political circus" that is politicizing the Agency as well as the Senate committee. Given the way the process had been conducted he would have a hard time working with the committee even if he were confirmed. Hopefully, he concluded, "people of all political views . . . will demand that Washington give priority to policy over partisanship, to governing over 'gotcha.'"[29]

On 21 April 1997, Clinton nominated George J. Tenet, who had been serving as acting DCI since Deutch's departure the previous December, to be the DCI in his own right.[30] Prior to this, Tenet had been DDCI to Deutch and had served on the NSC staff during Woolsey's tenure. From 1985 until 1993, he had been a member of the staff of the SSCI, serving as its staff director between 1989 and 1993. While other staff of the intelligence committees had gone on to senior positions within the Intelligence Community, none had ever risen to the DCI's position.

The committee held only one day of public hearings on the Tenet nomination. Shelby signaled at the outset that he would not challenge the nominee, and other Republicans fell in line.[31] One pointed out the need to put someone into the job after a five-month hiatus. While the nominee was asked substantive questions, the vitriol that marked the Lake hearings was conspicuously absent. No issue of significance emerged.

The day after the hearing, however, the committee was informed that the attorney general, in response to a request from the White House counsel's office, had opened a preliminary investigation into whether Tenet had failed to disclose ownership of certain stock and real property in filling out a government financial disclosure form in 1993. Tenet's father had purchased the assets at issue without his son's knowledge. Tenet's brother had apparently discovered them in 1994 — after the father's death — in a safe deposit box in Athens, Greece. After the discovery and his interest in the assets had been determined, Tenet had reported them on his financial disclosure statement.

---

[29] Anthony Lake, "Letter to President Clinton," reprinted in the *New York Times*.

[30] For an account of how this came about, see Tenet, *At the Center of the Storm*, 5–10.

[31] *Washington Post*, "In Turnabout, GOP Senators Welcome CIA Nominee."

The White House counsel reviewed the matter in 1995 in connection with Tenet's appointment as DDCI and did not believe a referral to the Justice Department was required. Now the lawyers at the White House were saying that such a referral was required.

The leaders of the SSCI were briefed on the matter and immediately indicated they did not see it as an obstacle to Tenet's confirmation. However, the Justice investigation had to run its course before a vote on the nomination could be taken. This did not occur for two months. On 8 July 1997, the committee was told that Tenet had been cleared of any wrongdoing.[32] He was unanimously voted out of committee and approved by voice vote of the full Senate on 11 July, almost seven months after Deutch had resigned.

Tenet was DCI until 2004, second in longevity only to Allen Dulles. He also became the first DCI since Richard Helms to be held over from one administration to another.

Porter Goss: 2004

Tenet resigned as DCI on 11 July 2004, as the investigations of the Agency's failure to predict the 9/11 terrorist attacks were coming to an end and as its evident miscalculations with respect to Iraqi weapons of mass destruction (see chapters 7 and 8) were being publicly documented.

To replace him, President George W. Bush nominated Porter J. Goss, a Florida congressman who for the preceding seven years had chaired the HPSCI. He was the second nominee for DCI to have served in Congress (Bush's father was the first), but the first to have also served as an overseer of the Agency. Goss also had the distinction of previously having served as a case officer in the DO during the early part of his professional career.

Making his appointment all the more extraordinary, it came at a time when Congress was debating whether to create a new director of national intelligence (DNI), as recommended by the 9/11 Commission, with responsibility for the Intelligence Community as a whole (see chapter 2). Thus, at the time his nomination was announced, Goss did not know if the new position would be established or, if it were created, whether he would be named to it.

Goss had chaired the HPSCI since 1997 and by most accounts had run the committee in a bipartisan manner, particularly compared to the operation of most House committees. In 2004, however, he announced his decision to retire; 2004 was also a year marked by a hotly contested presidential election.

---

[32] *Washington Post*, "Tenet Cleared for Panel Vote on CIA Post."

Earlier in the year, Goss had criticized the putative Democratic nominee on several occasions, as well as the Democratic Party itself, for their lack of support for intelligence. He had taken unusually partisan positions (for him) in defense of the Bush administration's performance on Iraq, causing the SSCI's Democratic vice chairman to explicitly warn Bush not to appoint him as Tenet's successor.[33]

Bush ignored the advice and nominated Goss anyway. Not surprisingly, at the confirmation hearings that followed, several Democrats on the committee took him to task for his earlier rhetoric. In more than five hours of grueling questioning, Goss recanted some of his earlier partisan attacks, admitting at one point that he did, in fact, believe the Democratic Party "strongly supports the Intelligence Community." He also conceded that "at times, perhaps, I engaged in debate with a little too much vigor or enthusiasm." Assuring the committee that he had a "commitment to nonpartisanship," Goss promised to run the Agency without regard for politics.[34]

With the support of several Democrats, the committee reported Goss's nomination to the full Senate by a vote of 12 to 4. On 22 September 2004, he was approved 77–17, as both houses were attempting to craft legislation to overhaul the government's intelligence apparatus.[35] On 17 December, this effort came to fruition when President Bush signed into law the Intelligence Reform and Terrorism Prevention Act of 2004. As a result, the office of Director of Central Intelligence, which had served as the focal point of US intelligence for 58 years, was abolished. Goss was reappointed as director of the CIA while he waited for a new DNI to be named. His former post would be abolished upon the swearing in of the new DNI. That occurred on 21 April 2005.

AUTHOR'S COMMENTARY

Openness of the Confirmation Process

No other country in the world brings the director of its national intelligence service before its legislature (and the world) for a public examination before taking the reins of power. But Congress wanted a measure of control over who was appointed to run the CIA, and the only way to accomplish this under the Constitution was to enact a law requiring the Senate to "advise and consent" to the appointment. Necessarily, confirmation by the Senate is an open process:

---

[33] See Press Statement of Senator Jay Rockefeller, June 25, 2004.

[34] *Washington Post*, "At Hearing, Goss Vows Nonpartisan CIA Leadership."

[35] *Washington Post,* "Senate Confirms Rep. Goss as Intelligence Director."

the president must name the appointee and the Senate must publicly vote to confirm or reject the appointment, implying that there be a record open to all 100 members of the Senate who ultimately must cast a vote on the nomination.

Occasionally, however, the requirement to have an open process creates problems for the committee handling the nomination (since 1976, the SSCI). Nominees who have had roles in the intelligence business may not be able to be questioned about all of them in public. Similarly, the rules of security classification might constrain witnesses who might wish to testify for or against the nominee. Members might also find it difficult to question nominees without intelligence experience about how they would handle a matter that is still classified. While the committee has the option of going into closed session to take testimony from the nominee or other witnesses, it must still find a way to make relevant information public if it has the potential for affecting the vote of the full Senate on the nomination.

Significance of the Confirmation Process

Considering that the confirmation process has never failed to confirm a DCI whose nomination has come to a vote, one might be inclined to dismiss it as a sideshow. It is anything but that.

Nominees for the director's position are first vetted by the executive branch. Security issues are considered; conflicts of interest, adjudicated; and potentially embarrassing personal situations, identified. If a nomination goes forward, the results of these inquiries are furnished the committee handling the nomination, which has the option of reopening matters of concern to it. The committee also requires the nominee to respond to a questionnaire designed to elicit information apart from that it receives from the executive branch. The responses to this questionnaire can sometimes raise new issues.

The committee may also have issues raised by third parties who wish to testify. Typically, the staff evaluates the allegations the committee has received and recommends to the leaders of the committee whether any of these issues deserve airing at the hearings.

The nominee typically arranges "courtesy calls" in advance of the hearings with all committee members willing and able to see nominee. These meetings usually take place in private in the senator's office, giving each participant an opportunity to size up the other outside the glare of the public spotlight and before the nominee formally appears at his confirmation hearing. If a senator has concerns about the nomination, he or she will typically raise them in this initial meeting and have the nominee respond informally. If the senator is satisfied with the response, the issue is not likely to be pursued at the hearing.

The confirmation process will typically address issues that have been identified in the course of this preliminary process. Although issues are sometimes surfaced for the first time at the confirmation hearings themselves, this is rare. If the preliminary process did not identify issues of significance, the hearing will likely consist of opening statements by the members and nominee, followed by questions which, to the outside world, seem desultory and perfunctory. The committee may appear to be letting the nominee off the hook, when, in fact, it has conducted a thorough inquiry and found nothing significant. On the other hand, if the preliminary inquiry identified issues, the hearing process will expand as necessary to flesh them out to the satisfaction of the members concerned.

Confirmation hearings are also occasions not simply to elicit information from the nominee but also to extract commitments in terms of future relationship with the committee. Since the Iran-contra scandal, for example, every nominee for DCI has been asked whether he will commit to notifying the oversight committees within 48 hours of a covert action finding being signed by the president. While the law does not expressly require this, any nominee who answers that question in the negative is creating a significant obstacle to confirmation. Moreover, assuming the nominees know that if they violate this pledge, the committee will hold them to account.

Since only the SSCI conducts confirmation hearings, its members are given a "leg up" on their counterparts on the HPSCI. By dint of the confirmation process, they are given an opportunity to acquaint themselves with the new director before they have to deal with him or her on substantive issues. Of course, this can be either a benefit or a detriment depending upon what kind of initial impression the new director has made. The confirmation process sets the tone for what the director's relationship is apt to be with the SSCI. For the HPSCI, it takes a bit longer.

The Ideal Nominee?

Administrations generally seek to appoint people whose nominations, they believe, will not be controversial and will sail through the confirmation process. Where the DCI job is concerned, however, this is apt to be shortsighted. Nominees without experience in intelligence may not have a track record they can be questioned about, but they may also lack the knowledge and aptitude to be an effective director. Nominees who have no prior personal relationship with the president they serve may escape being asked whether they would ever shape analysis to support the president's policy preferences, but they may later find it difficult to relate to the president, unable to influence policy at all.

Occasionally, administrations have looked for "managers" to fill the DCI position—people with proven management skills. But these skills, too, may not translate well into the intelligence environment. Nominees from the business world may be frustrated by the rules and pace of the federal bureaucracy, and their experience in the private sector may subject them to special scrutiny during the confirmation process. Nominees from the military, whose management skills and patriotism might augur well for their confirmation, may not possess a background or aptitude in foreign affairs.

It is difficult to glean much wisdom on this subject by looking at the past. Only five nominees for the DCI's position generated much controversy during their confirmation process: McCone, Colby, Gates (twice), Lake, and Goss. Of these, one was a businessman (McCone); two had spent most of their careers as intelligence professionals (Colby and Gates); and two were serving in high-ranking governmental posts when they were nominated (Lake as national security adviser and Goss as chairman of the HPSCI). Of the five, the one who generated the most controversy (Gates) was arguably the best qualified, being both a career intelligence officer and a confidante of both presidents who appointed him.

Experience does seem to suggest, however, that the timing of nominations may have as much to do with the degree of controversy generated by the confirmation process as the nominees themselves. The nominees who received the largest number of negative votes in the Senate all came along in the midst or aftermath of a major scandal or intelligence failure: McCone, after the Bay of Pigs; Colby, in the midst of Watergate; Bush, in the midst of the Church and Pike Committee investigations; and Gates, in the middle of, and again after, the Iran-contra scandal. On the other hand, all of the nominees who came along after a prior nominee had withdrawn (Turner after Sorensen; Webster after Gates; Deutch after Carns; and Tenet after Lake) have benefited from the desire of the committee considering their nomination to "get someone in the job" without further delay.

Experience also demonstrates that partisanship must be taken into account, both with respect to the nominee's past and with respect to the political makeup of the committee considering the nomination. Nominees who are viewed as overly partisan, either because of their relationship with the incumbent president (Lake) or because of positions they have previously taken (Goss), can expect to encounter hostile questions from one side of the committee or the other. How serious a concern this is likely to be in a particular case will depend upon how partisan the committee itself is at this juncture.

APPENDICES

APPENDIX A. DIRECTORS OF CENTRAL INTELLIGENCE

RADM Sidney W. Souers . . . . 23 Jan 1946–10 Jun 1946

LTG Hoyt S. Vandenberg . . . . 10 Jun 1946–1 May 1947

RADM Roscoe H. Hillenkoetter . . . . 1 May 1947–7 Oct 1950

GEN Walter Bedell Smith . . . . 7 Oct 1950–9 Feb 1953

Allen W. Dulles . . . . 26 Feb 1953–29 Nov 1961

John A. McCone . . . . 29 Nov 1961–28 Apr 1965

VADM William F. Raborn, Jr. . . . . 28 Apr 1965–30 Jun 1966

Richard M. Helms . . . . 30 Jun 1966–2 Feb 1973

James R. Schlesinger . . . . .2 Feb 1973–2 Jul 1973

William E. Colby . . . . 4 Sep 1973–30 Jan 1976

George H.W. Bush . . . . .30 Jan 1976–20 Jan 1977

ADM Stansfield Turner . . . . .9 Mar 1977–20 Jan 1981

William J. Casey . . . . .28 Jan 1981–29 Jan 1987

William H. Webster . . . . .26 May 1987–31 Aug 1991

Robert M. Gates . . . . .6 Nov 1991–20 Jan 1993

R. James Woolsey . . . . 5 Feb 1993–10 Jan 1995

John M. Deutch . . . . 10 May 1995–15 Dec 1996

George J. Tenet . . . . 11 Jul 1997–11 Jul 2004

Porter J. Goss . . . . .24 Sep 2004–21 Apr 2005

APPENDIX B. COMMITTEE CHAIRMEN WITH RESPONSIBILITY FOR THE CIA (1947–2004)

SENATE ARMED SERVICES COMMITTEE (1947–75)

John Chandler "Chan" Gurney (R-SD) 1947–49

Millard Tydings (D-MD) 1949–51

Richard Russell (D-GA) 1951–53

Leverett Saltonstall (R-MA) 1953–55

Richard Russell (D-GA) 1955–70

John Stennis (D-MS) 1970–75

SENATE SELECT COMMITTEE ON INTELLIGENCE (1976–2004)

Daniel Inouye (D-HI) 1976–78

Birch Bayh (D-IN) 1979–80

Barry Goldwater (R-AZ) 1980–84

David Durenberger (R-MN) 1985–86

David Boren (D-OK) 1987–92

Dennis DeConcini (D-AZ) 1993–94

Arlen Specter (R-PA) 1995–96

Richard Shelby (R-AL) 1997–2001

Bob Graham (D-FL) 2001–2002

Pat Roberts (R-KS) 2003–2004

SENATE APPROPRIATIONS COMMITTEE (1947–2004)

Styles Bridges (R-NH) 1947–55

Kenneth McKeller (D-TN) 1949–53

Styles Bridges (R-NH) 1953–55

Carl Hayden (D-AZ) 1955–69

Richard Russell (D-GA) 1969–70

Allen J. Ellender (D-LA) 1971–72

Warren G. Magnuson (D-WA) 1978–81

Mark O. Hatfield (R-OR) 1981–87

John C. Stennis (D-MS) 1987–89

Robert C. Byrd (D-WV) 1989–95

Mark O. Hatfield (R-OR) 1995–97

Ted Stevens (R-AK) 1997–2004

SENATE APPROPRIATIONS SUBCOMMITTEE ON DEFENSE (1975–2004)

John McClellan (D-AR) 1975–77

John C. Stennis (D-MS) 1978–80

Ted Stevens (R-AK) 1981–85

John C. Stennis (D-MS) 1986–87

Daniel Inouye (D-HI) 1988–94

Ted Stevens (R-AK).. 1995–2001

Daniel Inouye (D-HI) 2001–2002

Ted Stevens (R-AK) 2003–2004

HOUSE ARMED SERVICES COMMITTEE (1947–1977)

Carl Vinson (D-GA). 1949–53

Dewey Short (R-MO) 1953–55

Carl Vinson (D-GA) 1955–65

L. Mendel Rivers (D-SC) 1966–71

F. Edward Hebert (D-LA) (full committee) 1971–75

Lucien Nedzi (D-MI) (subcommittee). 1971–75

HOUSE PERMANENT SELECT COMMITTEE ON INTELLIGENCE (1977–2004)

Edward P. Boland (D-MA) 1977–84

Lee Hamilton (D-IN) 1985–86

Louis Stokes (D-OH) 1987–88

Anthony Beilenson (D-CA) 1989–90

David McCurdy (D-OK) 1991–92

Dan Glickman (D-KS) 1993–94

Larry Combest (R-TX) 1995–96

Porter Goss (R-FL) 1997–2004

HOUSE APPROPRIATIONS COMMITTEE (1947–2004)

John Tabor (R-NY) 1947–48

Clarence Cannon (D-MO) 1949–53

John Tabor (R-NY) 1953–54

Clarence Cannon (D–MO) 1955–64

George Mahon (D–TX) 1964–79

Jamie L. Whitten (D–MS) 1979–93

William H. Natcher (D–KY) 1993–94

David R. Obey (D–WI) 1994–95

Robert L. Livingston (R–LA) 1995–98

C.W. "Bill" Young (R–FL) 1999–2004

APPENDIX C. HEADS OF THE CIA OFFICE OF CONGRESSIONAL AFFAIRS (1947–2004)

Walter L. Pforzheimer 1946–55

Norman Paul 1956–57

John Warner 1957–68

John Maury 1968–74

George Cary 1974–77

Frederick P. Hitz 1977–80

J. William "Billy" Doswell 1981–82

Clair E. George 1982–84

Charles Briggs 1984–86

David Gries 1987–88

John Helgerson 1988–89

E. Norbert Garrett 1989–91

Stanley M. Moskowitz 1991–94

Joanne O. Isham 1994–96

John H. Moseman 1996–2001

Stanley M. Moskowitz 2001–2004

APPENDIX D. LIST OF ABBREVIATIONS

SAC: Senate Appropriations Committee

SASC: Senate Armed Services Committee

SFRC: Senate Foreign Relations Committee

SSCI: Senate Select Committee on Intelligence

HAC: House Appropriations Committee

HASC: House Armed Services Committee

HFAC: House Foreign Affairs Committee

HPSCI: House Permanent Select Committee on Intelligence

JAEC: Joint Atomic Energy Committee

BIBLIOGRAPHY

Public Documents

CIA. "Family Jewels," FOIA electronic reading room, www.foia.cia.gov.

US Congress. House. Select Committee to Investigate Covert Arms Transactions with Iran; Senate. Select Committee on Secret Military Assistance to Iran and the Nicaraguan Opposition. *Report of the Congressional Committees Investigating the Iran-Contra Affair.* 100th Cong., 1st sess., 1987. H. Rep. 100-433; S. Rep. 100-216.

US Congress. House. Permanent Select Committee on Intelligence; Senate. Select Committee on Intelligence. *Report of the Joint Inquiry into Intelligence Community Activities Before and After the Terrorist Attacks of September 11, 2001.* 107th Cong., 2nd sess. December 2002. H. Rep. 107-792; S. Rep. 107-351.

US Congress. House. Permanent Select Committee on Intelligence. Subcommittee on Evaluation. *Iran: Evaluation of U.S. Intelligence Performance Prior to November 1978.* 96th Cong., 1st sess., January 1979. Committee print.

————. *U.S. Counterintelligence and Security Concerns — 1986.* 100th Cong., 1st sess., February 1987. H. Rep 100-5.

————. *Investigation into the Iranian Arms Shipments to Bosnia: Report of the Permanent Select Committee on Intelligence.* 105th Cong., 2nd sess., 9 October 1998. H. Rep. 105-804.

————. *Intelligence Authorization Act for fiscal year 2005: report together with minority views (to accompany H. R. 4548) (including cost estimate of the Congressional Budget Office).* 108th Cong., 2nd sess., H. 108-558, 21 June 2004.

US Congress. House. Committee on Armed Services. *Crisis in the Persian Gulf: Sanctions, Diplomacy, and War: Hearing before the Committee on Armed Services. Testimony of DCI William Webster.* 101st Cong., 2nd sess., December 1990. HCAS 100-57.

———. *Intelligence Successes and Failures in Operations Desert Shield/ Desert Storm.* 103d Cong., 1st sess., 1991. Committee Print 5, 16 August 1993.

US Congress. Senate. Select Committee to Study Government Operations With Respect to Intelligence Activities [Church Committee]. *Alleged Assassination Plots Involving Foreign Leaders: An Interim Report of the Select Committee to Study Government Operations With Respect to Intelligence.* 94th Cong., 1st sess., 20 November 1975. S. Rep. 94-465.

———. *Covert Action.* Hearings, Volume 7 [Chile]. 94th Cong., 1st sess., 4 and 5 December 1975.

———. *Final Report, Book 1, Foreign and Military Intelligence.* 94th Cong., 2nd sess., 1976. S. Rep. 94-755.

US Congress. Senate. Select Committee on Intelligence. *Nomination as Director of Central Intelligence of Adm. Stansfield Turner: Report of the Select Committee on Intelligence of the United States Senate.* 95th Cong., 1st sess., 22–23 February 1977. S. Rep. 95-5.

———. *Report on the Casey Inquiry.* 97th Cong., 1st sess., 1 December 1981. S. Rep. 97-285.

———. *Meeting the Espionage Challenge: A Review of U.S. Counterintelligence and Security Programs.* 99th Cong., 2nd sess., 7 October 1986. S. Rep. 99-522.

———. *Nomination of Robert M. Gates to be Director of Central Intelligence: Report of the Select Committee on Intelligence, Together with Additional Views.* 102nd Cong., 1st sess., 1991. Exec. Rep. 102-19.

———. *The Intelligence Community's Involvement in the Banca Nazionale del Lavoro (BNL) Affair: Report / Prepared by the Staff of the Select Committee on Intelligence.* 103rd Cong., 1st sess., 1993. Committee print. S. prt.103-12.

———. *Nomination of R. James Woolsey: Hearing before the Select Committee on Intelligence of the United States Senate.* 103rd Cong., 1st sess., 2–3 February 1993. S. hrg. 103-296.

———. *An Assessment of the Aldrich H. Ames Espionage Case and its Implication for U.S. Intelligence: Report / Prepared by the Staff of the Select Committee on Intelligence.* 103rd Cong., 2nd sess., 1 November 1994. Committee print. S. prt. 103-90.

———. *Intelligence Analysis of the Long-Range Missile Threat to the United States: Hearing before the Select Committee on Intelligence of the United States Senate.* 104th Cong., 2nd sess., 1996. S. hrg. 104-854.

———. *U.S. Actions Regarding Iranian and Other Arms Shipments to the Bosnian Army: Report of the Select Committee on Intelligence.* 104th Cong., 2nd sess., S. Rep. 104-68.

———. *CIA's Use of Journalists and Clergy in Intelligence Operations: Hearing before the Select Committee on Intelligence of the United States Senate.* 104th Cong., 2nd sess., 17 July 1996. S. hrg. 104-593.

———. *Nomination of Anthony Lake to be the Director of Central Intelligence: Hearing before the Select Committee on Intelligence of the United States Senate.* 105th Cong., 1st sess. 11–13 March 1997. S. hrg. 105-424.

———. *Committee Activities.* 107th Cong., 1st sess., 3 August 2001.

———. *Review of United States Assistance to Peruvian Counter-Drug Air Interdiction Efforts and the Shootdown of a Civilian Aircraft on April 20, 200: Report of the Select Committee on Intelligence of the United States Senate.* 107th Cong., 1st sess., October 2001. S. Rep. 107-64.

———. *U.S. Intelligence Community's Pre-War Intelligence Assessments on Iraq (unclassified version).* 108th Cong., 2nd sess., 9 July 2004. S. Rep. 108-301.

———. *The Use by the Intelligence Community of Information Provided by the Iraqi National Congress: Report of the Select Committee on Intelligence of the United States Senate.* 109th Cong., 2nd sess. 8 September 2006. S. Rep. 109-330.

US Congress. *Congressional Record.* 103rd Cong., 1st sess., 20 October 1993. Vol. 139, S13978–9.

National Commission on Terrorist Attacks Upon the United States. *The 9/11 Commission Report.* Washington, DC: GPO, n.d.

Commission to Assess the Ballistic Missile Threat to the United States [Rumsfeld Commission]. *Executive Summary.* 15 July 1998.

National Intelligence Council. *Foreign Missile Development and the Ballistic Missile Threat through 2015* (unclassified summary of NIE). December 2001, http://www.cia.ic.gov/new_nic/pubs/2001nic/nie/12-01/4287731/4287731.html

Intelligence Oversight Board. *Report on the Guatemala Review* (declassified). 28 June 1996. The report is available on-line at several web sites, including http://www.ciponline.org.iob.html.

Oral History Interviews

(Copies of all transcripts are in the CIA History Staff unless otherwise indicated.)

George L. Cary (by Robert Hathaway), n.p., 30 September 1983.

George L. Cary (by Ralph E. Weber), McLean, VA, 24 November 1987.

Richard Helms (by R. Jack Smith), n.p., 3 June 1982.

Richard Helms (by Robert Hathaway), n.p., 4 November 1983.

Walter L. Pforzheimer (by Robert Hathaway), n.p., 8 March 1983.

Walter L. Pforzheimer (by Ralph E. Weber), McLean, VA, 11 January 1988.

Walter L. Pforzheimer (by Woody Kuhns), Washington, DC, 9 July 1996.

John S. Warner (by Ralph E. Weber), McLean, VA, 9 October 1987.

John S. Warner (by Woody Kuhns, Britt Snider, and Sherry Long), n.p., 27 September 1996.

John S. Warner (by Ed Dietel), n.p., 2 November 1997.

Lawrence K. "Red" White (by Jim Hanrahan) n.p., 7 January 1998.

Other Interviews

George Jameson (by author), n.p., 28 December 2006.

John H. Moseman (by author), n.p., 28 and 29 December 2006 and 31 March 2006.

Walter L. Pforzheimer (by author), n.p., 15 October 1996.

Senator Richard Shelby (*New York Times*), 10 September 2002.

Senator Richard Shelby, American Morning, CNN, 17 July 2003, transcript. http://www.cnn.com.

William Webster (by Stephen Knott and Marc Selverstone), Miller Center of Public Affairs, Presidential Oral History Program, University of Virginia, 21 August 2002. Transcript found at http://webstorage3.mcpa.virginia.edu/poh/transcripts/ohp_0821_webster.pdf.

Books, Articles and Unpublished Manuscripts

Ambrose, Stephen. *Ike's Spies: Eisenhower and the Intelligence Establishment*. Garden City, New York: Doubleday & Co., Inc., 1981.

Andrew, Christopher. *For the President's Eyes Only: Secret Intelligence and the American Presidency from Washington to Bush*. New York: HarperCollins, 1995.

Associated Press. "CIA Searching for Answers behind its India-nuclear failure," 16 May 1998.

Barrett, David M. *The CIA and Congress: The Untold Story from Truman to Kennedy*. Lawrence: University of Kansas Press, 2005.

Bearden, Milt and James Risen. *The Main Enemy: The Inside Story of the CIA's Final Showdown with the KGB*. New York: Random House, 2003.

Braden, Tom. "The Birth of the CIA" *American Heritage Magazine* 28, no. 2 (February 1977). Available on-line at http://www.americanheritage.com/articles/magazine/ah/1977_2_4.shtml.

Bryan, Richard. Press release. 22 February 2000.

Carns, Michael. Press release. 11 March 1995

Cassidy, John, and Marie Colvin. "Accusations Fly as Iraq Cancels White House Meeting with Bush," *Sunday Times,* 16 December 1990.

CNN. "CIA Caught Off Guard on India Nuclear Test, Hearings Inquiry," 12 May 1998.

CIA. "Jeremiah News Conference." Transcript. 2 June 1998.

Conboy, Kenneth and James Morrison. *Feet to the Fire: CIA Covert Operations in Indonesia, 1957–1958*, Annapolis, MD: Naval Institute Press, 1999.

Colby, William and Peter Forbath. *Honorable Men: My Life in the CIA*. New York: Simon and Schuster, ca. 1978.

Conner, William E. "Reforming Oversight of Covert Actions After the Iran-Contra Affair: A Legislative History of the Intelligence Authorization Act for FY 1991," *Virginia Journal of International Law* 32 (Summer 1992).

Crile, George. *Charlie Wilson's War: The Extraordinary Story of the Largest Covert Operation in History.* New York: Atlantic Monthly Press, 2003.

Dujmovic, Nicolas, ed. "Reflections of DCIs Colby and Helms on the CIA's 'Time of Trouble,'" Unclassified extracts from *Studies in Intelligence* 51, no. 3 (September 2007): 39–56.

Dulles, Allen. *The Craft of Intelligence.* New York: Harper & Row, 1963.

Gates, Robert M. *From the Shadows: The Ultimate Insider's Story of Five Presidents and How They Won the Cold War.* New York: Simon & Schuster, 1996.

———. "The CIA and American Foreign Policy," *Foreign Affairs* 66, no. 2 (Winter 1987/88): 215–30.

Glass, Andrew and Gerald Grant. "NSA Officers Describe Aid Given by CIA," *Washington Post,* 15 February 1967.

Gordon, Michael R., and Bernard E. Trainor. *The Generals' War: The Inside Story of the Conflict in the Gulf.* Boston: Little, Brown, ca. 1995.

Hamilton, Lee. "Letter to the editor." *Washington Post*, 20 March 1986.

Hathaway, Robert M. and Russell Jack Smith. *Richard Helms as Director of Central Intelligence, 1966–1973.* Washington, DC: CIA Center for the Study of Intelligence, 1993. (Declassified in 2007)

Helms, Richard. *A Look Over My Shoulder: A Life in the Central Intelligence Agency.* New York: Random House, 2003.

Hersh, Seymour. "Huge CIA Operation Reported in U.S. Against Anti-War Forces, Other Dissidents in Nixon Years." *New York Times*, 22 December 1974.

House Permanent Select Committee on Intelligence. "Evidence Does Not Support Allegations of CIA Participation in Drug Trafficking," *New York Times,* 11 May 2000.

Jehl, Doug. "The Reach of War; Congressional Criticism; House Committee Says CIA Is Courting Disaster by Mismanaging Its Human Spying." *New York Times*, 25 June 2004.

Karalekas, Anne. *History of the Central Agency*. Laguna Hills, CA: Aegean Park Press, 1977.

Kennedy, David. "Sunshine and Shadow: The CIA and the Soviet Economy. Case Study C16-91-1096.0 for the Intelligence and Policy Project," John F. Kennedy School of Government. Cambridge, MA: Harvard University, 1991. [Title also appears as "Feat or Failure?: The CIA and the Soviet Economy."]

Kennedy School of Government. "James Woolsey and the CIA: The Aldrich Ames Spy Case. Case study C115-96-1339.0." Cambridge, MA: Harvard University, 1996.

Kinzer, Stephen. *All the Shah's Men: An American Coup and the Roots of Middle East Terror*. Hoboken, NJ: John Wiley & Sons, 2003.

Knaus, John K. *Orphans of the Cold War: America and the Tibetan Struggle for Survival*. New York: Public Affairs, 1999.

Lake, Anthony. "Letter to President Clinton," reprinted in the *New York Times*, 19 March 1997.

Lardner, George. "No Iraq Move Seen Until Attack Near; CIA Expects Saddam to Extend Crisis." *Washington Post*, 15 December 1990.

Leary, William M., ed. *The Central Intelligence Agency, History and Documents*. Tuscaloosa: University of Alabama Press, 1984.

Los Angeles Times. "U.S. Dispute Holds Up Covert Iraq Operation," 5 January 1999.

Lundberg, Kirsten. "The SS-9 Controversy: Intelligence as Political Football. Case Study C16-89-884.0 for the Intelligence and Policy Project," John F. Kennedy School of Government. Cambridge, MA: Harvard University, 1989.

———. "CIA and the Fall of the Soviet Empire: The Politics of 'Getting It Right.' Case Study C16-94-1251.0 for the Intelligence and Policy Project," John F. Kennedy School of Government. Cambridge, MA: Harvard University, 1994.

———. "Politics of a Covert Action: The US, the Mujahideen, and the Stinger Missile. Case Study C15-99-1546.0 for the Intelligence and Policy Project," John F. Kennedy School of Government. Cambridge, MA: Harvard University, 1999.

———. "Congressional Oversight and Presidential Prerogative: The 1991 Intelligence Authorization Act, Case Study C14-01-1605.0 for the Intelligence and Policy Project," John F. Kennedy School of Government. Cambridge, MA: Harvard University, 2001.

Maury, John, "CIA and the Congress." *Studies in Intelligence* 18, no. 2 (Summer 1974): 1–14. (Declassified September 1993; also printed in the Congressional Record, 18 September 1984)

May, Ernest and Philip Zelikow. "Prelude to War: US Policy Toward Iraq 1988–1990. Case Study C16-94-1245.0 for the Intelligence and Policy Project," John F. Kennedy School of Government. Cambridge, MA: Harvard University, 1991. (Revised in 2000 by Kirsten Lundberg with the assistance of Robert David Johnson.)

McLaughlin, John. Press Conference (transcript). 9 July 2004.

Meddis, Sam. "Critics Charge CIA Analysis is Politically Biased," *USA Today*, 14 January 1991.

Mendez, Antonio J. *The Master of Disguise: My Secret Life in the CIA*. New York: William Morrow & Co., c1999.

Miller, Lyle. *Legislative History of the Central Intelligence Agency: National Security Act of 1947*. Central Intelligence Agency (Office of Legislative Council), 25 July 1967. (Declassified draft)

Montague, Ludwell L. *General Walter Bedell Smith as Director of Central Intelligence, October 1950–February 1953*. University Park, PA: Pennsylvania State University Press, c. 1992.

Moore, Molly. "Schwarzkopf: War Intelligence Flawed; General Reports to the Congress." *Washington Post*, 13 June 1991.

New York Times. "Royalists Oust Mossadegh; Army Seizes Helm," 20 August 1953.

———. "Moscow Says U.S. Aided Shah's Coup," 20 August 1953.

———. "Officials Say CIA Did Not Tell FBI of Spy Case Moves," 11 October 1985.

———. "Bush Urges Effort to Press Noriega to Quite as Leader," 10 May 1989.

———. "Bush Aide and Senator Clash Over Failed Coup in Panama," 9 October 1989.

———. "Administration is Fighting Itself on Haiti Policy," 23 October 1993.

———. "U.S. Plan to Change Iran Leader Is an Open Secret Before It Begins," 26 January 1996.

———. "More Delays in Hearing to Confirm CIA Chief," 12 February 1997.

———. "Leaders in Senate Demand FBI Files on CIA Nominee," 28 February 1997

———. "Defining Goal in Iraq," 23 December 1998.

Ott, Marvin. "Partisanship and the Decline of Intelligence Oversight," *International Journal of Intelligence and Counterintelligence* 16, no. 1 (Spring 2003): 69–94.

Pedlow, Gregory W., and Donald E. Welzenbach. *The CIA and the U-2 Program, 1954–1974* (declassified 1998). Washington, DC: CIA Center for the Study of Intelligence, 1998.

Pincus, Walter. "2 CIA Officers Choose Retirement over Demotion." *Washington Post*, 14 October 1994.

Prados, John. *Lost Crusader: The Secret Wars of CIA Director William Colby.* New York: Oxford University Press, 2003.

———. *Presidents' Secret Wars.* Chicago: Elephant Paperbacks, 1996.

Public Broadcasting Service (PBS). "The Online News Hour with Jim Lehrer." Transcript. 3 June 1998.

Ranelagh, John. *The Agency: The Rise and Decline of the CIA.* New York: Simon & Schuster, 1986.

Rockefeller, Senator Jay. Press release, 25 June 2004.

Royce, Knut. "Damage Reports That Don't Add Up," *Newsday,* 19 February 1991, p.5.

Risen, James. "CIA Chief Is Asked to Stay On and Agrees."

Sciolino, Elaine. "The 43rd President; The Intelligence Director; As Bush Ponders Choice of Intelligence Chief, Some Suggest that No Change Is Needed." *New York Times*, 29 December 2000.

Shenon, Philip. "Bush Says He'll Seek to Revive Intelligence Bill House Blocked," *New York Times*, 22 November 2004.

Smist, Frank J., Jr., *Congress Oversees the United States Intelligence Community, 1947–1994*. Knoxville: University of Tennessee Press, 1994.

Snider, L. Britt. "Congressional Oversight of Intelligence After 9/11." Chap. 14 in *Transforming US Intelligence: Challenges for Democracy*, edited by Jennifer Sims and Burton Gerber. Washington, DC: Georgetown University Press, 2005.

———. *Sharing Secrets with Lawmakers: Congress as a User of Intelligence*. Washington, DC: CIA Center for the Study of Intelligence, February 1997.

———. "Creating a Statutory Inspector General at the CIA." *Studies in Intelligence* (Winter-Spring 2001). Available on-line at https:www.cia.gov/library/center-for-the-study-of-intelligence/csi-publications/csi-studies/winter-spring01/ir.

Stockwell, John. *In Search of Enemies: A CIA Story*. New York: Norton, 1978.

Studeman, William. *Testimony to the Senate Select Commitee on Intelligence* (Open Hearing on Guatemala). 4 April 1995. http://www.cia.gov/news-information/speeches-testimony/1995/dci_testimony_4495.html

Tenet, George. *At the Center of the Storm: My Years at the CIA*. New York: HarperCollins, 2007.

———. "DCI Statement on the Belgrade Chinese Embassy Bombing: House Permanent Select Committee on Intelligence Open Hearing." 22 July 1999. Copy available at www.cia.gov/news-information/speeches-testimony/1999/index.html.

Troy, Thomas F., *Donovan and the CIA: A History of the Establishment of the Central Intelligence Agency*. Washington, DC: CIA Center for the Study of Intelligence, 1981.

Turner, Stansfield. *Burn Before Reading: Presidents, CIA Directors, and Secret Intelligence*. New York: Hyperion, c2005.

Warner, Michael, ed. *Central Intelligence: Origin and Evolution*. Washington, DC: CIA History Staff, 2001.

Washington Post. "Nunn Regrets Vote on Gulf War," 26 December 1966.

———. "Carns Withdraws as CIA Nominee," 11 March 1995.

———. "Tenet Cleared for Panel Vote on CIA Post," 9 July 1997.

———. "At Hearing, Goss Vows Nonpartisan CIA Leadership," 15 September 2004.

———. "Senate Confirms Rep. Goss as Intelligence Director," 23 September 2004.

———. "In a Turnabout, GOP Senators Welcome CIA Nominee."

Weiner, Tim. "Agency Chief Pledges to Overhaul 'Fraternity' Atmosphere at C.I.A," *New York Times*, 9 July 1994.

———. "CIA Is Working to Overcome Sex and Race Bias, Chief Says," *New York Times*, 21 September 1994

———. "CIA Mission: Strengthen Ties on Capitol Hill," *New York Times*, 21 February 1995."

Woodward, Bob. *Veil: The Secret Wars of the CIA, 1981–1987*. New York: Simon & Schuster, 1987.

INDEX

D

N

R

S